The Saxophone

THE YALE MUSICAL INSTRUMENT SERIES

The Saxophone

Stephen Cottrell

Yale University Press
New Haven and London

For information about this and other Yale University Press publications please contact:
U.S. Office: sales.press@yale.edu   yalebooks.com
Europe Office: sales@yaleup.co.uk   www.yalebooks.co.uk

Set in Columbus MT by IDSUK (DataConnection) Ltd
Printed in Great Britain by TJ International Ltd, Padstow, Cornwall
Library of Congress Control Number

Cottrell, Stephen, 1962–
    The saxophone / Stephen Cottrell.
      p. cm.
    ISBN 978-0-300-10041-9 (cl: alk. paper)
1. Saxophone—History. 2. Sax, Adolphe, 1814–1894. I. Title.
    ML975.C67 2013
    788.7—dc23

                                                              2012028346

A catalogue record for this book is available from the British Library.

10 9 8 7 6 5 4 3 2 1

For my parents, Dennis and Eunice Cottrell

Contents

Illustrations, music examples and tables

Illustrations

Music examples

Tables

Preface

The saxophone is one of the most recognised musical instruments in the world. Loved by many, loathed by some, in the early twenty-first century it has both a musical and symbolic significance far beyond that for which its inventor, Adolphe Sax, might reasonably have hoped. It has been the instrument of choice for luminaries such as the American President Bill Clinton and King Bhumibol Adulyadej of Thailand. Performers such as Charlie Parker, John Coltrane or Kenny G have become household names around the world. It has been used in numerous musical genres, often very different from those for which it was originally intended, and the instrument is matched by few others across the globe in terms of the different musical uses to which it is put.

So why has so little been written about it?

Of course, it is not really true to say that little has been written about the saxophone; it is more accurate to observe that most writing about the instrument occurs in newspapers and magazines or, more recently, on forums and blogs. There is also a significant amount of pedagogic material to help students learn the instrument, and supplementary information accompanying recordings. But there has been comparatively little *scholarship* devoted to the saxophone. Whereas instruments such as the flute, clarinet or trombone, and particularly the guitar, violin and piano, have numerous different volumes to which an aspiring scholar might be directed, the saxophone has nothing like this bibliographic hinterland. Kool's 1931 volume is historically significant but obviously now quite dated. Ventzke et al. (1987) and Dullat (1999) are both valuable, although both reflect the organological inclinations of their authors and are very focussed on the development of the instrument itself; they are both also only available in German, putting the English reader at something of a disadvantage.[1] Beyond this there are a small number of volumes and papers that address specific aspects of the saxophone's history and development, annotated catalogues of particular collections, and some good detective work undertaken in pursuit of American DMA qualifications in the last few decades. Like any scholar endeavouring to stand on the shoulders of those who have come before, I have gratefully availed myself of this work where appropriate, and the details of these publications can be found in the endnotes and bibliography. But serious saxophone scholarship remains rather underdeveloped in comparison with other instruments. Why?

I suggest this is largely a consequence of the saxophone's earlier reputation. As later pages will show, the instrument has, until quite recently, struggled to be taken seriously, particularly by the kinds of scholars most likely to produce a volume of this sort. Just as popular music and jazz have taken many years to become properly accepted within a musical academy that has conventionally focussed on the Western classical tradition, so the instruments seen as peripheral to that tradition have also been marginalised as legitimate objects of scholarly enquiry. One of the main aims of this book, therefore, has been to lay out a scholarly and authoritative history of the saxophone in English, bringing together the facts as I understand them, while also endeavouring to provide a critical reading of those facts in order that their broader significance may be more clearly appreciated.

About this book

Who, then, is the book written for? Firstly, it is not intended to be an exhaustive organological study, although Chapter 2 concentrates particularly on issues relating to the saxophone's technological development. I am not an organologist. Indeed, I would have some sympathy with the view – given the effectiveness of Sax's original vision and the saxophone's relative lack of mechanical transformation over its lifetime when compared to other instruments – that the organological details pertaining to the instrument's history are perhaps less significant than other aspects. This is not to diminish the achievements of those who have pioneered organological research on the saxophone, and from whose knowledge and talents I have benefited both through their written work and in direct correspondence. It is simply to observe that their expertise in this area is greater than mine, and that setting out these developmental details here has involved a personal journey of understanding and discovery from which I hope others will benefit.

Instead my imagined readership comprises those who have an interest in learning more about the saxophone's overall historical trajectory, while at the same time understanding something of the changing social, cultural and musical contexts within which that trajectory has been played out, and which have impinged on the instrument's development and its global dissemination. Inevitably, therefore, there is a strong narrative thrust to the book, and indeed the saxophone, perhaps more than many instruments, lends itself to such an approach: it has an identifiable beginning; its early development is wrapped up with the life of its inventor (biography being itself almost inevitably narrative); and its major successes occurred during the course of the twentieth century, a century not only sufficiently close to us at the time of writing that its unfolding still appears as recent memory, but also one extensively supported by the explosion of mass media – newspapers, film and television, sound recordings, the internet – through which it has been heavily documented, and from which a sense of narrative is easy to construe. There is a risk that such an approach may make it appear that events unfold in a neat historical sequence. This is, of course, not the case and what may appear as a convenient chronological relationship between instruments, individuals, works, or performances, frequently masks a considerable overlap of musical influences and social networks.

I have endeavoured to write an authoritative academic text, but not one couched in dense academic prose that is inaccessible to the general reader. I have consciously introduced many other voices into the text, whether those of other scholars, journalists or critics, and indeed of saxophonists themselves when expressed through printed sources. I have also introduced brief biographies of many of the leading classical and jazz performers. While more extensive jazz biographies abound, the details of the classical players are often harder to uncover. In both cases, however, I have used these sketches to make broader points about the instrument's social and musical significance. I have also endeavoured to accommodate as much empirical data as possible, believing that the broader sweep of history is often most usefully illuminated by focussing on significant but revealing historical details (scholars will recognise this 'thick description' as an approach emanating from anthropologists such as Clifford Geertz or social historians such as Cyril Ehrlich).

I hope the book will appeal to saxophonists keen to learn more about the history and development of the instrument they play, but no special knowledge of the saxophone is needed to understand many of the points being made, and the book is aimed at the general reader not the specialist. However, for those unfamiliar with saxophone specifics, the Introduction provides a rapid summary, outlining the main members of the family, and in very general terms how the instrument works and how performers control it. Chapter 1 then provides an overview of Adolphe Sax's life, by way of contextualising the invention and early development of the instrument. Sax was a remarkable figure in many ways, and one possibly now deserving of a more extensive biography than those provided by Malou Haine and Wally Horwood around 1980, fine though those books may be.[2]

Chapter 2 provides the major organological overview of the instrument. It begins by considering what led Sax to invent the saxophone, and what he identified as the specific deficiencies in other instruments that he thought might be remedied through the invention of a new one. It explains the particular cultural and technological forces that led to the saxophone's ultimate design as a single-reed instrument with a conical bore, details the steady development of the overall family over the following two decades, and reviews the efforts of those who came to the instrument after Sax and who sought to improve or modify it in some way.

Chapter 3, covering the nineteenth century, was one of the more difficult chapters to write, in part because, at first glance, the saxophone appears to have only a small role in Western music-making during that century, and the historical record is often focused elsewhere. But dig a little below the surface and there is a more significant story to be told, albeit one that demonstrates a relative lack of overall interest in the instrument until the last two decades of that century when, on the back of military and colonial expansion, and the early growth of certain types of popular music, the saxophone began its inexorable rise to global domination.

Chapter 4 is the longest chapter, largely because of the enormous significance of the period from around 1885 to 1930, when the saxophone went from being a musical instrument relatively unknown to most of the world's population to one that became, as Jane Austen might have put it, universally acknowledged. This happened largely because of developments in popular music in the United States. During this period the musical fabric of the USA was woven from a remarkably rich tapestry of different styles and genres. This chapter illustrates how the saxophone's golden thread was woven through that tapestry, and shows how crucial the period was for both the pride and the prejudice that the instrument may be said to have experienced in the years that followed.

Chapter 5 deals with jazz. So intertwined is the relationship between the saxophone and the development of jazz that some would assert that a history of the saxophone is little more than the history of jazz itself. One of the aspirations of this volume as a whole, however, is to demonstrate the need to take a broader view of the instrument than this, but it is indisputable that jazz has given the saxophone its most signal identity, and has contributed greatly in turning it from a relatively obscure and little-used instrument into a distinctive musical icon. Equally, the saxophone has proved to be the instrument of choice for many of the most significant jazz innovators, such that the development of the jazz tradition can to a considerable degree be followed through a lineage of distinguished saxophone players, many of whom have played musically pivotal roles.

The same could not be said for the Western art music tradition, which is the focus of Chapter 6. Notwithstanding Sax's original aspirations for the instrument, it is only in the last few decades that the saxophone has come to be seen as anything other than an exotic visitor to the concert hall or the opera house. This chapter considers why that is so, while also reviewing the ways in which the instrument has been used by composers, and the roles played by those individuals and ensembles who have – now – successfully established a vibrant classical tradition for it.

Chapter 7 brings up to date the more recent developments in the popular, jazz and art music genres covered previously, while also providing an overview of the saxophone's role in various 'non-Western' musics. When writing about recent events we are inevitably denied the benefit of historical perspective, and it may be only a few years before the individuals, repertoires and trends to which I have drawn attention here appear rather out of date. Nevertheless, some account must be made of the recent past in this volume, if only because the last few decades have seen a significant resurgence of interest in the instrument, and much of this interest has been stimulated by its use in the mass mediated musics considered in this chapter.

Chapter 8 provides the conclusion to the volume as a whole, and takes a more critical look at the saxophone's place in a variety of twentieth-century contexts. Musical instruments around the world are frequently assigned symbolic meanings in the cultural contexts in which they circulate, which gives them a significance that goes beyond their function as tools to create musical sounds. The saxophone appears particularly rich in this respect, and over time the instrument has been subject to a variety of – sometimes profoundly negative – cultural constructs. Thus the volume ends by exploring the disparate and changing meanings that have accrued to the instrument in some of these different contexts.

Acknowledgements

This book has taken much longer to complete than I anticipated, but that is no fault of the many people who have facilitated its progress along the way. To all of them I offer grateful thanks, while acknowledging that whatever strengths the book may have is partly due to their efforts, and its remaining weaknesses are due to mine alone.

Much of the book was written during my time on the staff at Goldsmiths College, London, from which I received not only institutional support through a period of research leave and help with research travel costs, but also much informal support from my academic colleagues. My more recent employer, City University London, supported some of the permissions and copyright costs. The Arts and Humanities Research Council also funded a term's research leave, and both the British Academy and the University of London Central Research Fund supported the costs of research trips to libraries in Europe and the USA.

Several individuals read portions of the manuscript and provided valuable feedback on it, often to a much greater degree than I had any right to expect. I am particularly indebted in this respect to Kevin Dawe, John Harle, Robert Howe, Ignace de Keyser, Colin Lawson, and Albert Rice.

Staff at many libraries and archives provided helpful support: the Bibliothèque nationale de France in Paris, the British Library in London, New York Public Library, the Horniman Museum in London (particularly Bradley Strauchen), the Musée des Instruments de Musique in Brussels (particularly Gèry Dumoulin and Anja Van Lerberghe), the Farmer Collection at the University of Glasgow, Pedro Belchior at the Villa-Lobos Museum, Rio de Janeiro, and the staff of the libraries at Goldsmiths College and City University.

A wide range of people in other organisations also provided different forms of help: Stéphane Gentil and Catherine Georgoudis at Henri Selmer, and Jean Marie Paul at Vandoren, all in Paris; Adrian Woods at sax.co.uk in London; Malcolm Gerratt and Steve Kent, who smoothed the book's progress through the Yale University Press machine; Liz Dean, who helped with image copyrights, and Rick Campion, who set the musical examples. Nigel Simeone gave outstanding assistance with the final copy-editing, including providing a masterly eye for historical detail. Other individuals who have generously given of their time and expertise in different capacities include Trevor Herbert, Bruno Kampmann, William McBride, Malcolm McMillan, Leo van Oostrom, Vera Ruel-Wunsch, Thomas Smialek, and Tom Wagner (and his mum). My thanks to all of them for their support; and to any whose names I may have forgotten, my apologies for the oversight.

Grateful and loving thanks are also due to Eva Mantzourani, who was my muse and companion as we jointly struggled through the last few years towards the completion of our individual book manuscripts.

Abbreviations and conventions

Citations

To save space I have used a slightly unconventional referencing system, in which sources in endnotes are given using the author-date system, and are listed in full in the bibliography. Sources not otherwise listed in the bibliography are given in full in the relevant endnote. I have given dates of birth and death (where known) only for saxophone players themselves; similar details for composers or others are not given unless important for context. They can easily be pursued elsewhere.

Abbreviations and nomenclature

The details of the initial ambiguity surrounding saxophone nomenclature are given in Chapter 2, but since the names with which we are familiar today became reasonably settled in the mid-nineteenth century I have usually been able to use them consistently without difficulty; any further ambiguities are detailed in the text. I have used the following abbreviations to indicate particular members of the saxophone family:

Sn: sopranino; S: soprano; A: alto; T: tenor; B: baritone; Bs: bass; Cbs: contra-bass

Numbers preceding these letters indicate the numbers of that particular family member in a given context. Thus, 2S/2A/T/B indicates a group comprising two sopranos, two altos, one tenor and one baritone saxophone. All saxophones should be presumed to be of the E♭/B♭ tonalities – as itemised in the Introduction – unless otherwise indicated.

   La Revue et Gazette musicale de Paris is an important journal when considering musical life in nineteenth-century Paris; references to it here are consistently abbreviated as *RGMP*. The *Journal des débats politiques et littéraires* is always shortened simply to *Journal des débats*. Other journal titles are given in full.

Illustrative material

Illustrations, music examples and tables are numbered sequentially throughout the text, even when the illustration is a copy of sheet music (i.e. an image).

Translations

All translations are mine unless indicated, with the source reference given in an endnote.

Pitch level indicators

For the presentation of pitch levels I have adhered to the Helmholtz system of pitch nomenclature, in which middle C is taken as c¹. Pitch levels are thus indicated as follows:

B_I = the note B two octaves and a semitone below middle C
C = the note C two octaves below middle C
c° = the note C one octave below middle C
c¹ = middle C
c² = the C one octave above middle C
c³ = the note C two octaves above middle C

Ex. 1. Pitch level indicators.

Sharps are indicated with a ♯ and flats with a ♭; so, for example, the conventional written range of most saxophones is given as b♭° to f♯³.

Introduction: Saxophone essentials

The saxophone family

The saxophone is not one, but many. The generic term describes a family of related instruments, unified by their shared acoustic properties, similar designs and performance characteristics, and their collective roots in the vision of the man who invented the instrument, Adolphe Sax.

The most common members of the family are today designated as soprano, alto, tenor and baritone, but others often encountered include sopranino and bass; contrabass and sub-contra-bass models can also occasionally be found. Additionally, some saxophones exist in both straight and curved versions, and manufacturers also offer a range of lacquers to finish their instruments, which can make them look very different. The uninitiated may be forgiven for thinking that to peer into a saxophone shop window is not so much to gaze upon a family as to confront a zoo.

Notwithstanding this variety of models, all instruments use essentially the same fingering. Once this fingering is learned it can be easily transferred across the family, though modifications must be made to the player's embouchure (mouth shape) and posture in moving between instruments of different sizes.

Saxophones are transposing instruments: although each model sounds different – higher or lower according to whether they are smaller or larger – they are all notated the same way. The saxophonist today always reads from the treble clef, and the transposition is done by the instrument. Thus the written range of most saxophones is from $b\flat^\circ$-$f\sharp^3$, but the pitches heard will vary according to the model played; saxophonists therefore distinguish between 'written' and 'sounding' pitches.

The instrument's range of a little more than two-and-a-half octaves is not especially large when compared to others such as the clarinet or the violin, although skilled players can extend the upper limit beyond $f\sharp^3$ by the use of special fingerings, together with consequent changes in embouchure tension and position. These force higher harmonics out of the overtone series, allowing the range of each instrument to be extended by a fifth or so in the case of the soprano, to more than an octave in the case of the baritone.

Visually, the saxophone may appear to be technologically complex, but its design is fundamentally quite straightforward. The main body is in one piece, although instruments are manufactured in different sections and joined in the factory, as a cursory inspection reveals. From the alto downwards the performer attaches to the top

1.   Six members of the saxophone family, from left to right, sopranino, soprano, alto, tenor, baritone, bass.

Ex. 2.   Written and sounding pitches for the six most common saxophones.

of this body a neckpipe, which is usually curved in some way to facilitate easier entry to the mouth. A mouthpiece then slides over a cork sleeve on the end of the neckpipe, and a single reed is bound to the mouthpiece by means of a ligature. The smaller instruments usually dispense with this neckpipe, and the mouthpiece fits straight on to the end of the body.

The keywork is organised around the disposition of the two hands (more details on the specifics of the keywork are given in Chapter 2). In general terms, the left hand controls the keys for $c\sharp^2$-g^1, together with additional palm keys for notes from d^3-f^3; an additional stack operated by the left hand little finger also controls most of the low notes of the instrument, from $c\sharp^1$-$b\flat^\circ$. The right hand controls the keys operating $f\sharp^1$-d^1, together with keys for c^1, e^3, $f\sharp^3$, and a variety of additional keys for chromatic notes. The move from the low register to the middle register occurs between $c\sharp^2$

and d², and is facilitated by a key controlled by the left thumb. The right thumb is placed under a thumb hook to help steady the instrument, but it does not normally provide support except in the case of soprano and sopranino. The other saxophones are sufficiently heavy that a neck strap (sling) needs to be used to take the weight. On some baritone models the right thumb also controls a key that provides a low a°.

The fingering for the saxophone is not particularly difficult to learn, especially for those who already have some expertise on flute, clarinet or oboe, with which the fingering patterns share some similarity. Nor is it difficult to blow – and as anguished parents around the world will attest, it is possible to get considerable volume from the instrument long before a performer acquires any real expertise. These twin traits – being comparatively easy to learn and easy to play – have underpinned much of the instrument's popularity over the last century or so, and are recurrent themes in this book. But as saxophone teachers will often caution, it is also an easy instrument to play badly.

Mouthpieces and reeds

The characteristics of mouthpiece and reed have a significant impact on the sound and behaviour of the instrument. Performers notice considerable differences when changing mouthpieces, not only on the effect they may have on intonation, but also on timbre, sound production, and so forth. There are many elements of mouthpiece design that can be manipulated to produce different effects, and the variety of musical

2. A miscellany of saxophone mouthpieces, demonstrating the wide variety available to performers today.

contexts in which the saxophone is now played, and the diversity of timbres thus required, means that performers have a bewildering array of mouthpieces to choose from, much greater than for other similar instruments (see ill. 2).

The tip opening, chamber and other elements of the mouthpiece may vary greatly, but as a general principle the wider the tip opening, the softer the reed that may be accommodated; too stiff a reed relative to the tip opening makes it difficult to achieve the periodic closure that is necessary to get the sound column vibrating. In general, classical players tend to favour medium tip openings with medium or medium soft reeds. Early jazz and popular music performers favoured more open lays with softer reeds, but over time they have moved towards mouthpieces with longer and narrower chambers, in part to produce the harder, edgier sounds necessary to compete with amplified instruments. The baffle, the underside of the sloping top of the mouthpiece, is particularly important in determining sound quality. The different shapes afforded to this baffle play a significant role in the many different types of sound that saxophonists are able to coax from the instrument. A slightly concave baffle, for example, produces a darker sound with less projection, and is often favoured for classical playing in orchestras. In contrast, a step baffle reduces the aperture at the tip end, restricting the air flow at this point and increasing the brightness of the sound quite significantly. This type of mouthpiece is often preferred by players working alongside amplified instruments.

The table and rails of the mouthpiece must be absolutely flat, to allow the reed to fit closely, with the reed itself being held in place by a ligature. A conventional two-screw ligature remains widely used, but has now been joined by a number of other designs, including those that use a screw plate to clamp the reed, and some that use a thick textile binding rather than the traditional metal cage. While the changes in sound quality resulting from these small differences may not be recognisable to any but the most discerning ear, they can significantly affect the feel of the instrument in the performer's mouth, and hence the manner in which the reed and embouchure are manipulated.

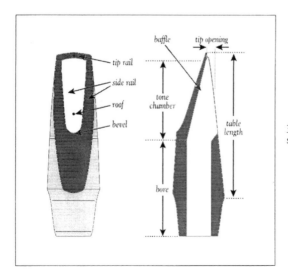

3. The various components of a saxophone mouthpiece.

The reed itself is cut from the large semi-tropical grass *arundo donax* or *arundo sativa*, sometimes referred to as 'cane'. This is indigenous to many countries, but is cultivated for the express purpose of providing clarinet and saxophone reeds in the Var region of France. The stems are cut before they are ripe, then allowed to mature in the open air. These are then cut to length, flattened on one side, and scraped down to a feath-ered edge on the other. The scraped sides are given different profiles ('cuts') by different manufacturers, with some leaving more of the heart of the reed in place and others tending to cut the reeds flatter. Performers evolve different preferences, which are again related to mouthpiece design and timbral aspiration. Unlike double-reed players, saxophonists tend not to make their own reeds from reed blanks, relying instead on purchasing them ready made from manufacturers. Many players do, however, indulge in a degree of manipulation, scraping and sanding various parts of the reed in order to encourage it to respond according to their preferences. Long-suffering players, who constantly bemoan the variability of the reeds they purchase, will be heartened to learn of similar concerns expressed as early as 1867 by Sax's biographer Oscar Comettant, who commented on the declining quality of reeds avail-able to performers even then, as a result of the move away from hand-made reeds and towards their mechanical production.[1]

The saxophone embouchure

The historical development of the saxophone embouchure, and its current practice, are more complex than is initially apparent. The saxophone follows the clarinet in having the mouthpiece oriented so that the reed is on the underside, resting on the lower lip, notwithstanding that until the late 1830s some clarinettists in France were still playing with the reed on top of the mouthpiece. The former practice was only officially adopted by the Paris Conservatoire from about 1830,[2] and many players who had built their technique around the 'reed on top' principle would most likely have continued playing in this fashion for several years thereafter. Nevertheless, Sax, an accomplished clarinettist, almost certainly learned the clarinet with the reed resting on the lower lip, and an 1846 method by Jean Cokken explicitly asserts that the saxophone mouthpiece should be placed in the mouth with the reed at the bottom; Georges Kastner, a close colleague of Sax who wrote the first authoritative method, also in 1846, similarly notes that the instrument was 'naturally' played in this fashion.[3]

The exact embouchure employed is less clear. Many clarinettists of the time played with a double-lip embouchure, whereby the reed rests on the lower lip, which is taken back over the teeth to provide a cushion, and the top lip also covers the upper teeth, providing a similar cushion between these teeth and the top of the mouthpiece. Certain players, however, advocated a single-lip embouchure, in which the lower lip similarly provides a cushion between the reed and the lower teeth, but the upper teeth are placed directly on the top of the mouthpiece itself, without the intervention of the upper lip, the latter being used only to form a seal around the mouthpiece. Kastner appears to have presumed that the double-lip embouchure would be the norm for the saxophone, since his method notes that Sax himself suggested that in some cases positioning the top teeth on the mouthpiece might reduce fatigue.[4] Cokken's method appears to suggest a single-lip embouchure, noting that the 'the upper lip envelops the mouthpiece without touching the teeth since it harms the quality of the sound'.[5] Various later methods published in the nineteenth century argued for or against these different embouchures. Louis Mayeur's 1867 method provides an example, noting that 'many clarinettists play the saxophone placing the upper teeth on the mouthpiece; this means is good for the clarinet but not for the saxophone. First one has less strength and much less sound, and in this manner one gets tired more quickly.'[6]

The double-lip embouchure could be found well into the twentieth century; Rudy Wiedoeft noted as late as 1925 that although 'I personally rest my upper teeth lightly on the mouthpiece [...] many good saxophonists use both lips'.[7] In contrast, Ben Vereecken's 1917 method advocates the single-lip embouchure, noting that the player should 'draw the lower lip easily over the teeth so that the reed does not touch the teeth. The upper teeth are applied to the mouthpiece'.[8] Vereecken's approach is grounded in classical training and a pedagogic orthodoxy designed to produce maximum pitch control and a centred, focused sound.

During the 1920s, and possibly earlier, a third type of embouchure evolved, one which more easily facilitated the kinds of flexible phrasing and control that jazz and dance music players required on the instrument. It first appears in 1925 in the method by Walter M. Eby, and relies on the performer *not* taking in the lower lip over the teeth, instead leaving it slightly puckered in front of the lower teeth, thus providing a cushion for the reed to rest on. In this fashion the player could achieve maximum lip flexibility.[9] Ben Davis argued for a similar embouchure in his 1932 method. Asserting that the embouchure advocated by Vereecken was 'extremely tiring to the lip, [so that] the embouchure soon weakens, with consequent lack of control over the reed and resultant poorness of tone and harsh low notes' he also advocated a lip-out embouchure that required the performer to 'rest the lower lip against the lower teeth, then lower the reed on to the rim of the lip, so that the inside of the lip forms a cushion between the teeth and the lip.' Davis emphasises that the player should '*not draw the lip in over the teeth*' but that the lip should 'form a sort of support for that part of the reed which is immediately outside the mouth.'[10] Both Eby and Davis are likely to have been formalising an embouchure that was already employed among dance band and jazz saxophonists, which may have arisen among those who were largely self taught, or taught by imitation and oral tradition, rather than more literate approaches relying on existing methods.

These two different types of embouchure are still in evidence today, with the lip-in type being largely the preserve of classically-trained players, and the lip-out version usually preferred by jazz players. The lip-out embouchure allows more malleability of the sound, and increases the importance of lower jaw movements in shaping musical phrases; this would have aided the pitch bending and novelty effects that were popular at the time it evolved. It is certainly an important component of much contemporary practice in jazz, rock and pop today, where flexibility of the neck and lower jaw to induce pitch bending and other phrasing effects have become central to individual and generic styles of performance. Among classical players the lower jaw stays rather more fixed.

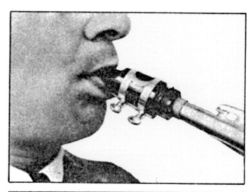

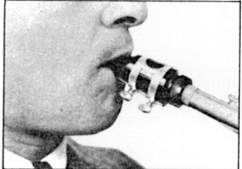

4.   Images from Ben Davis's 1932 'Comprehensive Course' for saxophone (p. 41), showing the three different saxophone embouchures. From top to bottom these are: the more modern 'lip out' embouchure; the conventional classical 'lower lip in' embouchure; and the now obsolete 'double lip' approach.

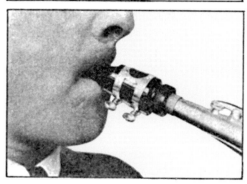

Saxophone acoustics

Despite the instrument usually being made of brass, the saxophone is technically designated as a woodwind instrument because of its single reed. In acoustic terms the instrument functions as a simple coupled system. The body contains an air column that is excited into vibration by the reed attached to the mouthpiece. The reed is itself excited by the air blown past it by the player, and closes against the mouthpiece briefly as it vibrates; the tip of the mouthpiece curves away slightly from the reed in order to facilitate this. The vibrations of the reed are controlled by the player's lips – largely the lower lip, in fact – since uncontrolled vibrations lead to squeaks. Significantly, the performer's oral cavity constitutes a further couple on the outside of the reed, and this plays an important role in determining both the precise pitch of the note and its timbre.

The saxophone has a conical bore and thus overblows at the octave, like the oboe, rather than at the twelfth, like the clarinet. In practical terms this means the player uses many of the same fingerings in the upper and lower registers, with the thumb operating a key that opens a small vent towards the top of the instrument, thus facilitating notes in the upper registers. Modern manufacturers use two carefully placed octave vent holes: the first provides the overtones for the upper register notes d^2 to $g\sharp^2$, and the second for all notes above this (usually a^2 to $f\sharp^3$). Earlier saxophones had two (and on a few of Sax's earliest models, three) octave keys, but all modern saxophones now have a mechanism operated by a single key, which automatically opens the required octave vent hole.

It is the combination of a conical bore with a single-reed mouthpiece that gives the instrument its not inconsiderable volume. The expansion rate (conicity) of the saxophone – the rate at which the conical bore expands from the proximal point (nearest the mouth) to the distal (farthest) end – is far greater than for other woodwind instruments. Whereas oboes and bassoons have expansion rates of between 1 and 2 per cent, the saxophone bore expands at a rate of about 7 per cent.[11] The conical air columns contained within all these instruments are truncated at one end to facilitate the mouthpiece and any crook upon which it sits. Acoustic theory dictates that the internal volume of the crook and mouthpiece must be equal to the 'missing' portion of the cone. It is for this reason that modern mouthpieces may be very unsatisfactory on earlier instruments – and vice versa – since the internal dimensions of the mouthpiece may not complement those of the main body of the instrument. Early saxophones sound softer and less resonant than their modern successors, but they play equally well, providing they are equipped with the correct mouthpiece.

The effective length of the saxophone air column is altered by opening and closing toneholes covered by large pads operated by the keywork. Although the flared bell is an important and iconic part of the saxophone's morphology, it does not in fact play a significant acoustic role, except in the case of the lowest notes. The majority of the saxophone sound emanates from the holes immediately beneath the lowest closed hole of any given note. For example the fingering for g^1, which leaves all the right-hand toneholes open, means the note is largely heard through those right-hand holes (used for the notes f^1, e^1 and d^1 etc.) rather than the lower holes found along the bell. As with other wind instruments these open holes provide what is known as a tonehole lattice, which in practice filters out or reduces low frequencies and boosts high frequencies. Although many of the saxophone's keys are closed when not in use, twelve rest open. This means that certain notes sound slightly stuffier than others because, although the tonehole immediately below them is open, the one below that may not be; later saxophone designs that endeavoured to remedy this problem are considered in Chapter 2.

The particular conical bore of the saxophone gives it certain characteristics that are not found on similar instruments. As already noted, both the bore diameter and the rate at which it expands are markedly greater than for other woodwind instruments, and this means that the toneholes needed are also large, since the size of such holes is determined by the bore diameter at the point where they are placed. The acoustic significance of this large bore in relation to the overall length of the instrument is that the fundamental tones are more easily produced, and it is this characteristic that gives each note of the saxophone a particularly rich harmonic spectrum – its 'fruitiness'. But a further problem arising from this rapidly expanding bore is that the degree of conicity determines the veracity of the harmonics, and thus the accuracy of the tuning. If the cone is too closed the upper harmonics become progressively sharp, whereas if it is too open they become flat. Furthermore, each tonehole is lipped by a small rim or chimney upon which its covering pad sits. This increases the effective volume of the cone and again affects the tuning of particular notes, either up or down according to the relationship between that tonehole and the sound waves inside the instrument. Adolphe Sax was clearly aware of this problem, since a prototype bass saxophone survives from around 1850 that does away with these chimneys, having instead curved pads that follow the shape of the body of the instrument. This innovation appears to have proved problematic and it did not enter production.[12]

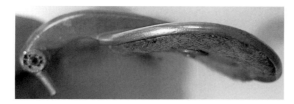

5. A curved keypad from a c. 1850 saxophone by Adolphe Sax. The key was designed to sit flush to the body, rather than resting on a soldered chimney.

Chapter 1

The life and times of Adolphe Sax

Dinant and Brussels

The small Belgian town of Dinant lies some 60 miles south-east of Brussels on the banks of the River Meuse. Nestling in the foothills of the Ardennes forest it is an attractive but unremarkable town with a long history of metalwork craftsmanship, having achieved a reputation in the Middle Ages for the production of what became known as *dinanderie*: fire irons, candlesticks and similar, and ecclesiastical objects such as fonts and lecterns. At the peak of its manufacturing success in the fifteenth century the town's population may have reached as many as 60,000, although today it numbers some 13,000 inhabitants. But its place in the cultural history of Europe is assured perhaps less through its mercantile past, and instead because it is the ancestral home of one of the most remarkable and innovative families involved with instrument manufacturing. Just as the later names of Sousa or Martenot live on at least in part through the names of the instruments in which they are incorporated, so too the name of the Sax family remains in the public consciousness through the several types of instrument for which it acts as a prefix: the saxhorn, the saxotromba, and above all the saxophone.

The head of the family, Charles-Joseph Sax, was born in Dinant on 1 February 1790. Like many in Dinant he was a craftsman, apprenticed to a cabinet maker in Brussels at the age of fifteen, and his occupation on his eldest son's birth certificate is listed as 'Joiner and Cabinet Maker'. He was also a keen amateur musician, taking part in the Dinant Société d'Harmonie (a wind band) in which he played the serpent, an S-shaped wooden instrument with a cup-shaped mouthpiece similar to that of the trombone. Rather than purchase a serpent he decided to use his carpentry skills to make his own, modelling it on an instrument by another Belgian maker.[1] It is probable that this was the first of several such instruments, and that he developed some self-taught skills as an instrument maker over the following years, in addition to his formal apprenticeship.

In his late teens Charles-Joseph took a job in a local factory making spinning machines, and in 1813, aged 23, he married a local girl, Marie-Joseph Masson. Almost exactly a year later their first child was born, a son, on 6 November 1814. He was christened Antoine-Joseph, the same name as Charles-Joseph's father, although he appears from a young age to have been accorded the moniker by which he was to become more widely known: Adolphe. He was to be the first of eleven children born to Charles-Joseph and Marie Sax, five girls and six boys, although only three would survive past their thirtieth birthday.

Adolphe was the only one of these many siblings to be born in Dinant as Charles-Joseph moved the family to Brussels in 1815. The fall of Napoleon after the battle of Waterloo and the subsequent demise of the First French Empire had led to the closure of the factory in which he worked, and he now found himself unemployed. Turning instead to his skills as an instrument maker he established a small business in the Belgian capital. Although his initial output was confined to serpents and flutes the operation flourished, and he gradually expanded to produce clarinets, bassoons and brass instruments. The birth and death certificates of subsequent children show numerous different addresses, from which it can be inferred that his successful and expanding business was frequently outgrowing its working premises.

In Charles-Joseph's personality and attitude to his work we can see a number of characteristics that his eldest son would inherit. He was inquisitive, restlessly seeking improvements to the instruments he manufactured. He was extremely perseverant but could also be obstinate to a fault. He was keen to learn more about the acoustic principles underlying instrument design. He explored how the positions of finger holes might be calculated more scientifically, determining in advance where the holes should be rather than relying on trial and error or the ergonomics of the hand, and

6.   Charles-Joseph Sax.

he was one of the first designers to work in this way. He took out a number of patents to protect inventions and innovations across a wide range of instruments, including the piano, the guitar, and particularly the horn. His posthumous reputation as an instrument maker rests in large part on his 1824 invention of the *cor omnitonique* (omnitonic horn).[2] This instrument incorporated all the crooks into the horn itself, which more easily facilitated chromatic passages that had previously required the interchange of such crooks during appropriately placed rests in the music; it was ultimately made redundant by the invention of the valve, which was developed around the same time.

According to Sax's first biographer, Oscar Comettant, Adolphe was an accident-prone child. Comettant's account of Sax's life is often romanticised and not entirely reliable, but the list of calamities he attributes to the infant inventor is striking: he tumbled down three flights of stairs and cracked his head on a stone floor; he drank a mixture of vitriol and water, mistaking it for milk; he was burned in a gunpowder explosion, and then again when a frying pan was knocked over; a falling roof-stone caused a lifelong scar on his head; he once went to bed in a room where newly-varnished objects were drying, but was discovered before he had expired through inhaling the noxious fumes.[3] If true, his fortitude in surviving such a litany of potential disasters was a characteristic that was to resurface frequently in later life, if only because it was to be much called upon.

Unsurprisingly, given the predispositions of their father, both Adolphe and his brothers were musically well educated. Adolphe enrolled in 1828 at the Royal School of Music, a precursor to the Royal Brussels Conservatoire, the latter not being established until 1832. Here he studied flute, in addition to solfège and harmony. He took private lessons on the clarinet with Valentin Bender, who was later Director of the *Musique Royale des Guides*, and became something of a virtuoso on the instrument. The visiting German composer Joseph Küffner was sufficiently impressed by Sax's abilities that he dedicated a work for two clarinets to the young performer in 1834.[4] Had Sax's life taken a different route, or his inclinations been otherwise, he might have made a successful career as a virtuoso clarinettist. But the lure of the family workshop and the environment of innovation and enquiry that surrounded him at home had already shaped his future trajectory. Following the patrilineal conventions that characterised many craft families of the time, Adolphe and several of his brothers chose to make careers as instrument makers themselves, with varying degrees of success.

Given Adolphe's expertise as a clarinettist it is unsurprising that his first forays as a designer and manufacturer were with that instrument; his own practical experience would obviously have given him particular insights into whatever deficiencies he might have felt the instrument to have. Even so, Sax *fils* made a precocious start to his manufacturing career, allegedly exhibiting his first designs while still only fifteen. These were shown at the Brussels Industrial Exhibition of 1830 and, according to Comettant, consisted of two flutes and a clarinet crafted in ivory.[5] However, there is no mention of Adolphe's name in the official catalogue, and it is probable that his father still had a considerable hand in the making of these instruments, since Adolphe was effectively a foreman in his father's workshops at this time.[6]

More significant is the later exhibition of 1835, in which Sax *père* displayed 25 brass instruments and 16 woodwind instruments, including, according to the exhibition catalogue, 'a boxwood clarinet with 24 keys, invented and perfected by Sax *fils*'.[7] It was later suggested that Sax had received an honourable mention for this instrument, but there is again no evidence for this in the official list of awards made at the exhibition.[8] Nevertheless, the instrument attracted considerable approval from many who saw it, with explicit attention drawn to it in the report of the Exhibition the following year; it was also praised by Sax's clarinet professor, Bender.

Over the next few years Sax devoted much of his energy to improving the bass clarinet. At this time the bass version of the clarinet family was a rather unsatisfactory instrument, notwithstanding that attempts had been made to improve it by Heinrich Grenser in 1793, Desfontenelles in 1807, and Georg Streitwolf in 1828. Sax, drawing on his father's knowledge of bore sizes and acoustic theory, produced a much improved model with a larger bore and toneholes in the correct places, the latter being closed by means of covered cups. He also added a second speaker key to aid sound production in the top register. The final result was an instrument producing a much richer sound as well as being better in tune and more easily facilitating rapid passagework.[9] The new instrument was patented in 1838, and its success established Sax's reputation as an instrument designer and innovator, bringing him to the

7. Caricature of Adolphe Sax astride his redesigned bass clarinet, c. 1850.

attention of musical circles in both Brussels and Paris. In 1842 Berlioz wrote that 'the new bass clarinet of M. Sax preserves nothing of the old one except the name [. . .]. What distinguishes it above all is its perfect intonation and its uniform temperament in all degrees of the chromatic scale.'[10]

In 1839 Sax made a brief trip to Paris in order to promote this new bass clarinet, and used the opportunity to become acquainted with composers such as Berlioz, Meyerbeer, Halévy and Kastner. Brussels was considerably less significant as a musical centre than the French capital, and it is likely that Sax was already beginning to feel torn between his family ties in Belgium and the possibilities offered by one of the major centres of mid-nineteenth-century European music-making, less than 200 miles away.

By the time of the Belgian Industrial Exhibition of August 1841 Sax was established as an inventor and manufacturer in his own right. His name is listed separately from that of his father among the official exhibitors. The Exhibition catalogue indicates that Sax displayed a number of instruments and accessories, including his new bass clarinet, several other clarinets, and 'a bass saxophone in brass'.[11] This is an intriguing entry, and it is the first record we have of Sax using the word saxophone. But it is not entirely clear whether the saxophone was actually displayed at this time, or indeed if it was even ready for display; these issues are dealt with in more detail in Chapter 2.

The reception given to Sax's display at this exhibition was apparently controversial. The official report notes the quality of Sax's work, the considerable progress he had made in making woodwind instruments, and the fact that he was awarded a silver medal for his exhibits. However, two of Sax's contemporaries recount that the examining jury relating to musical instruments at the Exhibition recommended Sax for the gold medal, but that the central jury overruled them on the grounds that Sax was too young, and that if he were awarded the gold medal this year there would be nothing to give him on subsequent occasions. Sax's response was, allegedly, 'if I am too young for the gold medal, then I am too old for the silver'.[12] This is an engaging story and one that suggests something of Sax's fiery temperament, a trait that was to become a feature of his dealings with others. But Sax's early biographers were also some of his most ardent supporters. They were often guilty of embellishing the facts in order to put the case more strongly for Sax's abilities, and there is no independent documentary evidence to support this anecdote.

If Sax had been slighted in this way by the Exhibition's central jury it may have contributed to his plans to move to Paris. These intentions were further reinforced by a visit from a high-ranking officer in the French army, Lieutenant-General Marie-Théodore Gueilly, Comte de Rumigny. De Rumigny was concerned at the poor state of France's military bands, and made it his business to visit Sax's workshops in Brussels in the summer of 1842. Enthused by what he saw, he became convinced that Sax and his instruments could play an important role in raising the standard of French military music, and his encouragement of the young inventor no doubt reinforced in Sax's mind the idea of a permanent move to the French capital. With a contact such as de Rumigny, Sax probably foresaw the possibility of a financially rewarding relationship with the French military establishment, enabling his business to grow well beyond what was possible in Brussels.

Paris – the early years

The period from the Revolution of 1789 to the fall of the Second Empire in 1870 was a time of considerable social ferment and political insecurity in France. The Revolution itself had at first a negative impact on Parisian cultural life, but the establishment of the Conservatoire national supérieur de musique in 1795 provided salaries and prestige for certain more fortunate musicians, and this helped in part to reinvigorate the capital's musical life. The advances of the first decades of the nineteenth century in areas such as manufacturing, transportation, and science and technology – particularly in relation to the development of steam-driven engines – led to fortunes being made by industrialists, bankers and others. All this, together with a trend towards urbanisation and the rise of an affluent middle class, made Paris a wealthy city. This in turn generated greater musical patronage, and figures such as Berlioz, Chopin and Liszt would soon benefit from the largesse of the newly-monied middle classes, either through direct employment in salons and concert halls or through private teaching.

In 1814 Napoleon I abdicated and the Bourbon monarchy was restored, first with the weak Louis XVIII and then in 1824 with the repressive Charles X. The latter's more draconian and right-wing policies led to a further revolution in 1830, resulting in the so-called 'July Monarchy' of Louis-Philippe, which lasted until 1848. Louis-Philippe's encouragement of middle-class business and commerce provided a fertile environment for aspiring merchants such as Sax. It was therefore a matter of concern to such businessmen when the monarchy was again overthrown in 1848, and Louis Napoleon, nephew of Napoleon I, was installed as President, eventually proclaiming himself Emperor Napoleon III in 1852. This Second Empire lasted until 1870. As will become apparent, the ebb and flow of these political tides were to impact on Sax's own fortunes to a considerable degree.

There were two other discrete yet related parts of Paris's social landscape that would influence Sax's fortunes over the coming decades. The first comprised those significant musical figures who formed part of the musical oligarchy in the French capital, but who were favourably disposed towards the ideas of the Belgian inventor. Foremost among these was Hector Berlioz, now remembered as one of the most important French composers of the nineteenth century but also a highly influential writer and music critic. Also notable were Jean-Georges Kastner, a composer and theorist who was one of Sax's most ardent supporters and who is credited with first using a saxophone in his opera *Le Dernier Roi de Juda* (1844); and Oscar Comettant, a critic who became an enthusiastic advocate for Sax, as well as writing the 1860 biography. Other composers such as Adam, Halévy, Donizetti, Meyerbeer, Thomas and Rossini also supported Sax by scoring for some of his instruments, and by making public statements in his favour. François-Joseph Fétis, a Belgian composer and writer who, like Sax, had established himself in Paris, also wrote an extensive and important biography of his compatriot.[13] When the *Revue et Gazette des Théâtres* reproduced a collection of different letters commending Sax's work in 1843, it was no surprise that they bore the signatures of many of these individuals.[14]

The support of such figures was essential to Sax because it helped counter the opposition he faced from more hostile elements in Paris, particularly from the instrument makers with whom he was in direct competition. Some of these were very influential in France's expanding market, with long-established and lucrative businesses. Sax most likely realised before he moved to Paris that he would face significant opposition from those keen to protect their interests. As early as 1841 a letter appeared in the *RGMP* claiming that Sax had copied innovations already devised by one M. Lefèvre, an oboist in Nantes, and had claimed them as his own.[15] Similar accusations would become a familiar feature of Sax's later career.

But the generally positive responses Sax received on his visits to Paris must have removed any lingering doubts he had about moving there, and after a brief trip to Berlin to study German methods of instrument manufacture, he moved permanently to Paris in October 1842. He established his first workshop, in a modest building at 10 rue Neuve-Saint-Georges in July 1843. But his business grew quickly. That same year he filed his first French patent (an improved generic system for closing keys on wind or metal instruments)[16] and by 1844 he was already exporting instruments to Germany, Belgium, Holland and England; Rossini was also advocating the adoption of his instruments by the Conservatory in Bologna.[17]

Sax's apparently unceasing flow of invention and innovation was a characteristic he retained throughout his working life. By the time the saxophone was patented in 1846 it had already been preceded by two other families of instruments: saxhorns and saxotrombas. The first of these – the second patent filed in 1843 – was arguably an evolution of existing brass technology, albeit radically modernised by Sax to create a homogenous family of valved brass instruments; these began as forward pointing trumpet-shaped instruments (valved bugles) but evolved into upward pointing tuba-shaped instruments. There remains considerable confusion over the names given to

8. Adolphe Sax c. 1841, lithograph by Baugniet.

these various types, a confusion furthered by the use of different names in different countries to describe the same instrument. The debate as to whether this family of instruments could actually be described as an invention provided the basis for many of Sax's legal disputes over subsequent decades, since it was widely claimed that these instruments largely used existing technology. Indisputably, however, Sax brought new levels of workmanship, timbral homogeneity and organisation to this particular group of brass instruments. Sax himself did not use the description 'saxhorn' in his patent, preferring instead to describe them as 'a system of chromatic instruments'.[18] This uncharacteristic reticence was not evident with his second group of new instruments, the saxotromba family, patented two years later in November 1845.[19] These differed from the saxhorns: whereas the latter had an entirely conical bore, saxotrombas comprised a mixture of cylindrical and conical bores. They made less impact than the earlier group and were more or less obsolete by the 1870s. Another family, the so-called saxtuba – again, this term is not used in the patent – suffered a similarly short-lived existence after being patented in 1852.[20]

Sax's predilection for designing musical instruments in families was neither coincidental nor the result of any hegemonic tendencies, although this was precisely the accusation many of his opponents levelled at him. Perhaps his greatest single contribution to instrument design was to have realised the importance of the relationship between bore size and tonehole size and placement, an insight that in part enabled him to create uniform families of instruments. Such uniformity not only facilitated a particular homogeneity within each family (and by extension other ensembles in which they might be employed), but it also made performers' lives easier. By unifying the approach needed to play different instruments – for example, by retaining the same fingering system among different members of the same family, as with the saxophone – a musician who learned to play one member of a family could easily transfer to another.

Sax's inventions went beyond these instrumental families. He continued to make improvements to the clarinet, enhancing the designs of toneholes and keys. He renovated the bassoon, inspired by the work of the German inventor Theobald Boehm. He spent some time considering the problems of various percussion instruments, and registered several patents for the improvement of timpani, including one in 1855 relating to chromatic timpani.[21] There were also a number of patents relating to non-musical items. In 1863, after a bout of illness, he patented a 'Goudronnière-Sax', a machine for disseminating antiseptic vapours around a room.[22] In 1866 he proposed a novel design for a concert hall, based on parabolic principles and shaped like an elongated egg, which he suggested would have acoustic properties far superior to halls then in use.[23] And there were some ideas that were considerably less practical, notably the unpatented 'Saxocannon', a proposal for a cannon with a bore of ten metres that would fire a shot weighing 550 tons.[24] Sax registered more than 40 original patents in total, not including duplicates taken out in Belgium or England to protect items already patented in France.[25]

One way in which Sax was able to demonstrate the advantages of his instruments was by organising concerts at his workshops in the rue Neuve-Saint-Georges. To these he would invite friends and acquaintances, as well as others whom he felt might be

9. Lithograph of a concert of new Sax instruments at Salle Sax, rue Saint-Georges, published in *L'illustration*, 16 July 1864. Several saxophones can be clearly distinguished.

useful to him as he attempted to establish his business. The first of these appears to have taken place in December 1843.[26] In front of an audience that included Meyerbeer, Berlioz, Kastner, General de Rumigny and numerous journalists, Sax himself illustrated the advantages of his clarinet, bass clarinet, and saxophone. The great French trumpet virtuoso Jean-Baptiste Arban, who was frequently employed by Sax to demonstrate his brass instruments, played a variety of trumpets and cornets. At a later event, on 3 February 1844, Berlioz arranged a short piece, his *Chant sacré*, to be played entirely on instruments Sax had invented or perfected, including the saxophone. François-Antoine Habeneck, a renowned violinist and conductor, expressed his admiration for this ensemble.[27]

These occasions made favourable impressions on many of Paris's most illustrious musicians, and Sax nurtured the relationships that arose from them. For example, in late 1846, after the unsuccessful premiere of Berlioz's *La Damnation de Faust*, Sax lent the composer 1,200 francs to enable to him to travel to Russia, even though Sax's own financial position was by no means secure at the time.[28] In later years, when the opposition against Sax was at its height, Berlioz railed in support of the inventor, asserting with characteristic hyperbole that 'it is scarcely to be believed that this gifted young artist should be finding it difficult to maintain his position and make a career in Paris. The persecutions he suffers are worthy of the Middle Ages and recall the antics of the enemies of Benvenuto [Cellini], the Florentine sculptor. They lure away his workmen, steal his designs, accuse him of insanity, and bring legal proceedings against him. With a little more dash they would assassinate him.'[29]

Sax and the French military

Part of Sax's motivation for moving to Paris was the possibility of developing a potentially lucrative involvement with the French army. Military bands were maintained throughout France and its burgeoning empire, and this offered a large prospective market for wind and brass instruments. General de Rumigny's enthusiasm for Sax's innovations was already evident, and he moved in the highest circles of the French military elite, taking a particular interest in the state of military music provision. De Rumigny and others were becoming increasingly concerned with the poor state of French military music-making, although the Gymnase de Musique Militaire had been established in 1836, under the direction of the clarinettist Frédéric Berr, in part to address these deficiencies. In particular, the military authorities were aggrieved that the bands of Prussia and Austria were so demonstrably better than those of France, and such concerns were shared by the then sovereign, King Louis-Philippe.

Prussian superiority in military music was largely due to the German instrument maker Wilhelm Wieprecht. Wieprecht had systematically overhauled Prussian bands in the 1830s, reorganising the instrumentation of the bands as well as developing several of the brass instruments used in them. Wieprecht and Sax shared a mutual distrust of each other's work, and the former's antipathy towards the saxophone in particular was one reason why the instrument was less popular in Germany in the nineteenth century.[30] However, Wieprecht's skill as an organiser of military ensembles was reflected in the widespread adoption of his approach throughout Germany when the German Empire was created in 1871. French disquiet with the standards of military bands was not confined only to the upper echelons of the army; other writers openly expressed their concerns in the most robust manner. The journal *L'Illustration*, for example, wrote of one performance in 1845 that 'the bass, bellowed out by the ophicleides, carried everywhere, yet covered everything. As to the intermediate parts, at fifteen feet you could not even tell they were there. You would hear piccolo, the ophicleide, bass drum and cymbals and the rest would be completely lost.'[31]

In 1844 Sax, mindful of the opportunity at hand, wrote three letters outlining what might be done to improve the situation: these went to de Rumigny, Marshal Soult, the Minister of War, and the King himself. The latter was already familiar with Sax's work, having visited his stand at the Industrial Exhibition earlier the same year, probably at the behest of de Rumigny.[32] Marshal Soult asked Sax to demonstrate his instruments, so that he might hear them at first hand. This then led to a live comparison being staged between 32 bandsmen representing the established military instrumentation and nine musicians playing Sax's instruments.[33] Even with such numerical disparity Sax's instruments were deemed superior; the suitably impressed Minister of War convened a special commission, chaired by de Rumigny, to investigate the matter. The commission began its work early in 1845.

Sax's proposed overhaul of French military band provision, and the degree to which this would be built around his own instruments, can be understood by comparing the following two lists; the first was given by Léon Kreutzer as being the typical instrumentation of a military band prior to 1845, in an article published later that year in the *RGMP*:[34]

Table 1: Typical instrumentation of a French military band prior to 1845.

1 piccolo	4 piston cornets	4 trombones
1 E♭ clarinet	2 valve trumpets	4 horns
12 B♭ clarinets	1 regular trumpet	6 ophicleides
2 oboes	1 keyed bugle	5 percussion
2 bassoons		

Total = 45 players

The second is drawn from one of Sax's submissions to the commission, and was subsequently published by Berlioz in the *Journal des débats* in April 1845:[35]

Table 2: French military band instrumentation proposed by Adolphe Sax in 1845.

1 E♭ piccolo	2 B♭ 3-valve baritone saxhorns	2 B♭ ophicleides
1 E♭ clarinet	2 B♭ 4-valve saxhorns	1 snare drum
6 unison B♭ clarinets	4 E♭ 3-valve contrabass saxhorns	1 bass drum
6 three-valve trumpets (Sax system)	2 three-valve cornets	1 tenor drum
2 small E♭ saxhorns	2 valve trombones (Sax system)	2 pairs of cymbals
4 B♭ saxhorns	2 slide trombones	1 triangle
4 B♭ tenor saxhorns		

Total = 46 players

In Sax's list, the numbers of clarinets and ophicleides have been reduced, and the oboes, bassoons and horns have all been replaced with Sax instruments of some kind; his belief that only first clarinets should be retained (not second, third or fourth clarinets) is evident. The retention of even two ophicleides is perhaps surprising since Sax was no fan of the instrument. It is also curious that Sax did not at this stage include saxophones, particularly since he appears to have had a clear view of the potential role the instrument might play in such bands, as the saxophone patent, also initially submitted in 1845, makes clear (see Appendix). The instrument's omission is not easily explained unless – since the patent had yet to be granted – Sax was reluctant to allow it to be seen by potential competitors. Alternatively, given the developmental state of the instrument at this time, it is possible that he felt it not ready to be included, or that it would not be well received, or indeed known at all, by some of those scrutinising his proposals.

Sax faced opposition to his proposals from Michele Carafa, the director of the Gymnase de Musique Militaire since 1839, despite Carafa's earlier endorsement of Sax's innovations.[36] Carafa was against Sax's radical plans and preferred a more conservative approach, arguing that with the correct balance and proportions the existing instrumental disposition was perfectly adequate. In order to be seen to be fair, the commission arranged a public competition in the Champs de Mars on 22 April 1845. One band would employ Carafa's proposed instrumentation, the other would be under Sax's control. Not only would the commission be in attendance but the event would be open to members of the public, who would be free to voice their own opinions.

Today the Champs de Mars lies in the shadow of the Eiffel Tower, with the River Seine at one end and the École Militaire at the other. In 1845 it was an even larger space, used for military reviews, often before troops were sent into battle. On the day in question it was to see combat of a rather different type. There was significant public interest in the event, and a large crowd assembled to hear the two bands, in addition to the commission members, other senior officers, eminent artists and journalists.[37] Carafa's group was constructed along traditional lines, including oboes, bassoons and numerous clarinets. Sax's band was intended to follow closely the instrumentation given in Table 2, with one notable exception: he had, finally, abandoned the ophicleides that he so disliked and replaced them with two unspecified saxophones. He also exchanged the Eb piccolo for a Db version.[38] However, when it came to the performance itself seven of his musicians – including the saxophonists – failed to appear, having been persuaded to stay away, possibly bribed by Sax's opponents.[39] The event lasted more than four hours,[40] since various permutations of instruments, particularly all-brass bands, were being scrutinised, to cater for the different demands of the various French regiments. But the day was a significant success for the Belgian inventor. The crowd was soon convinced of the superiority of his instruments. The press caught the public mood and developed the analogy of a battle between the two camps. *Le Charivari* (a model for the famous British satirical magazine *Punch*) likened the victory of 'Les Saxons' over 'Les Carafons' as equalling any victory of Napoleon.[41] *L'Illustration* proclaimed that 'we have the right to hope that our brave army will now be able to defy its rivals in concerts as in battle.'[42] Kreutzer, writing in *La Quotidienne*, was even more effusive, observing that 'a Stradivarius violin compared with a violin from the village, a glass of generous Bordeaux next to an adulterated beverage made in Suresne, that is the difference which exists between the old music and that proposed by M. Sax.'[43]

The commission inevitably took a more measured tone and a little longer over its deliberations, but eventually agreed on a compromise arrangement to be recommended to the Ministry, in which the number of players would be set at 54, to include two saxophones.[44] Oboes and bassoons would be retained. The Ministry of War itself, however, took a slightly different view. In the official instrumentation published on 10 September 1845 they largely followed the commission's recommendation, but omitted the oboes and bassoons. Infantry bands would have 50 musicians, including the two saxophones, and cavalry bands, composed entirely of brasswind instruments and without saxophones, would have 36 musicians.[45]

For Sax the outcome was highly satisfactory. His new instruments were all accepted into the different ensembles to varying degrees, and the final disposition of instrumental resources was constructed to a large extent upon the models he had advocated.

10. Exterior view of Adolphe Sax's workshops on the rue Saint-Georges in the mid-nineteenth century.

An entire family of saxhorns would now be required by each regiment, as well as pairs of saxophones, and the majority of other brass instruments required used his innovations. Military instruments suffered high degrees of wear and tear, and would need constant replacement, thus securing the future of his business. Furthermore, since these new instruments were now to be officially adopted by the military, they would need to be taught at the Gymnase de Musique Militaire. This required new staff, and thus a series of auditions was held to decide on the new appointments. In November 1846 the *RGMP* announced that Monsieur Cokken, also a Professor of Bassoon, had been named as the first Professor of Saxophone at the institution, together with several other new appointments, including that of Arban as Professor of Alto Saxhorn.[46] Cokken's skills as a teacher must have served him well: less than a year later the *RGMP,* commenting upon the graduation performances of the school, wondered how his initial class of five students had 'obtained in so short a time such marvellous results'.[47] After the initial euphoria, however, the reality was that the saxophone was only rarely employed in most bands in the years immediately following this event, and it was to take considerably longer before the instrument became a widespread feature of French military music-making.

Competition and litigation

Sax's triumph with the French military establishment should have secured his position in Paris as the pre-eminent maker of brasswind and woodwind instruments, as well as giving him a strong financial basis on which to plan for the future. In fact it brought more sharply into focus the two factors in his life that so frequently undermined his career: his own relative lack of business acumen coupled with a tendency to resort to hasty litigation; and the conspiratorial opposition of his many enemies in Paris, particularly other instrument manufacturers, who feared that Sax's ambitions would be the foundation of their own demise.

Sax's success at the Champs de Mars, and his subsequent control, amounting to a virtual monopoly, over the supply of instruments to the French military establishment, threatened the livelihoods of several long-established and influential Parisian instrument makers. Some of their names – for example the Buffet family and Gustave Besson – remain familiar today because of the legacies of the eponymous companies and marques they established.[48] Others such as Halary, Gautrot, or Raoux, several of them significant manufacturers in the nineteenth century, are less well remembered now.[49] Like Sax, many had been awarded medals and commendations at various exhibitions for their contributions to instrument design and development. But unlike Sax they were already running established and profitable businesses, supplying French musicians in general and the military in particular. Two of Sax's early supporters, Comettant and Pontécoulant, later suggested that the manufacturers organised themselves into a formally constituted body in order to oppose Sax's interests, although there is no hard evidence for this.[50]

While the dedication with which Sax's competitors pursued litigation against him may appear curious today, it must be seen in the context of the vigorous entrepreneurial climate that characterised Parisian instrument manufacturing at this time. Substantial profits, as well as reputations, were at stake. The industrial revolution was taking hold in France and fortunes were being made by certain industrialists, particularly in textiles and steel. This in turn led to increasing urbanisation and a significant boost for the construction industry, building factories and then houses for the people who worked in them. Speculators were keen to profit from these commercial enterprises, and entrepreneurs starting up new companies often financed them with the offer of shares in the company and the promise of handsome profits later on. Notwithstanding that many instrument makers were small-scale craft workshops rather than industrial enterprises, in the world of instrument manufacturing there seemed no more profitable prospect than the young Belgian inventor. Sax, subscribing happily to the new capitalist philosophy, had established his company in exactly this way, raising capital of 40,000 francs from ten shareholders contributing 4,000 francs each in December 1842.[51] Were he to prove the more attractive proposition for potential investors, it might be difficult for other manufacturers to expand their own businesses as they would have wished, in addition to combating the competition that Sax's company provided.

Sax's opponents reserved their most concerted opposition for the saxophone. By 1845 the instrument was sufficiently developed that Sax was ready to apply for a patent, though it remains a little puzzling that he waited so long. Given that he was demonstrating his invention in Paris from 1842 onwards, it might be thought he would wish to safeguard it at the earliest opportunity. Perhaps some of the delay was caused by the move to Paris in 1842, since Sax was unable to establish a proper workshop there until July 1843. Most likely, however, Sax was waiting until the instrument was developed enough for him to be confident that he could protect it adequately. Whatever the reason, his application was opposed by others on a number of grounds. It was suggested that the instrument was not original but in fact a copy of various pre-existing instruments; Sax had little difficulty in refuting these allegations. It was claimed that the instrument was not musical at all; the clarinettist of the Théâtre Français wrote that 'the saxophones sound hollow and wrong – they are noisy and blaring', an opinion which brought a sharp riposte from Berlioz.[52] The editor of *L'Europe musicale et dramatique* sided with Sax's opponents, facetiously referring to the 'manufacturing Messiah by the name of Bax, Fax or Rax who had created the Blaghorn'.[53] More sinister forms of subterfuge were employed than simple name calling: a number of saxophones were sent abroad to have the maker's engravings and identifying marks removed, then re-imported in an effort to show prior existence of the instrument. Pictures of them were even included in other makers' catalogues. Such forgeries were poorly done and quickly exposed as chicanery.

This chorus of negative criticism inevitably affected Sax. Although no legal proceedings were entered into until 1846, Sax did delay his saxophone patent application for one year, in the meantime issuing a challenge to his adversaries that if any of them could produce a saxophone within that year he would withdraw his application. None responded to the challenge, and on 21 March 1846 Sax submitted his application. Under prevailing French law, patents could be registered for 5, 10 or 15 years only, at an annual cost of 100 francs for each year of registration; the saxophone patent was granted for a duration of 15 years, on 22 June 1846.[54]

Sax's competitors began formal legal proceedings against him in March 1846, just as he was filing his patent application. This was the beginning of a series of legal battles that would consume much of his energy and finances over the coming decades. Although this first writ initially concerned Sax's earlier French patents of 1843 and 1845, for saxhorns and saxotrombas respectively, the new patent for the saxophone was quickly added to it.

Several of the accusations made against Sax simply repeated in more formal terms the objections noted above, which had already been made known verbally and in writing, and which Sax had little difficulty in rebutting; indeed, the court itself ruled that some of the accusations were contradictory and cancelled each other out.[55] A more serious challenge was presented by the assertion that Sax had violated a law passed in 1844, which stated that an invention could not be described as original if, before a patent had been taken out, it had received sufficient publicity to allow it to be copied or made.

The judges hearing the case would not commit themselves to a verdict, instead appointing a panel of specialists to advise them. This panel began collecting information from individuals who were in some way familiar with Sax's instruments. Of particular interest is the affidavit from Cokken, the Professor of Saxophone at the Gymnase de Musique Militaire. He was, unsurprisingly, effusive in his praise for the instrument:

> Having learned that some have denied the existence of the saxophone, I come to attest to you that this instrument really does exist, that I play it myself, and that I teach it at the Gymnase de Musique Militaire. I take advantage of this opportunity to add that the saxophone is an instrument as beautiful as it is good, of great power, of magnificent timbre, and finally the easiest to learn. I do not doubt that excellent results can be obtained from it in military bands as well as symphony orchestras.[56]

The panel also took evidence from those who had heard or written about the saxophone, all of whom claimed that they could not have passed on the technical information required to build one.[57] Accordingly, the panel stated their belief that the allegations against Sax were untrue, and that all his patents were valid and should be allowed to stand.

This ought to have been the end of the matter, with the court heeding the panel's advice and throwing out the case before them. But events beyond Sax's control conspired against him. Before the court could give its final pronouncement French political life was thrown into fresh turmoil and the decision was delayed. It would be another eight years before the case was finally settled.

Sax and the Second Republic

Sax's business prospered in the years immediately after the Champs de Mars event, notwithstanding the various legal challenges mounted against him. But his own success was in notable contrast to the worsening social and economic climate of the country as a whole, a deterioration that become increasingly evident as France approached the century's midpoint. A bad cereal harvest in 1845 was compounded by a much worse harvest generally in 1846. Bread and potatoes were in short supply and a full-blown agricultural crisis developed. Food prices rose at an alarming rate, and the population spent increasing proportions of their income feeding themselves. This led to less expenditure on non-essentials such as textiles or houses, reducing the manufacturing, construction and transport industries. By the end of 1847, 700,000 workers had been made redundant in the railway and steel industries alone.[58] Stockholders, speculators and finance houses were soon affected, and there were reports of banks themselves going bankrupt, when they became unable to return deposits to anxious clients. Political pressure mounted on the ageing King Louis-Philippe. In Paris, what began as a demonstration became a riot and then a revolution when a group of protestors was shot on the Boulevard des Capucines in February 1848. Within 24 hours the King abdicated and fled from Paris to England.

It is tempting to read the relationship between Sax, his opponents and his patrons as an example in miniature of the difficulties besetting the end of Louis-Philippe's reign. Many middle-class industrialists had prospered under the King's administration, particularly those receiving patronage from royalty, the government, or the military, whereas traditional workers had become marginalised and felt the need to fight for their rights through protective associations of various kinds. Sax himself was confronted by just such sentiments among his workforce. Comettant suggests that during the unrest created by the 1848 revolution, Sax's workers approached him and asked that in future the business should be run as a cooperative, a request that would have been much in keeping with the political sentiments of the times. Sax was ready to agree, but pointed out that if the company was to be structured in such a fashion, the workers would have to underwrite their share of any losses, as well as benefit from any potential profits. According to Comettant this was enough to subdue these radical plans, and no more was heard of the matter.[59]

In the immediate aftermath of Louis-Philippe's abdication Sax was confronted by a problem that presented a more fundamental threat to his financial security and the future of his business. The 1848 revolution that deposed the King had established a provisional 'citizen's government'. Sax had few connections with this new regime, unlike many of his opponents who now saw an opportunity to put him in his place. In particular, Carafa, over whom Sax had triumphed in the Champs de Mars and whose own plans for the organisation of military bands had thus been thwarted, was well connected with the new administration and seized his opportunity. The first decision of the new government in relation to music was to overturn the edicts issued in 1845 on the instrumentation of military bands, and to return them to something resembling their former disposition, including oboes, bassoons, ophicleides, and conventional horns and trumpets. Infantry bands would have 50 players and cavalry bands would have 36 players, and none of them would play any instrument made by Sax.[60] Fétis wrote scathingly of this decision in the *RGMP*, noting that it was based on little more than 'a miserable question of pride'.[61]

Sax was facing a potentially ruinous situation. He had a manufacturing operation to keep going and a skilled workforce to be concerned about, but his most lucrative market was under threat. Under its interim government France was experiencing severe economic pressures. Political instability continued and unemployment rose steeply. Once again Parisians took to the streets, and in June 1848 the Provisional Government was disbanded, having survived for only four months. Popular elections were held and Louis Napoleon (Napoleon III), the nephew of Napoleon I, became President. After a *coup d'état* in November 1852, Louis Napoleon proclaimed himself Emperor and the Second Empire was born.

These political upheavals had other ramifications for Sax's business. In the case of the ongoing 1846 court proceedings it meant that judgement had been deferred. By the time the case returned to court the original lawyer for the opposition had become Minister of Justice in the Provisional Government, an inauspicious turn of events from Sax's perspective. The lawyer who replaced him in the case now exploited Sax's connections with the recently deposed Louis-Philippe, in order to highlight his alleged anti-republican tendencies (although there is little evidence to suggest the true nature of Sax's political affiliations).[62] The expert panel's report was presented, but the new court disagreed with their findings. Sax's 1845 patent relating to the saxotromba was disqualified, as was part of the 1843 saxhorn patent. Only the patent covering the saxophone was upheld in full. Sax appealed, however, and the case had several further hearings before finally coming to a conclusion at Rouen in 1854, with the court finding in favour of Sax and deeming his patents to be valid. As part of the documentation presented during this last hearing Sax's lawyer's put forward a letter written by Meyerbeer in 1849 to the Chancellor of the Belgian Embassy, responding to the latter's request for his views on Sax's instruments, in which Meyerbeer observed that:

> I would limit myself to mention his bass clarinet, a formerly defective instrument, but today an achieved improvement, and his saxophones, comprising a family of six members from high to low, whose magnificent and particular sonority will be

of a valuable help to military bands and will even be able to be added to orchestras, therein furnishing composers with new combinations of instruments.[63]

Although the decision of the court in Rouen brought this particular piece of litigation to a close, Sax immediately filed a counter-suit against his opponents, in a series of actions that occupied him over the next decade. The last of these was not concluded until 1867. There were other legal proceedings too: in 1850 he successfully sued the maker Michel Rivet, based in Lyon, for counterfeiting a saxophone, something Sax only discovered when the unwitting soldier who had purchased it brought it to his factory in Paris for repair.[64] In 1866 he began another successful action against a singer, Marie Sasse, who had taken the name of Sax as her stage name. And in 1876 he was himself sued by the Society of Composers and Music Editors (SACEM), who claimed he owed royalties on account of the concerts he had organised.[65] From 1846 onwards Sax's involvement with judicial process became a recurrent feature of his life; despite his prodigious energy these proceedings inevitably drained him both emotionally and, because of the significant legal costs he incurred, financially.

Under the short-lived Provisional Government Sax and his employees had given up one day's pay to help those injured in the revolution. Sax had also offered the Première légion de la garde nationale mobile a set of his instruments.[66] Even so, it was becoming impossible to run his factory as a going concern. Sax wanted to reduce the number of workers employed in the factory, but was persuaded otherwise to avoid the risk of a backlash should he be seen to be cutting his workforce so soon after the worker-led revolution. Instead he accepted a loan of 30,000 francs from one of his associates, Paul Leroux, which allowed him to keep the factory open and retain his skilled staff. No receipt was required for this money, and thus it may have appeared to Sax as a gift rather than a loan. This unfortunate confusion had significant repercussions shortly thereafter, when the original donor died and his family demanded full repayment of what was now deemed unequivocally to be a loan. Sax was in no position to repay the money and on 5 July 1852 he was declared bankrupt for the first time. Sax reached an agreement with his creditors to pay the capital owed over the next eight years, and this allowed him to continue in business.

Notwithstanding these legal and political difficulties, Sax's name remained in the public eye, particularly through his success at various exhibitions. At the French Industrial Exhibition of 1849, for example, he was awarded the only gold medal to be given to a wind instrument manufacturer. More significantly, four months after this exhibition ended, he became a Chevalier of the Légion d'honneur, one of only three instrument makers to be so honoured.[67] it was an unusual distinction for a manufacturer to be given both awards at the same time, and Sax was understandably keen to draw attention to the achievement in his advertising. At the 1851 Great Exhibition in London Sax was the only French exhibitor in his category to obtain a Council Medal, awarded for his display of 85 instruments. While such successes in themselves provided little financial recompense, they undoubtedly helped Sax's trade connections and profile, as well as enhancing the reputation of his innovations.

Following the installation of Napoleon III as President of the Republic in December 1848, Sax felt it expedient to ingratiate himself with the new regime. The new President was already familiar with the inventor's achievements, since he had presented Sax with the Légion d'honneur. A military parade organised in May 1852 included a number of Sax's instruments, the sound of which apparently greatly impressed the President.[68] Napoleon III began to consider reorganising the military band of the Imperial Guard, largely for his personal use. Sax, using what connections he had in the new administration, provided a possible model for this new band, which he was then invited to audition in front of Napoleon himself. The inventor called upon the best players he could summon, and the ensemble, having previously been heard in front of a distinguished gathering at Sax's own workshops, was given a private audience on New Year's Day, 1853, only a few weeks after Napoleon had mounted the *coup d'état* that led to him pronouncing himself Emperor. Napoleon was suitably impressed by Sax's ensemble, and Sax now found himself with a new and very powerful patron.

This new situation was clearly much to Sax's advantage, and a number of benefits quickly followed. Several of his admirers, including Napoleon himself, made arrangements with Sax's creditors to pay off his debts, thus releasing him from bankruptcy and allowing him to revive his business. The following year Sax was honoured with the title of 'Official Musical Instrument Manufacturer to the Emperor', the decree being signed by Achille Fould, Minister of State, on 8 April 1854. Only three weeks later, on 1 May, a further decree came into force reorganising the band of the Imperial Guard in the fashion of Sax's instrumentation heard the previous year. This was followed on 16 August by yet another decree, ordering the reorganisation of regimental bands along the same lines as the Imperial Guard.

Sax's revised instrumentation for this ensemble built on the changes he had put forward in 1845, dispensing with ophicleides, reducing the number of double reeds, and incorporating many of his own instruments. In particular, a double quartet of saxophones was introduced, the family by now being more fully developed. The full list of instruments for infantry was to be as given in Table 3:[69]

Table 3: Revised instrumentation for French military bands proposed by Adolphe Sax in 1854.

2 flutes/piccolos	2 small Eb soprano saxhorns	2 cornets (piston or valve)
4 Eb clarinets	2 alto Bb saxhorns	4 trombones (including one bass)
8 unison Bb clarinets	3 Eb alto saxotrombas	1 bass drum
2 oboes	2 Bb baritone saxhorns	1 side drum
2 soprano saxophones	4 Bb bass saxhorns	2 pairs of cymbals
2 alto saxophones	2 Eb contrabass saxhorns	2 percussionists
2 tenor saxophones	2 Bb contrabass saxhorns	
2 baritone or bass saxophones	4 valve trumpets	

Total = 57 players

The smaller cavalry bands were to comprise 37 players, built around Sax's brasswind instruments, without any woodwind or percussion.

These revisions to military bands achieved almost everything that Sax had set out to accomplish a decade earlier. His ideas on the suitable instrumentation of such ensembles now lay at the heart of the Empire's military music-making. His own instruments were to be central to all military ensembles, and the future of his manufacturing enterprise appeared secure.

Sax's family in Paris

If the mid-1850s marked another period of success for Sax in his professional life, his personal circumstances were more complicated and occasionally traumatic. In 1853 Sax's mother and father left Brussels to join Adolphe and their three other surviving children, who by this time were all residing in Paris. Perhaps at the age of 60 Charles-Joseph Sax was finding it increasingly tiring to run his own business in Brussels. More compellingly, the couple had suffered a triple tragedy in late 1852, with three of their remaining offspring dying within the last four months of that year.[70] Adolphe's success at this time may also have influenced their decision. Charles-Joseph's enthusiasm for instrument innovation was undiminished, and before installing himself in the French capital he had patented a new type of piano, described, of course, as a 'Piano-Sax';[71] now he sought to exploit his invention. Clearly his well-connected son was of assistance in this respect, since early advertisements for the product carry the endorsement of several of Adolphe's long-standing supporters, including Berlioz, Kastner and Meyerbeer. But Charles-Joseph's business was unsuccessful and he was declared bankrupt in October 1857. From this point on he assisted his son in the rue Saint-Georges workshops – where he appears to have been given responsibility to oversee the production of saxophones[72] – until his death on 26 April 1865. His wife, Adolphe's mother, passed away some years earlier, on 1 November 1861.

While these losses were undoubtedly keenly felt by Adolphe Sax, he was not without family. His brother Alphonse had worked with him in his workshops from the mid 1840s. Alphonse sought to establish a reputation as an instrument maker in his own right, although his most significant contribution was a system of 'pistons ascendantes et descendantes omnitoniques-chromatiques' (resonant of his father's *cor omnitonique*) dating from the 1856.[73] Relations between the two brothers cooled in the early 1860s, when Adolphe appears to have attempted to block his brother's entry to the London International Exhibition of 1862.[74] Over the next few years Alphonse became particularly identified with a campaign to demonstrate that women were just as physically capable of playing brass instruments as men, and moreover, that such practice had moral and physical benefits. While somewhat paternalistic by today's standards, this attitude was ahead of its time.[75] Although Alphonse attempted to set up an instrument manufacturing business under his own name, this was unsuccessful, and he ceased to be listed as a Parisian manufacturer by 1867.[76] He continued his innovations in other areas, from women's hair-drying appliances to propulsion systems for fire engines, without much success, before his own death, aged 52, on 25 June 1874. Two other siblings also made the move to Paris at some point. Adolphe's brother Charles-Joseph is recorded as having died, aged 51, in Paris on 31 January 1871, while his sister Antoinette-Maria died before her parents, aged 29, on 17 May 1856. Little else is known about either of these two members of the Sax family.

Adolphe's own domestic situation was complex. Berlioz had complained as early as 1847 that one of the many charges laid against Sax by his competitors was not only that he was a foreigner but also a bachelor.[77] Used in this euphemistic yet faintly derogatory fashion, such a description was intended to convey a suspicion of homosexuality; this was a more scurrilous dimension of the opposition mounted against him and appears unsupported by any evidence. Sax was the father of five children between 1853 and 1859, two of whom died in childhood. His remaining progeny survived until the Second World War, with his youngest son, Adolphe-Edouard Sax, taking over the family business after his father's death in 1894. What is less clear, however, is Sax's relationship with their mother, since Sax himself appears never to have married.

The mother of his children was Louise-Adèle Maor, the daughter of a Spanish father and a French mother, born in Frévent in northern France on 26 August 1830. Little is known of her life, in part because the history of nineteenth-century France – as in so many other places – is seen through the activities of men; unless their contributions are in some way remarkable, women are often marginalised and frequently omitted altogether. But there is perhaps another reason why little is recorded about the mother of Sax's children, and that is because Sax himself appeared keen to downplay his relationship with her, even though she bore him five children over a period of six years.

The use of names already prevalent among both the Sax and Maor families provides a tangible link between children and parents:[78]

Table 4: The children of Adolphe Sax and Louise-Adèle Maor

Name	Date of Birth	Date of Death	Comments
Anna-Emilie (Maor) Sax	29.4.1853	Before 1945	Recognised by Sax 24.11.1886
Adèle-Marie-Amelie (Maor) Sax	14.12.1855	10.5.1856	Died aged 6 months
Adolphe-Charles-Antoine Sax	October 1856	6.6.1858	Died aged 20 months
Adèle-Marie (Maor) Sax	29.11.1858	1938	Recognised by Sax 6.11.1886
Adolphe-Edouard (Maor) Sax	29.9.1859	1945	Recognised by Sax 28.10.1886

Sax clearly had a complicated relationship with the mother of his children, quite apart from the fact that no record exists of their marriage. On the birth certificates of the three children who survived into adulthood the father is not named, only the mother, though each records the surname as '(Maor) Sax'. Only in the case of the baptism or death certificates of the two children who died in infancy was Maor listed as Sax's wife. The birth certificate of the first child (Anna-Emilie) declares the mother's address to be 50 rue Saint-Georges. This was the address of Sax's workshop, where he — and presumably Maor — lived.[79] Yet the certificates of some of the later children note the address as being at Neuilly-sur-Seine, on the outskirts of Paris. This may have been another house owned by Sax, or possibly the address of one of Maor's family. Certainly, when Maor herself died on 15 September 1860, only one year after the birth of Adolphe-Edouard, she was living at 7 rue Saint-Claude, and not, it would appear, with Sax.

Further evidence attests to the complex relationship between Sax and Maor. In 1856, at the time of the death of his sister Antoinette-Maria, Sax had acquired in perpetuity the rights to a burial plot in the cemetery at Montmartre. Here he constructed a sepulchre that accommodated various deceased members of his family over subsequent decades and, ultimately, himself. Those entombed include his parents, a number of his siblings and their relations, as well as several of his children. Maor was not buried here, nor the two children who died in childhood.[80] Sax only officially recognised his other three children much later in life, in 1886, when he made a declaration that he was indeed their father; this may have been prompted by the forthcoming marriage of his younger daughter, Adèle-Marie, later that year.

Sax's determination to distance himself in public from Maor almost certainly arises from his concerns about social rank and perceptions of middle-class respectability. It seems likely that Maor occupied a relatively humble position; she may have been one of Sax's workers or even a domestic at the rue Saint-Georges, which could explain how they met. In contrast, Sax generally moved in circles that would today be described as middle class, mixing with composers, writers, and various dignitaries of the Parisian artistic scene. Indeed, his connections with the upper echelons of the military and with the Emperor would have elevated his prestige considerably. For a man in his position the public profile he maintained would have been crucial to his reputation. As the historian Roger Price observes, for men such as Sax, 'it was important to appear daily to be part of the social group to which one claimed to belong — through habits of dress [. . .] speech, manners, accommodation, the employment of domestics, etc., i.e. by the ostentatious observance of particular norms of behaviour [. . .]. The choice of profession, of a place to live and especially of a marriage partner, were clear indicators of group membership.'[81] In post-revolutionary France membership of the group to which Sax aspired was earned rather than bestowed, and might easily be lost. As the *Journal des débats* noted at the time, 'the bourgeoisie isn't a class, it's a position; you acquire it, you lose it'.[82] Under such circumstances Sax's involvement with Maor would have been regarded by many as an unfortunate misalliance.

Regardless of his feelings for Maor, therefore — and this was obviously no passing attraction, given the longevity of their relationship and the number of children they had — Sax may well have felt that to acknowledge their relationship publicly, particularly by making it official through an act of marriage, would have jeopardised both his social position and his business. It is for this reason that he felt compelled to distance himself from her, both in life and in death. Thus poor Louise-Adèle Maor is given only a marginal place in the official record of Sax's life, and in its many retellings often no place at all.

The 1860s and 70s

The 1860s provided a mixed economic climate for instrument manufacturers in Paris. The decision to standardise French pitch at A = 435 in 1859, on the recommendation of a government commission, provided a temporary boom for many instrument makers as bands and orchestras with instruments set at other pitches sought to conform to the new standard. Sax, with a well-equipped factory and skilled staff on hand, is likely to have benefited from this decision.[83] Set against this, however, was the decision in 1860 to reduce the number of military musicians in each infantry band from 57 to 40. Cavalry bands were also to be reduced by ten players. Those instruments to be withdrawn included a number of Sax's models, although in neither case did it involve reducing the number of saxophones. The situation was made worse in 1867 by the abandonment of military music provision altogether in the cavalry divisions, a decision that sparked an outcry in the French press from Sax and other interested parties.

Sax also had other concerns. In 1860 the fifteen-year patents he had taken out for the saxophone and the saxotromba were due to expire, and he would thus have no legal protection against the exploitation of his inventions by other manufacturers. Furthermore, under prevailing French law it was very difficult to extend patents. In fact this had been achieved only once previously, by an inventor who had patented a system of wood preservation in 1841 and had been given an extension for a further five years in 1856. Extensions were technically possible, but two important conditions had to be satisfied: that the inventor had made a substantial contribution to a particular art or industry, and that he had not been able to profit from his invention through exceptional circumstances that were beyond his control. Sax clearly felt he had good cause on both grounds, particularly in light of the long series of legal proceedings with which he had been engaged for many years, and what he saw as the undermining of his business by his competitors. After numerous discussions with the necessary legal authorities an extension was granted by imperial decree, for both patents, on 1 August 1860, giving Sax the sole rights to manufacture saxophones for another five years.[84]

The Paris Exposition Universelle of 1867 was the last major event at which Sax exhibited. It was a significant occasion, with some 42,000 participants, including more than 11,500 French exhibitors. 486 names are listed under the section devoted to musical instruments, with 201 of these being French manufacturers.[85] Despite the large number of potential competitors, however, the exhibition was a considerable success for Sax. Although his most significant patents had by now expired and instruments such as the saxophone could legally be manufactured by other makers, it was Sax who was given the highest award by the International Jury: the Grand Prix. The superiority of his brasswind instruments can be discerned from the fact that no manufacturers in this category were awarded gold medals, the only prizes given being silver medals and below. Only one gold medal was awarded to a woodwind manufacturer (Triébert), the rest being awarded silver or below. The jury clearly felt there was a considerable difference between the quality of Sax's products and those of his competitors. The Exhibition authorities also ran a competition for the best 'fanfare' (small brass ensemble), and Sax, with a group of fifteen players, was awarded the first prize of 3,000 francs. His triumph was complete.

11. Promotional material noting Sax's achievements at the 1867 Paris Universal Exhibition.

ADOLPHE SAX ✿ ✠
1er Grand Prix de la Facture Instrumentale
Exposition Universelle, Paris 1867.

During the exhibition the president of the International Jury judging Sax's work recommended that he should be promoted to the rank of Officier of the Légion d'honneur, observing that this would be 'the most honourable compensation for all the grievances, all the losses which have accompanied his inventions, [and] the fairest reward for his admirable and useful work for the future of instrumental music'.[86] Sax had already been made a Chevalier of the Légion d'honneur in 1849; he now expected to be given the higher award. However this appears not to have happened; nor, according to his own account, did he receive the 20,000 francs due to him for the Grand Prix. Both of these slights were to be bitterly recalled in later years.[87]

Sax's activities went well beyond those ordinarily expected of a manufacturer, particularly in relation to the promotion of his own instruments. His abilities as a skilled performer developed into work as a conductor. As early as 1847 he had been engaged by the Paris Opéra to supply a stage band for a performance of Verdi's opera *Jérusalem*, and this connection with the Opéra was maintained for many years, with Sax contracted to oversee such ensembles. He frequently used these occasions as an opportunity to employ his own instruments, although his conducting skills appear questionable. Wagner observes in his autobiography that for the Paris production of *Tannhäuser* in 1861 he 'had to deal with the terrible man Sax, the celebrated instrument-maker. He had to help me out with all kinds of substitutes in the shape of saxophones and saxhorns; moreover, he was officially appointed to conduct the music behind the scenes. It was an impossibility ever to get this music played properly'.[88]

Sax was also involved in teaching the saxophone. Again there was a degree of self-interest in this, since the instrument could only be properly established if there were performers who were willing and skilled enough to play it. Classes in the instrument had been established in the Gymnase de Musique Militaire in 1846, but these appear to have been short lived since there is no record of them after 1850.[89] In 1856 this school was closed, and responsibility for the education of military musicians passed to the Paris Conservatoire. At this point a number of teachers were employed to teach military students, and Sax wrote to a commission set up to examine military music provision, asking that he be appointed to teach the saxophone:

> Among the artists who today play the saxophone, there is not one who is equipped to teach all individuals of the whole family, from the soprano to the bass, and none of those who play possesses the best sound (the quality of the timbre) because of the instrument they practised previously and which they are obliged to continue to play every day. If therefore the teaching of the saxophone were abandoned to a professor other than myself, the timbre would inevitably deviate from that which I wanted and have achieved [. . .]. It is not only to prevent the torture of me hearing all my life a timbre different from that which should be obtained that I insist upon this point; you know, gentlemen, how important are the posture and sound production in relation to the human voice [. . .] you appreciate even more this importance with regard to a new family of instruments.[90]

Sax was duly appointed, although military music teaching was regarded as tangential to the main work of the Conservatoire, and those who taught such classes were not regarded as full professors; Sax's name does not appear on a list of teachers who had worked at the Conservatoire compiled in 1900,[91] and no saxophone class was opened at the Conservatoire proper during Sax's lifetime, in spite of Berlioz's recommendation as early as 1848 that one should be established.[92] This did not prevent Sax rather ingenuously styling his letterhead 'Maison Adolphe Sax, Professeur au Conservatoire national de musique' on his letterheads.[93] From 1858 to 1878 Sax also ran a publishing business, again primarily to produce music for his new instruments (see p. 99).

These multi-faceted business activities do not appear to have been enough to secure his financial position. The expiry of his patents probably contributed to his difficulties, but it was the 1870 French defeat in the Franco-Prussian war, and the subsequent cuts in expenditure on military music, that were more problematic. Sax later claimed that after this war he had been able to supply a total of less than 2,000 francs' worth of instruments to the army.[94] The defeat also led to the closure of the Conservatoire saxophone class, compounding his problems. His influence in the French capital was also waning, and many of those who had previously supported him could no longer help: Kastner had died in 1867, Rossini in 1868, and Berlioz in 1869. These setbacks, combined with the perpetual drain of ongoing legal proceedings and the non-payment of damages made in his favour, eventually resulted in Sax being declared bankrupt for a second time, in 1873. Again he came to an agreement with his creditors, and somehow found additional funds that enabled him to carry on for a further four years. But the situation was precarious, and he was declared bankrupt for a third and final time, at the age of 63, on 14 May 1877. This time Sax's creditors forced him to sell his prized collection of musical instruments, containing 467 examples not only of his own work (95 instruments), but also examples from many other different periods and cultures. Among those listed in the auction catalogue were an experimental saxophone, the first versions of C soprano, E♭ alto and E♭ baritone saxophones, and several gold- and silver-plated saxophones that had been exhibited at the International Exhibition of 1849, and for which Sax had received the gold medal and subsequently the Légion d'honneur.[95]

The loss of the many instruments with which this energetic man had surrounded himself throughout his life must have had a profound emotional affect, particularly since the sum raised, 12,000 francs, was a pitiful amount for such an important collection.[96] From this point on Adolphe Sax, who had held such a visible position in Parisian musical life for nearly 40 years, appears to have retreated into comparative obscurity. He attempted to enter the 1878 Paris International Exhibition, but was unable to raise the amount needed to pay the exhibitor's entrance fee. He protested angrily to the Minister of Agriculture that he was being denied the opportunity to show his new designs, that the public would think his company had ceased production were he not allowed to exhibit, and that other manufacturers were being permitted to demonstrate their versions of instruments he had himself invented.[97] The last point is particularly ironic. The Exhibition jury, comprising such luminaries as Franz Liszt and the critic Eduard Hanslick, awarded a series of gold, silver and bronze medals to other manufacturers specifically for their excellent saxophones, and in one case for well-manufactured saxophone reeds. Sax's feelings of injustice and maltreatment were not without foundation.

Sax was also obliged to sell his music publishing rights, but the small amounts of money raised by this and by the sale of his instrument collection did at least allow him to reach an agreement with his creditors. In March 1878 he agreed to pay 25 per cent of his remaining debts over a period of five years. This meant he could continue in business, albeit on a much reduced scale. He forfeited his workshop in the rue Saint-Georges, and was obliged to move to smaller premises; this was only the first of a series of moves for Sax and his company over the next fifteen years or so, probably because of the increasing difficulty in keeping the company solvent. Although he is not on the list of Parisian instrument manufacturers for 1881, his name does appear again in 1890 and 1893.[98] Aged 78, the extent to which Sax was still involved in the company is unclear; more likely his son Adolphe-Edouard was now the driving force, since he continued his father's work after the latter's death.

The final years and Sax's legacy

In his final years Sax's financial position was constantly precarious. Following his bankruptcy in 1877 he had been awarded a small annual pension of 300 francs by the Association des artistes musiciens, an organisation to which he had contributed since its foundation in 1843. But the lack of resolution to his earlier legal conflicts, and particularly the non-payment of damages, contributed to both his difficult financial position and his increasingly embittered state of mind. In 1887 he published an

'Appeal to the Public', in which he pleaded publicly for the damages arising from the court case concluded in 1860 to be agreed and paid.[99] Sax also recounted the many injustices that he felt had been perpetrated against him over the years, and argued that he sought their resolution primarily so that 'this would permit me before dying to pay others what I owe them, and give myself a few hours of peace in a life consumed by trouble'.[100]

His plight did not go entirely unnoticed by Paris's musical community. In August 1892 the composer Paul Lacôme apparently had plans to rehabilitate Sax, and Emmanuel Chabrier wrote to fellow composer Vincent d'Indy about 'Poor *père* Sax! When one thinks that this talented man has passed his life to become a bankrupt in order to enrich men who today have decorations and are millionaires [. . .] it is disgusting, but very human.'[101]

Adolphe Sax died at his home, 16 rue Frochot, on 7 February 1894. He had made and lost several fortunes, but in his later years had derived very little financial benefit from his numerous and influential inventions. He was buried on 10 February in the family tomb he had established in the Montmartre cemetery. The tomb is in the form of a chapel but with few distinctive markings other than the simple inscription 'Famille Ad. Sax', underneath which is the name of Sax's son-in-law, Millet de Marcilly.[102] It lacks any other decoration, reflecting the near anonymity into which Sax had himself retreated by the end of the century.[103] As a brief obituary in the London *Times* put it on the day he was buried: 'His inventions attracted the attention of Berlioz, Auber, Halévy, and other composers. His influence upon military music was first brilliantly seen under the Empire, when all his ideas were adopted. He perfected also the bassoon [. . .]. He reformed modern orchestras, and yet died poor.'[104]

12. Advertisement for 'Adolphe Sax – Father and Son' intended to demonstrate the continuation of Sax's work by his son Adolphe-Edouard.

Sax's work was continued after his death by his son Adolphe-Edouard. The latter took over his father's position as director of stage music at the Paris Opéra, as well as his manufacturing interests. A new plant was built at 84 rue Myrha, but both this and the Sax company were eventually purchased by Selmer in 1929.

Sax's name has remained in the public consciousness since his death largely because of its perpetuation in his most successful and significant invention, the saxophone. Yet his diverse innovations profoundly influenced various aspects of music making in the nineteenth and early twentieth centuries, in brass and wind ensembles, in orchestras, and in the technological development of musical instruments.

Sax can also be seen as something of a romantic figure, particularly at a time when Romanticism itself became such an integral component of nineteenth-century French culture. His struggles against the various fates that befell him, his rise from humble origins to gracing French corridors of power, his legal battles with those who conspired against him, his idiosyncratic genius and fiery temper, his impoverished final years, even his affection for a woman he felt unable to marry, could all contribute to a reading of his life which sees him as that quintessentially Romantic character: the artist as hero. But perhaps this is too generous an interpretation; certainly many of his contemporaries would be surprised by it. In the decades immediately after his death his name was compromised by the increasingly dubious reputation enveloping the saxophone. 'Posterity will never forgive you, Adolphe Sax!' the *Saturday Review of Literature* asserted sometime in the first part of the twentieth century, beneath a cartoon of Sax surrounded by saxophones in his workshop.[105]

Yet the reception afforded to Sax after his death was by no means entirely negative. The town of Dinant acknowledged his importance by erecting a memorial plaque on the house in which he was born; this was replaced by a stained-glass window in his honour after the original building burned down during World War II. Today the town is adorned by several statues commemorating the connection with its most famous son.

In April 1933 a musical gala was held at the Institute of Fine Arts in Paris in Sax's honour. The event provoked a substantial editorial in the London *Times* a few days later which, while making some rather trenchant observations on the various abuses of the saxophone itself, noted that Sax could no more be blamed for this than could Shakespeare for all the bad Hamlets. The editor's final observation provides a suitable epitaph for this complex but fascinating man: 'He deserves, poor ghost, his musical gala, and recognition from genuine musicians as one of themselves'.[106]

Chapter 2

The saxophone family

Inspirations and antecedents

What led Adolphe Sax to create a new, hybrid musical wind instrument? Sax himself provided several answers to this question in the explanation he attached to the saxophone patent (see also Appendix):

> One knows that, in general, wind instruments are either too loud or too soft in sonority. It is particularly in the basses where one or the other of these faults is most appreciable. The ophicleide, for example, which reinforces the trombones, produces a sound by nature so disagreeable that one is obliged to banish it from closed rooms, for lack of being able to modify the timbre. The bassoon, on the contrary, makes a sound so feeble that one cannot use it except to fill out the accompaniment. And for particular loud orchestration effects it is perfectly useless. Note that this last instrument is the only one which blends with string instruments.
>
> It is only the brasswind instruments that give the most satisfying effect in the open air. Also a wind group composed of these instruments is the only orchestral combination that has the power to be used in such circumstances.
>
> As for string instruments, everybody knows that, in the open air, their effect is useless because of the feebleness of their sound. This makes them nearly impossible to use in such conditions.
>
> Struck by these various drawbacks, I have sought a way to remedy this by creating an instrument which, by the character of its voice, can blend with string instruments, but which possesses greater strength and intensity than these. This instrument is the Saxophone. Better than any other, the Saxophone can finely modify its sounds to give them the qualities just mentioned and to preserve a perfect evenness throughout its range. I have made it from brass in the shape of a parabolic cone.[1]

Although the patent deposition was written some time after a prototype saxophone had been developed, it makes clear the musical problems Sax was endeavouring to solve. In the late 1830s he had already been addressing what he perceived as deficiencies in the lower winds, hence the innovations he brought to the bass clarinet patented in 1838. Notwithstanding his improvements, however, the bass clarinet's relative lack of power meant that it alone could not compensate for the deficiencies that Sax identified in the lower woodwind and brasswind instruments.

These deficiencies were felt to be particularly acute in relation to the ophicleide, but Sax's somewhat disparaging remarks about this instrument should not obscure its importance in the historical development of the saxophone. The ophicleide is a type of a keyed bugle – now largely obsolete – with a conical bore and a moderately flared bell. Patented in 1821 by the French maker Halary, the name ophicleide was intended only to refer to the bass version of a family of instruments, although in time it came to be used for all its members. The bore of the instrument was large, relative to its length, as is typical of members of the bugle group. Although played with a cup mouthpiece, like all brass instruments, the effective length of the tube was altered by keys rather than valves (it was not until the 1850s that valves became more reliable and widespread). These keys, initially simple flat discs faced with leather but later formed of cupped key-heads with pads, rested on raised collars soldered onto the instrument. However, the collars altered the acoustic properties of the conical bore; although the fundamental tones were broadly in tune, many of the harmonics were not, and the instrument was noted for its unreliable tuning. Additionally, the holes furthest from the bell produced notes that were weaker and poorer than others, leading to uneven tone production. Playing the ophicleide thus required both a strong lip and a well-trained

13. An ophicleide in C, made by Charles-Joseph Sax.

ear – not always to be found among those who performed on it, though the fact that the instrument proliferated at all is a testament to its more skilled players.

Sax was very familiar with the ophicleide. His father Charles-Joseph made them from at least the 1830s and the instrument's merits and demerits would undoubtedly have been subjects of conversation between father and son. In 1842 Sax *père* had taken out a Belgian patent to protect a system of 'cylinders' added to the instrument intended to address some of its deficiencies,[2] and there are extant examples made by Adolphe himself dating from the early 1840s.[3] The ophicleide may itself have been related to an upright version of the serpent, a wooden instrument with a cup mouthpiece made in a snake-like shape from which it takes its name. Later versions of the serpent had used keys to cover those holes previously closed by the fingers, and it is possible that Halary had developed the idea for the ophicleide from this instrument; the word 'ophicleide' literally means 'keyed serpent'.

Sax's ambivalence towards the ophicleide was shared by others of the time. Berlioz, for example, in one of several diatribes against the instrument (which he had employed in the *Symphonie fantastique*) wrote in 1842 that ophicleides were 'poorly studied. Good performers are rare; in general they leave much to be desired [. . .]. One uses them in military music to fill out the harmony or to double the melody; but their timbre is generally very unpleasant, and they lack exactness'.[4] In 1843 the critic Blanchard, using text remarkably prescient of Sax's own patent description, observed that:

> The ophicleide, which plays forte with the trombones, often makes sounds that are raucous, uneven and especially unpleasant in a room and even in the open air; it is very difficult to modify them. The bassoon, on the contrary, is only good for accompaniment and for certain effects that are particular to it; it is nearly useless in fortes. Except this last instrument, there are none that blend pleasantly with string instruments, and these are a nuisance outside whereas the strident voices of the brass instruments resound. The saxophone remedies these inconveniences: with more intensity in its sound, it could not blend better with the string instruments; it can modify its sounds better than any other.[5]

Blanchard's words are sufficiently close to Sax's patent deposition that one wonders whether he had seen the patent, or a text similar to it, as early as 1843; or – more likely – whether Sax borrowed Blanchard's review in constructing the patent. But however their shared dislike of the ophicleide was arrived at, sentiments such as these were not confined to France. In London the *Musical World* of June 1841, commenting on an improvement to the serpent made by Thomas Key, observed that 'thus the fine quality of tone of the serpent may, henceforth, be available in the orchestra, and the hog-song of the ophicleide will, we fervently hope, be speedily tacitted or banished altogether'.[6] Such was the widespread antipathy towards the instrument that it was unkindly (and infamously) referred to as the 'chromatic bullock' by George Bernard Shaw.[7]

Sax's prototype saxophone entailed removing the cup mouthpiece from an ophicleide and replacing it with a single-reed mouthpiece. Although he left no account of his invention it is highly likely that this prototype was arrived at by adding a bass clarinet mouthpiece to an ophicleide.[8] The coupling of a single-reed sound generator with a large conical-bore instrument such as the ophicleide certainly produces a sound that distinctly suggests the tessitura of the baritone/bass saxophone. Berlioz, writing in March 1842, confirms the genesis of this 'ophicléide à bec', observing that the instrument involved 'replacing the cup mouthpiece with the mouthpiece of a clarinet. The ophicleides thus become brass instruments with reeds; the different sonority and timbre which results from this system is so much to their advantage [. . .] that, most probably, the ophicleide with a reed mouthpiece will come into general use in a few years.'⁹

Creating a new musical instrument through such hybridisation was not unusual in nineteenth-century Paris, and other inventors endeavoured to amalgamate a piano with an organ, a harmonium with a piano, or a piano with percussion instruments.¹⁰ Sax's innovation and enterprise was thus very much of its time, but his experiment with the 'ophicléide à bec' was not arrived at by chance. As the patent deposition makes clear, it was the product of logical reasoning and reflection, a point underlined by Sax's son Adolphe-Edouard in later life.¹¹ Nevertheless, several of Sax's competitors attempted to demonstrate that the saxophone was not an original instrument and was therefore not eligible to be protected by a patent; as part of the legal proceedings taken against him several forerunners were suggested as possible models for the saxophone.

The principle of adding a single reed to a conical-bore instrument was by no means novel, and it has been suggested that similar instruments existed in ancient times.¹² There were certainly late-eighteenth- and early-nineteenth-century attempts to secure clarinet-type mouthpieces to conical-bore woodwinds. Johann Wilhelm Hesse, a clarinettist in the court orchestra of Braunschweig, Germany, in the late eighteenth century, is listed as having attached a clarinet mouthpiece to a bassoon; observers are reputed to have remarked that the new instrument surpassed the woodwinds both in looks and in sound.¹³ Another bassoon-related instrument, the alto fagotto, invented by the Scotsman William Miekle probably sometime in the early nineteenth century, was also advanced as a prototype saxophone. It comprised a conical wooden tube shaped like a bassoon, but sounded by a single reed attached to the instrument by means of a bassoon-like crook.¹⁴ Miekle's invention appears to have been refined by the London manufacturer George Wood around 1830. Wood published a method for the instrument in the early 1830s, the title page of which observed – in the somewhat longwinded fashion of the time – that it was *An Instrument which Embraces the Sweetest & Most Admired Notes of the Clarinet & Bassoon, & Eminently Calculated to Accompany the Human Voice, or to Perform Solos & Concertos in Orchestras or Military Bands*. It seems unlikely that Sax knew anything about this instrument,¹⁵ but the range of possible uses implied by this title is surprisingly consonant with Sax's own ideas about what the saxophone might achieve, and demonstrates that he was not the only inventor addressing these issues at the time.

There are other instruments worth noting because of the associations previously made between them and the saxophone. Constant Pierre (1855–1918), a French musicologist who was no fan of Sax, drew attention to an instrument made by the French clockmaker Desfontenelles in 1807, largely on the grounds of its morphological similarity to the saxophone. However, later tests indicate that the instrument overblows at the twelfth, like a clarinet, and not at the octave, as the saxophone does. It also sounded one octave lower than the clarinet, suggesting that it was an early bass clarinet.[16] An instrument called the bathyphon, invented in 1839 by Sax's German adversary Wieprecht and the Berlin maker Skorra, was also put forward as a progenitor of the saxophone.[17] But the bathyphon is a contrabass clarinet, described as such by its inventor; in fact the panel of experts selected for Sax's trial of 1847 concluded that the German instrument was itself an imitation of Sax's bass clarinet, patented in 1838.

Another instrument often presumed to have some connection with the saxophone is the Hungarian tárogató, largely on account of its resemblance to the soprano saxophone, since it too has a straight tube with a discernible conical bore to which a single reed mouthpiece is attached. But this manifestation of the tárogató did not appear until the late nineteenth century. Its original incarnation was as a shawm-like instrument with a double reed. It was not until the Hungarian instrument makers Stowasser and Schunda developed it in the cause of Hungarian nationalism – submitting a series of patents either side of the turn of the twentieth century – that it took on its present form.[18] Much though his competitors endeavoured to prove otherwise, it is clear that Sax's new instrument was indeed very largely an innovation of his own making.

No specific date can be ascertained for the invention of Sax's prototype. Although the patent for the saxophone was originally intended to be submitted in 1845, the instrument had been demonstrated before this date. It seems likely that the initial development occurred in the late 1830s. Maurice Hamel, whose father Henry was a close friend of Sax, suggests in a series of handwritten notes (now in the archives of the Selmer company in Paris) that Charles-Joseph Sax indicated that the saxophone was created in 1838, while Adolphe was still working in his father's workshop.[19] This was the year that Sax patented his new bass clarinet, reinforcing the idea that the young Belgian was preoccupied at this time with the lower part of the orchestral wind texture. Furthermore, in 1847 Charles-Joseph Sax, in a series of polemics published in *La Belgique musicale* in which he supported his son against accusations made by the German maker Wieprecht, stated that the saxophone was already invented by 1838. Such assertions must be treated warily, however, since a polemical exchange, by its very nature, encourages writers to be liberal with the truth.

The prototype is likely to have been invented before the term 'saxophone' was conceived and it is not clear when the word itself was first used. J. B. Jobard, the Belgian government's commissioner in Paris, wrote a report of an 1839 industrial exhibition in the French capital, in which he observed that Sax had invented 'a contra-bass clarinet in brass [. . .] the *saxophone* is the Niagara of sound'.[20] Quite what the commissioner meant by the use of the word at this point is unclear; it is possible that he had attributed it to describe Sax's new bass clarinet, or perhaps a contra-bass clarinet.[21] However, Jobard's report was not published until 1842, and may well have been written some time after the exhibition itself, so even if he was using the word as we understand it, we cannot be completely sure whether the term was in circulation in 1839.

But we can be confident that the saxophone was invented between 1838 and 1840, since in 1841 we find the instrument listed as part of Sax's participation in the Belgian Industrial exhibition held in Brussels. For the first time Adolphe registered separately from his father Charles-Joseph. The catalogue demonstrates that he was exhibiting a variety of clarinets, a bass clarinet and 'un saxophone basse en cuivre' – a bass saxophone in brass.[22] It is not entirely clear whether the instrument was in fact properly displayed. The exhibition's official report states that the instrument was not presented because it was not finished in time, but it also suggests that Sax did play the instrument before the jury of the music section.[23] Why Sax might demonstrate the instrument but not officially enter it is a matter for conjecture. Most likely, as the report implies, he felt it to be not sufficiently finished to warrant public appraisal or critical scrutiny. Another explanation was provided by the Belgian organologist Charles Mahillon in 1847. Mahillon stated that Adolphe Sax had wanted his latest invention be placed behind a curtain, to prevent it being copied by a rival manufacturer before Sax had the opportunity to protect it with a patent.[24] This appears plausible in light of the constant litigation in which Sax was later embroiled, although it does beg the question as to why Sax waited until 1845 to submit the patent. In 1848 Georges Kastner offered a more romanticised reason for the instrument's non-participation in the 1841 exhibition, suggesting that 'an instrument wrapped in a cloth that Sax had wanted to present or at least to make heard before the admission jury, was sent flying with a violent kick at a moment when the inventor Adolphe Sax was absent.'[25] Kastner makes clear that he is referring to the saxophone; however, given his partisan support of Sax and his instruments, such a story must be treated with caution.

Whatever the veracity of these individual tales, it is clear that a prototype saxophone was in existence while Sax was still in Belgium, before his move to Paris in 1842.

Developing the saxophone family in Paris

Sax had made one trip to Paris in 1839 to promote his new bass clarinet, but considerably more important was his visit of June 1842. This resulted in two significant meetings at which he demonstrated his various instruments: one with Berlioz, at that time music critic of the respected *Journal des débats*; and one at the initiation of François-Antoine Habeneck, conductor at both the Paris Opéra and the Orchestre de la Société des Concerts du Conservatoire, who invited Sax to perform at the Conservatoire before various luminaries such as the composers Auber and Halévy, the writer Éduard Monnais and the flautist Louis Dorus. Clearly these presentations made good impressions, for on 12 June 1842 no fewer than three articles appeared in different publications lauding Sax's achievements. A news article in the *RGMP* noted that:

M. Sax (son), the skilful instrument manufacturer from Brussels, has been in Paris for some days. He has made heard at the Conservatoire, before the director M. Auber and some professors, the bass clarinet and the new ophicleide of which he is the inventor. Full justice has been rendered to the beauty of these instruments, to which no other can be compared for the range, power and infinite variety of nuances of which they are capable.[26]

The editor of *La France musicale* similarly reported Sax's presentation at the Conservatoire, and observed that 'his third invention is destined to replace the ophicleide. This brass instrument is played with a clarinet mouthpiece and its range is close to two and a half octaves, beginning from the B♭ of the bassoon. One can have no idea of the beauty of the sound and the power of the notes in the lower octave.'[27]

Perhaps the most extensive and influential eulogy, and certainly the article that has been subsequently most widely quoted, was written by Berlioz for the *Journal des débats*. It is a long piece in which Berlioz notes that considerable progress had been made in the art of musical instrumentation in the previous twenty years, and he lavishly praises the contributions Sax had made, as well as asserting the further contributions Berlioz felt he was likely to make. After outlining for the reader Sax's development of the clarinet family, and particularly his bass clarinet, he draws attention to the saxophone:

> The saxophon [*sic*], named after its inventor, is a brass instrument somewhat similar in shape to the ophicleide, and equipped with nineteen keys. It is not played with a mouthpiece like other brass instruments, but with a mouthpiece similar to that of the bass clarinet. The saxophone will thus be the head of a new family, that of brass instruments with a reed. Its range is three octaves, beginning with the low B flat below the stave (bass clef); its fingering is more or less the same as that of the flute or the second register of the clarinet. As for the sound, it is of a nature that I don't know a low instrument currently in use to which, in that respect, it can be compared. It is full, mellow, vibrant, extremely powerful, and capable of being soft. It is much superior, in my view, to the low notes of the ophicleide, for the precision and consistency of the sound, the character of which is in any case totally new and does not resemble any of the timbres that one presently hears in the orchestra, with the exception of the low E and F of the bass clarinet. Thanks to the reed with which it is provided the saxophone can increase and decrease its sound; it produces, in the high register, notes of penetrating vibration that could be successfully applied to melodic expression. Undoubtedly it will never be appropriate for rapid lines or complicated arpeggios; but low instruments are not intended for such rapid movements. Therefore, instead of complaining, we should rejoice in the impossibility that one will be able to abuse the saxophone and destroy its majestic character by giving it musical futilities to perform. Composers will be much indebted to M. Sax when his instruments come into general use. May he persevere; he will not lack encouragement from friends of art.[28]

Although Sax was demonstrating the instrument at this time, it was clearly still in development. In June 1842 Michele Carafa, the director of the Gymnase de Musique Militaire with whom Sax would later clash over the reorganisation of military bands, wrote the inventor a letter in which he observes that 'your brass instrument which uses a clarinet mouthpiece will become a very good instrument. I regret not having seen it finished; in the state that I have heard it, I cannot express enough the advantages which it will offer.'[29] Furthermore, the various observations that the saxophone was 'similar in shape to the ophicleide' suggests that at this time (mid 1842), the ophicleide-saxophone was the only shape in existence, and the S-shaped instrument of today had yet to evolve. The editor of *La France musicale* cited above notes that the instrument had a range of some two and a half octaves, starting from B♭$_1$, indicating that the instrument was a bass. We cannot be sure in what key this prototype was pitched, but C or B♭ appear the most likely options, if only because these were the keys in which bass ophicleides were made (with C being more common than B♭).[30]

By 1843 the instrument had evolved further. The critic Henri Blanchard, writing in *RGMP* in September of that year, noted that the saxophone 'is equipped with nineteen keys, which close the holes, of which some are nearly two inches in diameter. Its fingering resembles that of the second register of the clarinet, and its mouthpiece is, more or less, similar to that of the new bass clarinet. Its range is three octaves, the lowest note being A'.[31] Similarly, Berlioz, in a late addition to his *Grand Traité d'instrumentation* in December 1843, observed unambiguously that 'the saxophone is a transposing instrument in B flat; its [written] range is [B$_1$-c¹].'[32] Thus the first working saxophone was an ophicleide-shaped saxophone, pitched in B♭, with the lowest written note of B$_1$, sounding A$_1$. The choice of this low note, a minor third below that available on the cello, is unlikely to have been fortuitous. The equivalent note on the ophicleide in B♭ was unreliably sharp, while the bassoon could descend only as low as B♭$_1$, and many bassoons of the time lacked the B$_1$ and C♯ pitches. Given his aspirations for the saxophone, Sax would have wanted to ensure its obvious advantages over those instruments he hoped it would replace.

By 1843 evidence emerges of Sax's intention to create a family of saxophones. While such plans were obvious in the 1846 patent – the various designs sketched there make this clear – we cannot know whether such a family was part of Sax's original intention. By the mid 1840s, however, Sax increasingly conceived his instrumental innovations in groups, as evidenced by his various families of saxhorns, saxotrombas and so forth. The saxophone was to follow a similar path. Castil-Blaze in *La France musicale* speculated that the saxophone family would be 'completed by an alto and two sopranos of the same type. The effect of three or four saxophones introduced into a large orchestra would be delightful.'[33] In the same journal a few months later the Escudier brothers wrote that they had heard only the bass version of the instrument, but that 'one can imagine a quartet of saxophones, soprano, tenor, bass and contrabass; this is a new world that is opening for instrumental art'.[34]

In 1844 Sax's supporter Kastner produced supplements to two of his own texts on orchestration, both of which now included information on families of saxophones rather than suggesting only the prototypical bass. His *Cours d'instrumentation*, originally published 1839, was amended to suggest the availability of a family of soprano, alto or tenor (an early indication of the uncertainty of nomenclature), bass, and contrabass saxophones. More explicitly, however, the 1844 supplement to his 1837 *Traité général d'instrumentation* listed two complementary 'families' of saxophones: soprano in C or B♭, alto/tenor in F/E♭, bass in C/B♭, and contrabass in F/E♭. Musical examples accompanying the text indicate the ranges of these various instruments. Kastner contradicts Blanchard by asserting that at this stage the instrument had seventeen rather than nineteen keys. But he includes advice on how to score for the instruments, warning that the illustrated three octave range 'can barely be used by virtuosos

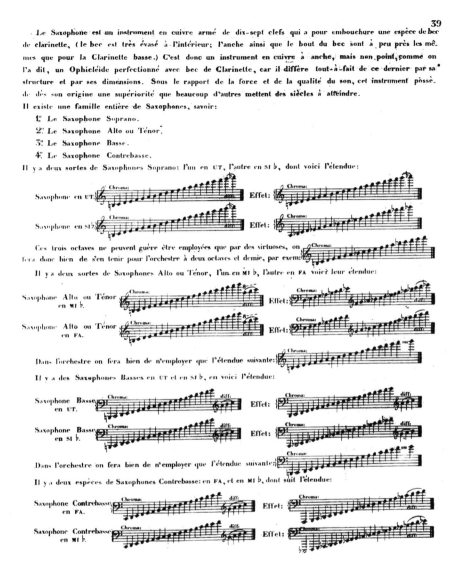

14. Theoretical ranges of various saxophones, given in Kastner's 1844 supplement to his orchestration treatise.

and one would therefore do well to limit oneself in the orchestra to two and a half octaves.'[35]

But it is inconceivable that the many different versions of saxophone listed by Kastner were in fact available in 1844. The various writers describing a family of instruments were doubtless both repeating Sax's aspirations and outlining theoretical possibilities for the development of the family. There are few explicit references to saxophones other than the bass prior to the submission of the saxophone patent in 1846, and the patent itself makes clear that although two members of the family were at an advanced stage the rest were insufficiently developed to be precisely described. A sales brochure from Sax's company dated around 1845 mentions only a single otherwise unspecified saxophone for sale.[36]

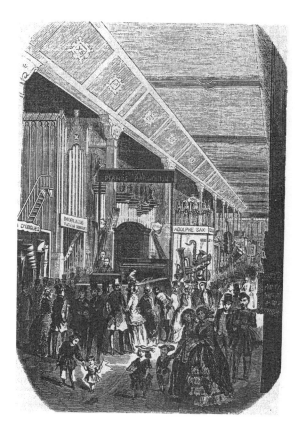

15. Lithograph of Sax's display at the 1844 Paris Exhibition, published in *L'Illustration*, 11 August 1849.

Of the two more developed instruments the Bb bass retained the ophicleide form, but the other, pitched in Eb, probably resembled the S-shaped instruments with which we are familiar today. The historical record reveals no verifiable sightings of the S-shaped saxophone at this point, however. A letter from the instrument maker Charles Finck in 1844 mentions both bass and tenor saxophones (the term tenor being used to describe an Eb baritone model),[37] and a lithograph that illustrates Sax's display at the 1844 Paris Exhibition clearly shows an S-shaped saxophone standing behind what may well be an 'ophicleide à bec', although the image was not published until 1849 and was possibly completed after the event, so there must be some doubt as to its accuracy.

One final detail suggests that two members of the saxophone family were in existence prior to 1846. In the autograph score of the 'Epilogue (Dans le ciel)' to *La Damnation de Faust* (1845–6), Berlioz allocated two staves to saxophones. They are marked in pencil, but crossed out, as 'Saxophone ténor en Es Mib'[38] and 'Saxophone basse en Bb', and given treble and bass clefs respectively. Despite his description of the Eb instrument as 'ténor', Berlioz was referring to what would today be described as the Eb baritone. Although not used in the final scoring of the piece these are exactly the two instruments most clearly identified in Sax's patent of 1846. Sax may well have been working on other members of the family when time and other commitments would permit, but none would come into the public domain until after the patent itself had been approved.

The 1846 saxophone patent

As noted in Chapter 1, Sax's patent for the saxophone was intended to be submitted in 1845, but was withheld for a year before eventually being submitted on 21 March 1846. It was granted on 22 June of the same year. Of the various sketches it provides only two are filled out with detailed keywork (see ill. 16). One of these (no. 1) bears enough similarity with contemporary saxophones to be recognisable today, whereas the other (no. 2) clearly resembles an ophicleide. The instruments numbered 3 and 4 demonstrate larger versions of number 2; they are simply sketched in silhouette, and this lack of detail again suggests they were hypothetical at this stage. Numbers 5–8, similarly apparently hypothetical, are more closely related to number 1. A mouthpiece, labelled 'bass saxophone', is also sketched.

The two most detailed instruments in the patent sketches are provided with numbered keys that correspond to the fingering descriptors Sax also supplied. In devising his keywork for the saxophone Sax recycled fingering patterns already employed successfully on other instruments of the time. Keys were often grouped on pivoting rods in the manner Theobald Boehm had developed for his 1832 flute, rather than having individual levers as on an ophicleide.[39] The fingering pattern as indicated on sketch no. 1 remains remarkably similar to modern saxophones, demonstrating the ergonomic efficiency of Sax's original design, although it appears also to owe something to early nineteenth-century oboes.[40] There are eighteen touches in all, acting on a total of twenty keys. While the fingering indications supplied in the patent are rudimentary, a fingering chart in the saxophone method published by Georges Kastner the same year, clearly based on an instrument almost identical to the one indicated in the patent, gives more insight into Sax's intended fingering design.

The left hand touches are 1, 2, 3, producing b^1, a^1, g^1 in the lower register, with the left hand little finger controlling $g\sharp^1$ and the lower notes b^0 and $c\sharp^1$. The right hand touches 4, 5 and 6 produced the notes f^1, e^1, and d^1 in the low register, with $f\sharp^1$ produced using 123_5_ or 123__6 as on a Boehm flute. Low c^1 and $e\flat^1$ were played by the right-hand little finger, and an alternative side $b\flat$ fingering was controlled by the right-hand index finger. The instrument lacked the now common front f^3, side c and chromatic $f\sharp$ alternatives. The articulation between the left hand $g\sharp$ key and the low b^0, $b\flat^0$ and $c\sharp^1$ keys is a later innovation not found on Sax's original design. Two alternative fingerings are given for c^2, neither of which is orthodox today; the first is for touch 3 alone, the second for the more usual touch 2, but with the addition of the first octave key. The latter was not high enough on the instrument to produce c^3, and this alternative fingering may have been identified for tuning purposes.[41] The middle d^2 was produced using a 'short' fingering that employed the first left-hand palm key, more normally reserved today for d^3; $d\sharp^2$ is given in both the short version, using only the $d\sharp^3$ palm key, and the now usual long version employing the first octave key, operated by the left-hand thumb.

The high c^3 fingering replicated the two alternative fingerings of c^2 plus the second octave key, with $c\sharp^3$ played open, using just this octave key, which then remained open for all higher notes. These high notes show some variation from those familiar today: all notes from d^3 to f^3 were played by keys operated by the left-hand palm, but the combination of keys deployed was rather different from the additive arrangement

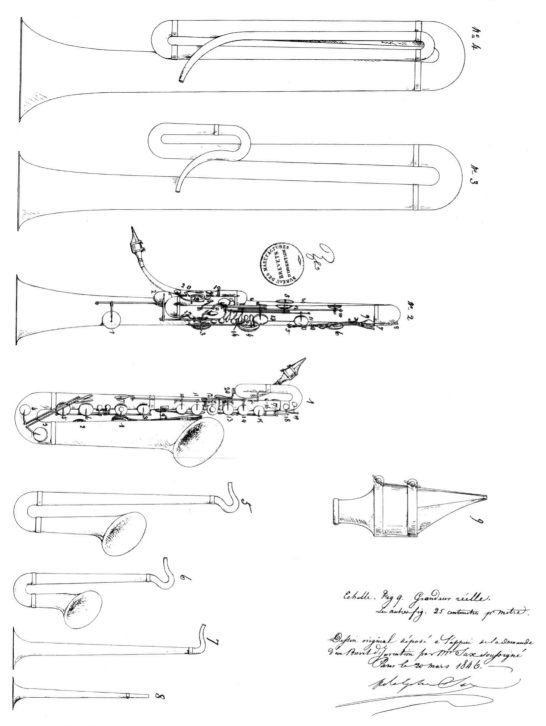

16. Sketches submitted as part of the 1846 saxophone patent.

TABLATURE DU SAXOPHONE.

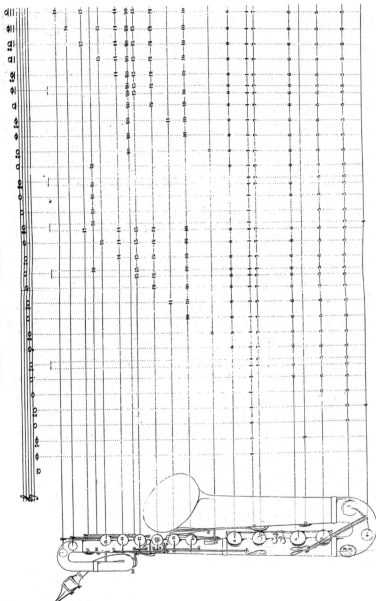

(*Note*) Les chiffres placés dans une colonne verticale au dessous des notes, indiquent chaque fois les clefs à prendre pour faire la note qui les surmonte; on remarquera que les chiffres correspondent aux clefs de l'instrument, en partant de celle qui est placée le plus près du pavillon, et en remontant vers l'embouchure.

*Lorsqu'*il y a un double doigter pour faire la même note, nous l'avons indiqué par une seconde colonne verticale parallèle à la première.

(*Observation essentielle*) Le doigté est le même pour tous les saxophones, sans exception.

17.   Saxophone fingering chart from Kastner's 1846 method.

– each key remaining open when the one above it is brought into use – common on modern saxophones. Thus d^3 and $d\sharp^3$ were played by separate keys (15 and 17 respectively, the former *not* being employed when the latter was required); e^3 had its own key (18) added to that of d^3 (15); f^3 had its own key (19) added to that of $d(^3 \sharp17)$. This rather cumbersome arrangement of the palm keys would be refined over the following years (see Table 5, p. 56).

The bass in patent sketch no. 2 has three octave keys, a point reinforced in Sax's description accompanying the diagram. However, both the S-shaped saxophone in the patent and the fingering chart in Kastner's 1846 method indicate an instrument with two octave keys (numbered 16 and 20), with the changeover between them occurring at $g\sharp^2$. The three-octave key arrangement appears to have been deemed impractical and two octave keys quickly became standard. It is conceivable that the third octave key was something of a late and possibly experimental addition, since in 1843 the writer Castil-Blaze had noted that the saxophone was equipped with nineteen keys, not the twenty illustrated in the patent.[42]

The nominal playing pitches Sax stipulates for the instruments in his patent bear only a passing resemblance to today's saxophone family. Saxophone number 1 is described as an 'E♭ tenor saxophone', the lowest note of which was written b°, sounding D; the highest note $d\sharp^3$, sounding $f\sharp^1$. This would make the instrument equivalent to today's baritone saxophone. Saxophone number 2 was not given a descriptive title but was pitched in C, with a written lowest note of $B\flat_1$. This low fingering appears quickly to have been left behind as the instrument developed; in all other cases the lowest note on early saxophones was written b° (modern instruments descend to $b\flat^\circ$ or a°). Sax notes that this instrument could also be made in the key of B♭, in which case its lowest note would sound $A\flat_1$. Such an instrument would be equivalent to today's bass saxophone. Sax's placing of it in this order shows that he also thought of it as such, even if he omitted the name at this point. Why this instrument should be indicated as a C bass rather than the B♭ of the prototype is unclear.[43] Saxophone number 3 was described as a 'Contrabass saxophone in G', which could also be made in A♭, and number 4 was described as a 'Bourdon' (in this sense meaning 'large' or 'low') which was again pitched in C, with a possible version in B♭ listed. The other four models were described as being 'in the same keys as the preceding instruments, but one octave higher'. Thus, at this stage some fourteen models of saxophone were theoretically available, or under consideration; however only two were laid out in any detail, again suggesting strongly that Sax had plans for a larger family of related instruments but that the necessary development of the others had yet to be completed.

Even Sax appears not have been quite clear what might be possible, since the patent itself is inherently contradictory. Sax suggests that numbers 5–8 are at the same pitch as numbers 1–4, but one octave higher. This, however, would mean that a saxophone made one octave higher than number 4 (the Bourdon) would duplicate exactly saxophone number 2, the unnamed 'bass' saxophone. One possible explanation is that the intended higher instruments were a modern B♭ tenor (no. 5, an octave higher than no. 2), an E♭ alto (no. 6, an octave higher than no. 1), a B♭ soprano (no. 7, an octave higher than no. 5), and an E♭ sopranino (no. 8, an octave higher than no. 6).[44]

Not only does Sax's patent explicitly demonstrate the connection with the ophi-cleide, it also shows the relationship between these early saxophones and Sax's 1838 bass clarinet. In particular, the curved bell of saxophone number 1 is reminiscent of the alternative curved bell Sax had proposed in 1838, and the swan-shaped crooks of saxophones 5 and 6 also demonstrate clear parallels with the crook drawn in the bass clarinet patent.[45]

By the time the saxophone patent was granted, in June 1846, the S-shaped 'tenor-baritone' saxophone appears to have been supplanting the larger 'ophicleide' version. The patent itself suggests an evolution from one to the other, since it makes clear the different arrangement of octave keys on the two instruments, and the different ranges available. The ongoing evolution of the instrument is also evidenced by the oldest surviving saxophone (serial no. 4634), one of these S-shaped 'tenor-baritone' models most likely dating from 1846–8. The instrument shows some variation from the patent sketch, particularly in being made from 5 sections rather than 6, in the shape and position of the low b° key behind the bell, and in having rather different keywork for the low c^1 and eb^1 linkages. The pillars holding the keys are soldered directly onto the body of the instrument rather than being attached to small platforms as on later models, and the instrument has a mix of flat springs and needle springs, whereas the latter would subsequently become the norm. Significantly, the fingering for e^3 has changed. Whereas this had previously been fingered entirely with the left hand palm

18. The oldest surviving saxophone, dating from c. 1846–8.

keys, a right-hand side key had now been added for this note. This reduced the ergonomic demand on the player's left palm and facilitated more fluent passagework
among these high notes; this key arrangement was sufficiently successful that it has
been retained on modern saxophones.[46]

The increasing dominance of the S-shaped 'tenor-baritone' member of the saxophone family may be attributed to a number of factors. It was less prone to damage
than the ophicleide-shaped bass instrument, as well as being lighter and more easily
played while marching. The lowest notes offered by the bass had not previously been
part of wind band textures, and were therefore not missed. Other instruments such as
contrabass saxhorns were being developed at the same time, and these more comfortably provided the lowest voices in the bands, as well as being more rugged than either
ophicleides or saxophones.[47]

The importance of the S-shaped model can also be inferred from its centrality in
three saxophone methods published in 1846, by Kastner, Jean Cokken, and an
otherwise unidentified 'Hartmann'.[48] Of these, Kastner's is the most significant. Given
his close relationship with Sax, Kastner's *Méthode complète et raisonnée de saxophone* –
dedicated to Sax and doubtless approved by and probably written in collaboration
with the inventor – provides considerable insight into the state of the instrument at
this time, and Sax's thoughts on its future. Kastner's *Méthode* appears to have been
written at the behest of the French Minister of War shortly after the instrument's
adoption by the French military. It was originally published by Eugène-Théodore
Troupenas in 1846, but a revised edition was issued by Louis Brandus in 1850, after
Troupenas's death. The difference between these two editions indicates the development of the saxophone family over this period.

That Kastner's 1846 method includes a fingering chart based on an Eb tenor-
baritone saxophone similar to saxophone no. 1 in Sax's patent suggests that in his
(and by implication Sax's) mind this was now to be seen as the 'standard' saxophone;
even at this comparatively early stage the ophicleide-shaped instruments were being
left behind. This perception is reinforced by Kastner's statement that 'the fingerings
are absolutely the same for all the saxophones, low or high',[49] thus conveniently
ignoring the three octave keys still clearly evident in the sketch of the bourdon. The
other diagrams from Sax's original patent are also included and named. The names
given are now (in order of size from lowest to highest), 'bourdon' (patent sketch
no. 4), 'contre basse' (no. 3), 'basse' (the prototype ophicleide, no. 2, and the only one
other than the Eb baritone in Kastner's method with keywork drawn in), 'soprano'
(S-shaped, no. 5), 'saxophone aigu' (no. 7), and 'saxophone sur aigu (piccolo)' (no. 8,
having a straight body). While these names may have made sense to Kastner and Sax
they bear little relationship to contemporary nomenclature: the name 'soprano' is
allocated to an instrument looking more like today's tenor, while the modern Eb
alto and Bb tenor instruments are missing entirely. But the keys in which the
instruments might be available – still largely hypothetical at this stage – are more
settled and consistent than those given in the patent, with each of the seven sizes of
instrument offered either in C and Bb or F and Eb, making a total of fourteen
possibilities in all. The ranges of the top four pairs are notated in the treble clef, while
the lowest three pairs are in the bass clef. All instruments are indicated as having a

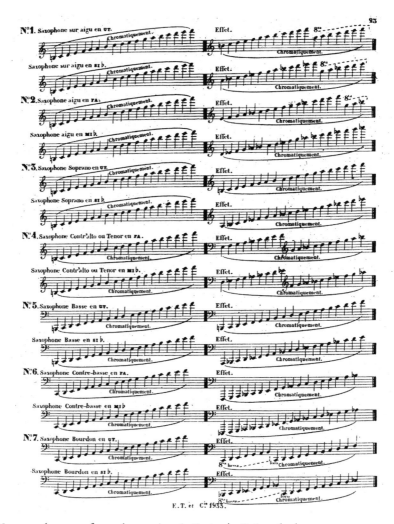

19. Names and ranges of saxophones given in Kastner's 1846 method.

range of some two and a half octaves, written as $b°$ to f^3 for the treble clef instruments, B_I to f^1 for the basse, and C to f^1 for the contre-basse and bourdon. There is no mention in this method of possible extensions to these ranges into the altissimo register, which Kastner had suggested in the 1844 supplement to his orchestration treatise.

The new edition of Kastner's method published by Brandus in 1850 includes different nomenclature for the various instruments and a revised fingering chart. The saxophones now listed bear a much closer resemblance to those familiar today. There are nine sizes given (compared to eight in the patent and seven in the 1846 edition), each of which is described as being in either Bb or Eb, with a note at the bottom of the page indicating that all instruments are also available sounding one tone higher, that is, in C or F; the majority of these are still likely to have been speculative at this stage. The names used also more closely resemble those with which we are familiar today: a 'Petit Saxophone suraigu' in B♭ (theoretically sounding a minor seventh above its notated pitch), a 'Petit Saxophone aigu' in E♭ (today's sopranino), 'Soprano' in B♭, 'Alto' in E♭, 'Ténor' in B♭, 'Baryton' in E♭, 'Basse' in B♭, 'Contre-basse' in E♭, and 'Bourdon' in B♭, the latter somewhat improbably having A_2 as its lowest note. The written ranges of each instrument have been standardised as b° to f³, and all are now written in the treble clef.

The differences between the revised fingering chart and the 1846 original again reveal the ongoing development of the instrument at this time, particularly in relation to the placing of toneholes. The two alternative fingerings for c² remain (and are replicated for c³, with added octave key), suggesting again a linkage between the

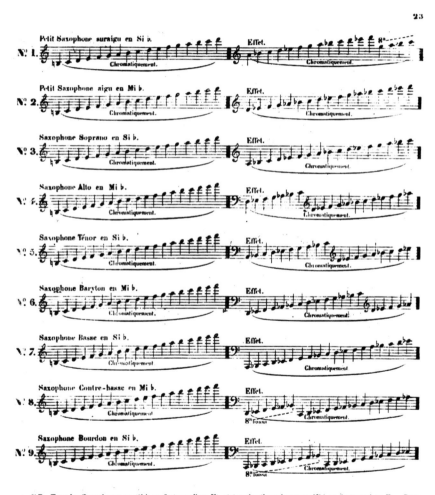

N.B. Tous les Saxophones en Si♭ se font aussi' en Ut et tous les Saxophones en Mi♭ se font aussi en Fa. Dans ce cas l'effet réel est d'un ton plus haut que pour les Saxophones en Si♭ et en Mi♭.

20. Revised saxophone names and ranges given in the 1850 Brandus edition of Kastner's method.

second and third left-hand touches that was eventually deemed redundant; the previous addition of the octave key with touch 2 to produce this note has been removed. There are three alternate fingerings for written c♯²: the conventional open tube; the same with the right-hand keys added, this being a modification probably intended to help with tuning, as is the case today, and perhaps a formalisation of performance practice already extant; and a 'long' fingering arising from adding the octave key to the same fingering as c♯¹, which is today seen as unorthodox. The change between octave keys is now indicated as occurring at written a♯², not g♯² as previously (today's automated mechanisms normally change over at a²), suggesting that the holes covered by these keys had been repositioned. The short d² fingering has been replaced by today's long version, and the alternative short d♯² fingering has similarly disappeared. Three possibilities are given for d³, one of which is an over-blown fingering that dispenses with the palm key more normally used for that note. The fingering for the highest four notes has been slightly simplified, with d³ also obtained via its own discrete key (15), which then remains open while other keys are added to it to obtain the remaining notes: d♯³ from keys 15 plus 16, e³ from 15 plus 17, and f³ from 15 plus 18.[50] A comparison of these fingerings relative to their 1846 equivalents is given in Table 5.

Table 5: Comparison of fingerings required for the highest four notes on the saxophone in 1846 and 1850 (shaded columns indicate 1850 fingerings).

		Pitches desired (written)							
		d³		d♯³		e³		f³	
Palm keys opened	d³	X	X		X	X	X		X
	d♯³			X	X			X	
	e³					X	X		
	f³							X	X

By the time of this 1850 publication it might be inferred that Sax was thinking of two families of saxophones, one pitched in F/C and the other in B♭/E♭. Many commentators have suggested that these were designed to function as 'orchestral' and 'band' families' respectively.[51] However, there is no compelling evidence to support the assertion. Very few F/C saxophones were actually made by Sax,[52] his competitors, or later manufacturers, with the exception of the tenor saxophone in C – the C-melody – made in significant numbers in early twentieth-century America.[53] The F/C instruments were planned and advertised by Sax at a time when the family itself was still in development and its most useful sizes not yet known. As the E♭/B♭ instruments became increasingly employed in French military bands, Sax appears to have realised there was little demand for saxophones pitched in F and C, and concentrated his efforts on developing and promoting the more saleable instruments. Nevertheless,

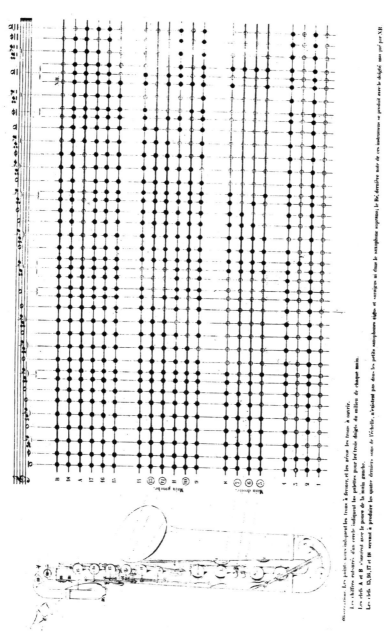

21. Saxophone fingering chart as given in the 1850 Brandus edition of Kastner's method.

he retained a personal preference for the F alto as an orchestral instrument. In a letter written to the composer Ambroise Thomas in 1883, Sax observes that:

> The saxophone in F appears to me to be the true type which should be adopted for the symphony. Some time ago I had the opportunity to demonstrate this instrument separately for two of our young masters, Mr. Massenet and Mr. Saint-Saëns. They were so taken by the timbre, the penetrating charm, and the extraordinary novelty of this orchestral voice that they immediately conceived the project of using it (as Meyerbeer had done at the beginning of *L'Etoile du Nord*). Mr. Massenet introduced it in one of his symphonic pieces; Mr. Saint-Saëns immediately composed a solo for *Henry VIII*. But both composers clashed with the bad feeling or inability of a saxophonist accustomed to his saxophone in E♭, and both of them were forced to retreat and entrust their solos to other instruments: Mr. Massenet to the clarinet, and Mr. Saint-Saëns to the oboe.[54]

Sax's observation that the player involved preferred to retain the E♭ instrument rather than change to the unfamiliar F alto reinforces the idea that the B♭/E♭ family was quickly deemed to be standard. Even if Sax *had* at some stage conceived of separate families for different contexts, this was clearly never put into practice. Although a small number of composers such as Ravel and Strauss later called for saxophones in F and C (see p. 230) this was likely to be on the basis of erroneous information received. They may have been influenced by the inclusion of a sextet at the end of both editions of Kastner's method, composed by Kastner himself, for two sopranos in C, one F alto, two C basses and an F contrabass saxophone (although there is an accompanying note suggesting that the composition can also be performed by equivalent members of the B♭/E♭ family). Since many of these instruments were hypothetical when Kastner's method was written, the fact that composers may have scored for them – either at the time or later – cannot be taken as evidence that the instruments ever existed, or that Sax conceived of them as being assigned to separate families designated for specific purposes.[55]

Given the authoritative nature of Kastner's method it is unsurprising that neither of the methods by Cokken or Hartmann published in 1846 provides significant further information on the development of the instrument. Cokken suggests the E♭ tenor-baritone instrument as being 'the one most used up to the present', although he describes it as the 'contralto or tenor';[56] like Kastner he describes the mechanism as being the same for all saxophones, again reinforcing the view that the B♭ bass ophicleide-shaped instrument was already discarded. Hartmann's method is less polished than the other two, but the only organological difference is that the fingering chart it contains indicates the changeover point from one octave key to the other as taking place at written g♯² rather than a♯². Whether Hartmann felt this was more effective or he was simply not familiar enough with the instrument to understand its proper functioning is unclear; the latter is most likely, since his fingering chart is somewhat inconsistent and idiosyncratic.

By 1847, therefore, it appears likely that only the bass (ophicleide-shaped) and E♭ tenor-baritone (S-shaped) instruments were finished and available for use, and the

22. A rare tenor saxophone in C, made by Adolphe Sax in 1879.

tenor-baritone was increasingly viewed as the 'definitive' instrument, partly on account of its greater suitability for military bands – its superior portability would have counted in its favour – and partly because it was more technologically refined and therefore likely to be more usable and manageable than the prototypical bass.

Over the next few years Sax developed further members of the saxophone family. The ophicleide-shaped bass appears to have been withdrawn and redeveloped as an S-shaped instrument.[57] A sales brochure for Sax instruments from February 1850 shows a revised bass in C – albeit that it is listed separately from the other saxophones – now with a range written from b°-e³ (sounding B$_I$-e¹). Redesigning the bass in this fashion was possibly intended to distance the saxophone from its ophicleide forerunner, in order to rebut more effectively the claims made by Sax's competitors that the saxophone was not in fact his invention, particularly since writers such as Berlioz had originally described it as an 'ophicléide à bec'. It might be further explained by Sax's known aspirations to facilitate as easily as possible the change for performers between similar instruments, as well as the economic and manufacturing benefits that would accrue from having workers in the same factory skilled at producing comparable instruments, particularly since the S-shaped bass had all its keywork on a single tube rather than distributing it across 4 parallel tubes as on the ophicleide version. This redesign of the bass saxophone permanently established the range of the instrument as being approximately the two and a half octaves common today. As already noted, in its initial incarnation this instrument, with its third octave key, had been identified as having a range of 3 octaves, and the 1844 supplement to Kastner's orchestration treatise claims a three-octave range for all saxophones. But as the family evolved the need for these higher notes was obviated by the development of other models, and Sax appears content to have reduced the range of the bass saxophone accordingly.

The parabolic bore

Sax observes in the patent that he had constructed the saxophone 'in the form of a parabolic cone', and this application of parabolic shapes in musical contexts was one of his recurring interests. He was not alone in this. Both the influential German flute maker Theobald Boehm (1794–1881) and the Belgian organologist and instrument maker Victor-Charles Mahillon (1841–1924) argued at different times in the nineteenth century for the effectiveness of the parabolic shape as an appropriate basis for the calculations underpinning musical instrument design. Sax was a firm believer in such arguments. His last patent, submitted in 1880, involved redesigning the bells of brass instruments to incorporate a parabola, and he had previously, in 1867, put forward a suggestion for an enormous egg-shaped concert hall, the guiding principles of which were based on parabolic curves.[58]

Nevertheless, Sax's apparently simple statement about the saxophone bore has at times caused confusion.[59] Jaap Kool, a composer and musicologist who wrote an early book on the saxophone, appears to have provided the most convincing explanation. Kool, writing in 1931, examined one of Sax's original alto saxophones and observed that two of the walls of the instrument were not straight, but formed a slight curve. That is, the wall with the toneholes and the wall opposite curved back in on themselves slightly towards the distal end, rather than continuing in a straight line as a simple cone would require. The other two walls were, however, straight. Thus, although a cross section of the instrument appeared almost circular at the point at which the neck was inserted, as the tube progressed it became increasingly elliptical.[60] Sax had felt that making the bore parabolic in this fashion helped to ensure the higher notes of the instrument were better in tune. Furthermore, Kool measured the diameters of the toneholes and found that certain holes were smaller than the ones preceding it, when on a perfect cone each successive descending hole should have increased in size, in proportion to the increasing diameter of the bore. At these places Kool observed that Sax had 'once again employed small parabolic bulges in the opposite direction of the overall curve which extends across the entire instrument'. These he describes as concave and convex parabolas.[61] Therefore, in addition to the basic conical shape of the instrument, Sax appears to have used a variety of parabolas to change the nature of the reflected waves within it at particular points along the expanding bore.[62] Sax also appears to have gradually reduced the expansion rate of his saxophone bores over time, since the bell diameters demonstrate a consistent reduction on all models from the early 1850s through to the late 1870s, together with a concomitant reduction in bell sizes.[63]

These parabolic curves are no longer found on modern instruments, which are now constructed as pure cones, to the regret of some. Even in 1931 Kool lamented that both American and European firms were increasingly putting 'inexpensive saxophones on the market, which often forego the parabolic shape' and he complained that such instruments sounded 'harsh and slightly raspy', whereas the original saxophone sound he found 'uniquely sonorous, mellow, and at the same time somewhat hollow'.[64] The demand in the 1920s and 30s for more powerful and penetrating instruments is likely to have contributed to this development. Sax did not invent, nor did he claim to invent, a musical instrument that combined a single reed with a conical bore. It was the addition of such a reed to a *parabolic* conical bore that he construed as the instrument's most innovative acoustic feature, a feature that has been lost on modern instruments. Nevertheless, a more recent study of saxophone acoustics has suggested that the parabolic bore produces only a negligible effect on frequency placement when compared to a pure cone, and that 'the unique qualities associated with saxophones of this shape (and era) are most attributable to other factors, as well as further possible bore deformities'.[65]

The mouthpiece

The mouthpiece sketched in the 1846 patent is described as 'a single reed mouthpiece with a very flared interior which tapers to the part that fits the body of the instrument'.[66] It is designated as being for the bass model, although Sax notes that it could be made in different sizes for the other saxophones. Both Berlioz and Kastner

23. A pair of original saxophone mouthpieces made by Adolphe Sax.

observed in the 1840s the similarity between the bass clarinet mouthpiece and that of the saxophone, thus underlining the chronological and developmental relationship already noted between these two instruments.[67] Early saxophone mouthpieces were made of wood, although Cokken's 1846 method indicates that they might be made from either wood or metal;[68] Vulcanised rubber, popularly known as ebonite, the material from which many modern mouthpieces are made, was not widely used for the manufacture of single-reed mouthpieces until the last quarter of the nineteenth century. Although crystal mouthpieces were also available by 1873, Sax continued to use wooden mouthpieces: his 1881 patent includes a sketch of a wooden mouthpiece, though he writes that it could be galvanised with brass and then coated with gold, silver or nickel.[69] This coating was an attempt to reduce the impact upon the mouthpiece from changes in humidity and moisture.

Later innovations by Sax

In 1850, only four years after the original French patent, Sax was granted a Belgian patent to protect his rights when exporting his instruments into Belgium, and a comparison of these two patents provides further evidence of the saxophone's development in the late 1840s.[70] Six instruments are listed in the later patent – C bass, E♭ baritone, B♭ tenor, E♭ alto, B♭ soprano and E♭ 'aigu', the latter again equivalent to today's sopranino – although only four are represented in diagrams; the sopranino and tenor are omitted, suggesting that these instruments were still, as previously, not fully developed at this stage. Obvious technical and morphological changes to the 1846 E♭ tenor-baritone instrument can be observed: the number of tube sections appears reduced from six to five, requiring less soldering and allowing more flexibility in the positioning of keywork; the pads for the lowest notes are worked by a linkage system, rather than being directly operated by means of long keys fixed to the bell; there is no longer an octave key at the bottom of the U-bend of the crook, where it would have collected water – subsequently deposited on the player's hand – and also deteriorated more quickly; the crook itself has rather different dimensions to the earlier patent, ensuring that the mouthpiece is presented to the player's mouth at a less acute angle and helping to reduce turbulence in the air column. The changed position for the e^3 key – now operated, as today, by a key adjacent to the right hand index finger – is recognised. The low b° key of the alto appears to have been moved from being directly behind the bell to a position on its left hand side; the baritone and bass models in the 1850 patent retain it in its original position, and the change was not effected on these instruments until some time later. The surviving c. 1850 bass saxophone in which the tonehole chimneys have been abandoned (see p. 9) is again indicative of the experimental state of saxophone construction at this time.[71]

Around 1847–8 Sax had begun production of the E♭ alto, which appears in an undated sales list from around this time, offered at a price of 200 French francs.[72] Initially the instrument had a neck with a double curve, but from some time in the early 1850s this was changed to a single curve. All saxophones prior to 1860 had large bells in comparison with today's instruments, and this is particularly noticeable on the alto versions. Bell sizes gradually decreased on all saxophones from the dimensions

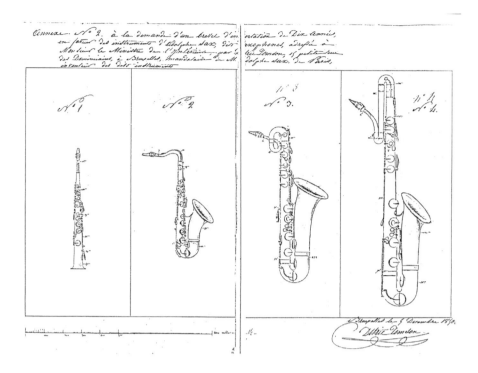

24. Sketches of four saxophones submitted as part of Adolphe Sax's 1850 Belgian patent.

found in the earliest models, but there is a particularly sharp reduction in alto bell sizes around 1860, with bell diameters changing from c. 140mm to c. 117mm.[73]

The soprano saxophone appears to have been sufficiently developed by 1849 that it could enter production, and the earliest surviving soprano possibly dates from that year.[74] It lacks palm keys for any notes above c♯³ (sounding b²) and thus added only three additional notes to the ranges covered by the existing members of the saxophone family, since the E♭ alto's written f³ sounded a♭². By 1860 Sax had added keys for d³ and d♯³, increasing the overall range of the family by five notes, but did not go beyond this for reasons that are not entirely clear. It is conceivable that these high notes, which are in any case often the most difficult part of the soprano instrument to control, were deemed to be insufficiently secure for some technological reason that has been subsequently overcome. The tablature provided for the 1850 Belgian patent reaffirms that the top note of the soprano was written c♯³ at that time.

The description 'ténor' had been applied by Kastner in 1844 and 1846 to an instrument approximating to today's E♭ alto – described as an alto-ténor – and by Sax himself to the E♭ baritone model in 1848 and 1850, which he described as baryton-ténor. Appending the description 'ténor' to these two other instruments indicates not only that Sax felt that between them such instruments might adequately cover the tenor range, but also that no separate instrument bearing this nomenclature was yet in circulation. Sax did show a B♭ tenor saxophone at the Paris Exhibition in 1859, although it does not feature in his 1850 *prospectus de vente*, suggesting that it was not

25. Bb soprano (1867) and Eb alto (1861) saxophones, both made by Adolphe Sax.

in production at this time. In 1853 Sax established a *Société de la Grande Harmonie* – a mixed wind band of a type that became increasingly popular in mid-nineteenth century France – largely to act as an advertisement for the capabilities of his own instruments; a poster from December 1853 advertises performances by the group, but does not give full details of the instrumentation. However, two undated posters clearly indicate the presence of a tenor saxophone, played in both instances by Monsieur Lépine,[75] and it was also unambiguously listed in the decree of 16 August 1854 reorganising the band of the Imperial Guard. Thus, while the tenor instrument was probably still being developed in 1850, it was almost certainly in production by sometime in 1853, and possibly earlier. One further indicator that the tenor model was still being developed in 1850 is provided by Sax's Belgian patent of that year, where it is clearly indicated. The fingering charts accompanying the patent indicate a small divergence in relation to the tenor instrument. Whereas the changeover point from one octave key to the next is indicated as $a\sharp^2$ on all other saxophones, on the tenor it is described as occurring at c^3, again suggesting that the instrument was still under development at the time this patent was submitted (the different changeover points of the two octave keys is explained by the different positions occupied by the vents they cover on early Sax instruments, when compared to modern instruments).[76]

In 1855 Berlioz revised his *Grand Traité*, substantially reworking his chapter on the saxophone. He now noted that there were six kinds of saxophones, listing them as sopranino ('aigu'), soprano, alto, tenor, baritone and bass. He also observed that Sax would shortly produce a contrabass member of the family, an indication that no such instrument was in production at that time – occasional earlier references to it must have related to prototypes or hypothetical designs. Berlioz's observations on the timbre of the sopranino – '[it] is much more penetrating than that of the clarinets in B♭ and C, without having the piercing and often harsh outburst of the small clarinet in E♭' – are sufficiently accurate to indicate that he must have heard the instrument.[77] It can therefore reasonably be inferred that the sopranino was available by this time, even though no specimen remains and there is no iconographic evidence to support its existence.

Sax's original French saxophone patent was valid for fifteen years, with an extension granted – somewhat unusually – for a further five years (see p. 32). This extension expired on 11 May 1866. Two months prior to this, however, on 19 March, Sax submitted a further patent application outlining a range of modifications and improvements to the instrument, which was approved a few weeks later on 31 May.[78] This list of alterations appears a curious mixture of work already undertaken combined with what were presumably technological aspirations: Sax was protecting not only what he had achieved but what he hoped to achieve. The patent details six proposed changes to the instrument: i) an elongation of the instrument (without changing its sounding pitch) which Sax felt would increase the number of harmonics in the sound, particularly the harmonic at the twelfth, thus bringing something of the clarinet's character into the saxophone sound; ii) a revision to the mechanism of the left hand keys, to make the fingering easier and more regular; iii) the somewhat inconceivable addition of 'pistons' (i.e. valves) to the instrument, albeit without changing the fingering required from the player; iv) the addition of 'one or two' new octave keys, the first, which would be sufficiently high so as to require a vent hole through the mouthpiece aligned to one on the neck, would facilitate notes in the upper register, the second was designed to improve middle d^2 and eb^2; v) intriguingly, Sax proposed a c^1 hole in the middle register, which might be covered either by the thumb of the left hand or a key operated by this thumb. Sax had perhaps returned to his clarinet models here for inspiration, since from his description one may assume he had something similar to the clarinettist's left hand thumb/key arrangement in mind. Sax's observation that the saxophone could be made 'in wood or any other suitable material' again suggests that his work on clarinets was not far from his mind; vi) revisions to the bore of the instrument, suggesting that the existing shape which 'approaches a parabolic cone' could be modified into a right cone or a retractable or concave cone. It is unclear what Sax meant by this, but the fact that none of these proposed modifications appears to have been employed in production indicates their provisional and hypothetical nature. Realising that his patent was about to expire, Sax was most likely speculating on any conceivable development that might have been introduced by other manufacturers, as well as protecting potential innovations that he himself might wish to exploit commercially.

Sax submitted only one further patent relating to the saxophone, granted on 16 January 1881, which again proposed a series of largely speculative modifications. Noting that the E♭ alto saxophone was by then the instrument most commonly used, especially by military bands, Sax equated this instrument with the role of the viola in a string quartet, but observed that its range did not go quite as low as the viola, whose lowest string then as now was tuned to c°. Accordingly, Sax proposed increasing the range of the alto by two semitones, down to b♭° (recalling the lowest note of the bass saxophone in the original patent) and a°; these extra notes sounded the low d♭° and c° respectively, and would thus also allow the instrument to double the viola line in the orchestra. Similarly, Sax proposed adding keys to facilitate high f♯³ and g³, the first of these being played with the right hand (as on modern saxophones), the second with the left hand. He also suggested having as many as four octave keys, the fourth of which would not be controlled by the thumb, but could be brought into use by the keys of the upper notes themselves. Sax envisaged that such a mechanism could only apply to the very highest notes, from e³ to g³, since these keys were not used for any other notes on the instrument. A key operated by the left hand thumb could be added, which would allow c² to be played without the need for any other keys to be closed, and would also more easily facilitate a trill from b¹ to c² simply by using this thumb key (in a manner analogous to the modern flute). Sax also proposed a linkage such that the notes achieved by depressing the left hand fingers could be lowered by one step when adding either the first or second fingers of the right hand; versions of this mechanism are still used today (saxophonists will know this as the long B♭ fingering). One final and rather curious addition proposed by Sax was the diametrical insertion of a membrane inside the saxophone's crook; this would be covered by a key-operated pad. Opening the hole while the instrument was being played would cause the membrane to vibrate and 'modify the sound of the instrument while producing a sort of grinding in order to get particular effects'.[79] The effect proposed would presumably have added a kazoo-like quality to the instrument, perhaps reminiscent of the throat growl sometimes used in contemporary and popular music today. Thus the manipulation of the instrument's basic timbre, which was to become such a widespread feature of saxophone performance in the twentieth century, might reasonably be said to have started with the inventor himself, in theory if not in practice.

Patents and developments by other Europeans

One of Sax's most significant achievements was his development of families of instruments whose individual members were comparatively uniform both in their acoustic behaviour and the techniques required to play them. This not only ensured a good degree of timbral homogeneity but also made it easy for musicians to move from one instrument to another, since both the fingerwork and the methods of sound production were essentially the same. This holistic approach was construed by Sax's opponents as demonstrating a megalomaniac attitude towards instrumentation, with the Belgian endeavouring to dominate all musical ensembles by giving his instrumental families central roles within them. Yet the advantages of such families were not lost on other manufacturers, whatever their public misgivings. The most obvious aping of Sax's approach was developed by his most implacable opponent, Pierre-Louis Gautrot. In 1856 Gautrot patented the first of a family of instruments called sarrusophones, which were designed to compete with the saxophone. As with saxophones, the family was developed over many years, and appears not to have been completed until 1867, when a complete set was demonstrated at the *Exposition universelle* in Paris. The instrument was moderately successful during the nineteenth century, and its success may well have dissuaded Sax from further developing the lowest proposed members of the saxophone family.

The sarrusophone was named after, and may have been invented by, a French band-master, Pierre-Auguste Sarrus. Like Sax, Gautrot was seeking a substitute for the comparatively weak oboes and bassoons in marching bands, and needed an instrument that could provide greater volume; the instrument would therefore require a large bore and large toneholes; it should be easily played while marching, and produce a homogenous timbre across a range of models. Almost inevitably, the sarrusophone shared a number of characteristics with the saxophone. It was a brass instrument of conical bore, albeit coupled to a double rather than a single reed. It was ultimately available in alternating Eb/Bb tonalities in a full range of sizes from sopranino to contrabass. Although initially offered with a range of three octaves this was eventually standardised at two octaves and a sixth, and because each was written in the treble clef (apart from the C contrabass) the written range became bb^0 to g^3, almost exactly that of the saxophone. In keywork and fingering the sarrusophone also bore more than a passing resemblance to Sax's prototypical bass saxophone, though its narrower bore and smaller conicity made the larger sarrusophones more manageable than saxophones covering the same range, particularly for a marching musician.[80]

Although for most models the sarrusophone retained the upward-pointing ophicleide shape that Sax had moved away from, a 1911 variant, the Rothophone, produced in Italy, was nothing less than a sarrusophone made in the shape of a saxophone.[81] These later developments only serve to reinforce the close relationship between the two instruments. Pontécoulant, in his *Organographie* of 1861, notes that 'Gautrot, seeking to counterbalance the success and vogue of the *Saxophone*, thought of producing a crude imitation under the name *Sarrusophone*'.[82] Sax, seldom hesitant in resorting to litigation, filed a suit for copyright infringement within three days of Gautrot's patent being granted, on 12 June 1856. This resulted in a three-year legal battle that was finally resolved – in Sax's favour – on 8 July 1859. Sax, undoubtedly piqued at having his innovations appropriated by a rival manufacturer, responded not only with legal action but also by including in his 1866 saxophone patent the idea of attaching a saxophone mouthpiece to Gautrot's sarrusophone, thus changing it from a double-reed to a single-reed instrument.

The litigation between Sax and Gautrot is indicative of the fierce competition between brasswind instrument manufacturers in Paris at this time, and the importance they attached to patenting even the smallest innovation. The expiry in 1866 of the five-year extension to the original saxophone patent meant that Sax's rights in relation to the instrument were no longer protected, and other manufacturers were now legally permitted to develop and patent their own models and modifications. That relatively few chose to do so may be taken as evidence both of the effectiveness of Sax's original

26. A bass sarrusophone in C and an alto rothophone in E♭ (dates unknown).

design and of the instrument's comparatively marginal position in the world of French music at this time; more manufacturers would doubtless have been interested in developing the instrument had the potential commercial benefits been greater. Nevertheless, several manufacturers did demonstrate an interest in taking the instrument forward. On 7 August 1866, only a few months after the expiry of the original patent, Millereau and Company submitted a patent for an instrument to be called a 'Saxophone-Millereau'.[83] Unsurprisingly, Millereau's instrument was similar to Sax's design, except that the two octave keys were mounted on a single post rather than each having its own fixing, although they remained independent rather than interchanging automatically, as modern systems do. Another modification included mounting the low c^1 and eb^1 keys on a single rod, allowing the provision of an alternative low $c\sharp^1$ key below these. In the same sketch Millereau added a key between the e and d finger touches. This key does not appear in the other sketches and its possible function is not clearly explained in the patent.

It was not only Parisian instrument makers who endeavoured to capitalise on the expiry of the original patent. Five hundred miles further south in the town of Toulon on France's Mediterranean coast, a maker by the name of Claude George also put forward in 1866 a revised system of keywork for the saxophone. George's revisions grouped sets of keys together for the purpose of mounting them more effectively on the body of the instrument, although there was no impact on the disposition of the fingering system itself. In particular, the keys of each hand were grouped together on the same rod, whereas Sax had mounted some of them on separate rods; this innovation, now commonplace, was considerably ahead of its time. Further refinements to George's system were patented in 1869 (including the addition of a single post for the octave keys, as with Millereau) and in 1870. The diagram accompanying the latter amendment appears to indicate the addition of rollers to the c^1 and eb^1 keys, something which is again common on modern saxophones but was also ahead of its time; however, surviving instruments suggest that this idea never made it into production.[84]

Notwithstanding his earlier promotion of the sarrusophone, Sax's long-standing opponent Gautrot also took the opportunity in 1868 to submit a saxophone patent, possibly to pique the Belgian inventor yet further.[85] Gautrot claimed in the patent text

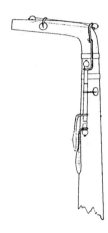

27. Sketch from Millereau's 1866 saxophone patent, showing revised right hand $c^1/c\sharp^1/eb^1$ arrangement, and the single post mounting of two octave keys.

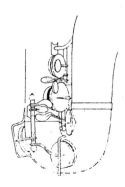

that Sax's instrument had undergone few significant changes since the original 1846 design, but that he, Gautrot, had improved tuning and sonority through simplifying the mechanism. Gautrot's modifications were largely related to the interior dimensions of the bore and the placement of toneholes, and he gives detailed calculations of these for Bb soprano and Eb alto and baritone instruments. He proposed minor changes to certain key placements and the manner by which these were attached to the body. Gautrot also advocated redesigned pads, in which a stiffening mechanism was introduced between the pad and the cup in order to keep the pad itself flatter. In exterior appearance and range (b° to f³) the instrument appears largely unchanged from Sax's own.

Between 1875 and 1879 Pierre Goumas applied for four patents relating to the saxophone, under the name of Goumas et Cie (although Goumas had taken over the operations of the Buffet Crampon company at this stage, and continued to use the latter's trademark). Goumas's concern was with the operation of the left-hand keys, especially the notes between b^2 and d^3, and particularly the perennially problematic $c\sharp^3$. Observing that the fingering of the left hand had 'always been very difficult, and that not until after years of study could one become a master',[86] Goumas proposed a system based on the left hand of Boehm's clarinet fingering. Specifically, he designed a left-hand thumb key to be operated separately from, and in addition to, the two existing octave keys. By means of a carefully constructed linkage d^3 appears to have been accessed by using the second octave key only; $c\sharp^3$ was produced by the index finger of the left hand, simultaneously raising the thumb from the new thumb key. Pressing the thumb key alone produced c^3, while adding the index finger produced b^2. An additional palm key (similar to today's d^3 key) could be used with the new thumb key to provide a semitone trill from c^3 to $c\sharp^3$. Again following the Boehm system, Goumas introduced a linkage so that bb^2 could be produced by adding the right-hand index finger to the b^2 fingering, as is common today (as well as having the same effect on bb^1). Goumas appears unsatisfied with the outcome, however, and submitted three further amendments to this patent, one in 1878 and two in 1879, which continued to address the problematic $c\sharp^2$. His final attempt at a solution was to incorporate a right hand side key, in the position in which a side c trill key is today more commonly provided, with which the $c\sharp^2$ could be obtained. Goumas's patents may have partly inspired Sax's 1881 patent, which addresses several similar issues.

In 1886 the Association générale des ouvriers en instruments de musique, an organisation involving several of the manufacturers who had taken legal action against Sax, proposed a number of modifications.[87] These included: a long bb^1 fingering which could be played by depressing any of the first, second or third fingers of the right hand plus the first finger of the left hand (thus extending Goumas's and Sax's innovation); two half-holes on the keys for the left hand index finger (b^1) and the right-hand middle finger ($f\sharp^1$) – the first was intended to function as an octave vent key for the notes $g\sharp^2$ to b^2, and the second an alternative way of playing d^3 and $d\sharp^3$; a lever added below the right-hand first finger – to provide a trill from f to f$\sharp$ – and another below the right-hand middle finger – to provide an alternative f natural fingering; the addition of what appears from the patent sketches to be a right-hand trill key from b^1 to c^2; an additional low $c\sharp^1$ key, to be played by the right-hand fourth finger; and an additional left-hand fourth finger key, which provided an alternative eb fingering (similar to the e/b^1 cross

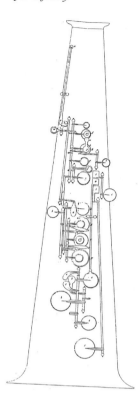

28. Soprano saxophone sketch from the 1886 patent by the Association générale des ouvriers en instruments de musique.

fingering available on the Boehm clarinet). The Association included a diagram of a soprano saxophone to illustrate these developments.

A subsidiary patent of 1887 repeated much of the information from the first patent, while proposing yet more innovations, now illustrated with both soprano and alto saxophone diagrams.[88] Keys were now arranged such that the depressed g♯ key remained closed while playing f♯, more easily facilitating f♯/g♯ trills. A further linkage between the low c♯^{1} and c^1 keys, which normally stood open, allowed both to be played with the right hand little finger only, with c^1 automatically closing the c♯^{1} key as required. A right-hand g♯ key was added to aid trills from g♯ to a. The f³ key was linked to the other palm keys, thus requiring only the opening of this one key to render accurately this top note (rather than necessitating the manual opening of all the other palm keys). An alternative left-hand fingering was given for e♭^{1}, in addition to the normal right-hand fingering. A separate diagram illustrated the addition of a moveable brass tuning slide fitted onto the neck of the saxophone, to which the mouthpiece was attached, which allowed the instrument to be tuned without a space developing between the exit point of the neck and the chamber of the mouthpiece.

Millereau, who had submitted the first non-Sax patent in 1866, proposed a further development in an 1888 patent, extending the range of each saxophone down to written b♭°.[89] To produce this note he devised, in conjunction with the renowned Parisian saxophonist Louis Mayeur, a mechanism operated by the thumb of the right hand, normally used only to support the instrument rather than having an active role. While the extension down to b♭° eventually became commonplace, the

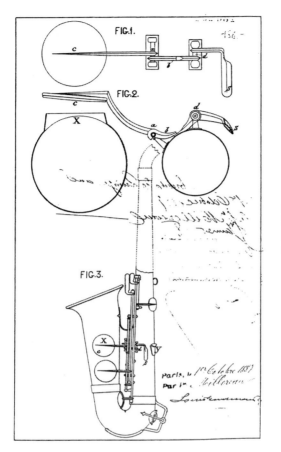

29. Sketch from the 1887 Millereau-Mayeur patent showing proposal for a right hand thumb key to extend the saxophone range down to b♭°.

Millereau-Mayeur thumb mechanism did not (although it might be argued that it paved the way for the later addition of the low a° left-hand thumb key, now common on many baritone saxophones).

Pierre Goumas sold the Buffet Crampon marque to his former pupils Paul Evette and Ernest Schaeffer in January 1885. From 1887 to 1912 Evette and Schaeffer submitted a series of patents and amendments in relation to saxophone construction that, taken as a whole, provided perhaps the most radical rethinking of saxophone keywork of any manufacturer at that time. Their first patent of 1887 extended the g♯ linkage devised by the Association, so that this key would be closed by any of the right-hand keys, not just the f♯, thus enabling a range of trills between all these keys and the g♯. Like Millereau, they extended the range of the instrument down to b♭°, but this lowest note was now produced by the left hand little finger (unlike Millereau's thumb mechanism), which automatically closed the b° key in the process, in the manner of modern saxophones. The tonehole for this lowest note was on the opposite side of the bell to the b° tonehole. Elsewhere, a small extension to the pad covering the b♭¹ tonehole, normally closed by the left-hand middle finger, allowed this pad to be closed by judicious placing of the left hand index finger; this is the origins of the

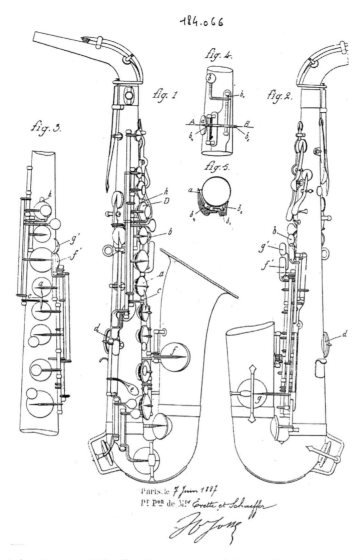

30. Sketch from Evette and Schaeffer 1887 patent: key g' closes pad g, producing low b°; key f' closes pad f, producing low b♭° (also closing key g' in the process). Key e provides the chromatic f♯. Pad D is extended slightly by touch h, which provides the button b♭ fingering.

button b♭ key familiar today. This provided a third manner of playing this note (in addition to the extant 'long' and 'side' fingerings).

A further Evette and Schaeffer patent of 1885 introduced a front f key, linked to the highest palm key of the instrument, which provided an alternative and more straightforward fingering for e³ and f³. Later the same year an amendment proposed an extension of the bis b♭ principle to the middle finger of the right hand, where an additional touch depressing a half-hole mechanism on the d¹ key was designed to produce e♭¹ (duplicated in the upper octave) as an alternative to the conventional right-hand little finger option. Later patents submitted by Evette and Schaeffer proposed:

further revisions to the mechanism of those keys controlled by the left-hand little finger (two patents both submitted in 1896); a reconfiguration of the neck and higher octave key of the baritone saxophone (1901); improvements to the perennially problematic middle c♯² (1907); a complex reconfiguration of the little finger mechanisms for both left and right hands, including the addition of a third key for the right-hand little finger such that low b° could also be played with this finger only, in the manner of a Boehm clarinet (previously it could only be produced by the left-hand little finger), an addition that also facilitated easier trills between the lowest notes on the instrument (1907); and yet more refinements to the neck of the saxophone, intended to make the instrument more comfortable for the performer (1912).⁹⁰

From about 1910 to 1930 this collection of innovations was sold under the Buffet marque as the Evette and Schaeffer 'Apogée' system.⁹¹ The keywork now included an additional right-hand g♯ key similar to that introduced by the Association some years earlier, and also added a rather curious long key operated by the first finger of the right hand, which produced d² or d³ as required, apparently to simplify certain awkward fingerings for passagework around the breaks between registers. Although more complex and therefore expensive to produce than other saxophone keywork, the 'Apogée' system was very sophisticated. The system was considered sufficiently workable to be emulated in part by the Holton company on their 'Rudy Wiedoeft' models produced in the late 1920s, but most of Evette and Schaeffer's innovations have not been retained by modern manufacturers. Even the front f³ key introduced by them as early as 1895 and now considered commonplace, was not standard on the majority of saxophones until the 1970s.

The Couesnon company joined forces with Dolnet, Lefevre et Pigis to submit a joint patent outlining various minor innovations in 1888.⁹² These included an extra key for the low c¹ played by the little finger of the left hand, again reminiscent of similar alternate fingerings on the Boehm clarinet, and a further additional key beneath the right-hand side b♭ key, which more easily facilitated a g-g♯ trill.

The innovation that had the most profound impact on saxophone performance was contained in a different 1888 patent, submitted by Arsène Lecomte.⁹³ Lecomte claimed to have successfully modified the saxophone's Boehm system fingering, and that the result was sufficiently distinguishable from Sax's original that these instruments should henceforth be known as a 'clarinophones', not only because of their new fingering but also, so he claimed, because of their altered bore dimensions. This neologism was unnecessary, since his instruments remained quite clearly saxophones. But Lecomte made one particularly significant contribution to the development of the instrument by combining the two previously independent octave keys into a single automatic key operating two vents according to context; the correct octave vent would automatically be opened depending on the note required, rather than the vent having manually to be opened by the player's left thumb choosing between two separate keys, as on Sax's system. This undoubtedly facilitated easier playing, and would soon become an integral part of saxophone design.⁹⁴ Lecomte also installed rollers on the low e♭¹ and c¹ keys, enabling the right hand little finger to slide between them more easily, and providing explicit evidence of the innovation already implied in Claude George's patent of 1869.

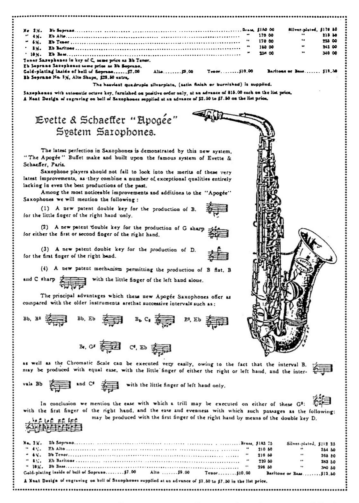

31. Evette and Schaeffer catalogue from c. 1912 proclaiming the advantages of the 'Apogée' system.

Lecomte does not appear to have sole claim to the automatic octave mechanism, however. In 1890, shortly after his patent was accepted, the German company of Heckel produced an instrument they described as a 'heckel-clarina', which closely resembled the soprano saxophone but was fitted with traditional German oboe fingering; this was intended to meet the demands of German players of the period. While the instrument itself was not patented, the company did seek to protect its own automatic octave mechanism, which it claimed to have invented.[95]

It would take quite some time before this automatic octave mechanism became standard. Ben Vereecken's method *Foundation to Saxophone Playing*, for example, published nearly 30 years after Lecomte's patent in 1917, contains separate exercises for the first and second octave keys, demonstrating that at that date there were still many players performing on instruments that made such skills necessary.

Late nineteenth- and early twentieth-century innovations in the United States

For most of the nineteenth century European companies dominated saxophone manufacturing, but from about 1888 Conn became the first American maker. Conn's early saxophones largely followed European models, but the company was keen to innovate and, like others, to draw attention to such innovations in its marketing. From the mid 1890s its 'Wonder Improved' models were available in soprano, alto, tenor and bass versions, and although advertised as having a compass of bb^0 to f^3, only the alto and tenor models in fact appear to have had this range, the others being limited to eb^3 at the top.[96] Rollers on the key clusters operated by the little fingers of both hands were now standard. Around 1906 the company moved to a single automatic octave key, which again soon became standard on all models.

Conn offered its saxophones in both high pitch and low pitch versions. This reflected the various pitch standards prevailing in different parts of the world, and was an attempt on Conn's part to increase international sales. Pitch standards had fluctuated throughout the nineteenth century, notwithstanding efforts by the French government to standardise them in 1859 at $a^1 = 435$ Hz; this pitch standard was more widely adopted in 1887. But many military bands in France, England and the United States were playing to higher pitch standards; official British army pitch from the 1890s to 1928, for example, was as high as $a^1 = 452.5$ Hz. Hence the need for Conn and other manufacturers to produce instruments that could be played in tune at these different levels; Conn's own definition of low pitch was $a^1 = 440$ Hz and high pitch $a^1 = 452.5$ Hz.[97] Pitch standards became more uniform over the course of the 1920s, and so production of different versions of the same model was gradually phased out (the now familiar 'concert pitch' of $a^1 = 440$ Hz was widely adopted in 1939 before becoming internationally standardised in 1955).

Conn instigated a further innovation in 1919, by introducing drawn toneholes for the instrument. Saxophone toneholes had previously been created by soldering a ring of metal onto the saxophone body at the required point, then cutting out the metal sheet within the ring, before smoothing off the inside. Following a manufacturing process introduced by William S. Haynes (patented in 1914),[98] Conn manufactured saxophones by drawing the toneholes from the same sheet of metal from which the saxophone body was made, rather than soldering the flanges on separately. Not only was this method more robust and less likely to develop imperfections during the manufacturing process, it also ensured that the metal flanges were the same thickness as the instrument's body, resulting in better acoustic performance. Since the body of the instrument could now be made in one go, with tools designed specifically for the purpose, there were also considerable savings in labour and material costs, savings that could be passed onto the purchaser.

The Conn company instigated further innovations over the following years. From the late 1910s it incorporated into the neck of its instruments a microtuner, which endeavoured to compensate for the overall impact on the bore of the small positional changes of the mouthpiece on the neck, recalling the similar innovation put forward by the Association générale in 1887. In order to tune the instrument saxophonists

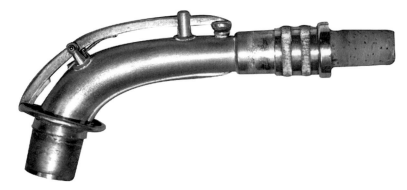

32. A Conn microtuner, designed to make variations in saxophone tuning more uniform.

move the mouthpiece forward or back a little along the neck, thus raising or lowering its overall pitch slightly. However, this has a greater effect on toneholes closest to the mouthpiece than it does on others, and this disturbs the overall integrity of the instrument's intonation; it was this imbalance that Conn's microtuner sought to alleviate. The device was considered sufficiently successful to be retained on Conn models until the mid-1950s.

In the early 1920s Conn established an 'Experimental Laboratory', which underpinned their work in instrument design and development. One of the engineers who worked in this laboratory, Allen Loomis, had already been developing the saxophone prior to joining Conn in 1926, and he continued his innovations thereafter. Loomis was particularly preoccupied with refining the automatic octave mechanism, and patented a number of changes to this. Whereas Sax had at an early stage reduced the number of octave vents from three to two, Loomis proposed to reinstate the third and ultimately a fourth octave vent, since he knew that acoustic theory dictated that, ideally, each higher note should have its own separately positioned octave key. On his proposed four-vent model two of the vents would be on the body of the instrument, and two on the neckpipe; they would operate automatically in the respective ranges of $d^2–d\sharp^2$, $e^2–g\sharp^2$, $a^2–c\sharp^3$, and $d^3–f\sharp^3$. Loomis's proposals were too complex and costly to be put into production at the time, and only a few prototype models were built with a three-vent octave mechanism; but Conn did produce commercially a similar three-vent mechanism on its Connstellation range, introduced after World War II.[99]

During World War II the Conn factory was given over for military use, and subsequently the company never regained its previous stature. Although it remained an important American instrument manufacturer until the late 1950s, competition from abroad, particularly from the exceptional popularity of the Mark VI model produced by Selmer in the 1950s and 60s, obliged the company to concentrate more on student instruments, and its formerly pre-eminent position among North American manufacturers was lost.

Conn's first 1888 saxophone is likely to have been developed by one of its foremen, Ferdinand August Buescher, but he left Conn in 1893 to form his own business, the Buescher Manufacturing Company. Like Conn, this was located in Elkhart, Indiana,

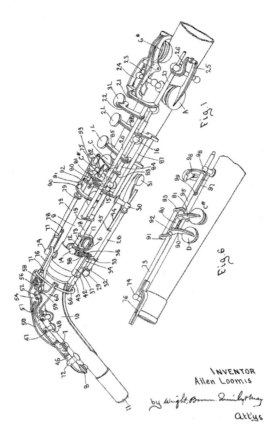

33. Patent sketch including Allen Loomis's triple octave mechanism, 1925. Two octave vents can be discerned on the neck (nos 7 and 8) while the third is below the neck joint (no. 6).

and the company soon rivalled Conn in its importance for the domestic American market. Although it did not produce a full line of saxophones until 1914, under its 'True-Tone' marque,[100] by 1918 the company was offering a range of eight models, including three sopranos in E♭, C and B♭, the latter being curved and the first two being straight. All models had a written range of b♭° to e♭³.

As might be expected, the production methods and some of the underlying design features of Buescher's instruments were similar to those of Conn. Buescher used a mixture of drawn toneholes and the older soldered type, and from 1921 all models were offered with an automatic octave key as standard.[101] A g♯ trill key was introduced in 1925 and remained on all Buescher saxophones until being gradually phased out in the 1950s. Later developments, such as changing the placing of the lowest keys or developing new bell proportions, might be construed as matters of detail rather than substance, notwithstanding the enthusiastic claims made for them in advertising copy. Perhaps the company's most significant innovation of the 1920s was its introduction of snap-on pads, for which Ferdinand Buescher himself submitted three patents between 1921 and 1929.[102] Previously, the saxophone pads seated inside the cups that covered the toneholes had been glued in place. Buescher's 'snap-on' arrangement comprised a fastener fixed to the underside of the cup, onto which a pad could easily be pressed on or prised off; a further fastener held the pad in place once fitted. This meant the player

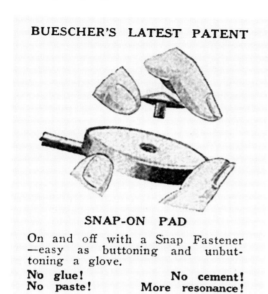

34. A 1923 advert for Buescher's snap-on pads.

could themselves comfortably undertake the changing of pads when necessary, rather than requiring a specialist repairer. The arrangement worked well until the key itself became misaligned, at which point the seal between the pad and the tonehole would become ineffective. Buescher's third patent sought to remedy this by introducing a tilting mechanism that would allow the pad to adjust itself automatically to the disposition of the tonehole rim, even if the key was out of alignment. Although these snap-on pads were not widely taken up by other manufacturers, Conn did produce a 'Res-O-Pad' in the 1930s; this had a large central metal plate designed to keep the leather pad taut, and was similarly designed to be easily adjusted by the saxophonist.

The increasing popularity of the saxophone in America from c. 1915 to c. 1925 led to booming sales, and other companies began to design and manufacture the instrument. The Holton company had begun making saxophones in 1901. They pre-empted Buescher's use of the g♯ trill key by adding it to all their saxophones, as well as a customised c^2-d^2 trill key placed alongside the right-hand side keys. From 1927 Rudy Wiedoeft endorsed Holton saxophones, and these models, as noted above, emulated the articulated g♯ mechanism found on Evette and Schaeffer's earlier 'Apogée' models, whereby the low b♭°, b° and c♯¹ keys all opened the g♯ key, more easily facilitating slurs between these notes. Holton was sufficiently pleased with the musical possibilities the arrangement offered that the company asked Wiedoeft to write eight exercises that would specifically demonstrate its advantages; an articulated g♯ mechanism of a similar kind remains standard on modern saxophones. Holton also mounted an additional key on the bow of the instrument from 1928. Described by the company as a 'low-octave' key, it was designed to aid production of the notes e^1-$c♯^1$ (which were liable to split or warble on saxophones of the time), but was closed by the c^1 key for the lower notes. The addition was of questionable value, however, and not adopted by other manufacturers.

Towards the end of the 1920s, as the fashion for saxophone ownership in the USA waned, sales began to fall rapidly. This sudden decline naturally posed significant challenges to manufacturers, and in some cases provoked them to design increasingly exotic instruments in a bid to counteract the receding commercial tide. In 1928, for example, Conn introduced two rather idiosyncratic and short-lived instruments, the 'mezzo-soprano' saxophone and the 'Conn-O-Sax' (also known as the 22-M). Curiously, both of these instruments were pitched in F. The former, as its name suggests, was a hybrid between the soprano and alto members of the family. It retained the curved alto shape and keywork, although the smaller bore was more reminiscent of the soprano. It was in many ways similar to its E♭ cousin but it had a lighter, sweeter tone, something that may explain Adolphe Sax's earlier fondness for the F alto. Conn made great claims for the instrument in its advertising copy, observing, for example, that the instrument's smaller size would make it ideal for children; the company also somewhat optimistically suggested that the new instrument would be easier to use in orchestral contexts, since 'a great deal of the classics for orchestras are written in sharp keys' and that because only one sharp needed to be added to the saxophone line – rather than the three required for an E♭ instrument – this would 'open up a wealth of classical music to the saxophone which has hitherto been out of reach'.[103]

The Conn-O-Sax was yet more curious (see ill. 35). Building on a patent filed by Charles G. Conn in October 1913, the instrument resembled a cross between a saxophone and a heckelphone, the latter being a double reed instrument with a conical bore, developed by the German manufacturer Heckel from 1904 and often used to play bass oboe parts.[104] The Conn-O-Sax retained both the straight conical bore and the flared bell of the heckelphone, but replaced the oboe fingering with standard saxophone fingering; the double reed arrangement was replaced by a single reed mouthpiece fixed to a curved neckpiece. Unusually the instrument had a range of nearly three octaves, from written a° to g³. In engineering and musical terms it was a successful and flexible instrument, with an idiosyncratic voice. But neither this instrument nor the mezzo-soprano saxophone was commercially successful, partly because of the rapidly shrinking market in which they were launched, and also because, in spite of Conn's enthusiastic advertising, there was no obvious market or musical role for them, nor any repertoire they might easily utilise.

Many manufacturers responded to ongoing customer demand for novel or distinctive saxophones by offering other innovations designed to make their products look unique. Some of these developments embodied genuine technological advances while others were largely superficial. Around 1922 Conn briefly introduced coloured lacquer saxophones, advertising that they could be purchased in 'rich purple, wonderful shades of rose, green or blue, a striking black and silver combination – *in fact most any color one may desire*';[105] Buescher followed suit. The demand for saxophones was so great in the 1920s that the major manufacturers such as Conn and Buescher followed European examples in providing stencils; distributors such as Continental, Sears & Roebuck, Selmer (US) and others provided saxophones to their customers stamped with their own insignia, even though the instruments were manufactured by other companies. This practice continues today, of course, and is not confined to saxophones.

35. A 1930 Conn-O-Sax.

The H. N. White company's Saxello, produced under its 'King' label in 1925, was a more interesting innovation (see ill. 36). The Saxello was a straight soprano saxophone in B♭ with the addition of a half crook added to take the mouthpiece, and a forward-pointing bell at the bottom of the instrument. The keywork was not otherwise substantially different from other soprano saxophones. The instrument's designer, Henry E. Dreves, argued in the patent that both the curved and straight versions of the soprano saxophone were flawed: the former because the bend disrupted the passage of air through the instrument and left it with a muffled sound, the latter because it needed to be pointed horizontally towards the audience but could not comfortably be supported by a sling, thus making it 'very difficult to hold while playing open tones'.[106] While modern players may find such claims implausible, the Saxello succeeded in combining an innovative and distinctive design with real practical application; as evidenced, for example, by the provision of a small v–shaped clamp at the back of the lower part of the instrument, which doubled as both a knee rest when the instrument was in use, and a floor rest when it was not.

36. A 1925 advert for the King Saxello.

The Buescher company also produced a 'tipped bell' B♭ soprano for some years in the 1920s, in which the bell of the instrument was slightly tilted forward, and the neckpiece slightly backwards towards the player's mouth. Buescher adverts of the time similarly suggested that the tipped bell model had the advantage that 'when in playing position, the bell rests comfortably on the player's knee, taking the weight of the instrument off the hands and leaving them free to manipulate the keys.'[107] For a limited time around 1927 Buescher also offered a straight alto saxophone in E♭, without the iconic U-shaped bend of most other alto and tenor saxophones, though the bell tipped away slightly from the player's body. Largely duplicating the conventional alto keywork, this well-made and well-regarded instrument suffered, like the Conn instruments in F, from being introduced at a time when the market for saxophones was rapidly contracting. Later in the century the jazz player Rahsaan Roland Kirk would modify both a King Saxello, adding a larger bell, and a Buescher straight alto, adapting the keywork to facilitate one-handed playing. He renamed

37. A 1926 Buescher 'tipped-bell' soprano.

these instruments the 'stritch' and the 'manzello' respectively, but the neologisms should not be taken to imply that these were anything other than individually customised factory models.

The tenor saxophone in C, widely known as the C-melody saxophone, became particularly popular during the saxophone 'craze' of the late 1910s and 1920s. Slightly lighter in both weight and tone than the normal B♭ tenor, its popularity stemmed in part from the fact that it was a non-transposing instrument. Players with rudimentary reading and performance skills could therefore perform directly from sheet music, playing the vocal line alongside the piano accompaniment, without need for the tiresome practice of transposition (although some players used E♭ or B♭ instruments for the same purpose, simply learning the 'wrong' fingerings so as to avoid transposing entirely). The C-melody saxophone became the quintessential amateur's instrument,

38. A 1923 Conn tenor saxophone in C (C-melody).

to the extent that many professionals disdained it. Ben Davis's observation in his saxophone method that the C-melody instrument was appropriate for a performer who had 'no desire to play in a band [...] but merely to amuse himself (or herself) and entertain friends in the home circle'[108] may be taken as typical of this attitude. Such comments arose from the often poor standards of those who performed on the instrument and the type of music they played, rather than any deficiency in the C-melody instrument itself, which in every other respect was as viable as any other saxophone. The instrument sold very well for some time, and most saxophone manufacturers of the late 1910s and early 1920s offered a tenor model in the key of C.

For those who couldn't or wouldn't engage with the intricacies of saxophone fingering, there were simpler alternatives such as slide saxophones. These were plain tubes with a piston, onto which a saxophone mouthpiece was attached by means of a side extension. As the slide of the piston was moved up or down, so the pitch changed, in some cases over a range of about two octaves, when fitted with an octave

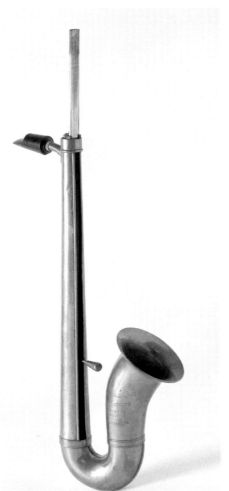

39. A 1927 slide saxophone.

key. The American company of Reiffel and Husted appears to have patented the first of these in 1924,[109] but other manufacturers followed suit, with such instruments being variously referred to as a 'Swanee Sax' in Britain or the 'Mellosax' in France. While differing in their details, the fundamental principle of altering the pitch by means of a hand-operated slide remains the same. The connection of these instruments with saxophones proper may be regarded as tenuous, arising simply from the addition of a single-reed mouthpiece to a tube with a conical bore; but the hype surrounding these simple instruments, and their nomenclature, demonstrates the perceived marketing potential of the word 'saxophone' at the time. As with their more serious counterparts, such instruments were frequently supported with associated merchandising, with one London publisher, for example, providing a method for the Swanee Sax in 1930.[110]

The novelty value demanded of popular entertainers resulted in a small number of customised instruments made for particular shows or tasks. Several specimens of one-handed saxophones exist, for example, in which the keywork has been ingeniously modified so as to be played by only the right or left hand. These were most likely made for vaudevillians who wished to demonstrate that they could play the saxophone with one hand while undertaking another activity, such as juggling, with the other.[111] A later invention allowed a single performer to play three saxophones simultaneously. Developed by its only known performer, Billy True, it arose from True's work as a saxophonist during the 1920s, but the device was not fully realised and patented until 1938, long after the decline of vaudeville.[112] It comprised an ingenious reconfiguration of two C-melody saxes and one alto, and allowed one of each to be played with the right and left hands, separated by the remaining saxophone which was controlled by foot pedals. The performer could play three-part harmony and counterpoint, and sound like a one-man saxophone section, thus prefiguring a similar approach by Rahsaan Roland Kirk in the latter part of the century.

Notwithstanding the peripheral nature of True's idiosyncratic invention, it demonstrates the technical experimentation and innovation that surrounded the saxophone from the late 1910s to the 1930s, underpinned by musical and technical curiosity, and compulsive popular demand. Occasionally this also impacted on the development of other wind instruments, such as the curious hybrid between oboe and saxophone known as the 'oboe sax'. Developed initially by the French firm Lorée in the late 1920s, these instruments were essentially Boehm-system oboes whose keywork was slightly modified so as to resemble saxophone fingering. The motivation for such instruments was straightforward: since so many people were learning the saxophone, perhaps some of them could be encouraged to transfer to, or double on, the oboe. A small number of other companies, including Boosey and Hawkes in London, developed similar instruments, but there was little interest in them and they quickly faded into obscurity.[113]

Further enhancements in Europe and America

As noted in the Introduction to this volume, one of the challenges of woodwind instrument design is to avoid the cross venting that arises from an instrument's tonehole lattice. This can make certain notes sound stuffier than others and lead to an uneven tone across the instrument. The problem was identified by Boehm in the early 1830s, and he endeavoured to solve it in the redesign of flute fingering he put forward in 1832. Since Sax had copied some of the principles of flute, oboe and clarinet fingering schemes onto the saxophone, some of the problems came with them also. In particular, the g♯, d♯ and c♯^{1} keys were all closed at rest, meaning that the notes immediately above them (a^1/a^2, e^1/e^2, and d^1/d^2 respectively) were prone to stuffiness.

Several designers have attempted to alleviate these problems. From 1924 King saxophones were for a while made with an open g♯ key, with the company advertising that this 'greatly improves the tone quality and makes the instrument in perfect tune'.[114] The following year Allen Loomis filed a patent (granted in 1928) that incorporated a more radical rethinking of saxophone fingering. Loomis had already patented a sophisticated revision of piccolo fingering in 1913, and now transferred these principles to the saxophone. His addition of extra octave keys has already been noted above, but he proposed a complete redesign of the fingerwork also. His 'double resonance' saxophone – so-called because of the elimination of cross venting, by having at least the next two toneholes open below that through which any given note was sounding – still had the notes g♯, d♯ and c♯^{1} closed in their normal position, but

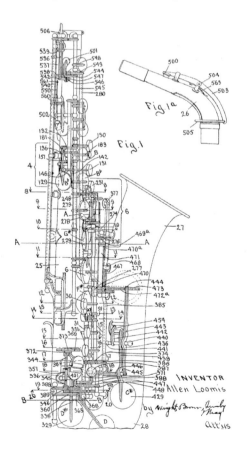

40. Patent sketch for Allen Loomis's 'double resonance' saxophone, 1925.

incorporated a new mechanism that opened them when the note above them was played. His design also had substitute cross-fingerings for the little fingers of both right and left hands, in the manner of a Boehm clarinet, as well as alternative trill keys for g♯¹ and d♯¹; and the bell of the instrument was extended to facilitate a low a° fingering. All of this required substantial rethinking of the normal saxophone layout, including, for example, moving the pads and toneholes for the primary notes away from the touches that operated them. Loomis's design was highly ingenious but also technologically complex and therefore expensive to manufacture, and he was unable to persuade any company to produce it commercially. Only six models were ever produced, of which only three are known to exist.[115]

A similar difficulty befell Charles Houvenaghel's 1931 design for the Leblanc company, which led to the relatively short-lived production of its 'Rationnel' saxophones in the 1930s. Like Loomis, Houvenaghel sought to design keywork that left as many keys as possible open in their resting position. He also added an ingenious linkage to the key operated by the right-hand middle finger, which would lower every primary note above it (g¹, a¹, b¹, c♯²) by one semitone when it was brought into play, or produce a fork e♭ note for the fingering pattern 1234_6. This latter arrangement more easily facilitated a d–e♭ trill, while its other uses greatly simplified trills on a range of other notes. A revised version of this key system was introduced by Leblanc in the 1950s, as model numbers 120 (tenor) and 100 (alto). However, as in the 1930s, and notwithstanding the obvious benefits it brought to the instrument and the fact that it required very little reorientation on the part of the player, it proved insufficiently popular and only a few instruments were made.

One innovation more widely adopted by manufacturers during the 1930s was the movement of the toneholes facilitating low b° and b♭° from one side of the bell to the other. Conventionally these had always been on the side closest to the player's hip, but the sound from these large toneholes had a tendency to be muffled by the body, and notwithstanding the use of key guards the player's clothing would occasionally catch in them. Although some of Conn's 'New Wonder' models in the early 1930s had been made with split bell keys, whereby the b° key would be on the closed side and the b♭° key on the open side, away from the player's body, as the 1930s progressed many manufacturers placed both keys on the open side; for example, King's 'Voll–True II' model from about 1932 and the Selmer 'Balanced Action' model from 1935. This disposition of bell keys, and the more effective key linkages that made it possible, remain the norm on saxophones today: toneholes producing notes from c♯¹ downwards are all on the side away from the player's body.

The use of leather pads to cover the toneholes of the instrument has remained largely consistent, and the innovations introduced by Buescher and Conn in the 1920s have not been widely pursued. One major exception was the 'padless' saxophone introduced by the American H. & A. Selmer Company in the early 1940s.[116] Instead of the toneholes being covered by pads located within the key cup, a thin leather ring or grommet was set within the rim of the tonehole itself, and flush to its surface. The key cup was then replaced by a thin metal disk, which closed against the grommet to form a seal. While this worked well when the key and the tonehole were perfectly configured, the slightest misalignment would prevent a good seal from being effected.

41. Part of a Selmer 'padless' tenor.

Although ingenious, the design proved insufficiently robust, and was neither widely proliferated nor, indeed, continued for very long by the company itself.

With the possible exceptions of the Conn-O-Sax and Leblanc's 'Rationnel' system, most of the innovations relating to the saxophone that were actually put into production during the twentieth century could be construed as refinements of Adolphe Sax's original conception for the instrument, making small adjustments to keywork or developing production techniques in a broadly incremental fashion. The Grafton saxophone, patented by Hector Sommaruga in 1946, is perhaps the one design that could claim to be truly different, while remaining recognisably a saxophone: it was the first such instrument to be made out of acrylic plastic, rather than brass.

Sommaruga realised in the final years of World War II that whereas brass sheets and tubes were expensive and in short supply, synthetic plastic technology had advanced to the stage where it could be used to manufacture musical instruments, thus potentially supplanting the more expensive traditional materials. He set about designing a saxophone in acrylic plastic. An initial patent was lodged in September 1945, with full specifications being added in December 1946; the patent was awarded in July 1948.[117] The patent text indicates that Sommaruga aspired to 'manufacture a saxophone possessing all the conventional playing facilities, and moreover with a more pleasing appearance, greater solidity, less liability to break-down, improved tonal qualities – and all this at a greatly reduced cost of production.'[118] The last point was particularly significant, since it was felt that an acrylic saxophone could be manufactured more cheaply than a metal one and would thus appeal particularly to the educational market. The patent also outlined various strategies by which the difficulties of working with plastic would be overcome. These included reducing the number of pillars and altering their position on the body, changing the system of guards used to protect keys, and adapting the body in order that pre-assembled unitary keywork could be fitted. The keywork was itself the subject of a further patent, and since the plastic body was not strong enough to take the conventional needle springs which normally provide the tension to keep keys open, these were replaced by coiled springs; this gave a slightly 'soggy' feel to the fingering, since the keys did not snap back as readily as a conventional instrument. Although the body was plastic, the neck remained made of brass.

Although an unplayable prototype was produced in 1946 it took a further four years of development to bring the idea to fruition. The Grafton Acrylic alto (ill. 42), advertised as 'a tone poem in ivory and gold', was launched in 1950 at a price of £58, about half the cost of a metal instrument.[119] It was not universally well received, but was adopted by certain players. The English jazz saxophonist John Dankworth was an early supporter, and both Rudy Vallée and Charlie Parker occasionally played one, although the latter only outside the United States due to endorsement obligations. Ornette Coleman was one of the most ardent supporters of the instrument and used

42. A Grafton acrylic alto saxophone.

it for many years, having replacements sent over from England when he needed a new instrument (which, by his own admission, was every year).

Although there was significant initial interest in the acrylic saxophone it did not carve out a permanent niche for itself. Its radical appearance was felt to be out of place in musically conservative arenas such as swing bands and orchestras. The instrument was not particularly sturdy and if dropped the body might crack. While the manufacturers in London operated an efficient repair system, other repairers were less willing to engage with the instrument because of its unfamiliarity and the intrinsic difficulties of repairs. The Grafton also needed constant adjustment, which was not always practicable for a touring musician. By 1967 production had ceased, and in 1968 the specialist tools and jigs required to produce it had been mistakenly thrown out as scrap metal, ensuring that none can ever be made again. Graftons are now seldom played although there are still some in good condition. Their 1940s design retains a certain 'retro' stylishness, a legacy perhaps of the designer's Italian roots. Grafton Acrylic alto saxophones have become collector's items: the one played by Charlie Parker sold at Christie's in London in 1994 for the not inconsiderable sum of £93,500.[120]

The normal range of the saxophone has expanded marginally in the last few decades, and the conventional written range of most instruments is now taken to be $b\flat^0$ to $f\sharp^3$. There are exceptions: baritone models having an additional lower note, written a^0 (sounding C, the lowest note of the cello), were introduced in the early 1950s, and this extension has become increasingly common on professional instruments. This low a^0 has sometimes been offered on other models, notably on some alto versions of the famous Mark VI model from Selmer during the 1960s. The extension to the high $f\sharp^3$ became increasingly the norm from the 1960s onwards, albeit that it was initially offered by most manufacturers as an option rather than as a standard addition. Detachable necks for soprano saxophones have become fashionable. Initially introduced by the Japanese manufacturer Yamaha, these allow the player to choose between a perfectly straight neckpipe or one that slightly curves towards the mouth, thus changing the angle at which the instrument is held relative to the body. A few recent soprano models have also added a top g^3 key to the instrument, located adjacent to the now customary high $f\sharp^3$ key.

At the risk of generalisation, while the earlier half of the twentieth century was marked by significant innovation and experimentation in saxophone design, there have since been fewer changes to the instrument. In part this reflects an increasingly stable design in which manufacturers have addressed and solved many of the more significant challenges presented by earlier instruments. But it is also perhaps a by-product of an increasingly globalised musical world, wherein, as with other wind instruments, individual idiosyncrasies relating to particular models are less widespread than before, as internationalised ideas about tonal homogeneity and equally-tempered tuning become ever more prevalent.

Chapter 3

The saxophone in the nineteenth century

Social transformations in mid-nineteenth-century France

The saxophone may be said to have appeared at a time when Paris was in the throes of revolutions that were political, social, economic and aesthetic in nature. The political tides that ebbed and flowed through nineteenth-century France reflected the significant social and economic changes that gripped the country in general, and Paris in particular, at that time. As in other parts of Europe, increasing economic prosperity was founded upon colonial expansion, the rapid growth of manufacturing industries, and a developing transport infrastructure. Much of the expansion in industrial fields was driven by developments in steam engine technology. Sax himself harnessed the power of steam-driven machines in his Parisian workshops. Arguably, the impact of these evolving technologies on business, commerce and society at large would not be equalled until the computer-led digital revolution of the late twentieth century.

The economic benefits of this first technological revolution encouraged the development of increasingly affluent and influential middle classes. At the end of the eighteenth century these had been relatively small and inconsequential. Unlike the aristocracy and upper classes they had little control over concert practice, seldom influenced musical taste, had little influence over communications media, and musicians themselves demonstrated very little in the way of entrepreneurial leadership. All this changed in the 1830s and 40s, and these changes had a profound effect on the environments in which the saxophone was first introduced. The increased spending power available to these middle classes further underpinned the expansion of commerce and trade, and also created the notion of 'leisure time'. Music-making at home became an important domestic activity, particularly for women, and the piano especially came to be seen as a respectablising instrument, connoting a sense of refinement and achievement among those seen or aspiring to be middle class.[1] The working classes seldom shared in the financial benefits of this economic success, and thus began to form organisations and unions to protect their rights and interests. But they, too, participated in musical leisure activities, particularly in promenade concerts in the parks and other open spaces, albeit of a rather different type and cost to those catering for the middle classes.

This increasing involvement of the general population in the appreciation of art and light classical music – whether as audience members or amateur performers – was allied to the growing commercialisation of the channels through which such music was disseminated. The number of concerts given in Paris grew from 78 in the 1826–7 season to as many as 383 in the 1845–6 season – an increase of nearly five hundred per cent.[2] Particular arenas of musical taste evolved. Opera was especially significant and popular, and provoked much commentary in the musical press, more so than the style that, even then, was described as 'classical music', based on the Germanic heritage of Haydn, Mozart and Beethoven. This last tradition was particularly conservative, seldom presenting the virtuosi popular in other contexts, nor even performing much new music from those composers influenced by their Austro-German forebears. This style was little known in Paris up until 1830, and although it became increasingly popular over the next two decades, not until the end of the nineteenth century did it achieve the level of importance in concert programming it occupies today.

The expansion of the middle classes inevitably led to more fragmented patterns of musical consumption; as in other urban Western centres, taste, particularly taste in music, increasingly became a marker of class. Aficionados who were familiar with one repertoire or style at times regarded other genres with suspicion, particularly in relation to the commercialisation, flamboyance and overt virtuosity that often characterised those concerts more frequently enjoyed by the working classes. Similarly, those whose tastes were addressed more adequately by the popular categories viewed the aloof and ascetic stance of the classical music devotees with equal disdain. This tension between art music and other more popular genres continued throughout the century, and in this bifurcation appear the roots of a conflict between forms of art and popular cultures within which the saxophone was to become entangled for the next hundred years.

These changes were perhaps most profoundly felt in Paris, since the capital city was the economic and cultural hub of an increasingly centralised French society; but whatever happened there radiated throughout the rest of the country, and indeed to other parts of the French empire. Military music-making provided a particularly significant outlet for Sax's manufacturing activities, and later in the century larger ensembles, both military and civilian, would play a central role in bringing the saxophone to a wider public in Europe, America and beyond.

Thus the social frameworks surrounding the production and consumption of music in mid-nineteenth-century France were changing rapidly, and all this affected how the saxophone was seen and heard by the French public (and beyond), and the ways in which the instrument was made, sold, bought, and played.

Industrialisation and manufacturing

By the middle of the nineteenth century musical instruments had become tradable commodities, manufactured and sold in large quantities, with significant potential profits to be made if the right combination of design and affordability could be matched to consumer demand. Paris was the pre-eminent centre of instrument manufacturing at this time; hence Sax's desire to become permanently established there in 1842. The scale of expansion can be judged from the increasing number of exhibitors at the national exhibitions that were regularly held there throughout the century.

In 1827 some 72 instrument manufacturers exhibited; this rose to 109 in 1834 and then to 243, the largest number recorded, in 1855; thereafter numbers show a gentle decline.[3]

Successful innovations assured considerable prestige (through the award of honours at these exhibitions, for example), as well as, in some cases, considerable financial benefits. There was great competition between Parisian manufacturers to develop new instruments and improve existing ones. Patents for brass and wind instruments were especially popular: in the years 1840–70 they considerably outnumbered all other types of patent except those relating to the piano. Sax alone took out more than twenty music–related French patents over the course of his lifetime; his father and brother Alphonse took out a further two each.[4] While historical perspective may allow us to construe the saxophone as one of the more important and influential musical developments of the time, it was in fact only one of many innovations put forward by ambitious inventors. The accordion provides a useful point of comparison. Invented simultaneously in both Vienna and London in 1829, it was subject to a number of improvements and modifications by Parisian manufacturers in the 1840s, and quickly established itself as the instrument of choice among the popular dance venues in the French capital. By 1847 there were no less than 62 accordion manufacturers registered in Paris.[5] The saxophone had to wait until the turn of the century before it achieved anything like this degree of widespread recognition and production.

Improved transportation links underpinned technological developments and facilitated the distribution of new products, thus opening up new markets. The railways played an important role in saxophone manufacturing. In 1850 Buffet Crampon established a factory for its instrument-making activities in Mantes-la-Ville, some 30 miles to the north-west of Paris, building on the town's long tradition of wind and brass manufacturing established by Louis XIV in the early eighteenth century. Mantes was on both the railway line and the river between the port of Le Havre and the capital Paris; raw materials and finished products could be easily acquired and distributed via these important transportation routes. Buffet Crampon began to manufacture saxophones there from 1866, before being bought out by Evette and Schaeffer in 1885. In 1880 Dolnet and Lefévre founded a factory close by, employing 50 to 100 workers producing woodwind instruments and saxophones;[6] the town thus became the pre-eminent centre of saxophone manufacturing in the nineteenth century. When Henri Selmer was looking for somewhere to establish a new factory away from his Parisian base in 1919, he similarly chose a vacant site in Mantes; the presence of the other manufacturers in the town ensured a readily available, trained workforce, in addition to the ideal transportation links.

Nevertheless, the impact of industrialisation on instrument manufacturing in the mid-nineteenth century should not be overstated. The majority of Parisian manufacturers were small or medium-sized enterprises, maintaining traditional approaches, upon whom modern methods of production had only a limited impact. Not all manufacturers were able or willing to make the capital investment necessary for large-scale operations, and the larger factories were usually allied to the manufacture of pianos, organs or brass instruments. Of this latter group Sax's factory was one of the more significant operations, but it was by no means the largest. By 1846, the year the saxophone patent was finally granted, Sax was employing some 70 workers, whereas his long-time rival Gautrot already had about 200.[7] By 1862 Gautrot was employing 700 workers at his factory in Paris, and a similar number at a second factory in Château-Thierry; he also had two further factories employing another 200 people. In total this amounts to some 1600 people employed by one instrument manufacturer.[8] Although Sax's business doubtless expanded and contracted over the years as his commercial fortunes waxed and waned, it was Gautrot who was the true businessman, with the largest operation. Most other manufacturers, including Sax, came from performance/teaching backgrounds, and many lacked the necessary business acumen to expand or sustain their enterprise, regardless of their musical or technological skills.

Only in certain areas did newer industrial practices evolve, and this was particularly evident among the larger piano and organ manufacturers. But the production of brass instruments was also significantly affected, and in this respect Sax's company in general, and the saxophone especially, were very much caught up in the modernising industrial tendencies of the time. In particular, assembly methods changed. Whereas instruments had previously been made individually by small teams of skilled craftsmen, now the manufacturing process could be broken down into various stages: one individual or small group would be responsible for making only one component of the finished article, and everything was assembled at a later stage of the production line. The manufacturing of musical instruments lends itself particularly well to this kind of division of labour, since the techniques involved in making the various parts of an instrument such as the saxophone require rather different skills, and can thus be accomplished on different parts of the factory floor: shaping the brass to form the body sections, assembling them, cutting toneholes and soldering chimneys, fixing

43. The instrument manufacturing process in Sax's workshop, as published in *L'Illustration* on 5 February 1848.

keys, springs and pads, and testing the finished product, could each be accomplished by different workers. Producing an instrument such as the saxophone remained relatively labour intensive, although in general workers were poorly paid and labour was comparatively cheap. Child labour was often used in instrument manufacturing, not only because these smaller hands could deal with more delicate tasks, but also because they were cheap to employ. Prisoners were also used to keep labour costs low: Sax himself employed 30 or so inmates of Melun prison.[9]

Engineering procedures also advanced rapidly. Previously the brass body of an instrument such as the saxophone had to be hand cut, beaten, and shaped. Now some stages of the manufacturing process could be achieved mechanically, with the still relatively novel steam engine driving machines on the factory floor via sophisticated systems of driveshafts, belts and wheels. Sax was himself something of a pioneer in developing new techniques for making brass musical instruments, and these skills contributed greatly to the superior quality of his products; they also made possible some of the technological innovations underpinning the saxophone, such as the relatively sophisticated keywork superimposed upon a brass body.

Commerce and trade

The rapid expansion of the middle classes in the mid-nineteenth century provided a growing number of individuals with small but meaningful amounts of disposable income, who were keen to demonstrate their newly acquired purchasing power. The acquisition of musical instruments became one way in which this new status could be demonstrated. As already noted, this was particularly true of the piano, which over the course of the century became a ubiquitous and quintessentially bourgeois instrument: an icon of middle class respectability. In contrast, the saxophone was a more utilitarian instrument, useful in military and harmonie bands certainly, and occasionally in the orchestra pit, but not an instrument that would have found widespread use in the parlour rooms of the domesticated middle classes.

The cost of certain instruments could be prohibitive. This was particularly the case with pianos, which might cost anything from 1,000 to 2,000 francs, at a time when an average annual working class salary might be 3,000 francs. Middle-class salaries would start a little above this, and a few middle class elite might earn as much as 25,000 francs.[10] To mitigate purchase costs, payment by instalment and the renting of instruments (especially pianos) became established practice, allowing families of limited means access to instruments that might otherwise be beyond them. Competition between manufacturers also drove prices lower. A basic flute might range from as little as five to perhaps 140 francs, while superior models might cost as much as 230 francs. Whereas Gautrot in the late 1840s was selling trombones between 22 and 60 francs,[11] Sax's models cost from 50 francs to 95 francs. The size of Gautrot's operation may well have enabled him to keep these prices low, whereas Sax positioned himself as a provider of better quality instruments, albeit on a smaller scale.

Saxophones were considerably cheaper than pianos but more expensive than most brass instruments, and about the same price as a basic version of Sax's bass clarinet. Sax was listing an (unspecified) saxophone in the *RGMP* for 200 francs in

44. Detail from Adolphe Sax's 1850 price list, showing the names and ranges of three saxophones, and prices in different currencies.

1848, replicating the price on an undated sales list from about the same period;[12] an illustrated sales list from 2 February 1850, demonstrating the instruments and their ranges in more detail, similarly advertises E♭ alto and E♭ 'baryton-ténor' saxophones for sale at 200 francs, with the B♭ soprano available at 160 francs and a bass in C, listed separately from the others, at 250 francs.

These were significant amounts, and Sax's monopoly over the saxophone probably underpinned his price setting. Equally, few economies of scale were available since demand for the instrument was low. The financial importance of the saxophone in Sax's business was marginal, and it formed a relatively insignificant part of his commercial activities. Although between 1843 and 1860 Sax made over 20,000 instruments in total, only 945 of these – less than five per cent – were saxophones.[13] This equates to an annual production of slightly fewer than 60 instruments (and probably less than this in the early years). In July 1852, when Sax was made bankrupt for the first time, there were more than 1,000 finished instruments in his workshops, of which 182 were saxophones.[14] This rather higher percentage (18 per cent) of unsold stock suggests that although the instruments were being made in the early 1850s, they weren't being purchased in significant numbers.

Notwithstanding the opposition that Sax faced from many Parisian instrument manufacturers, it would be wrong to assume that none would have dealings with him. In fact, for the period during which Sax's new instruments were protected by patent, several rival manufacturers felt it expedient to enter into commercial arrangements to manufacture instruments under licence, rather than miss out entirely on the sales to be made from the popularity of some of Sax's instruments.[15] Instruments manufactured under licence were stamped differently (indicating that they had been 'authorised') than those manufactured by Sax's company. The list of manufacturers with whom he agreed contracts in the 1850s and 60s includes some – such as Halary – who in the 1840s had joined in legal proceedings against him. However, it appears that such contracts only covered the saxhorns and saxotrombas; none related to the saxophone, again demonstrating the relatively small role the instrument played in Sax's commercial activities. The demand for saxhorns and saxotrombas was clearly much greater than for saxophones at this time, and Sax probably agreed to these licences because his own company was unable to meet this demand.[16]

From 1850 onwards, international markets became increasingly important for brass and woodwind instruments, because of the rising popularity of brass and military bands worldwide. Sax and other manufacturers entered into licensing agreements with agents in many countries for the better sale and distribution of their products. It is noticeable that Sax's 1850 brochure shows prices not only in French francs, but also English pounds, German and Prussian thalers, shillings and silbergroschen, and Spanish reales. England represented the most significant export market for French instrument manufacturers in general. From 1846 the London-based brass instrument specialists Distin & Sons were Sax's agents in England, and their stock lists included a saxophone from at least 1849.[17] From 1853 Sax gave Rudall, Rose, Carte and Co. in London sole agency to import his entire range. An 1854 advertisement in the *Musical Times* proudly announced that they had 'just received a great variety of soprano, alto, tenor and bass of Sax's new and beautiful-toned instruments, the Saxophone.' By way of endorsement the advert displayed an extract from the Jurors' report of the 1851 Great Exhibition in London, which had noted that 'these new instruments (brass and

45. Example of an Adolphe Sax stamp.

played by a reed), possess a charm equal to the originality of their tone, and they carry to the highest degree of perfection, *la voix expressive.*[18]

Once the patent for the saxophone expired in 1866 other manufacturers were at liberty to produce the instrument. Companies such as Buffet Crampon, Besson and Couesnon in Paris, the then separate companies of Hawkes and Boosey in London, Eugène Albert in Brussels, and others, all made and sold instruments under their own name during the second half of the nineteenth century, particularly from the 1880s onwards. Buffet Crampon appears to have been the most commercially successful, possibly manufacturing as many as 6,000 instruments up until 1885 (many presumably for the French military), before being taken over by Evette & Schaeffer, who then continued to develop the business into the twentieth century.[19] Other dealers would purchase instruments direct from these manufacturers and sell them on at a profit, or have them stamped with their own insignia and sold as their own (such instruments are often referred to as 'stencils'). Driven particularly by the expanding market for band instruments, dealers advertising saxophones could eventually be found in several major cities in France, England and Italy, but also more sporadically in Germany, Spain, the United States, and even Russia.[20] While Sax may not have benefitted greatly from his invention of the saxophone, as the later decades of the nineteenth century progressed, others clearly did.

Music publishing and journalism also grew significantly in mid-nineteenth-century France. Sax benefitted from the exposure offered through commentaries on his activities in print media, particularly journals such as *RGMP* and *La France musicale.* He also ran his own publishing house from 1858 to 1878, providing another outlet for his entrepreneurialism. Inevitably, publications were intended to support sales of the instruments he was manufacturing, and the saxophone was particularly promoted, with names such as Arban, Demersseman, Chic, Savari, and especially Singelée composing a variety of works for the instrument, normally accompanied by piano. The titles of these pieces – such as *Fantasie brillante, Caprice, Solo sur la Tyrolienne, Freischütz Fantasy* and so forth – betray their intentions: this was relatively lightweight music, designed to show off the capabilities of the new instrument and those students at the Paris Conservatoire and elsewhere who had recently mastered it. There were also works written for saxophone quartet, such as Singelée's *Premier quatuor* (1858) or Cressonnois's *Les Pifferari* (c. 1861). Savari wrote several works requiring larger numbers of saxophones, including an octet (c. 1861, for 2S/2A/2T/2Bs). At an auction of Sax's assets in 1878 there were 189 plates of published material for the saxophone, including some 35 works for saxophone and piano, and one work for two saxophones (S/A) and piano.[21] Prices for this material ranged from 5 to 7.5 francs – relatively expensive in comparison with sheet music today, but commensurate with similar publications at the time. These prices appear to have remained reasonably consistent during Sax's time as a publisher.[22]

Pedagogic methods provided an obvious mechanism through which a music publisher might profit from the invention of a new instrument. The saxophone has often been described as being relatively easy to play, and this was thought to be the case even in the mid-nineteenth century. In 1852 the *RGMP* observed that a musician already competent on the flute, clarinet, oboe or bassoon 'would need no more than eight days of study to familiarise themselves with [the saxophone]'.[23] Nevertheless, no fewer than three methods appeared in 1846, the year Sax's patent was approved. These were by Kastner, Cokken and Hartmann (see also pp. 53–8). Kastner's method, published by Troupenas, is the most complete and authoritative, undoubtedly because Sax provided much of the information for it. When it was reprinted by Brandus in 1850 the cover price was reduced from 40 francs to 30, as was common publishing practice at the time. Cokken had been appointed the first Professor of Saxophone at the Gymnase de Musique Militaire in 1846; his method, published by Meissonnier, was probably intended to capitalise on his position, as well as supporting his students through their studies at the Gymnase. Both Kastner's and Cokken's methods provide a range of instruction in basic musicianship and specific saxophone technicalities, as was common in such publications. The third method, supposedly by 'Hartmann *aîné* and published by Schonenberger, is more curious. Closely based on the same publisher's method for ophicleide it is clearly an amalgamation of material from other publications. It also appears to have been published in some haste, since several of the

46. The title page of the 1850 printing, by Brandus, of Kastner's Saxophone Method.

exercises given require the saxophone to go down to low a° or even g°, contradicting the range of the instrument explicitly given earlier in the method (and suggesting that they were in fact written for other instruments). Comparison of the plate numbers relative to other works by the same publisher suggests that Hartmann's method may even have appeared prior to the other two. This could indicate some hasty opportunism on the part of both author and publisher, which would account for the mistakes and somewhat slipshod nature of the publication.

Early reception history of the saxophone

Given the increasing attention devoted by composers to instrumental timbre in the mid-nineteenth century, it is unsurprising that much of the early commentary on the saxophone centred around the instrument's new and unfamiliar sound. Composers were by now required to be masters of instrumentation, capable of exploiting different orchestral colours as part of their compositional practice, in addition to their customary reliance on harmonic and rhythmic invention. As Dahlhaus observes, 'this "emancipation of timbre", initiated by Berlioz, freed tone colour from its subservient function of merely clarifying the melody, rhythm, harmony, and counterpoint of a piece, and gave it an aesthetic raison d'être and significance of its own';[24] and in this, as Dahlhaus also notes, we can see the roots of musical modernism as heard in the twentieth century. Thus the particular role ascribed to the saxophone by many twentieth-century orchestral composers, who frequently use the instrument as a distinctive soloistic colour within the ensemble, has its roots in those explorations of orchestral texture that were occurring just at the time at which the instrument itself was invented.

The growing importance attached to orchestration is further demonstrated by the appearance at this time of the first publications devoted entirely to this subject. Sax's close friend Kastner was central to these developments, with his *Traité général d'instrumentation* of 1837 being followed by a more substantial *Cours d'instrumentations* in 1839 (supplement 1844). Berlioz's well known *Grand traité d'instrumentation et d'orchestration modernes* appeared only a few years later, in 1843. Berlioz's opening line – 'Never in the history of music has so much been said about instrumentation as at the present time' – illustrates just how significant he felt the subject had become.[25] The large number of French musical instrument patents registered in the middle years of the nineteenth century may also be attributed in part to this quest for new sounds and a growing interest in being able to manipulate and exploit familiar ones. Sax, along with other inventors of the time such as Boehm, had already contributed to these aspirations by improving the capabilities of various wind and brass instruments, allowing them to be used more successfully in a variety of contexts, particularly for solo passages. Now Sax's new hybrid brass/wind saxophone, while seen as offering very practical solutions to a number of instrumentation problems in both the wind band and the orchestra, also enthused composers and critics because of the possibilities presented by its completely new sound.

The unfamiliar sonority of this new instrument clearly made a great impression on those who heard it. Henri Blanchard, for example, writing in the *RGMP* in 1843, noted that 'from its low sound, resounding, solemn and striking like the organ, to the intonation of the human voice spinning out a sound *perdendosi*, it combines all kinds of sonority. This beautiful and curious instrument is so to speak an eclectic compound of the purest and smoothest effects of a sonorous body.'[26] Berlioz was similarly impressed. Having already lauded the instrument's particular sonority in his *RGMP* article of 1842 (see p. 44), he drew further attention to the instrument's characteristic sound in the first edition of his *Grand traité* the following year, before refining his metaphors in the 1860 revision: 'It is in short, a timbre *sui generis*, offering vague analogies with that of the cello, the clarinet and the English horn, and taking on a brassy hue, that gives it a particular tone [. . .]. The timbre of the high notes of the low saxophones has something of pain and sorrow, whereas that of their bass notes has, so to speak, an imposing, papal calm.'[27] Comettant reported that Rossini had described the saxophone as having 'the most beautiful sound that I know',[28] while Meyerbeer is also reported to have said that the instrument was 'the beautiful ideal of sound'.[29] Escudier, writing in *La France musicale,* observed that 'one cannot imagine the beauty of sound and the power of the notes in the low octave'.[30]

These interests in the unusual sound of the instrument must also be seen in the light of the extensive interest in novelty and innovation that characterised much of western Europe in the mid-nineteenth century. In this sense the saxophone was very much an instrument of its time, and can be seen as emblematic of a general attitude in urban western European centres in which the unusual and unique were highly valued and, if commercially oriented and successful, offered significant financial rewards. Such was the nature of nineteenth-century entrepreneurialism that inventors often highlighted the original nature of even the most minor amendment or innovation, so that they might tempt potential purchasers and raise the profile of their name or company. Of none was this more true than musical instrument manufacturers. The critic Eduard Hanslick commented scathingly on such practices in a review of the 1863 International Exhibition in London:

> Each proud father of a young brass instrument is particularly concerned to think up a new outrageous name. If there are ten new improvements invented for the common flugelhorn, or the ophicleide, so they are introduced into the musical world as ten new instruments, often under the most arbitrary and incomprehensible names. One finds in the catalogue of exhibited brass instruments, among others, the following: schwannenhorn, glyceide, euphonion, tritonikon, phonicon, trompettin, zvukoroh, baroxyton, sarrusophone, pelitticon, königshorns, helicon, and a half-dozen compounds including the name 'Sax,' etc., etc. All these fabulous creatures could be easily brought under two or three more familiar designations.[31]

While Hanslick's scepticism reveals a great deal about nineteenth-century neologistic tendencies, it also demonstrates that Sax's own practice, in seeking to draw attention to his latest innovations by devising new and unusual names for them, was not particularly unusual for the time.

Classical and operatic performance contexts

Within Parisian classical music concerts built upon the Austro-German tradition the saxophone made very little impression. The essential instrumentation of the orchestra was already established, and this lent a certain conservative momentum to the tradition that militated against the introduction of new instruments such as the saxophone. Certainly there were innovations in symphony orchestra instrumentation, but these tended to be differences of degree rather than kind: Sax's renovation of the bass clarinet, for example, made it more widely used in the orchestra, and the percussion section also began to expand in range and function. Yet even the natural French successors to this Austro-German tradition, composers such as Gounod and Saint-Saëns, showed little inclination to include the saxophone in their concert works, and it would be well into the twentieth century before the saxophone was seen as anything other than an exotic and occasional visitor in such contexts.[32]

This is not to suggest that the saxophone was never heard in French concert halls. Bizet's *L'Arlésienne* (1872) – albeit originally conceived as incidental music for a stage drama – later spawned an orchestral suite that provides perhaps the most well-known example (see also p. 230).[33] Paul Dukas's recently rediscovered concert aria *L'Ondine et le pêcheur* (1884) also begins with an alto saxophone solo. But these occasional glimpses of the saxophone in the symphony orchestra provided neither significant sales for manufacturers nor introductions to a wider listening public; notwithstanding their curiosity value they are largely incidental to the instrument's development and dissemination in the nineteenth century.

The saxophone did penetrate the operatic world to some degree, and with good reason. The popular (and populist) operatic environments were more accommodating of musical innovation, and relied in part on a sense of novelty and spectacle to attract their audiences. The occasional introduction of new instruments and sounds contributed to an environment of musical and dramatic experimentation and innovation. Operatic performances were also more central to Parisian musical life. They drew larger audiences, provided more newspaper commentary, and were generally seen to be more significant than concert performances and thus attracted greater attention and investment. Significantly, Sax himself held a position at the main Paris Opéra as director of the *banda*, or fanfare. The *banda* were musicians who performed at stage level, either in view of the audience or off stage. They were to some extent independent of the main orchestra, with their director frequently called upon to score music for the ensemble according to the composer's wishes. Sax was appointed as director of the Opéra's *banda* in November 1847, relinquishing the post in May 1892, only two years before his death. Despite this opportunity, however, Sax continued to find it difficult to get his instruments accepted within the Opéra, in part because of opposition from the musicians themselves; and when his instruments were used they hardly ever included saxophones.[34]

Given frequent opposition to his inventions, and the highly politicised environments that surrounded classical music-making in general and the Opéra in particular, Sax was doubtless gratified by whatever support he did receive. In the case of the saxophone, however, while such support was strongly expressed through letters, criticism and treatises, it was not necessarily manifested in much actual scoring for the instrument. Berlioz represents perhaps the most extreme example of this trend. His writings express nothing but admiration for Sax's instruments in general and the saxophone in particular. He was one of Sax's major musical allies in Paris, and included many of the latter's instruments in his *Grand traité* of 1843.[35] In his theoretically ideal orchestra of 467 instruments he advocated having five saxophones. Yet despite this level of support Berlioz in fact never scored for the instrument. He arranged a short vocal piece, probably his *Chant sacré*, which he refashioned under the title *Hymne* into a sextet for three saxhorns, clarinet, bass clarinet and saxophone, performed in Sax's workshop on 3 February 1844. The performance was intended as a demonstration of the capabilities of Sax's instruments, and the saxophone was probably played by Sax himself.[36] Berlioz may have intended to use the saxophone in his *La Damnation de Faust*, but appears to have changed his mind (see p. 47); he also made unfulfilled plans in 1851 to employ the instrument in a forthcoming concert.[37] Berlioz himself was aware of the contradiction between his advocacy of Sax's instruments and his own reluctance actually to use them. In his *Memoirs* he observes – apparently discounting his earlier arrangement of the *Chant* – that he had often been criticised for 'excessive use of Sax's instruments – no doubt on the sound principle that I have often praised them, even if I do not happen to have employed them anywhere except in one scene of *La Prise de Troie*, an opera of which no one has yet seen a note.'[38]

Quite why Berlioz never scored for the saxophone remains a point of conjecture, but the reasons are likely to be largely pragmatic. For most of the 1840s and 50s Berlioz was better known in Paris as a writer and critic than as a composer. His operas were either unperformed or poorly received, and he exerted only limited influence upon a musical arena that was so central to Parisian musical life. Instead it was Rossini, to whom Berlioz was passionately opposed, who made the greater artistic and political impact. To have begun to score for an exotic instrument such as the saxophone, particularly in light of the antipathy demonstrated towards Sax by many musicians, might have further limited Berlioz's chances of performances. Berlioz gained increasing success abroad as the century progressed, both as composer and conductor, particularly in Britain, Russia and Germany. But in these other countries, had he scored for a saxophone, the problem would have been finding suitable players for an instrument which, to the extent that it was known at all, remained confined to military bands and occasional novelty appearances in popular music events. Even if players could have been found, standards of execution were likely to have been poor, as Berlioz would have known.

But other composers were in a position to demonstrate a more explicit commitment to the saxophone, and the instrument began to appear in a variety of operatic scores, performed not only at the main Opéra but also elsewhere in Paris. Georges Kastner claimed to be the first composer to score for it, in his opera *La dernier roi de Juda* (1844). Kastner was generally better known as a theorist than a composer, and his first three operas were never fully staged. *Le dernier roi* received only a single concert performance, on 1 December 1844, in the concert hall of the Paris Conservatoire. Notwithstanding Berlioz's assertion in his *Grande traité* that the saxophone was pitched in B♭, Kastner's score in fact calls for a bass saxophone in C.[39] The instrument is written in the bass clef, and is scored sparingly as an additional bass brass voice rather than as a member of the woodwinds. This appears to accord with Kastner's (and Sax's) view of the intended role for the instrument at this time, and its provenance as a replacement for the ophicleide. In two later works, his two *Ouvertures de festival* from 1858 and 1860, Kastner calls for a B♭ bass and, unusually, two alto saxophones in F.

In 1851 Armand Limnander de Nieuwenhove, a Belgian composer who, like Sax, had settled in Paris in the 1840s, scored for an E♭ alto saxophone in his opera *Le Château de la Barbe-Bleue*, performed at the Opéra-Comique on the eve of Louis-Napoleon Bonaparte's *coup d'état* on 1 December 1851. Although used sparingly, the instrument is given several lyrical solos, most prominently a lilting 6/8 melody at the opening of the second act (see ex. 3).

Limnander was presumably satisfied with the effect, since he scored a further solo for the same instrument the following year, in *Le Maître chanteur*. Also in 1852, J. F. Fromental Halévy, another of Sax's circle and something of a minor innovator in instrumentation, included a quartet of saxophones (B♭ soprano, 2 E♭ altos, and a bass

Ex. **3.** Entr'acte from Act 2, no. 8 of Armand Limnander's *Le Château de la Barbe-Bleue* (1851).

in C) in the fifth act of his opera *Le Juif errant*, premiered at the Opéra on 23 April 1852. The quartet was part of the *banda*, and Sax himself was one of the players at the premiere.[40]

For the remainder of the century the saxophone continued to be occasionally heard in operatic scores by French composers, with varying levels of participation. It was scored as an alternative to the bass clarinet in Meyerbeer's opera *L'Africaine* (1865), although this detail appears to have been introduced by Fétis, who produced the first performing version of the work after Meyerbeer's sudden death in 1864; Saint-Saëns later argued that the result was not very satisfactory.[41] Meyerbeer does appear to have wanted to score the cello solo in the 'Adagio' of the trio in Act V of another opera, *Le Prophète* (1848) for the saxophone; however, the resistance of the Opéra musicians prevented this.[42] Ambroise Thomas called for both alto and baritone saxophones in *Hamlet* (1868) and baritone alone in *Françoise de Rimini* (1882); the former includes a notable cadenza for the alto instrument, now frequently omitted in performance (see ex. 4). Both this and the Limnander example demonstrate how the saxophone was now conceived by composers to have a distinctive and flexible melodic voice, far removed from the essentially supportive role as an ophicleide substitute for which the instrument was first intended.

A variety of saxophones appeared in different works by Jules Massenet between 1871 and 1899, notably the E♭ alto in *Werther* (1892), although the latter was premiered in

Ex. **4.** Alto saxophone cadenza from Ambroise Thomas's *Hamlet* (1868).

Vienna rather than Paris. Saint-Saëns scored for a full quintet of saxophones (S/2A/T/B) as part of the *banda* for *Henry VIII* (1883).[43] Moreover, by 1879 the saxophone was sufficiently established at the Opéra that it was listed as part of the official instrumentation of the resident orchestra, played by the bass clarinettist Louis Mayeur (1837–94);[44] this may also help explain the alto saxophone solo in the barcarolle of Delibes' ballet *Sylvia*, which was premiered at the Opéra a few years earlier, in 1876.

Notwithstanding the initial reluctance of musicians in the Opéra orchestra to be involved with Sax and his instruments, it is clear that other renowned composers beyond the inventor's immediate Parisian circle were familiar with the saxophone. Liszt promoted the instruments during his period as a conductor in Weimar in the 1850s. He was introduced to Sax in Paris in late 1853, and shortly afterwards wrote to the violinist Joachim that he had heard '[Sax's] large family of Saxophones, Sax horns, Sax Tubas, etc., etc. Several of these (especially the Saxophone Tenor and the Saxophone Alto) will be exceedingly useful, even in our ordinary orchestras, and the ensemble has a really magnificent effect.'[45] Berlioz reveals in a letter of 1855 that he took the trouble to chase up Sax, who had failed to send a promised case of saxophones to Liszt in Weimar; Berlioz later returned to Sax's factory to ensure that they really had been sent.[46] Why Liszt ordered them is not clear; like Berlioz, he never scored for the instrument.

In 1861 Wagner presented to the Opéra a list of supplementary instruments required for the Paris production of *Tannhäuser*. This included a request for an additional 12 horns at the end of Act 1, to play horn calls. Wagner observed that 'since there won't be enough horns in Paris, M. Sax should be asked to replace a portion with some instruments of the same timbre of his invention, perhaps saxophones [*sic*].' Sax would have realised that the saxophone would be inappropriate for the idiomatic horn material at this point, and this, together with the misspelling of the instrument's name, suggests that Wagner was unfamiliar with the instrument, which would not have been common in Germany at the time (nor Switzerland, where he had been exiled for much of the 1850s); it is likely that Wagner, like many others, was confusing the saxophone with the saxhorn.[47]

The classical and operatic contexts in which the saxophone occasionally surfaced in the nineteenth century were undoubtedly important to Sax and others because of the legitimisation they appeared to confer upon this novel instrument. For those harbouring what would have appeared at the time as a perfectly natural presumption that Western art music was superior to all other kinds, the importance of having the saxophone accepted in these fields would have been unquestioned. Yet the instrument did not penetrate these musical environments to any significant degree, to the obvious frustration of its inventor, and had it not found rather quicker acceptance in popular and military contexts it is possible that the saxophone would have ended the century as little more than an obscure and seldom-heard musical curiosity.

Light classical and popular music – European soloists

Notwithstanding the expansion in concert activities in mid-nineteenth-century Paris, concerts involving the saxophone as a solo instrument were infrequent in the 1850s and 60s. They were largely given by a small number of instrumentalists (predominantly clarinettists) who had taken the time and trouble to develop their performance expertise on the saxophone in addition to their first instrument, or those who had developed saxophone skills beyond the basic standard required for participation in military ensembles. Sax himself gave demonstration recitals on the instrument in the performance space in his factory on the rue Saint-Georges and elsewhere, and should be considered the first soloist on the instrument. No commentary appears to have been left on his performances, and we might assume that whatever his earlier prowess as a clarinettist, the time-consuming nature of his work as an inventor, businessman and entrepreneur are likely to have prevented him from attaining high-level expertise on the instrument, notwithstanding his enthusiasm for it.

Cokken's and Sax's activities as teachers also ensured there was a steady supply of saxophonists with at least average skills on the instrument, and some must have achieved more than this. In common with other instruments, prizewinners from some of these classes were listed in the musical press. Thus in 1862, for example, we find *La France musicale* listing prizewinners from the 'military saxophone class' at the Conservatoire as being Eyckermann, Géraud and Simon (first prize) and Hausser, Dagard and Gluck (second prize), with the paper further observing that the class as a whole had been 'quite remarkable'.[48] Performers such as these were almost certainly giving occasional solos in the bands in which they played.

These classes ran until 1870 when, together with the other classes for military students, they were suspended following France's defeat in the Franco-Prussian war. Even then Sax offered to teach the classes for free, an indication of their value to him in seeking to establish and disseminate the saxophone. As late as 1883 Sax was still writing letters to the Director of the Conservatoire (now Ambroise Thomas, one of his erstwhile supporters) pleading for the opening of a saxophone class on the grounds that composers were having to substitute other instruments in their scores when they had originally written for saxophone, because of a dearth of suitably trained players.[49] Sax's complaints were to no avail, and despite a review of the Conservatoire's practices in 1892, which suggested that a class for the saxophone should indeed be restarted, this did not happen until 1942. Sax's frustration at the state of affairs in relation to the Paris Conservatoire may well have been compounded by the knowledge that the saxophone was being taught at the Brussels Conservatoire, by Nazaire Beeckman, from 1867 until his death in 1900.[50]

But as early as 1850 there were performers who had developed enough expertise on the saxophone to become internationally-renowned soloists. Two saxophonists in particular, Charles-Jean-Baptiste Soualle and Henri Wuille, are notable for the influence they had on the development and dissemination of the saxophone in the 1850s and 60s. Both gave occasional concerts in more formal contexts, and both are important figures in the early evolution of the concert saxophone in France, Belgium, England, the United States and, in Soualle's case at least, further afield. We know about their activities in part because of their association with one of the great musical showmen of that period, Louis Jullien, and his renowned series of promenade concerts. These proved to be among the most important of the early contexts in which the saxophone was heard, largely on account of the size of the audiences they often attracted.

Promenade concerts arose from the traditions of informal music-making among the lower-middle classes in taverns, cafés and parks. During the 1830s and 40s such venues were no longer provided with background music by itinerant street musicians, but by aspiring and ambitious professionals, the more popular of whom were able to attract large crowds. Promenade concerts transformed these informal occasions into large-scale commercial enterprises. The size of the audiences went far beyond those of other concerts, ranging from 1,500 to 5,000, with an average of perhaps 2,500.[51] These were people who could not afford – and were not predisposed – to attend the rather more sophisticated classical music concerts, but could manage the much lower prices for a promenade concert. Informality and entertainment were the defining characteristics, and programmes were undemanding. Solos played by star performers were a significant feature, and would be mixed with popular ballroom dances of the time – waltz, polka, quadrille, galop – as well as selections from well-known operas; even in these operatic extracts instrumental soloists might be used for the vocal lines, or play themes and variations upon them. The venues themselves promised a degree of escapism from the mundanities of everyday life, with statues, fountains and floral decorations adorning the hall. The overriding artistic criterion for this audience was novelty, not only new instruments, of which the saxophone was an obvious example, but also the dazzling new effects and extremes which particular virtuosi strove to achieve. Such pyrotechnic individual displays served several functions: they enhanced the reputations of performers, thus hopefully leading to more bookings and increased fees; they brought specific pieces into a wider public domain, leading to reproduction and marketing in modified editions for amateurs to perform at home or in the salon; and they demonstrated the efficacy or potential of the latest instrumental innovations, allowing manufacturers to profit from increased sales. While a number of musicians, including Sax himself, were proficient enough on the saxophone to fulfil the occasional demands of the opera house or the military band, the first truly notable exponents were those soloists with sufficient ability to attract and retain the audience's attention in the often more frenetic and display-oriented environments of the promenade concerts and similar.

In Paris such concerts were established by Philippe Musard, a showman and an able if somewhat eccentric and idiosyncratic conductor. Musard set many precedents in these concerts, including that of incorporating large numbers of diverse instrumentalists as well as the latest instrumental fashions. Thus innovations such as recently-developed valved brass instruments (like the *cornet à pistons*) or the still relatively new ophicleide were often to be seen at his events. Nor was Musard averse to augmenting the large forces available to him with sounds such as the crash of broken chairs, or pistol shots to signal the final galop of the quadrilles. But his success was waning by the mid 1840s and he retired into obscurity in 1852. Musard's real significance lies in his influence upon those who sought to emulate him, and of these by far the most important was Louis Jullien.

Jullien had been appointed conductor of the Paris Opéra balls in the mid 1830s, and by the late 1830s his fame rivalled that of Musard. By 1840 he had moved to England, and it was here that he made the greatest impact, becoming renowned for the kind of promenade concerts that Musard had first developed in Paris: a large

47. Louis Jullien.

orchestra would play arrangements of popular songs, dances and light classical fare, as well as accompanying soloists whose virtuosic turns were again designed to enthral and entertain the crowds. Although these promenade concerts were initially centred upon London, it was Jullien's prodigious touring activities that brought him wider recognition, and which had the greater consequence for the saxophone. He would play a season of four to six weeks during the winter in London, and spend the rest of the year touring the provinces and abroad.

Following a breakdown Jullien died in a French lunatic asylum in 1860, but he is a key figure in the early dissemination of the saxophone, because from the late 1840s he featured the instrument in many of his concerts, in both Europe and the United States. He thus facilitated many of the events in which the saxophone was first heard by the general public as a solo instrument, and particularly in major international centres such as London and New York. In so doing, Jullien unwittingly provided an identity for the saxophone that would persist for much of the half century that followed: playing light classical and popular music, albeit accompanied by occasional forays into more 'serious' classical music, as part of larger military and wind band ensembles. And his star saxophonists were Charles-Jean-Baptiste Soualle and Henri Wuille.

Soualle now appears something of an exotic figure. Born at Arras in 1824 he graduated from Klosé's clarinet class at the Paris Conservatoire in 1844 before becoming clarinettist in the orchestra of the Opéra-Comique. After the uprising of 1848 he took refuge in England as first clarinet at the Queen's Theatre, before then joining Jullien's orchestra. Soualle appears on a programme of 1850 as a performer in one of Jullien's monster quadrilles (requiring 207 instrumentalists), playing an instrument described as a 'corno musa', accompanied by a harp.[52] This 'corno musa' was undoubtedly the saxophone, although Soualle and Jullien appear to have persisted in using this description on various later occasions; the *Manchester Guardian* was still using the term two years later, as was the *New York Times* in 1853, and such usage is likely to have replicated the information given out at concerts.[53]

Soualle's 1850 performance would have been one of the earliest appearances of the saxophone in England, although Adam Carse notes that the previous year, in 1849, a London critic had castigated Jullien for adding to the instrumentation of Beethoven's Fifth Symphony, asking where in the score he had found the parts for 'four ophicleides and a saxophone, besides those of his favourite regiment of side-drums?' It is conceivable, though, that the critic had confused the saxhorn with the saxophone, like so many others. However, the Distin family, who had the first licence to import saxophones into England, were advertising them in the *Musical World* as early as 1849,[54] and the saxophone had been used by the Royal Artillery Band since 1848 (see p. 125); the critic's observations may indeed have been accurate, the more so since the *Illustrated London News* had carried a woodcut illustration of the instrument that same year.[55] The same publication observed in November 1850 that the instrument 'partakes of the volume and richness of the clarinet and the bassoon', while two years later the *Musical World* somewhat unflatteringly noted that the 'corno-musa' was 'made of brass, has the reed and mouthpiece of a clarinet, bristles with keys, and has the bowl or bell of a horn. It has a mellow rich tone – a compound of the clarinet and the cornet.' Notwithstanding that the instrument 'was beautifully played by M. Soualle' it appeared to the reviewer as 'a musical monster, neither fish nor flesh, nor good red herring.'[56]

Soualle's expertise on the instrument in the early 1850s provoked a number of favourable reviews in Paris and London that suggest he achieved an expertise on the instrument that compared favourably with the prevailing woodwind performance standards of the time. In Paris, Henri Blanchard, commenting in the *RGMP* of 1851 on Soualle's performances at the *Union musicale*, noted that although the velvety, suave tone of the saxophone was well known, Soualle had demonstrated that the instrument was equally capable of detached notes and fast, complicated movements: 'A clarinet, a flute would not have played better. We don't doubt that after this decisive test, skilled virtuosos will hasten to adopt an instrument that promises to produce new effects.'[57] Two months later, Berlioz, describing the same performance in the *Journal des débats*, noted that Soualle, 'recently returned from London, produced a great sensation in making heard for the first time in Paris, with all its advantages, the saxophone, masterpiece of Sax'.[58] Berlioz's words should not be taken too literally, since he was aware of its use in military band environments and Sax's own events. He was almost certainly alluding to its first significant concert performance: the *Union musicale* presented a rather more sophisticated ambience for such concerts than those offered in London by Jullien, and provides a relatively rare example at this time of a saxophone recital in a formal context.

But Soualle's concert giving, and hence his promotion of the saxophone, went beyond London and Paris. He was an inveterate traveller, and undertook tours to areas which in the mid-nineteenth century would have been considered highly exotic: Java, Shanghai, India, Mauritius and South Africa, for example, and he gave concerts in many of these places. He most likely introduced the saxophone to Australia, on 11 June 1853, when the *Melbourne Argus* noted the arrival of 'a newly-invented and most remarkable instrument styled the saxophone', before observing that 'no such music was ever before heard in this colony'.[59] Soualle is not mentioned by name, but it seems improbable that it could have been anybody else; he certainly spent time in both Australia and New Zealand over the following two years.[60]

In 1856 Soualle met with rather less acclaim when he performed in China and Hong Kong, in concerts for the expatriate European communities there. Contemporary reviews give fascinating insights into the reception of both the performer and the instrument at this time. Having previously described the saxophone as the 'corno musa' in London, Soualle now claimed to performing on the 'turcophone', and also on the turcophono and the turcophonini. These names were allocated to the different types of saxophone in place of alto, tenor and so forth. Soualle's deliberate neologism was probably further designed to reinforce the exotic novelty of the saxophone, as well as acknowledging a growing interest in musical exoticism in nineteenth-century France. This was an important component of his act. In many performances he adopted the moniker 'Ali Ben Sou Alle', even travelling under that name, and at least one contemporary engraving shows him in 'oriental' costume, holding an instrument that vaguely resembles a soprano saxophone. The roots of these name changes may well lie in changes that Soualle himself made to the instrument. In 1860 and 1861 he submitted patents to protect certain modifications to Sax's design: a single octave key replaced the two octave keys Sax's instruments were still employing, and the fingering for the lower notes of the instrument was revised, drawing on Buffet's Boehm-system clarinet keywork.[61]

Few international critics were sufficiently familiar with the saxophone so as to make the connection between Soualle's 'turcophone' and Sax's original, but they show a decidedly more lukewarm approach to the instrument than Sax's Parisian circle. The *North China Herald* observed that 'the compass of the instrument is very great but we confess to some disappointment as regards its quality of tone, and correctness of tone also, in some few notes, and altogether we think it an imperfect

48. Charles-Jean-Baptiste Soualle, in typical orientalist costume.

instrument – it may however, improve on further acquaintance'. The writer suggested that the turkophoni (most likely the soprano saxophone) was 'by far the most perfect and pleasing instrument of the two', whereas the *China Mail* rather patronisingly asserted that 'the instrument is well adopted for that class of music'. The latter publication still felt unable to speak of the instruments 'in *very* warm terms of praise at least as regards their suitability for solo performances'.[62]

Another expatriate publication, the French-language *Moniteur officiel* of India, reviewed two concerts given by Soualle in Pondichery, in 1857. While the *Moniteur* replicated the other Asian publications in using the term 'turcophone', the *RGMP*, reprinting the articles for its Parisian audience, also included the more familiar term saxophone in their copy.[63] But Soualle persisted with his description. An 1864 poster for one of Alfred Mellon's popular concerts at the Royal Opera House in London again advertises Soualle playing a set of variations on 'In My Cottage', on the 'Turkophone'.[64] A review in the *Musical Times* sniffed that this 'vapid fantasia' was played on 'a new instrument [by] a gentleman with the unmistakably Oriental name of Ali ben Sou-Alle'. Earlier the reviewer had noted of such concerts that 'in the attempt to offer sufficient attraction to the educated and uneducated in art, a middle course is pursued which has the effect of disappointing both'.[65] Such statements illustrate the often patronising attitudes of the musical establishment towards these popular concerts by impresarios such as Jullien and Mellon. The identification of the saxophone as a novelty act within such contexts is part of the reason why it struggled to become accepted as a serious concert instrument in Europe for much of the nineteenth century, as well as anticipating similar difficulties that would later beset the instrument in the twentieth century.

By 1865 Soualle's fame was such that he played for the Imperial family at the Tuileries in Paris and also for the Prince of Wales in London. To the latter he gave a bound collection of his published works. Different pieces in this collection indicate saxophone or turcophone as the melody instrument, probably depending on whether they were written earlier or later; there are also some songs and pieces for clarinet and for solo piano, demonstrating Soualle's wider musical gifts (see ill. 49).[66] Little is known of this colourful saxophonist after 1866, although he appears to have died in 1876.[67]

The other significant European saxophone soloist of the mid-nineteenth century, and one who appeared more frequently in Jullien's concerts and elsewhere in Europe, was the Belgian Henri Wuille (1822–71). Initially achieving recognition as a clarinet soloist he was equally in demand as a saxophone virtuoso; later in life he taught clarinet and saxophone at the Strasbourg Conservatoire. He first appears in the *RGMP* in 1851, in relation to a concert in Brussels, where he was solo clarinettist with the Brussels *Regiment des Guides*. Fétis, writing in 1851 but recalling Wuille's performances of the previous winter, observed that he was 'a very talented artist' and that he had performed on the saxophone 'the most difficult passages with great ease, to the unanimous applause of an appreciative public'.[68]

Wuille appears to have joined Jullien in London in 1852, and contemporary programmes list him in the orchestra alongside Henry Lazarus, the renowned clarinettist; indeed, Jullien advertised Wuille as 'the Belgian Lazarus' for his 1853 American tour.[69] Wuille's stature was such that his engagement by Jullien was recorded in the *RGMP*, and in August 1852 the paper noted that Jullien had hired both Wuille *and* Soualle for his

SOUVENIRS D'IRLANDE.

ALI-BEN-SOU-ALLE.

49. The first page of *Souvenirs d'Irlande* by Soualle, for turcophone and piano.

London concerts;[70] Wuille then played regularly with Jullien until at least 1856.[71] After this he appears to have returned to France, and by 1858 he was performing as a clarinettist with a theatre in Strasbourg. Kastner, writing that year in the *RGMP* after a concert in which Wuille had played on the saxophone a specially-commissioned fantasia by François Schwab on themes from Friedrich von Flotow's opera *Martha*, observed that he had joined 'perfect taste to a marvellous ability, and brilliant execution to the solid qualities of a good musician[;] M. Wuille enjoys a universal reputation justly acquired.'[72]

Notwithstanding the efforts of musicians such as Soualle and Wuille, and the commercial activities of Sax and others licensed to sell his instruments, in the latter part of the nineteenth century the saxophone went into something of a decline in Europe. While it remained a component of many military bands, elsewhere it appears to have fallen into relative disuse, once the initial novelty of the instrument had waned. It was not entirely forgotten, however. Promenade concerts continued in London after Jullien's demise, notably at Covent Garden, and those who followed endeavoured to emulate Jullien's flamboyant theatrical showmanship. Thus Alfred Mellon, staging a series of promenade concerts at Covent Garden in 1865, employed the services of a French saxophonist by the name of Cordier, and, as with Soualle previously, dressed him in a Turkish outfit for the performance of various saxophone solos, this time nominating him as 'Ali Ben Mustapha'. Similarly, Jullien's own son, attempting to follow in the footsteps of his impresario father, dressed a clarinet player by the name of Tyler in a Turkish costume, and obliged him to assume the equally improbable pseudonym of 'Ali Ben Jenkins' for a series of saxophone solos.[73] Such activities doubtless attest more to Soualle's legacy and an increasing fascination with – and idealisation of – the Orient than to a widespread interest in the saxophone itself, which continued to retain only a marginalised position within London's concert life. The relative unfamiliarity of the saxophone in much of Europe at the end of the nineteenth century is well summarised by George Bernard Shaw's 1885 observation that 'probably not one student in the Royal Academy or Royal College of Music could "spot" a saxophone blindfold'.[74]

Saxophone soloists in the United States

In August 1853 Henri Wuille travelled with Jullien to the United States as part of a nucleus of some 27 musicians for a four-week residency at the Castle Gardens in New York, which Jullien then planned to follow with a tour of other cities. American musicians, especially string players, would be booked to bring the orchestra up to the usual Jullien complement of approximately 100 players. The publicity for Jullien's first concert claimed that he had a repertoire of twelve hundred compositions, while also promising two instrumental solos for each programme.[75] Yet, while the programmes changed regularly, public interest in Jullien's events inevitably began to wane, and in December 1853 he decided to substitute his oft-performed and successful *American Quadrille* with his *Great Exhibition Quadrille*, which had been a success in London in 1851. Just as in London, particular attention was drawn to one part of the quadrille, the 'Aurora Serenade', which would feature Henri Wuille on the 'corno musa', the same curious misnomer that had been used previously. Thus on 19 December 1853 the saxophone made its debut in the USA, and a review in the *New York Daily Times* two days later dispels any remaining doubts as to the true nature of the instrument:

> A new instrument – new at least to a New York audience – is used in the introduction to the third figure. It is called the *corno musa* and is said to be of ancient origin. We are indebted for its present usefulness to Mr. Saxe [*sic*], a gentleman who has done for wind instruments what Erard did for harps – made them perfect. The corno musa is a brass instrument, but unlike any other with which we are acquainted, is played with a reed, the mouthpiece being, we fancy, similar to that of the clarionet. The tones which Mr Wuille elicited from the corno were beautifully sonorous and mellow [. . .] [he] performs on it in as masterly a style as on his own instrument, the clarionet.[76]

The reference to the instrument being 'of ancient origin' probably arises from misinformation put about by Jullien for the purposes of stimulating curiosity, or from the reviewer's lack of knowledge of musical instruments (and possibly both). Nevertheless, the occasion was significant enough to have been noted in Paris, where the *RGMP* recorded the enthusiasm that had greeted Wuille's performance in New York, while having no hesitation in replacing the term 'corno musa' with that of 'saxophone'.[77] If this was indeed the first time the saxophone had been heard in the US, it was only five days before it was incorporated for the first time into a work written by an American composer. William Henry Fry, a prominent New York music critic, wrote his *Santa Claus: Christmas Symphony* 'expressly for Jullien's Orchestra' and it was 'performed with the greatest applause for the first time on Christmas Eve, 1853'.[78] The following year Fry scored for saxophones in two further works: *Hagar in the Wilderness* (S/B) and *The Dying Soldier* (T).

Wuille's performances with Jullien, and Fry's use of the instrument in his scores, mark the beginning of a steady growth of interest in the saxophone in North America during the latter half of the nineteenth century. Early appearances were often the result of European connections, particularly through the migration of European musicians. But the acceptance of the saxophone in the USA, a country less constrained at the time by the kinds of social and musical hierarchies characterising cities such as London or Paris, was in notable contrast to the instrument's position in Europe, where it experienced something of a decline in the 1860s and 70s.

Reports of initial appearances are inevitably sporadic. In late 1862, Thomas Ryan, for example, undertook several performances on the saxophone as part of concerts given by the Boston Mendelssohn Quintet Club, of which he was a founder member and for which he also played both clarinet and viola. Ryan's repertoire comprised not only conventional clarinet concert material, but also transcriptions and operatic selections that were staple concert fare for wind soloists of the period, played on the saxophone: Schubert's *Serenade*, selections from Verdi's *Il Trovatore* and Donizetti's *Lucia di Lammermoor*, and so forth.[79] It may also have been Ryan who provided similar musical interludes for the commencement exercises at the University of Vermont in August 1866.[80]

Although the saxophone was by no means widespread at this time, Ryan's performances evidence an evolving concert tradition in the United States, one which was developed by determined individuals sufficiently enthusiastic about the instrument that they were prepared to generate both new repertoire and opportunities to perform it. Just as Americans settled and developed the territory around them, so too did they harness and exploit the new musical frontiers offered by the saxophone. Of nobody is this more true than Edward Abraham Lefebre (1834–1911), who was to become widely known as 'The Saxophone King' in late nineteenth-century United States.[81] This sobriquet was testament not only to his technical ability but also to his industrious development of new repertory for the instrument. And like Soualle some years before, he was also influential because of the extensive touring he undertook, largely in the USA but also beyond, promoting the saxophone in regions previously unfamiliar with it.

Lefebre was born on 15 December 1834 in The Hague, Holland, but little is known of his early years. He may have worked in Paris in the 1850s, but he emigrated to Cape Town, South Africa, in 1859, where he ran a music store, among other activities. It appears likely he gave concerts involving the saxophone in that country in the early 1860s.[82] He returned to Holland in 1863, and spent most of the rest of the decade there, before taking a position as a saxophonist in the orchestra of the Royal Alhambra

Palace in London in 1869. Just as Wuille and Soualle had previously found employment in the many promenade concerts offered in London at the time, so too did
Lefebre. At one such event, at the Royal Opera House, Covent Garden, he was
reputedly complimented by Charles Gounod, who gave Lefebre 'several friendly taps
of approbation on the shoulder, exclaiming, 'Bravo – saxophone!'[83] A subsequent
engagement with the Parepa Rosa English Opera Company as a clarinettist led to a
tour of the United States, after which Lefebre stayed on, becoming domiciled there
from about 1872.

Over the next 30 years Lefebre became the most renowned saxophonist in America.
He was hired by bandleaders such as Gilmore and Sousa to lead the saxophone
sections of their various bands (of which more below), undoubtedly increasing his
national profile; it was his tours and performances as a bandsman that provided the
platform for many of his performing activities. On 1 March 1875, for example, while
touring with the Gilmore Band, he performed a fantasia on themes from Bellini's
opera *Norma* at a concert in Boston. A reviewer writing in *Benham's Musical Review*
observed that Lefebre's performance was 'a treat, both from the excellence with which
the music was rendered, and from the fact that the instrument was previously
unknown among us.'[84]

Lefebre was industrious in generating chamber music opportunities for the instrument. Together with his saxophone colleagues in the Gilmore Band he formed the
New York Saxophone Quartette Club, which first performed in a Gilmore concert on
15 Jan 1874.[85] In addition to performing his own composition, *Swiss Air, with Variations*,
Lefebre also played as part of the quartet, performing two movements – Andante and
Allegro – from Jean Baptiste Singelée's *Allegro de Concert*.[86] Thus the professional band
movement in the United States provided in the nineteenth century the basis for the
saxophone to develop not only as a solo instrument, but in chamber music also.

Although the New York Saxophone Quartette Club was a pioneering group whose
profile was enhanced through its association with Gilmore, it was not the first

50.   The saxophone section from Gilmore's band in the late 1880s. E. A. Lefebre is second from
the left.

saxophone quartet in the United States. Eustach Strasser claims to have formed a group in Philadelphia as early as 1869 known as the 'The First Saxophone Quartette'.[87] Moreover, the St Louis Saxophone Quartet was working in the 1870s and performed regularly as 'an agreeable feature in the concerts of the Knights of Pythias Band at Schneider's Garden'[88] until disbanding sometime in mid-1880. But it was Lefebre who was most closely identified with the instrument – among those who recognised it at all – during these final decades of the nineteenth century.

In 1878 Gilmore's band undertook an extensive European tour that included many of western Europe's major cities. When the band returned to New York in September of that year Lefebre stayed in Europe and continued to give solo performances. Such was his stature that he appears to have been able to sustain several weeks of solo engagements, including a performance in front of Wagner in Leipzig.[89] Further concerts followed throughout Germany and Scandinavia, culminating in a four-week engagement at Kroll's Garden in Berlin as part of the variety performances sometimes staged there. At a time when established saxophone soloists in Europe would appear to be conspicuous by their absence from the historical record, Lefebre's concertising undoubtedly did much to keep the instrument in the mind of those who were fortunate enough to hear him play.

Lefebre was conscious of the need to generate new repertoire for the instrument. He collaborated with the otherwise little-known composer Caryl Florio, who, unusually for the time, wrote a series of works for the saxophone.[90] These included *Introduction, Theme and Variation* (1879) for E♭ saxophone and small orchestra, which lays some claim to being the first concerto-type piece written for the instrument,[91] and *Menuet and Scherzo* for saxophone quartet (1885). A *New York Times* review of a concert devoted to his music in 1880, in which Lefebre undoubtedly played but is not named, noted that Florio's *Allegro de Concert* (1879) for saxophone quartet was 'not specially interesting but exceedingly well performed'.[92] Lefebre also formed the Lyceum Concert Club in 1880, an enterprising if rather unorthodox instrumental group comprising himself as saxophone soloist, a flute soloist, a complete saxophone quartet (SATB), a flugelhorn and a contra bassoon, which provided concerts as part of the Lyceum movement.[93] This had developed from 1826 as a form of early, locally-driven adult education. It initially comprised lectures, instruction and debates, but eventually generated musical performances and lecture recitals, all of which were intended to be in some way educational. The movement provided one of the ways in which the saxophone became known to American audiences, not only through Lefebre's work but also later through the Clay Smith and Guy Holmes Apollo Concert Company (see pp. 140–2). The unusual instrumentation of Lefebre's Lyceum Concert Club suggests that the performers were drawn from Gilmore's band, with whom he was working at the time.

Although Lefebre had the highest profile of any saxophonist of the 1880s and 90s, naturally there were others, several of whom Lefebre worked with in Gilmore's Band or elsewhere. Like Lefebre many were migrant Europeans, and thus may have brought the instrument with them during resettlement; the otherwise unknown John Wirtz, for example, had performed a solo at the German Workingmen's Union (*Arbeiter Union*) in New York as early as 1870.[94] Johann Gottlieb Friedrich ter Linden (d. 1891), known as Fred ter Linden, was an early American saxophonist from Portland, Maine and later director of the US Army Principal Depot Band in New York. Linden taught the saxophone to his niece Louise Linden (dates unknown), and she went on to make some impression as a solo artist herself. She is listed as part of a benefit concert at the Park Theatre, NY, in the *New York Times* of 1 May 1881, and appeared alongside the Distin family and others at the opening concert of a new concert hall later the same year;[95] that she should be invited to share the same stage as the Distins attests both to her eminence and her competence. Undoubtedly she was known to Lefebre, since in 1878 she married Benjamin C. Bent, a cornettist with Gilmore's Band. Linden and her husband would give concert tours together when the latter's commitments to the band allowed. Her achievement is all the more remarkable given that at the time much of this kind of music making was, as in Europe, almost entirely male dominated.

Possibly more eminent still was Lefebre's own student, Bessie Mecklem (1875–1942), in part because in April 1892 she made some of the earliest recordings of any saxophonist, only two years after her teacher's first recordings. Mecklem and Lefebre performed together on several occasions in the late 1880s, and Mecklem also had a successful duo with her father Henry Clay Mecklem, a harpist. As with Louise Linden, that Lefebre should choose to share the stage with her at certain performances is testament to her abilities. Nevertheless, the saxophone remained relatively novel in the eyes of many, perhaps particularly when in the hands of a young female performer; one 1890 concert advert in the *New York Times*, drawing attention to the unusual nature of the performers, noted that 'the special attractions will be the boy violinist, Master Ghulka; Miss Bessie Mechlem [*sic*], saxophone soloist, and D.W. Robertson, manipulator of the musical silver sleigh bells.'[96] But Mecklem's abilities on the instrument must have transcended any curiosity value attaching to her work, and she was

51. Bessie Mecklem, who made the first solo saxophone recordings in 1892, pictured with her father Henry Clay Mecklem.

regularly employed: many of the references to the saxophone in the *New York Times* during the late 1880s and 90s refer to performances either by her or Lefebre.

Lefebre's influence as a teacher also extended to pedagogic publications. He composed original works and made transcriptions and arrangements that were published – by the Fischer company – in both Europe and the United States. These comprised typical fare for aspiring wind players of the time: operatic arias and sets of variations, light classics and other popular works. In the early 1900s these were augmented by a small number of arrangements for saxophone quartet, a medium that had achieved some popularity in the US by this time in part because of Lefebre's advocacy of it.

Following Gilmore's death in 1892 many of his musicians, including Lefebre, joined a similar band being run by John Philip Sousa, the US Marine Band. Sousa had taken over the leadership of this band in 1880, and by the time Lefebre joined in February 1893 it was the pre-eminent professional band in the country. But a dispute over his salary meant that Lefebre left the band the following year, in February 1894; his place was taken by the Belgian-born Jean Moeremans (see p. 160).

From this point until his death in 1911 Lefebre pursued a freelance career. He worked as a consultant to the Conn company, the first American saxophone manufacturer, whose instruments he endorsed. This was particularly true of Conn's 'Wonder' saxophones, advertised by them from as early as 1892. Lefebre's association with the company led to him create The Conn Wonder Quartette from the mid 1890s, as well as contributing to saxophone instruction at the Conn Conservatory of Music from at least 1896; through this latter role he again demonstrated his influence on a number of saxophonists who would later go on to be recognised performers in their own right.[97] After resigning his consultancy position with Conn in 1901 Lefebre rebranded the Wonder Quartette into the Lefebre Quartette. Under its new name the group toured the USA and Canada from 1901 to 1903, reinforcing Lefebre's personal reputation and national influence; the group was later observed to be 'the first saxophone quartette of note to make a transcontinental tour'.[98]

Notwithstanding increasing deafness in his later years, Lefebre continued to give concerts into his seventies, a consequence, no doubt, of economic necessity as much as artistic motivation. On his death in 1911 he was widely identified as the most eminent saxophonist across America, and he had played a significant role in laying the groundwork for the rapid popularisation of the instrument that would shortly follow.

European military and wind bands

The nineteenth-century context in which the saxophone flourished most widely, and which also provided the best economic returns for Sax's business, was in larger mixed wind bands and particularly military bands. Such bands were already undergoing transformation in the early part of the nineteenth century, moving towards instrumental combinations divided into homogenous families rather like orchestras (hence the later description 'symphonic wind band'). The implementation of valve technology for brass instruments and the timbral homogeneity arising from this were important aspects of this evolution. Sax's own predilection for developing instruments as homogenous families accelerated such changes, and the saxophone family took its place relatively quickly – albeit more often in theory than in practice – as a new but significant addition to many of these bands, particularly those in France or under French influence.

In the second half of the century the proliferation of military bands was matched by increasing popular interest in their activities, and particularly in the competitions and exhibitions in which such bands engaged. This in turn stimulated the formation of civilian wind bands in numerous towns and cities, many of whom took part in specially organised competitions. These bands took a variety of forms, and were inevitably rather less standardised in their instrumentation than their military equivalents, but saxophones were included if sufficiently enthusiastic performers could be found. In France, for example, these groups were largely divided into two types: *fanfares*, which were essentially brass bands with saxophones sometimes added, and *harmonie* bands, assembled from a more diverse range of wind, brass and percussion instruments. These became widespread in the mid- to late nineteenth century, with almost every French municipality proud of its own particular band. Their popularity led Sax to assemble his own group, which offered him an advertisement for his instruments, and one which would remain largely under his control. His *Grande société d'harmonie* gave a number of public concerts from 1853 onwards, with programmes comprising the now familiar mix of operatic extracts and items of solo virtuosity. In this particular case Sax had organised the ensemble along the lines of his proposed reorganisation of the Garde Impériale, and this further suggests that the group was being used as a shop window not only for his instruments, but also for his views on the correct instrumentation for such ensembles. A quartet of saxophones (SATBs) comprised an important part of this instrumentation, and the increasing number of named saxophone players is testament to the gradually expanding pool of trained performers from which Sax was able to draw. Their performances drew admiring comments from various critics, with the *RGMP* observing that 'nothing is more marvellous than the effect produced with these instruments, above all the saxophones [. . .]. M. Lecerf was strongly appreciated in the various solos on the alto saxophone, as was M. Auroux on the soprano.'[99]

Sax's expertise in the instrumentation of large wind ensembles did not go unnoticed by the then London-based Jullien. In 1856 Jullien developed, with Sax's assistance, a model military band which he toured under the name of the *Zouaves*, and which he hoped would impress the English military authorities sufficiently to encourage them to reform their ensembles as the French had done a few years previously (an aspiration doubtless shared by Sax and those English companies licensed to import his instruments). Sax's influence upon the instrumentation of the band was evident, comprising as it did numerous saxhorns and a full complement of five saxophones. Jullien wrote of his delight at the superior qualities of this group, and particularly of one player named Demange, whom he described as 'a bass, or rather, double bass saxophone player of prodigious talent'.[100] Further evidence of the connection with Sax may be inferred from Jullien's advertising of a similar group in 1858 as the *Société d'harmonie universelle*.[101]

But it was with military music-making that Sax mostly concerned himself. His victory on the Champs du Mars and the French government's decree that his plans for military bands should be implemented meant that saxophones became slowly more common in French military ensembles from 1845 onwards. Although initially set at only 2 saxophones per infantry band, by 1854 these had been considerably expanded to a double quartet. Although the numbers of musicians in French infantry bands were reduced from 57 to 40 by Government decree in 1860, the saxophones retained their place, and it might reasonably be assumed that by this time they were established constituents of a range of French military ensembles. Distribution was uneven, however, in part because of the initial lack of skilled players, the rescoring of extant repertoire required to incorporate new instruments, and the sometimes distant places in which military ensembles would be garrisoned, far from the influence of their Parisian masters. Notwithstanding the formal rhetoric, therefore, the deployment of saxophones in military bands was for many years inconsistent.

Nevertheless, military music provided an extremely important market for Sax and his competitors. In 1860 Pontécoulant estimated that there were 229 regiments requiring supplies of musical instruments, the latter being valued at more than 1.1 million francs; one estimate suggests that this amount would have been spent every five years on replenishing these supplies, given the average working life of a military instrument.[102] Because of the economic consequences, therefore, the further substantial reductions in the provision of French military music in 1867 provoked a notable backlash, not least from Sax himself, who was sufficiently concerned at the threat to his livelihood that he published an essay that year titled 'De la nécessité des musiques militaires'.[103] But certain flagship French military bands were spared from such economies. The protection afforded to these bands arose in large part because of the Paris Exhibition of 1867, at which an international competition was staged between invited international bands. France was naturally keen that it should be able to display large and competent ensembles at this event, and the bands of both the Guides de la Garde Impériale and the Garde républicaine de Paris took part. The instrumentation of these and other bands participating in this event allows us some insight into the patterns of dissemination of the saxophone at this time.

Table 6: Disposition of saxophones among the various bands competing at the Paris Exhibition of 1867 (adapted from Neukomm 1889).[104]

	Austria	*Baden*	*Bavaria*	*Belgium*	*France (Guides)*	*France (Garde)*	*Netherlands*	*Prussia*	*Russia*	*Spain*
Soprano	0	0	0	1	1	2	1	0	1	0
Alto	0	0	0	1	2	2	1	0	2	0
Tenor	0	0	0	1	1	2	1	0	2	0
Baritone	0	0	0	1	1	2	1	0	3	0
Bass	0	0	0	0	1	0	0	0	0	0

The lack of a bass in most of these sections demonstrates already how far removed was the role of the saxophone from Sax's original intentions for the instrument (as well as the impracticality of having in a marching band an instrument of the size originally conceived). Nevertheless, such a table can be misleading, and should not be taken to represent the position relating to all military bands in the countries represented. As with the French groups, these were showcase bands, demonstrating the best that any given country had to offer, and the inclusion of saxophones in other ensembles is likely to have been considerably more inconsistent, as well as varying greatly according to time and place. By 1884, for example, French infantry bands in general were listed as having only a single saxophone quartet,[105] although the Garde républicaine apparently continued to be considered a showpiece ensemble, retaining in 1889 the services of nine saxophones, albeit in a revised disposition of S/2A/3T/2B.[106]

In 1863 Hanslick had observed that the saxophone was little known in Germany, and that it was often confused with the saxhorn.[107] His assessment is borne out by the notable absence of saxophones in any of the Germanic bands at the 1867 exhibition, most likely because of Wilhelm Wieprecht's antipathy towards Sax and his instruments, and his influence on the organisation of military music in these countries. This state of affairs persisted for much of the nineteenth century and beyond. Although there is evidence of saxophone players in certain garrison towns around the turn of the century, saxophones did not become standard in German and Austrian military bands until a section (S/2A/T/B) was added to the Luftwaffe music corps in 1940.[108]

It is curious that the Spanish band in the competition is listed as having no saxophones since there is some evidence the saxophone was quickly assimilated into bands there. In 1852 the *RGMP* noted that the Spaniards, 'who search for and enjoy new musical effects, are passionately fond of this beautiful invention' and that 'most of their music is already provided with three or four saxophones in different keys'.[109] Even allowing for journalistic hyperbole the assertion is striking; saxophones were certainly available from a dealer in Madrid from at least 1857.[110] Similarly, Hartmann's saxophone method of 1846 has instructions in both French and Spanish, suggesting that the publisher thought there would be a Spanish market for the method, as had been the case with the ophicléide method on which it was clearly based. Thus their omission from this particular Spanish band line-up is possibly misleading. August Kalkbrenner, writing in 1884, noted that by then Spanish bands were including a double saxophone quartet (2S/2A/2T/2B), which would have been more in keeping with the *RGMP*'s earlier view.[111]

No Italian bands were present at the competition, although an 1850 Italian treatise on instrumentation by Antonio Tosoroni lists a potential family of 14 instruments, replicating information distributed by Kastner and Sax.[112] It is unlikely that the saxophone appeared in any Italian bands at this early juncture. The instrument is not listed in any of Tosoroni's models for various ensembles, suggesting that not only was he unsure how to score for it but also that it had yet to feature in any of them. The saxophone had been demonstrated by the clarinettist and maker Giovanni Bimboni at Florence's Accademia Filarmonica early in 1848.[113] But when Rossini included parts for saxophones in his 1868 *La Corona d'Italia*, written for military band and offered as a gift to King Victor Emmanuel II, the instruments had to be specially ordered from Paris for the first performance.[114]

No English bands were permitted to take part in the 1867 contest, but in fact the saxophone had appeared in them at an early stage. Henry Farmer records that:

> I can show from a list of the Royal Artillery Band in 1848 [. . .] that Henry Rigby was playing the saxophone in the band in that same year. I possess two programmes of the Band performing at Newcastle in September, 1855, which feature Rigby as a saxophone soloist, whilst the Band Fund Accounts, R.A., for the 1856–57 season prove that the band was in possession of two Alto and two Tenor Saxophones.[115]

This reference to a saxophonist in the Royal Artillery band in 1848 predates Soualle's performances in London under Jullien by two years. But more widespread adoption was slow to follow. The level and quality of military music provision in England lagged behind that of both Germany and France, although the creation in 1857 of a military music class at Kneller Hall (later the Royal Military School of Music) was designed to counter this. A further indication of the renewed seriousness with which the British Army viewed military music provision was the increase in size of the Royal Artillery Band (the country's leading military ensemble) from 43 to 74 players by 1863; saxophones, however, were no longer included.[116]

The increasing importance of Kneller Hall as an English military-music training establishment meant that its Director wielded considerable influence. Charles Mandel's appointment to the post in 1859 led him to publish that same year an extensive treatise on military band instrumentation that shows remarkable prescience and understanding of the potential use of the saxophone.[117] Whereas Kastner (1844) was only able to speculate on the instrument's use (since it was still under development), Mandel writes imaginatively of the possibilities the saxophone offered, suggesting that he was quite familiar with scoring for it, while at the same time retaining a somewhat dismissive attitude to the instrument:

> Except that is has a similar reed and mouthpiece, the saxophone does not bear the slightest resemblance to the clarionet, either in its compass, which is more like that of the oboe, or in its sound, which resembles a seraphim [. . .]. Its principal use should be limited to simple, choral-like melodies, and harmony; and, for this purpose, one saxophone alone cannot well be employed, but three, four, or, if possible, five, in different keys [. . .]. In extreme cases, however, the B flat soprano-saxophone may serve to replace the oboe, and the E flat alt-saxophone, the E flat alt-horn. The tenor-saxophone and the bass-saxophone have so peculiar and distinct a sound, that they cannot be employed as substitutes for any other instruments. In pieces for reed bands taken from operas, – as, for instance, Verdi's *Trovatore*, etc. – where there is an organ on the stage, the part for that instrument would, if arranged, in reed band, for four or five saxophones (pitched in various keys), produce a characteristic effect, although the same result might be obtained from flugel horns and trombones. Thus, the saxophone is only employed in reed bands of fifty performers and upwards, for the purpose of imparting greater variety

to the character of the general tone. In smaller bands, the use of it, in the place of other more practical instruments, would be attended with more disadvantage than advantage. It might be employed now and then, perhaps; but in that case, some of the performers would be burdened with two instruments.[118]

Despite Mandel's qualified advocacy, the saxophone did not become a regular constituent of English military bands for many years. Kalkbrenner's 1884 list shows a standard English band as having no saxophones, reinforcing an observation in the *Musical Times* of 1890 that the instrument had been 'little used in English bands until recently'.[119] Saxophones were eventually standardised in British military bands at a Kneller Hall conference in 1921, which decreed that one alto and one tenor instrument should be considered the minimum in any band with over twenty-five members.[120]

The saxophone's slow penetration into English bands provides a clear example of the difficulties of dissemination elsewhere in Europe and the USA: not only were there relatively few trained players, but many bandmasters considered there to be little gained by employing saxophones, because of the considerable amount of additional work involved in integrating them into existing repertoire. Band parts in the nineteenth century were not, on the whole, commercially printed and then distributed; they were largely bespoke, hand-written for a particular band, with instrumentation to match the available players. Integrating a new family of instruments such as the saxophone would have necessitated the rescoring of a considerable amount of material, together with the production of a new set of parts. The point was eloquently made by Kappey in his 1894 history of military music:

> As a military band instrument [the saxophone] is of great value when employed in a complete choir of soprano, alt[o], tenor, and bass, as its tone forms an admirable tonal link between reeds and brass. But the difficulty is, that such addition would render all the music hitherto accumulated, and which is arranged according to the prescribed regulation, useless. The loss of the large repertoire of many years' growth would far outweigh any gain from the adoption of the saxophone. As the compass of the saxophone is not very great – two octaves and two or three notes more – it is impossible to utilise it for the clarinet parts, which all require larger range. The addition of a 'set' would necessitate the great labour of writing parts for every piece desired by the conductor.[121]

George Miller's 1912 treatise *The Military Band* similarly warned aspiring orchestrators that saxophones could be employed for 'solo, melodic, or accompanying purposes; but it must be remembered that unhappily their use is not universal in our bands, and therefore they can only be allotted *ad libitum* parts'.[122]

As the nineteenth century progressed, however, the saxophone made slow but steady progress in the regular instrumentation of military bands. In particular, the colonial activities of several west European countries necessarily required the posting of military ensembles abroad, and these provided significant mechanisms through which the saxophone became more widely known. Notwithstanding the isolated international concerts given by performers such as Soualle and Lefebre, it was military music-making that began to make the saxophone more recognisable around the globe. International competitions and trade exhibitions also contributed to an increasingly globalised environment in which musical instruments such as the saxophone were disseminated as part of trans-national cultural flows. Gradually the instrument was adopted by band musicians far from the centres of western Europe. By 1884, for example, at least one Japanese band had as many as ten saxophones;[123] by 1885 the Mexican National Band is listed as having nine;[124] and by 1898 the 'Famous Military Band of Manila' in the Philippines was using eleven.[125] In Australia the New South Wales Police Band ordered its first set of saxophones in 1899, for the princely sum of £48.[126] Such examples provide evidence for the gradual dissemination of the saxophone around the world, and its developing profile and popularity. This was in turn reinforced by emigrant tradesmen seeking to establish themselves in these new environments, in order to service both military and civilian populations; Thomas Turrell, for example, was advertising saxophones as being 'in stock' in his warehouse in Auckland, New Zealand, as early as 1873.[127] But while European colonialism was undoubtedly significant for the introduction of the saxophone to some of the more far-flung corners of the globe in the late nineteenth century, it was the professional bands in the United States that were to prove most important with respect to its long-term development.

Bands in the United States

Military bands had been common in the United States since the mid-eighteenth century, expanding through the early part of the nineteenth century in both size and number. In the mid 1830s, partly in response to financial constraints and partly because of the introduction of valve technology, many bands became all-brass groups, eliminating the few reed instruments employed. During the American Civil War (1861–5) the number of bands again increased significantly, and although some included fifes, piccolos, and clarinets, with percussion instruments common, reed instruments remained in the minority. These bands were usually amateur, and the saxophone's absence arose not only because of widespread unfamiliarity with the instrument but also because of its relative expense. Saxophones were more complex to produce than the keyed bugles and similar instruments favoured by many amateur musicians, and were not manufactured in the United States until Conn started making them around 1888. All instruments therefore needed to be imported from Europe, adding to their cost. Even among those few musicians who knew of the saxophone, the price of acquiring one would often have been prohibitive.

Thus what progress the saxophone made in North America from the 1860s to the 1880s was largely related to the development of professional bands. These bands built on the success of Jullien's forays to the United States in 1853–4, and his large ensembles can be seen as the progenitors of an American professional band tradition that was to provide the most secure footing for saxophone in the latter part of the century. Such bands were remarkably popular over this period, often utilising large numbers of musicians and touring across the country, using the rapidly developing railroad network that serviced the growing urban centres. Harvey Dodworth appears likely to have been the first American bandleader to have introduced a saxophone, for his concert series given at New York's Central Park from 1858 onwards. In an 1873 interview he reflected on his reasons for introducing the instrument:

> I wanted to build up a popular taste for music, and I had fancies, magnificent visions, of the possibility of creating a splendid band – one which should rival the great band of the Guard Mobile – or, as it has since been called, the Garde Républicaine, of Paris; one of 85 musicians, playing the best music and maintained by the City. I imported two circular B♭ basses, a saxophone, and tenor clarionet expressly for these Central Park concerts. I looked forward to the time when from that beginning I should see developed a military band, built upon the orchestra principle of a full diapason of reeds, from top to bottom, to take the place of strings, the color tones to be supplied by the other instruments accordingly.[128]

Dodworth here touches upon several themes in relation to the saxophone that would be important for the remainder of the nineteenth century: the increasing popularisation of light classical music, particularly by professional bands, and the new audiences drawn to it; the saxophone's contribution to this popularisation, starting from a relatively peripheral role, but eventually leading to renowned soloists such as Lefebre achieving significant musical prominence; the symphonic aspirations of those creating a repertoire for the concert band, with the homogeneity of the saxophone family ultimately providing a distinctive part of the available timbral palette; and the significant influence of European models in band instrumentation and structure. Furthermore, the prevalence of European-trained saxophonists in many of these bands would provide another conduit through which European musical practice was transplanted to the United States. As in Europe, however, the saxophone took some time to become widely accepted, and for many of the same reasons: lack of familiarity, costs of acquiring the instrument, lack of skilled players, and the difficulty of accepting new instruments in contexts where a significant amount of hand-written music was already extant. Not until the 1870s were saxophones to become a regular feature of an American band, and their inclusion is due to that most famous of American bandmasters, Patrick Sarsfield Gilmore.

Like Jullien before him, Gilmore was as much an impresario and promoter as he was a bandmaster, and he was as fond as the Frenchman of mounting spectacular events with numerous participants. After successfully promoting band festivals in 1864 and 1869, he organised an International Peace Jubilee in Boston in June 1872, which involved bands from the United States, Britain, Germany, Ireland and, crucially, the French band of the Garde républicaine. On their arrival in the US it was observed that the Garde band included six saxophones.[129] On 20 June they performed a typically mixed programme including Rossini's overture to *William Tell* and Meyerbeer's *Fackeltanz*. The *Boston Evening Transcript* noted particularly 'those smooth saxophones, of which they play quite a number, transmitting tones of about the quality of a body of strings.'[130] Further concerts followed as part of the Jubilee, and then in Chicago, where the programme included the overture to Weber's *Oberon*. A critic of the *Chicago Tribune* noted that 'the Overture to *Oberon* had a nice solo for saxophone, the best yet assigned to that charming instrument, and a similar prominence was given it in the *Invitation to the Waltz.*'[131] The particular combination of saxophones used by the Garde band is not clear, but after a successful six weeks or so they returned to Paris. Yet their visit to Boston can be seen as indicative of the increasingly globalised environment in which such bands were now operating, with obvious consequences for the transmission of ideas on performance practice and approaches to scoring for instruments such as the saxophone.

Gilmore went on to form in 1873 the New York 22nd Regiment National Guard Band, a professional ensemble composed of many of the best musicians available to him. In due course this became the most highly respected band in America. Gilmore, undoubtedly influenced by the Garde républicaine's instrumentation, incorporated a number of saxophonists in the band, including Lefebre. It seems likely that he initially introduced just a quartet of saxophones; a programme for a concert at the Brooklyn Academy of Music in 1874 included a performance of Singelée's *Andante and Allegro* for saxophone quartet (S/A/T/B). These were also the saxophones Gilmore employed in his European tour of 1878. Gilmore was obviously pleased with the contribution of the saxophone family to the band's sound, and gradually expanded the section (see ill. 50). He enjoyed music-making on a large scale; notwithstanding his earlier extravaganzas, as early as 1875 his 'normal' band numbered 100 musicians, performing at the eponymous Gilmore's Concert Garden in New York. In September 1884 *Harper's Weekly* asserted that he was by then using a sextet of S/A/2T/B/Bs,[132] while at the St Louis Exposition in September 1892 he employed no less than 10 saxophones, distributed as Sn/2S/2A/2T/2B/Bs.[133]

Gilmore's band clearly provided an important platform for the saxophone in the 1870s and 80s, but not all his contemporaries were so enthused by the instrument. One 1889 commentator observed that Gilmore had 'always been an experimentalist, and is progressive in his theories concerning instrumentation. Unlike Signor Cappa and other great bandmasters, he believes in the employment, where permissible, of saxophones'.[134] Nevertheless, there were others happy to accommodate the instrument: Adolphe Neuendorff included four saxophones in his band of 43 musicians in 1880; the Fred Innes band included a quintet in 1887, and another band of his included a A/T/B trio in 1894; the short-lived Liberati band of 1883 featured F. A. Maginel as saxophone soloist; and so forth.[135] By the early 1890s, therefore, an ensemble of saxophones was common in many professional bands in the USA, and the instrument was fully established on American soil.

Just as the enthusiasm for military bands in Europe stimulated a growth in amateur music-making and the formation of *harmonie* and brass bands, so the success of professional American ensembles promoted interest among amateur bandsmen in the USA. And although the professional bands had an important role as cultural standard-bearers throughout the country from about 1875, because of their touring activities, they comprised only a small part of American musical life in rural areas that were far from the reach of the railways. In such places orchestras were rare, professional bands only occasional visitors, and homespun entertainment provided the central focus of musical activity. Following the end of the civil war in 1865, town bands in particular had proliferated, providing a focus for burgeoning civic pride in expanding communities, as well as musical functionality for parades and celebrations. One estimate suggests there were ten thousand so-called 'military' bands across the country in 1889 – the description 'military' being a reflection of their instrumentation rather than their status, since these were largely civic or corporate bands – and double that number by the turn of the century.[136] Many of these, remaining true to their Civil War roots, comprised only brass instruments. But as the century progressed woodwind instruments became more common. A typical band of perhaps twenty musicians in 1889 might comprise 65 per cent brass and 35 per cent woodwind;[137] but saxophones were again rare, their inclusion still held up through a lack of familiarity with the instrument and a lack of available music with parts for saxophone. There were exceptions: the Elgin Watch Factory Band of 1890, for example, was unusual in that reeds – including four saxophones – and strings outnumbered the brass instruments. As in several other cases, a European connection appears to have more quickly facilitated the introduction of saxophones in this band: the German-born bandmaster of the time, Joseph Hecker, had been a regimental bandmaster in England prior to migrating to the USA and Canada. The Parlin & Orendorff Company Band in Canton, Illinois also included saxophones from at least 1890. In general, however, the surviving pictorial evidence confirms that the saxophone was an uncommon addition to these amateur bands until the early twentieth century.[138]

After Gilmore's death in 1892 his mantle passed to the renowned John Philip Sousa. Sousa was an excellent all-round musician. Enormously successful as a bandleader, composer of light music (particularly marches and operettas), and musical entrepreneur, Sousa had used saxophones in the bands he directed from the early 1880s, and like Gilmore he contributed greatly to establishing the saxophone as an integral part of band instrumentation. Sousa had made his reputation as conductor of the US Marine Band, but was persuaded to resign from this ensemble and form a professional civilian band under his own name in September 1892. This band became one of the most well-known musical ensembles in the world in the early years of the twentieth century, and from its inception Sousa included saxophones in the instrumentation. Initially he used the same disposition of saxophones as he had in the Marine Band (A/T/B), with Gilmore's star saxophonist Lefebre taking over the alto

52.   The Elgin Watch Factory Band, sometime in the early 1890s.

position in 1893. By the time of his first European tour, in 1900, Sousa was using as many as five saxophones in a combination of 2A/2T/B, although four saxophones in an S/A/T/B combination appears to have been more usual.[139]

Sousa is an important figure in the dissemination and development of the saxophone in the late nineteenth and early twentieth centuries. His band and his music were remarkably popular at home and abroad, and the touring he undertook, in which he promoted the saxophone as both a solo and an ensemble instrument, would have introduced it to many who had not heard it before, or had not heard it so imaginatively and competently employed. He was profoundly patriotic, and a sense of 'American-ness' permeated both his compositions and the work of his band; his well-known march *Stars and Stripes Forever* (1896) provides an obvious example. By implication therefore, in the eyes and ears of those who heard the band and who were perhaps unfamiliar with the saxophone's European roots, the instrument itself would have been more closely identified with America, its musicians and its music – a not unreasonable association given the saxophone's success in its adopted country compared to its decline in Europe.

Sousa was a firm believer in musical variety and diversity, seeing these also as particularly American virtues, in contrast to what he construed as the national boundaries constraining much European music-making. He promoted virtuosity, employing expert soloists on a number of instruments – notably the renowned trombonist Arthur Pryor – and among his roster he recruited many of the best saxophone soloists of the time, even after Lefebre's resignation in 1894. By highlighting these saxophonists alongside other distinguished soloists he drew attention to the virtuosic potential of the instrument, as well as contributing to the development of performance standards on the saxophone itself. He promoted the saxophone section of the band – which later occasionally numbered as many as 10 – as a chamber ensemble in its own right, and they would give concerts by themselves away from the main band events. This was particularly true of the saxophone 'Octette' that was frequently featured during the concerts of the mid 1920s. Sousa also embraced the new technology of sound recording at an early stage, and made numerous recordings, thus producing some of the earliest surviving saxophone music on record (the saxophone section from his band recorded on the Victor label as early as August 1902, but there were many recordings undertaken prior to this by the band as a whole). He even composed an original piece for saxophone and band, *Belle Mahone* (1885), performed on several occasions by Jean Moeremans; unfortunately the work appears lost. The gradual emancipation of the saxophones as an independent section within a larger ensemble can also be seen in Sousa's scores through the early part of the twentieth century, even though he never ultimately treated them as a completely autonomous group.[140] One indicator of Sousa's influence on the development of American musical culture is that the 2A/2T/B combination of instruments he sometimes preferred would become almost universally employed in American swing bands of the 1930s and 40s, and the close harmony he occasionally scored for them would become an iconic twentieth-century musical sonority. Many of these points will be returned to in Chapter 4, since Sousa was an important contributor to the expansion of American popular music-making in the first quarter of the twentieth century.

By the end of the nineteenth century musicians such as Gilmore, Lefebre and Sousa had ensured that the saxophone was more familiar in the eyes and ears of many Americans than it was for most Europeans. The instrument was officially added to army bands as a result of an Act of Congress in 1899, an event that further expanded the market for the increasingly well-established American saxophone manufacturing industry. Nevertheless, few could have predicted just how popular and identifiable the instrument would become over the next three decades, as it was caught up in the enormous growth of American popular music in the early twentieth century.

Chapter 4

Early twentieth-century light and popular music

Vaudeville, circuses, minstrelsy and ragtime

It was the adoption of the saxophone in various popular genres around the turn of the twentieth century that introduced the instrument to a wider audience and gave it a more diverse profile. It became increasingly common among variety and vaudeville entertainers in the United States, and was also employed by band musicians supporting travelling circuses. In all these contexts it was often the essential novelty of the instrument, its unfamiliar sound and shape, that made it attractive. Variety entertainers were especially keen to emphasise this novelty. The *New York Clipper*, a predecessor to *Variety* magazine, advertised one duo who in 1891 offered 'a great variety of instruments including Trombone, Cornet, Staff Bells, Clarionet, Saxophone, Hand Bells, Musical Glasses, Violin, Guitar, Sleigh Bells, etc.'; an 1892 act which augmented its musical display on saxophones and assorted brass instruments with a novelty unicycle display; and an agent touting in 1893 for business for 'Henry Kniep's Saxaphone and Mandoline Quartet'; and so forth.[1]

The contexts in which many of these early variety turns appeared were often rowdy, even bawdy occasions deemed inappropriate for family participation. Thus from the early 1880s a New York impresario named Tony Pastor instigated a move towards more wholesome events. Such were the beginnings of the vaudeville circuits that were to become mainstays of North American entertainment either side of 1900, until their rapid demise during the Great Depression. Building on variety's twin traits of showmanship and novelty, and eschewing the need for the flimsy plots that sometimes characterised other forms of entertainment, vaudeville shows provided a chance for acts to demonstrate their prowess on new–fangled instruments. Thus Frank Mudge, described after his death in 1942 as 'the originator of the saxophone solo as a feature in vaudeville', began on the vaudeville circuits in 1896, and in 1905 Miss Nellie Graham, part of Gray and Graham's 'eccentric comedy musical act' felt able to offer 'wonderful work on the largest saxophone in the world'.[2] From its inception in 1905 *Variety* magazine listed various performers utilising the instrument, such as Newell and Niblo offering saxophone, violin and xylophone in 1906,[3] Garden and Somers, the 'World's Greatest Xylophonists' who also played trombone and saxophone in their act,[4] or Harry Batchelor, 'The Musical Rube' who in 1910 was deemed to be 'Positively the World's Greatest Saxophone Player.[5]

53. Variety act Newell and Niblo.

Acts featuring the saxophone were not confined to white performers. The *New York Age*, an influential African-American newspaper, carried advertisements for a variety of black entertainers, such as Mazie Moore, pictured with her flute and saxophone in 1912.[6] As the new century progressed the number of adverts for such acts multiplied, demonstrating the increasing use and dissemination of the saxophone in these contexts. Vaudeville shows were usually itinerant, moving across the country from one theatre to another, with each event seeking to entice a paying audience on the strength of the reputation or exoticism (or both) of its turns. Through such channels, in part, was the saxophone slowly but surely brought to the attention of the American public.

Nor was this pattern of dissemination confined only to the United States. The music hall circuits of Britain, continental Europe and beyond provided similar outlets for the instrument. The novelty of an all-women group including a saxophone possibly underpinned the success of The Biseras, for example, an ensemble of eight female multi-instrumentalists who toured the music hall circuits of Europe around the 1900s. Pictures from as early as 1905 show them including a saxophone among assorted other brass instruments and a side drum, in apparent imitation of a small marching band.[7] Similarly, The Elliotts were a novelty cycling act who also appeared as the 'Musical Savonas', in which guise they would play 50 instruments between them. Several of their publicity photographs show them dressed in faux eighteenth-century costumes, with each member of the seven-piece group holding a saxophone. The incongruity of the costumes and the instruments were doubtless intended to appeal to the public's taste for novelty and exotica in such contexts. The Elliott Savonas were heard on both sides of the Atlantic in the 1890s and 1900s; they appeared, for example, at the Olympia Music Hall in New York as early as 1896.[8]

Vaudeville circuits offered only one series of outlets for these multi-instrumentalists. Similarly itinerant were the circuses that criss-crossed the United States, and these provided considerable work for musicians of the period. They took their own performance spaces with them and often followed a fixed and predetermined route; whereas a vaudeville act might move once or twice a week, circuses and their bands could move every night. The daily routine for circus musicians was more arduous than for those in vaudeville. The day would begin with a parade through the town to attract attention, then perhaps a promenade concert provided for the audience as they filed in, followed by several hours of music to accompany the main show, which

54. The Elliott Savonas endorsing Buffet saxophones early in the twentieth century.

would normally be presented twice and might also be followed by a smaller after-show event. Circus musicians and their instruments needed to be very resilient to meet such demands, but the saxophone was ideally suited to this kind of work. It was reasonably robust, loud enough to project in the open air and the big top, comparatively easy to learn, could adequately cover a variety of musical styles, and was less physically tiring to play than trumpet or trombone.

Although take-up was initially slow, the saxophone did begin to make an impact, both musically and – at least as important – visually. One of the key moments of the circus day was the assembly on the bally, a platform outside the big top where performers would endeavour to attract the attention of potential audience members by creating a noisy spectacle (the ballyhoo). Here the unfamiliar sight and sound of the saxophone could be put to good effect. The trumpet player Leonard Phillips described his own contributions to a circus band ballyhoo in the 1920s: 'All the show would come out on the bally [. . .] the band too. They've got a big platform, you'd come out there and the band would play [. . .]. The people would be standing around on the ground looking [. . .] and they've got a spieler who would tell them about the show'.[9] In such contexts it is easy to understand how the unfamiliar saxophone might attract attention, or have attention drawn deliberately to it. Billy Young, father of the jazz player Lester Young, worked as a circus bandsman for a number of years in the 1920s, and used deliberately to hold his saxophone upside down as a means of attracting attention.[10] Another writer observed in a slightly different context that 'one of the first minstrel shows using the saxophone was Gorten's Golden Band Minstrels, and the crowd would usually gather open-mouthed and listen to the saxophone, being so unusual they attracted general notice.'[11] Thus the visual impact the saxophone created, with its new and unusual shape, was undoubtedly a factor in its adoption in a variety of popular genres.

The larger circuses carried with them numerous musicians. Pictures of the Ringling Brothers' circus parades during the period 1904–9 show at least four bands, one of which is on horseback, while the 1912 parade included five bands of between nine and fifteen musicians each.[12] Notwithstanding that the Ringling Brothers was one of the larger outfits, if the number of circuses in north America at the time is taken into account – eighty-nine in the 1901 season, for example[13] – it is clear that these provided employment for a substantial number of (usually young) musicians. While the names of many of these early circus saxophonists are lost, enough survive to illustrate that these were significant conduits of dissemination for the instrument in north America. In 1903 the Ringling Brothers were advertising Charlotte Rutherford as saxophone soloist in one of their sideshows, and had one F. Barney on their roster in 1905.[14] Tom Brown, who would go on to be the driving force behind the influential Brown Brothers saxophone ensemble, worked in various circuses in the early years of the century, and started on the baritone saxophone in 1904.[15] By the early 1920s the saxophone had become a mainstay of circus music-making. Billy Young's band, for example, comprised not only his son Lester, but also Lester's sister Irma – who would go on to become a fine jazz saxophonist in her own right – and two of their cousins and their wives, all of whom played the saxophone, among other instruments (see ill. 113).[16]

Yet including a new instrument such as the saxophone in these bands was not straightforward. Just as the symphony orchestra and the military band were based on a corpus of extant materials that militated against swift inclusion of new instruments such as the saxophone, so did the bespoke scores and parts used by circus musicians. Creating new parts and arrangements was an expense to be avoided if at all possible. If a musical director lost a particular instrumentalist, it was easier, for the sake of economic expediency, simply to replace him or her with an instrumentalist of similar type.

Minstrel shows also provided important musical outlets in North America during the nineteenth and early twentieth centuries. Blackface minstrelsy, a form of entertainment based on caricatures of African-American figures (an approach seen as less pernicious then than it is now), was an important component of this tradition. Whereas vaudeville owed much to the growing urban environments of turn-of-the-century America, and developed song repertoires that reflected this, minstrelsy remained characterised by rural images and songs. Reflecting these rural roots, the traditional instruments of the minstrel musician had been the banjo, fiddle and a variety of percussion instruments, although larger shows would employ more musicians and a wider variety of instruments.[17]

As with circuses, minstrel musicians worked hard, and followed a similar routine. Brian Klitz observes that a typical minstrel musician 'led the march to the town green that preceded the performance; played a concert, marched back to the hall and played a second concert to draw a crowd to the performance site, played the show itself [. . .] and finally played the post-performance concert.'[18] Musicians were again expected to be multi-instrumentalists and inevitably the saxophone began to make an appearance in some of these minstrel events. Minstrel troupes were less constrained by extant orchestrations, and preferred to write or arrange their own material for the instruments to hand. In his autobiography *Father of the Blues*, W. C. Handy recalls his use of a saxophone quartet during his leadership of the band of the Mahara's Minstrels, just after the turn of the century:

> In Chicago I picked up a quartet of saxophones who made the parade with us when we played Joliet, Illinois. I was featuring 'The Holy City' as a cornet solo and these saxophones contributed wonderfully to the religioso. That night I went to the box office and invited F. L. [Mahara] to come out and listen to my band concert with its remarkable reed section, only to find that my quartet of saxophones had left us [. . .]. Gone was my dream of scoring a sensation with a daring innovation, but I continued to encourage the use of the instruments.[19]

Handy's aspiration to create 'a sensation' underlines the point that, as in other contexts, the saxophone provoked welcome curiosity from the audience as well as fulfilling a range of musical duties.

The minstrel tradition declined in the early years of the twentieth century, before the saxophone achieved widespread popularity, and minstrelsy was overtaken by the more popular vaudeville shows (although individual minstrel acts could still be found within these). The saxophone was certainly part of this particular form of

American music-making but, with the sole exception of Tom Brown (of whom more below) – who drew upon the blackface minstrel tradition as an important part of his later act – minstrelsy itself was not, in fact, as important for the dissemination of the saxophone in the USA as were the other contexts in which the instrument could be found.

As American popular music moved towards the dance styles that would prove so successful in the 1910s and 20s, so the attraction of what was deemed to be 'syncopated' music took increasing hold in the popular imagination. In truth 'syncopation' became appended to almost any rhythmically vivacious music, but it was taken to be particularly characteristic of ragtime, and thus the word 'ragtime' was used to embrace almost any musical style that employed what was construed as syncopation. Although today ragtime is usually associated with particular piano pieces, especially those by Scott Joplin, at the end of the nineteenth century the description was applied more broadly, to cover so-called Coon Songs, arrangements of such songs for instrumental groups or bands, dance music or marches with high levels of syncopation, as well as a particular style of piano playing and associated repertory.[20] 'Ragging' music – even well-known classical tunes which non-literate pianists would learn by ear for precisely this purpose – became enormously popular in the years prior to the development of early jazz. An advertisement for a tutor titled 'The Rag-Time Saxophonist' by Kathryne E. Thompson in *The Metronome* in 1920 encourages the reader to 'learn to jazz on the saxophone', as well as suggesting that the book would provide 'a complete method on ragging the Saxophone'.[21] Such advertising copy demonstrates how the terms 'ragtime' and 'jazz' became conflated in the minds of many.[22] But this broader definition of 'ragtime' is significant for the development of the saxophone during this period, particularly since these syncopated musical styles underpinned the musical output of the most popular professional saxophone groups of the period from 1910 to 1930, and it was through these groups that, to a significant degree, the instrument was brought to the wider attention of the American public.

Early saxophone ensembles

Many of the earliest saxophone ensembles arose out of the multi-instrumental skills of the players involved, rather than being formed by saxophone specialists *per se*. The Elliott Savonas provide one example, and the Majestic Musical Four in 1903 similarly advertised themselves as a 'musical comedy act' playing not only saxophone quartet, but also quartets of brass, organ chimes and xylophones.[23] The group Klein, Ott Brothers and Nicholson were performing on 'Horns, Cornets, Trombones, Saxophones, Xylophones and Organ Chimes' at Broadway's New York Theatre and elsewhere in 1907.[24] Such groups were deliberately populist in orientation, and catered for the undemanding expectations of their vaudevillian audiences. In contrast, the 'New York' and 'Wonder' saxophone quartets formed by Lefebre in the late nineteenth century, and similar ensembles such as the American Saxophone Quartette, formed by saxophonists from the Sousa band in 1901, demonstrated to American audiences different musical possibilities offered by chamber groups comprised only of saxophones. These ensembles largely performed transcriptions of light classical repertoire, and the formal musical training their members had usually undertaken predisposed them to present their work as part of the 'legitimate' classical tradition. The American Quartette, for example, asserted in their advertising that their programmes were 'of high class, consisting of operatic and popular selections, which they render in a perfect manner'.[25]

The saxophone quartet proved to be surprisingly popular amongst professional and amateur performers alike in turn-of-the-century America. The in-house magazine of the C. G. Conn company listed a variety of ensembles around this time: the 'California Saxophone Quartette' formed by Frank Willard Kimball in 1896, was followed over the next decade by quartets in Cleveland, Ohio; Terre Haute, Indiana; Lebanon, Pennsylvania; Corydon, Iowa; and many more.[26] By 1905 the magazine was able to observe that 'Saxophone Quartettes are becoming the fashion. Even in the small towns where, perhaps, a band has not been organised, the Saxophone Quartette becomes a very popular musical organisation, always in demand.'[27] Their popularity continued to grow, and the same magazine boasted proudly in 1912 that 'Saxophone Quartettes have proven to be the most entertaining combination of reed instruments [...] and as a consequence quartettes are now being organised throughout the country'.[28] In many instances quartets would be formed within families, building on established Victorian traditions of parlour music. The Bohm family of Albion, Michigan, for example, created a quartet from brothers Albert, George and Gus, with their sister Mayta, in 1915 (see ill. 55). Pop Dorsey formed just such a quartet with his

55. The Bohm family saxophone quartet around 1915, in uniforms characteristic of band musicians of the period.

daughter Mary and both his sons Tommy and Jimmy around 1916; Jimmy would later become one of the saxophone stars of the dance band era.[29]

This widespread evidence of civic and domestic music-making based around small ensembles of saxophones demonstrates a social identity for the instrument that is different from both its largely military usage of the nineteenth century, and the overt reliance on novelty sounds and performance tricks that increasingly characterised the instrument in other contexts and with which it would become more closely associated in a few short years. For a while the saxophone was seen, like the piano, as connoting a sense of homespun respectability and shared community values, something that those who would shortly seek to vilify it appear quickly to have forgotten.

As the first two decades of the twentieth century unfolded, tensions between the different constituencies promoting the saxophone became increasingly manifest. On the one hand, growing familiarity with the instrument led to its widespread deployment in a range of popular music-making, and a developing identity as a 'fun' or 'novelty' instrument; on the other hand, there remained a group of committed and proficient performers who saw the instrument as a worthy addition to the orchestra or the concert stage, and who continued to argue for its accommodation in what they construed as a more serious classical tradition.

The tension between these two positions is evident in the work of Clay Smith and G. E. Holmes, multi-instrumentalists who worked in a variety of circuses, bands and minstrel shows before coming together to form a vaudeville company – the Apollo Concert Company – in 1905. In 1915 they left this group to form the Smith-Spring-Holmes Orchestral Quintet, whose subtitle 'The Company Artistic', indicates that the aspirations for the ensemble were rather different from the novelty-driven fare common on the vaudeville circuits. Instead, Smith and Holmes would target the Lyceum and Chautauqua institutions. These circuits comprised lectures and concerts or dramatic performances that took place either indoors, during the winter months (the Lyceum circuit), or in large tents on the outskirts of towns during the summer months (the Chautauqua circuit, which grew out of the Lyceum activities and which ran from the late nineteenth century through to the early 1940s). The initial intention behind both circuits was to provide community education, particularly in the more rural parts of America. Although over time the entertainment such events contained came to be more highly valued than the education they sought to provide, their loftier ambitions resulted in what the participants saw as more cultivated environments for musical performance.

In such contexts audiences would have perceived the saxophone and its music in a rather different light from that of the vaudeville circuits. Smith and Holmes were particularly keen to distinguish themselves from other vaudeville acts, positioning themselves as a rather more distinguished ensemble which sought to elevate public taste, especially in relation to the saxophone. In a letter to one manager Smith ordered that he should 'not let the word novelty appear in any of our advertising [. . .] there is no reason for the committeemen to get it into their heads that this is a novelty company [. . .]. Whenever [an] agent succeeded in talking this notion out of their heads we have always gone in and made big where they wanted high class music.'[30]

Smith and Holmes were convinced of the saxophone's potential as a serious instrument, and their influence upon its early development in America was furthered through a regular column they wrote for *The Dominant*, from July 1915 through to April 1924. These columns provide yet more evidence of their serious aspirations for the saxophone, as encapsulated in this observation made in 1917:

> The saxophone undoubtedly has its place in the orchestra and is worthy of being classed among the orchestral instruments, but it should be used properly and not abused and run in to take the place of every other legitimate instrument [. . .]. If played well it has a fine tone quality, which blends admirably with the modern orchestrations. But God save us from the hideous cat-calling that is so much in vogue at present termed 'Jassing.' The listener who hears some of these 'Jass' players and has never before heard a saxophone is liable to form some very erroneous opinions of the much talked of instrument [. . .]. Really, the 'Jasser' should be subject to the same quarantine restrictions as if he had the foot and mouth disease.[31]

Notwithstanding their occasional polemicism, Smith and Holmes's articles – they appear in fact to have been largely penned by Smith – served as important pedagogic material. They provided advice on tone development, articulation exercises, technique, reeds and equipment, and so forth, that would have been of great practical value for aspiring saxophone players of the time. Smith and Holmes were also active composers and arrangers for various ensembles involving saxophones. A sheet music cover from 1914 (see ill. 56) shows a substantial list of arrangements for saxophone quartet, including operatic extracts from Verdi, Wagner, Bizet and similar – indicative of their efforts to legitimise saxophone repertoire – with waltzes and other miniatures composed by Holmes.

Although Smith and Holmes endeavoured to move away from their vaudeville roots, as the century progressed other vaudevillians also began to conceive of themselves as saxophone specialists. Several of these groups offered mixed programmes of popular and light classical fare, such as the selections from Bizet's *Carmen* and similar that would comprise programmes by the Musical Cates. The Cates demonstrated, in their aspirations to move from small-time to big-time vaudeville circuits, a degree of showmanship that was emblematic of the age (see ill. 57). Thus they advertised themselves in August 1909 as 'America's Most Meritorious Musical Act', featuring the 'World's Greatest Saxophone Soloist' in Walter H. Cate.[32] Like others of the time, the Cates were keen to draw attention to anything that might be considered a novelty and which might thus offer an advantage over the competition. An advert taken out in *Variety* the following month announced, 'Just arrived from Paris, France, Two Mammoth Bass Saxophones, One B♭ Contra Bass, One Double E♭ Contra Bass, absolutely the largest saxophone and the deepest toned bass instrument in the world, also the only one of its size in the world. Height 6 ft 8 in. tall.' They then reminded readers that they also used the smallest saxophone made, in addition to having four extra-large xylophones.[33] The advert was provocative enough to elicit a response some weeks later from Gray and Graham, who were at pains to remind readers that Miss

56. Sheet music cover from 1914, listing some of the repertoire played by the Apollo Quartette.

Graham was in fact using 'the largest saxophone in the world', one which also measured 6 ft 8 in., and had been doing so for the previous eight years.[34] By now both
adverts were accompanied by pictures of the players and instruments concerned. Such
claims on behalf of the saxophone are reminiscent of those made for exhibits in a
travelling freak show, once again lending an exotic aura to the instrument, notwithstanding that advertising hyperbole of this kind – claiming the largest, smallest,
fastest, slowest, etc. – was perfectly normal for the time, and indicative of a general
approach among variety and vaudeville acts to draw attention to their own unique
selling point.

The Musical Spillers

Another saxophone group who achieved a high profile at this time were the Musical
Spillers. Originally a trio of singing, dancing, comic multi-instrumentalists, the
group's line-up later varied from five to thirteen players over the course of their

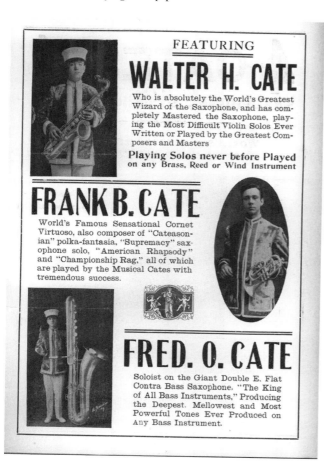

57. The Musical Cates, advertising in *Variety* on 18 February 1911, asserting that Walter H. Cate was 'absolutely the World's Greatest Wizard of the Saxophone'.

extensive career; at the height of their popularity they were performing as a group of six: three men and three women. Despite their versatile instrumental skills their act always contained a significant amount of work on saxophones, and it was frequently this that drew the attention of the critics; W. C. Handy claimed that it was the group's founder, William N. Spiller (1876–1944), who provided him with his first tenor saxophone in the early 1900s.[35] The Spillers were also keen to project what they felt to be their unique qualities, in this case their colour: 'Six Music Spillers, Greatest and Only Large Colored Musical Act in the World' ran their advertising in 1910, further informing that the group of 'Three pretty women and three men with plenty of classy wardrobe' offered 'original "rag time" music' involving six saxophones, three cornets, three trombones, and 'six hundred dollars worth of xylophones'.[36]

The use of the ragtime descriptor further underlines the importance of this style in the output of several of these early saxophone groups; for many people at this time the saxophone was most likely identified as a quintessentially ragtime instrument. The Spillers' press notices at home and abroad frequently drew attention both to their ragtime skills and the selection of light classical arrangements and ragtime music that was at the heart of their act: 'The talented negroes [. . .] created as much applause as any act on the bill. They play with equal ease, grace and correctness a selection

58.   The Six Musical Spillers.

from the Poet and Peasant and the St. Louis Rag';[37] 'The Six Musical Spillers have
an interesting mixture of rag-time and classical music, and prove extremely
entertaining'.[38]

Such was the affinity of the Spillers to ragtime that Scott Joplin prefaced his 1908
Pine Apple Rag with the words 'Respectfully dedicated to the Five Musical Spillers',
reflecting his close friendship with William Spiller, and the piece became a cornerstone of their routine. William Spiller also arranged excerpts from Joplin's opera
Treemonisha, thus presenting one of the first hearings of music from this historically
significant work. Whether this arrangement included saxophones is not clear, but it
seems highly probable. Spiller also shared some of Smith and Holmes's (and Joplin's)
aspirations to be seen as a 'serious' artist. Isabele Taliaferro (1888–1974), a female
member of the group who eventually married William Spiller,[39] later recalled that
he would resist the demands of theatre managers who told him to cut the classical
repertoire, but that they were subsequently 'amazed to hear the applause received after
the overture'.[40]

The Spillers toured prodigiously, and this itinerant lifestyle undoubtedly contributed to the increasingly high profile afforded to the saxophone. For the eighteen
months between November 1908 and July 1910, for example, the Spillers appear to
have had as few as nine weeks that cannot otherwise be accounted for with vaudeville
bookings. The list of states covered is impressive – Massachusetts, New York, Missouri,
Illinois, Wisconsin, Oregon and California.[41] – and while such a touring schedule

would have been common among many successful vaudeville acts at this time, it reinforces the importance of such circuits in bringing the saxophone to the attention of the wider American public. One can imagine the interest this still relatively unfamiliar yet distinctive instrument would provoke, as it arrived at the local theatre playing the latest fashionable, syncopated music.

The touring of the Spillers was not only confined to the USA and Canada, but also included Mexico, South America, Europe and Africa.[42] Unfortunately they were unable to gain the recording contract that their popularity deserved; this would have further increased their profile at the time, as well as providing a more substantial posthumous reputation. That they were not recorded is most likely due to the inherent racial discrimination of recording companies at the time. Very few African-American artists were able to make records before jazz became significantly commercialised from about 1918, and although the Spillers continued performing through the 1920s and, more sporadically, the 1930s, they were still unable to secure a recording deal. The Spillers were certainly distinctive among the largely white saxophone groups who dominated the vaudeville scene of the early 1900s, but while their skin colour provided them with useful advertising copy it also prevented them achieving greater recognition in other ways.

The Brown Brothers

Undoubtedly the most well known and influential of these early saxophone ensembles was the Six Brown Brothers, who achieved a higher profile than any of the other groups, both because of the popularity of their stage shows and through the numerous recordings they made.

The driving force behind the group was Tom Brown (1881–1950), the second oldest of seven siblings, of whom only one was a girl. All the children learned musical instruments, and the six brothers were all involved in musical entertainment for greater or lesser parts of their lives. The Six Brown Brothers did not always comprise these 'blood' brothers, but all six played with the group at some time, and there were four members – Tom, Alec, Vern and Fred – who were part of the group for most of its existence. They all fulfilled a variety of jobs in minstrel troupes and circuses in the first decade of the twentieth century, particularly with the Ringling Brothers Circus, for whom they worked extensively from probably 1904 through to 1909.[43] In 1908 they established what was then the Five Brown Brothers as a distinct entity. They made a small number of recordings in 1911 as a quintet, then expanded later that year to the sextet version with which they achieved their greatest successes; the Wall Street Crash of 1929 marked the beginning of their decline, and they disbanded in 1933 or 1934.[44]

The fundamental characteristics of the Brown Brothers' act – which several subsequent groups attempted to imitate – comprised low-brow musical compositions and arrangements with a significant proportion of lightly syncopated 'ragtime' material; a comedy routine that increasingly involved pantomime and visual gags rather than spoken material, supplemented by comic musical effects drawn from the saxophones by way of 'sobbing' and 'laughing' sounds, and similar; costumes that were initially military-band style but from 1914 gave way to more distinctive clown outfits; and the frontman Tom Brown, by way of acknowledging the group's minstrel roots, always appearing in blackface and, after the clown costumes had been adopted, oversized clownish boots.

It was a very successful combination, and made a good impression with reviewers from an early stage. Although they began as a multi-instrumental musical act – a 1910 advertisement lists saxophones, xylophones, steel organ chimes, novelty musical rattles, cornets, trombones and clarinets[45] – it was their saxophone work for which they became renowned. They made a particular impact through performing on the saxophones 'in one', that is, together at the front of the stage with a curtain down behind them (often covering scene changes for the following act). In 1911 *Variety* magazine observed that although the rest of their multi-instrumental act was routine, 'It is the work in "one" with the saxophones that makes them solid. The boys have wisely chosen selections and the way they can rip off "rag" on the instruments is a caution. The comedy is also good. They were forced to play themselves out before the audience was satisfied and even then they came back for three or four bows.'[46] A few months later the same magazine observed that the Brothers 'put on a battle royal with some rag music in "'one" that was right. They sparred with some comedy at first, but later scored a knock-out with those Saxophone "rags".'[47]

Reviews such as these reveal the growing popularity of the group, and would have reinforced perceptions of the saxophone as a characteristically ragtime instrument. They may also have been partly responsible for the Browns' decision to concentrate solely on saxophone work from about 1912. In 1914 they were put into the most successful show to open on Broadway that year, titled *Chin Chin*, a revue based very loosely around Chinese themes. The show occupied the Brothers for much of the period up to 1917, each year increasing their renown and profile in the various major

59.   Promotional image for the Brown Brothers, c. 1919.

cities to which it toured. By the time they moved on to other shows in the late 1910s and early 1920s they were a well-known and well-remunerated vaudeville act. In its endorsement of Buescher saxophones in 1921, the advertising copy noted that they earned 'the highest salary paid today for a musical act' and that 'the contrasting and harmonising tonal effects the Six Brown Brothers get from their sextette of gold-plated Buescher Saxophones surpass anything ever before associated with either the legitimate or the variety stage'.[48]

The Brown Brothers' reputation was further enhanced by the extensive recordings they made. From 1911 to 1917 they were the only saxophone group to be releasing recorded material, and their recording deals supplemented their income from live performance, as well as providing valuable publicity. This also made them valuable to promoters since the listening public's familiarity with the group through their recordings then led to larger audiences in the theatres where they were performing.[49]

None of the Brown Brothers would be regarded as virtuosi by today's standards, nor, indeed, by the standards of certain other players in the late 1910s. Their act relied not on individual virtuosity but on a carefully rehearsed routine that exploited the comic potential of the saxophone both sonically and visually. In their earliest 1911 recordings, made as a quintet, the instrumentation was 2A/T/B/Bs. The original sextet line-up, recorded in 1914–15, comprised 2A/T/2B/Bs, but this changed in 1916 to 2A/2T/B/Bs. Their ragtime style, with the musical texture anchored around the heavily articulated on-beat stabs of the bass saxophone, is often enlivened by comic effects: the bass made to sound like a bull frog, the clucking of farmyard hens in Tom Brown's alto line, or the occasional slightly drunk-sounding saxophone 'laugh' in some of the inner parts. All of these underline the important role that comedy played in the Brown Brothers routine, which led one reviewer to describe Tom Brown as being 'the melancholy one who stands apart and sobs with a saxophone and is funny beyond words'.[50]

So successful was the Brown Brothers' act that they engaged in a form of franchising, by organising satellite groups to which their name was attached; this was a common ploy among bandleaders with more engagements than they could reasonably discharge. Thus around 1916 Tom Brown authorised two other saxophone sextets – the 'Symphonic Sextette' and the 'Six Harvards' – and sought to entice the paying public to their concerts by advertising them as 'Tom Brown Presents . . .'. Like the Musical Spillers, the Brown Brothers also took full advantage of the increasing ease of international travel, touring the globe as ambassadors for American popular music in general and the saxophone in particular. They had already undertaken a successful tour of Britain in 1914, and added to this a coastal tour of Alaska in 1923 and a tour to Australia in the season 1923–4. The Brothers' performances were particularly successful in Australia, where vaudeville was still strong. In the United States, however, the success of the picture houses was rapidly diminishing the attraction of the vaudeville circuits; the stock market crash of 1929 and the ensuing depression effectively brought them to an end. The story of the Brown Brothers through the 1930s and 40s is an all too familiar one of previously successful artists struggling to make ends meet in their later years by taking a variety of non-musical and occasionally musical employment, and one or two failed business ventures. When Tom Brown died in 1950, the man whose influence on the dissemination of the saxophone during the first two decades of the twentieth century had been so profound was working as a night clerk in an obscure Chicago hotel.

The Brothers were successful enough to spawn a number of imitators: Billy Markwith had played with the Five Brown Brothers in 1909; he was the principal architect of 'The Saxo Sextette' and, like Tom Brown, appeared blackface in promotional photographs of the group in 1916; the Sextette recorded a number of sides for Columbia in 1916 and 1917, including a version of Tom Brown's *Bull Frog Blues*.[51] The Brown Brothers later took out an injunction against Markwith and an unrelated C. L. Brown, on the grounds that they were attempting to pass themselves off as the original Brown Brothers.[52] But there were many other groups attempting to replicate the Brown Brothers' formula, on both sides of the colour divide. The *New York Age* was advertising the African-American Byron Brothers saxophone quintet from at least 1914.[53] *The Musical Truth*, a house magazine for the Conn Corporation, featured a number of other imitators, such as The Six Nosses, photographed in clown outfits in 1917 with a line-up of S/3A/T/B, and the Kosair Temple Saxophone Sextette, from Louisville Kentucky, with a line-up of S/2A/T/B/Bs, who were also wearing polka dot clown costumes with cone hats.[54] The trend continued well into the 1920s, with the David J. Bolduc Saxophone Sextette, for example, still offering in 1925 'A Classy Attraction of Reputation and Merit backed by Years of Experience' from six similarly clown-garbed saxophone players (S/2A/T/B/Bs).[55]

This widespread association of the saxophone with comedy routines delivered by clownish instrumentalists undoubtedly established the instrument in the popular imaginary as both fun to play and funny to observe. While this certainly increased its popularity, it also provided those who later construed the saxophone as worthless or insubstantial with much ammunition for their cause, and it was to take many decades before the instrument finally divested itself of this reputation.

A saxophone craze?

The early decades of the twentieth century saw a significant growth in freestanding, large-scale saxophone groups in the United States, and a review of some of these demonstrates just how widespread was the use of the instrument by the mid 1910s, and how popular it had become with both amateur and professional musicians alike.

The first of these may have been O. P. Thayer's Saxophone Band in Rock Springs, Wyoming, advertised as 'The Most Unique Band of Wind Instruments in America' as early as 1902. The band comprised 18 saxophonists (4S/6A/4T/3B/Bs), in addition to two clarinettists, two drummers and a drum major. The band was the recipient in 1902 of the first bass saxophone made by the Conn company, who observed to Thayer that it was 'the largest saxophone ever manufactured and that the cost to produce it was a thousand dollars.'[56] While this is a particularly early example of a large saxophone group, by the mid-1910s they had proliferated throughout the country. In 1914 it was reported that 50 saxophonists had already been recruited for the hundred-strong ensemble planned as part of the Panama Pacific International Exposition in San Francisco in 1915;[57] a photograph of the Detroit Citigas Saxophone Band shows them

60.   Advertisement for the 110-piece Duane Sawyers Saxophone Band in *Metronome, April 1924* .

in 1916 having 24 players distributed as 4S/6A/8T/4B/2Bs;[58] the McMillin Saxophone Band from Cleveland, Ohio appears to have lacked the soprano line, but added 2 drummers to their 16 players of 7A/6T/2B/Bs in 1919;[59] the 1922 Denver Gas and Electric Saxophone Band had a similarly large contingent of 15 players, reasonably balanced as 4S/5A/4T/B/Bs;[60] a different type of balancing was achieved by the Zuriah Shrine Temple Octet of Minneapolis, who distributed their saxophones according to the size of the players, with the smallest individual taking the smallest saxophone;[61] Duane Sawyers's 110-piece Saxophone Band was advertised as part of an H. N. White advertisement in *Metronome* in April 1924.

Such groups were largely composed of amateur performers, but professionals could not afford to ignore their popularity. *Variety* observed in 1917 that Tom Brown himself was planning a saxophone band of some sixty performers, 'probably with the brothers as a nucleus'.[62] Although nothing appears to have come of this early attempt, the 'Six Brown Brothers and Their Thirty-Piece Saxophone Band' did come to fruition in 1924, making a number of successful appearances across the United States. Continuing the all-female theme of several smaller saxophone groups at the time such as 'The

BURT EARLE'S 20 SAXOPHONE GIRLS RECENTLY APPEARED AT THE PAGEANT
OF PROGRESS EXPOSITION, LOS ANGELES, CAL., ALSO UNDER EDWARD CAR-
RUTHER'S DIRECTION. BURT EARLE HAS 100 CALIFORNIA MUSICAL GIRLS
READY TO APPEAR IN ACTS FROM 10 TO 50, ALL TRAINED, COSTUMED AND
ROUTINED. SUITABLE FOR FAIRS, CIRCUSES, MOVING PICTURE, VAUDEVILLE
AND MUSICAL COMEDY THEATRES.

61.   Burt Earle's twenty saxophone girls, under the watchful masculine eye of their overseer.

Darling Four' and 'The Schuster Sisters Saxophone Quartette', the December 1922
edition of *Variety* carried a further advert for 'The Twenty Saxophone Girls', who had
made a recent exhibition appearance in Los Angeles; although the accompanying
picture showed only eight women, the male director, Burt Earle, offered combinations
of up to 50, as well as '8 Saxophone Girls and a Clown Comedian', an obvious allusion to the Brown Brothers act.[63] The Brothers' role in developing this trend is further
reinforced by a method on *How to Conduct Saxophone Bands*, published in 1921, which
has several pages of repertoire suggestions described as 'numbers featured by the Six
Brown Brothers Saxophone Act'.[64]

In late 1924 the first bassoonist of the Boston Symphony Orchestra, Abdon Laus,
who performed the saxophone solos in the BSO's concerts when required, began to
put together the 'Boston Saxophone Orchestra', drawn from professional and good
amateur players in the city. Over the next few months the ensemble rehearsed assidu-
ously, and also grew in size, with one concert comprising 85 players. On 10 February
1926 the group gave a concert in Boston's Symphony Hall, comprising a range of
classical transcriptions from Wagner, Beethoven, Gounod and others; for this concert
the group was made up of 4S/16A/8 C-melody/8T/4B/2Bs/1Cbs, together with
string basses, assorted percussion and the hall's large organ. The renowned soloist
Jascha Gurewich also performed with the group.[65] Given the ensemble's classical roots
it is perhaps unsurprising that, as with others of the time who sought to counter the
populist tendencies associated with the instrument, the Boston Saxophone Orchestra
was founded with the twin desires of 'lifting the instrument to a higher plane of
performance' and 'fostering better music for the instrument'.[66]

The substantial number of these large saxophone groups in the period from the mid
1910s to the late 1920s is reflective of a dramatic upsurge in the saxophone's popularity in the United States, and further reinforces that sense of communal and partici-
patory music-making that the instrument had by then come to connote. Many have

The Boston Saxophone Orchestra, Abdon F. Laus, Conductor

62. The Boston Saxophone Orchestra in *Metronome* in January 1926, whose classical roots and aspirations aimed to counteract what they saw as the populist agendas of other saxophone ensembles.

referred to this as a saxophone craze, and while such a description risks reproducing the kind of hyperbole that characterised the advertising of the time, it is certainly true that the saxophone enjoyed a wave of popularity that was not to be replicated by any other instrument until the arrival of the electric guitar in the 1960s. Terms similar to 'saxophone craze' were being used as early as 1914 by Smith and Holmes,[67] and the Buescher company also noted in a 1915 advert that 'the enormous demand for saxophone players in the last two years is one of the wonders of the music business'.[68]

Commerce and trade

The instrument continued to grow in popularity throughout the latter part of the 1910s, and more so during the dance band era of the 1920s, and this popularity was reflected in greatly increased sales. The production of domestically-manufactured saxophones significantly facilitated this trend, as well as reducing purchase costs. The C. G. Conn Company played a particularly important role, having established itself as the first American manufacturer of saxophones, probably around 1888, from its base in Elkhart, Indiana (see pp. 76–7). Its eponymous founder was elected to the United States Congress in 1892, and in 1899, in a manner reminiscent of Adolphe Sax's commercial enterprise half a century earlier, he introduced a bill requiring every US army regiment to be equipped with its own band. The Conn company, manufacturing a range of brass and wind instruments, naturally flourished, and again the saxophone benefited significantly through the strategic association of a manufacturer with the

63. The Conn saxophone factory c. 1912/13.

military establishment, with large quantities of the instrument being delivered to the US army around the turn of the century.[69] By 1905 Conn was the largest instrument manufacturer in the world, producing not only a complete range of wind and brass instruments, but also string and percussion instruments, phonographs and portable organs.[70] In 1922 the company asserted that it was producing as many as 150 saxophones a day, and some 75 per cent of the company's production capacity was diverted to saxophones.[71] Conn's ability to produce and distribute large numbers of saxophones for American consumption allowed it both to respond to and stimulate the growing domestic demand for the instrument.

The figures involved are revealing. Overall, whereas in 1914 around 6,000 new saxophones per annum were being sold in the United States, by the peak years of 1923 and 1924 this had risen to 100,000 saxophones.[72] By 1924 the Buescher company alone was making and selling instruments worth $3.5 million a year, the majority of these being saxophones.[73] From 1921–6 Buescher sold on average some 25,000 saxophones per annum, although by 1927 this had dropped to 13,000 and then only 4,000 in 1931, as the fashion waned. The Conn company similarly averaged 23,000 saxophones in the early part of the decade, dropping to 16,000 in 1927 and then 5,000 in 1931.[74] Other companies such as Martin, Holton and H. N. White also sought to profit from this rapidly increasing popular demand. The H. & A. Selmer company – an American offspring of the French company – later asserted that at peak times more than four thousand units per month were being produced.[75]

Saxophones were not the most expensive instruments of the time, but neither were they the cheapest. Imported instruments were inevitably more costly, because of import tariffs and transportation costs. A Carl Fischer advert from about 1908 indicates that an Evette & Schaeffer silver-plated alto, imported from Paris, would cost $183.50 and a tenor $190.[76] About the same time a flute could be bought as cheaply as $50, but better quality imports might fetch up to $400;[77] a piano from the Sears Roebuck catalogue could be had for as little as $87 in 1908.[78] But the increased demand for saxophones in the mid 1910s drove down prices, as locally-based manufacturers benefitted from economies of scale. Thus by 1918 Carl Fischer was advertising its own 'stamped' brass finish altos for $62.50, or $82.50 for the fancier silver-plated finish; tenors in either C or B♭ were similarly $65 or $87.50 respectively. Even a baritone could be had for a very reasonable $80 or $108.40.[79] The King company was similarly offering its named basic saxophones at prices ranging from $85 for a soprano up to $110 for a baritone.[80] These were list prices – in reality sale prices, as today, might well be lower, and second-hand prices lower still: Tom Brown recalled in 1923 how he had previously acquired a second-hand bass saxophone for as little as $60.[81] By comparison, quality flutes produced by the leading American flute maker William S. Haynes were available for $200, with imported English models costing $300;[82] the starting price for an upright piano from Sears Roebuck in 1919 was $248,[83] while grand pianos elsewhere were in the region of $590.[84] Thus a saxophone was affordable enough, and certainly not beyond the means of many of those who aspired to own and play one. Payment by instalments further tempted prospective purchasers. The 'Selmer Easy Payment Plan' of 1925 offered Selmer American sopranos in C or B♭ for only $20.86 down payment, followed by 10 monthly instalments of $6.26, a total of $83.46; an E♭ baritone was similarly offered at $30.04 down and $9.01 monthly ($120.04). Other models were available for amounts between these.[85] In contrast, the more expensive imported Selmer Paris models were offered at $114.95 or $31.61 down and 10 payments of $9.48 ($120.04) for a straight brass B♭ soprano, rising to $221.95 or $61.04 down and 10 payments of $18.31 ($244.24) for a silver–plated E♭ baritone.[86]

With sales tactics such as these, a plethora of pedagogic material and printed music increasingly available, and new factories and companies eager to capitalise on this latest fashion, the saxophone was once again caught up in a web of merchandising, commercial exploitation and mercantile expansion underpinned by a developing transport infrastructure; all of which was reminiscent of its original introduction in mid-nineteenth-century France, albeit now on a much greater scale. Furthermore, just as Buffet Crampon had established Mantes-La-Ville as the hub of French brass/wind manufacturing, so too did Conn's location in Elkhart, Indiana, act as a magnet for other companies such as Buescher, H. & A. Selmer and Martin. During the 1920s the great majority of American saxophone manufacture was undertaken in Elkhart, which in some quarters became known as 'The Saxophone City'.[87]

As the commercial frameworks surrounding the saxophone became more sophisticated, and the profiles of its leading exponents – underpinned by a range of mass media – became ever higher, the endorsement by saxophone celebrities of particular instruments was increasingly sought by the companies making them (this was equally

64. Conn sales advert from *Metronome* in February 1924, showing a range of classical and popular saxophone players as endorsers.

true of other instruments). Illustration 55 demonstrates the association of the Elliott Savonas with the Buffet company in France – an indication of the group's high profile at this time – and illustration 64 shows the wide range of both classical and popular saxophonists that the Conn company was able to call on to endorse its instruments.

Another reason for the saxophone's increasing popularity was that it was perceived to be a comparatively easy instrument to play, particularly by those who already possessed some level of musical ability. The Carl Fischer advert noted above also observed that saxophone fingering 'is so simple that any clarinetist can readily perform well after a few days' practice';[88] a 1915 publication suggested that 'greater progress is made and greater results obtained with a given amount of effort than upon any other instrument.'[89] Such attitudes to the saxophone are again reminiscent of those expressed in mid-nineteenth-century France.

Manufacturers seeking to profit from the saxophone's popularity were naturally keen to promote such characteristics. A 1923 information brochure circulated by the Buescher company observed that:

> if you can hum a refrain or whistle a tune with the band, then you can safely take up the saxophone with assured success. Learning to play the saxophone is [. . .] almost as simple as whistling a tune. Practically anyone can play the saxophone. Youngsters who never knew a note [. . .] have learned simple scales in an hour, played home melodies and popular airs in a week, learned new tunes every week, and in as little as three months have joined amateur orchestras or even the town band![90]

A 1926 advert by the same company went further. Under the title of 'It Put Him Where He Is Today' and a picture of a single saxophonist among a group of friends gathered around a piano, the advertising copy noted that 'His friends could hardly believe it. He had always been so uninteresting, such a dreg on the social market. But now, within six weeks, he had turned the tables. Now he's invited everywhere, and he's always the center of attraction, "the life of the party." He's popularity itself and he owes it all to his Buescher TrueTone Saxophone' (see ill. 65).[91] Musical instruments are seldom credited with such profound qualities of social transformation. But with such bold claims being advanced from so many different quarters, it is unsurprising that the saxophone achieved a reputation as a socially inclusive, fun and undemanding musical instrument, in contrast to its more longstanding competitors, which by comparison appeared weighed down by tradition and required years of specialist training in order to achieve basic levels of competence.

The increasing numbers of aspiring saxophonists turning to the instrument inevitably created greater demand for pedagogic materials. Jean White's *Elementary Method for the Saxophone* had been published as early as 1887 (although it was based on a French publication of 1881), and Otto Langey's *Practical Tutor for the Saxophone* published in London in 1889 appeared under the Carl Fischer imprint in the USA that same year. By 1889 Fischer was offering at least 40 separate titles published for solo saxophone, demonstrating the demand that the publisher perceived for such material even at this relatively early juncture.[92] Such publications reveal the nascent market among those bandsmen and other early pioneers who sought either to learn or to teach the instrument. But the popularity of the saxophone in the 1910s and 20s naturally created a much bigger market, and publishers quickly attempted to profit from it; from 1915 to 1930 more than seventy-five different methods, study books and

65. Buescher advert from *Metronome* in January 1926, asserting the transformative effects of playing the saxophone.

similar pedagogic materials directly related to the saxophone were published in the United States alone.[93]

Some of these methods demonstrate a certain anxiety towards contemporary saxophone practice from those who sought to establish a 'legitimate' tradition for the instrument. Since the writers themselves were usually schooled in the classical tradition, they took as their models methods for other instruments with longstanding pedagogic traditions: piano, clarinet, violin and so forth. Thus many saxophone methods include the rudiments of music, scales and exercises, and collections of classical transcriptions and popular tunes, which may have had only limited appeal to those who saw the saxophone as offering a short cut to possessing sufficient musical competence to play the latest popular melody.

The normal exhortations to regular and sustained practice are also found, doubtless conceived as further warnings to those individuals who wished simply to pick up a saxophone and have fun, rather than devote time to serious study. At the beginning of her 1922 *Progressive Method for the Saxophone* Kathryne E. Thompson somewhat maternalistically implores the student to:

> give to your saxophone the same consideration you would any other musical instrument, such as violin or piano or the human voice, and [. . .] not make the serious mistake of regarding it as TOO EASY to require practice. This is a mistake often made by the beginner, as the simple fingering of saxophone is quickly learned, and the student starts to play songs, etc, and to neglect tone and technical practice, and sometimes does not discover what a very serious mistake this is until he has wasted many months of valuable time.[94]

But the 'simple fingering of the saxophone' proved alluring to many, and for those who hoped to gain a degree of mastery in a rather shorter time than Thompson would have liked, there was plenty of printed support. The *Illustrated Five-Minute Course for Saxophone* was perhaps the most extreme example of this trend, but Bonnell's *Saxophone Made Easy: A New Method for Playing the Saxophone Without a Teacher*, or DeVille's *Eclipse Self-Instructor for Saxophone*, to name but two, provided plenty of competition.[95]

The notion that the saxophone was an easy instrument to play was not confined to the popular amateur market, but gained some ground in the military also. A diary belonging to the bandsman Phillip Jones gives some insight into how saxophone neophytes went about learning the instrument at the time. Jones later became a respected composer and conductor in New York, but in 1917, during World War I, he was drafted into the US Infantry. The day before joining up he was given a 'bright, shining B–flat Tenor saxophone [. . .] purchased at Carl Fischer Instrument Co.' He writes of his learning process:

> Miller [the bandleader] says my saxophone is a good one and easy to play. He showed me a lot about the instrument and had me practice in the band barracks [. . .]. At the end of six hours I had mastered the fingerings but have trouble with my lips in getting the tones. In other words I have no embouchure. Miller gave me a lesson at night and was most encouraging. He tells me that in a week, after I can play the 'Star Spangled Banner', he will make me a regular bandsman.[96]

The composer and scholar Walter Piston used a similar ruse, learning the saxophone at short notice in order to be accepted into a Navy Band, as did the young George Gershwin, who also anticipated being drafted at about this time and hoped to join an army band.[97]

Other methods were aimed at those with greater technical proficiency, either because they presumed some level of professional engagement – such as *The Ernst Modern System of Improvising and Filling in for the Dance Saxophonist*[98] – or because they encouraged advanced music reading skills: Thompson's *Practical Studies in Bass Clef for Saxophone* endeavoured to persuade saxophone players first to read and then transpose from the bass clef, to prepare for those occasions when it might be 'desired to substitute saxophone for cello or bassoon or trombone in [the] orchestra'.[99] Ben Vereecken's

Foundation to Saxophone Playing (1917) has a similar section offering 'Practical Hints regarding Transposition and Adaptation of Orchestra Parts to suit the Requirements, Character and Peculiarities of the differently pitched Saxophones'. Explicit instructions on transposing at sight are included, such as 'to read the Viola part properly, ignore the alto clef and substitute the treble clef and read and play the part one tone lower than written.'[100] His later 'advanced' method *The Saxophone Virtuoso* (1919) provides an extensive series of transposition exercises, and he observes in the preface that the ability to transpose was 'one of the most important and essential needs of the professional Saxophone player'. Successful completion of the method promised, perhaps a little optimistically, 'mastery of the clefs, transposition, technical control and every other problem of the saxophonist'.[101] These skills of musical adaptation and transposition at sight are less important today, when bespoke saxophone parts are the norm, but they would have been called upon quite regularly in the late 1910s and early 1920s. For several years stock arrangements for theatre and dance bands ('orchestras') included parts only for string instruments, and thus any saxophonists in these bands would have needed to read from the string parts, particularly the cello line. Unlike the symphony orchestra, where such instrument substitution would have been deemed inappropriate, these more utilitarian contexts welcomed the musical flexibility such skills afforded.

But for many the saxophone was first and foremost a novelty, fun instrument on which to play well-known tunes and from which one could easily obtain weird and wonderful noises. Hence the widespread identification of the 'moanin' saxophone, and the perception in some quarters that the instrument was good only for novelty sounds such as 'laughing' (a series of descending tones preceded by short upward glisses), 'slap tonguing' (a form of percussive attack not unlike string pizzicato), and other comic effects. Belwin published a method entitled *Sax-Acrobatix*, 'a book of saxophone stunts and tricks' that gave explanations and practice exercises that sought to help the saxophonist achieve, among other things, 'the laugh, the bark, the klack, the caw, the moan, the meow, the cry, the yelp, the sneeze' and so forth.[102]

Such characterisations were circulated even by those who had a vested interest in the instrument's overall success. A brochure produced by the Buescher company in 1921 observed that:

> Two saxophones, a piano and traps [i.e. drum kit], will by themselves make an excellent band producing all the necessary weird effects. In any town the talent can be found for a band of this character which will instantly leap into popularity for entertainments, concerts, and dance music. If more players are available, more Saxophones can be added – the more the merrier, and the greater number of grotesque effects it is possible to produce.[103]

A contemporary review of a 1912 Brown Brothers performance noted that 'the Saxophone [*sic*] is, unaided, a humorist. It looks like a sea horse and sounds like a canned fiddle. One, alone, gnaws at a funny bone, but six, ranging from a little one, with the voice of a deflating rubber bladder, to a paternal one that croaks like a musical bullfrog, are too much for any audience.'[104] With such sentiments so widely expressed, and with the visual association with clowning central to several variety acts, it is unsurprising that the saxophone should be seen as a comedic, novelty instrument. And while the exhortations of some musicians sought to downplay the saxophone's novelty value and reinforce its claims as an instrument worthy of serious study for serious musical ends, such voices were frequently lost among the chorus of others seeking to exploit for commercial gain the instrument's widespread popularity.

By the early 1920s the saxophone's adaptability was being harnessed in many contexts. In addition to the vaudeville, circus and minstrel circuits already noted, it was a constituent part of many cabaret bands. It was also heard in the picture houses, where its versatility could be put to good effect. It could be used to accompany the silent movies of the time: the Cincinnati Gem Theatre, for example, was using a saxophone trio for this purpose as early as its 1911–12 season;[105] or a vaudeville act like the Brown Brothers might form part of a series of entertainments that would include films interspersed with live acts.[106]

Above all the instrument came to be seen as quintessentially egalitarian. It was, in a sense, of the people and for the people: a mass-produced musical instrument catering for the musical aspirations of the masses. But it was this very egalitarianism, the notion that you could somehow be musically proficient *without* the need for intensive study supervised by authoritarian figures, that challenged conventional attitudes to musical learning and irritated those of a more highbrow musical disposition. These issues will resurface in Chapter 8, but it was to take the saxophone many years to lose such associations, and that this was achieved at all is due in large part to the arrival of several prominent virtuosos, who demonstrated how high levels of technical accomplishment could be achieved on the instrument without sacrificing popular appeal.

The rise of the saxophone virtuoso

Early performance standards on the saxophone in the more utilitarian contexts in which it was found were often not especially high. For example, recordings made between 1911 and 1913 by the English music hall artist Gertie Gitana, who played saxophone as one part of her act, demonstrate the very rudimentary skills that were probably typical of many of her ilk.[107] Even the recorded legacy of a group such as the Brown Brothers indicates technical abilities that today would be regarded as somewhat pedestrian, notwithstanding their enormous popularity at the time.[108] Elsewhere, however, much higher performance standards could be heard, particularly by saxophone soloists working with professional bands. Among the rank-and-file musicians within the saxophone sections standards were generally good, and, as already noted in Chapter 3 with respect to E. A. Lefebre, solo opportunities were occasionally available to those who were particularly talented. But the rivalry between players to obtain the most lucrative appointments, in addition to the competition often existing between professional musicians to outdo each other in the demonstration of technical excellence, all helped to increase performance standards in the early years of the twentieth century. Smith and Holmes noted in 1916 that 'there is no question but what the grand old LeFevre [Lefebre] was a great artist on the saxophone [*sic*], and perhaps no one has ever surpassed him in tone production. However, when it comes to execution, Harry Lewis, Ben Vereecken, Homer Dickinson, Tom Brown, Benne Henton and a score of others have him tied to a post.'[109]

Jean H. B. Moeremans (d. 1937/8?), in particular, demonstrated outstanding technique, and his position as soloist in the Sousa band, having succeeded Lefebre in 1894, meant that his performance skills were heard by a wide audience. Like Lefebre, Moeremans provides another example of a European-trained saxophonist finding a more natural home for his talents in the USA because of the greater employment possibilities the country offered. Born in Belgium, he appears to have either worked or studied in Paris in the early 1890s.[110] He was a member of the Belgian Guards band before emigrating to Canada.[111] He performed as a soloist with Sousa every year except 1901 for more than a decade, giving his final concert in 1905, and his repertoire comprised solos from mid-nineteenth-century composers such as Demersseman and Singelée combined with some of his own compositions and Sousa's *Belle Mahon*.

Although Moeremans had declined to take part in Sousa's long European tour of 1901, he did join him for a thirty-week tour in 1903, which began in England on 2 January of that year. The tour was ambitious, and although scaled down from its original aspirations the band still performed 362 concerts in 133 different towns, covering all the major cities of northern and central Europe.[112] Sousa's soloists included the outstanding trombonist Arthur Pryor and the renowned violinist Maud Powell. That Moeremans could comfortably share the stage with such luminaries is further testament to his abilities, and to Sousa's imagination in seeing the value of a saxophone soloist on the programme. The tour was a significant success, and we may assume that the praise heaped by the English press upon Moeremans's performances not only reflected his expertise but was also replicated in other European countries. The Sousa band's performance at the Queen's Hall in London met with observations such as: 'Mr J. H. B. Moeremans played a saxophone solo with extraordinary skill'; 'Mr J. H. B. Moeremans's fantasia on the saxophone was one of the striking features of the concert'.[113] In the provinces the novelty of the instrument still provoked commentary, and some critics continued to find it necessary to provide an introduction to the instrument for their readers. Thus the *Sheffield Independent* noted that: 'Mr J. H. B. Moeremans is a saxophone soloist. The saxophone is something like a big Dutchman's pipe, elaborately silver-mounted, the bowl curving up towards the mouthpiece. Its tone is that of the clarionet or the cornet, and at times of the bassoon.'[114]

Moeremans's profile with the Sousa band was such that he was asked to make a number of recordings as a soloist, for the Victor and Berliner labels, in addition to those he made with the band. Indeed, he was the most frequently recorded saxophonist in the early years of the recording industry, prior to about 1910 (see pp. 180–1). After he left the Sousa band in 1905 Moeremans continued to work as a soloist with other bands, albeit never achieving the same profile he had with Sousa; to a considerable degree he disappears from the historical record, and died in Belgium sometime in the late 1930s. But he had played a significant role in bringing a higher profile to the instrument in many contexts where it was still unfamiliar, and in demonstrating the high performance standards that might be achieved on it.

Sousa retained saxophonists in his band after Moeremans's departure, but without an identifiable soloist. The next saxophone player of significance to join the band was another Belgian, Benjamin Vereecken (dates unknown), albeit not until about 1910.[115] Vereecken joined Sousa, having been a flute soloist in the Arthur Pryor band (the famous trombonist having decided to run his own band by this time), and had previously worked in circus bands in Europe. Certainly Vereecken was the principal saxophone player during Sousa's renowned world tour of 1911, and he also supplied numerous arrangements for the band; however, there is no surviving documentary evidence that indicates he was performing prestigious solos as Moeremans was, nor does he appear to have made any solo recordings. Perhaps his most significant legacy was the two methods he wrote in 1917 and 1919, and he contributed a monthly series on saxophone technique in *The Metronome* in the early 1920s. His pedagogic work thus made him a significant influence on saxophone performance practice in the USA in the 1920s and 30s.

Two further Sousa soloists are also noteworthy. H. Benne Henton (1867–1938) was the first American-born saxophonist to achieve an international reputation. Like most saxophone players of the time he started on clarinet, before leaving home to join the Ringling Brothers circus band. Henton, like Vereecken, provides a specific example of a circus or vaudeville player whose talents allowed him to succeed in more musically demanding contexts. He was a founder member of the Bohumir Kryll band from 1906, then frequently a saxophone soloist with the Conway band between 1909 and 1918. Thus he already had a significant national reputation before joining Sousa in January 1919, and this was further enhanced by several recordings that he made for the Edison and Victor labels between 1910 and 1918. Henton had considerable technical ability. A supplement issued by the Victor company in October 1916 described him as 'the Paganini of the Saxophone';[116] even allowing for journalistic hyperbole the comparison is striking, and reflects something of his superior technical skills in comparison with other saxophone players of the time. Henton was perhaps the first soloist to make virtuosic use of the extended altissimo register (although the possibilities offered by this register had been recognised in the nineteenth century). As early as 1911 he was performing a cadenza as part of his own composition titled *Eleven O'Clock*, which was published the following year. The cadenza makes use of the

66.   Sousa's saxophone section in 1919, with H. Benne Henton standing third from the right.

Ex. 5. H. Benne Henton's alto cadenza to his own composition *Eleven O'Clock*, published in C. G. Conn's *Musical Truth* in 1912, demonstrating his use of the altissimo register.

altissimo register going up to d⁴, and although apparently never recorded, Henton did record a version of *Laverne* for the Victor label in 1918 that further demonstrated his facility in this extended register.

At a time when the saxophone continued to be associated with the novelty effects construed by many as 'jazz', soloists such as Henton demonstrated that there was another, more serious side to the instrument. An American critic, responding to one of Henton's performances in October 1919, made this very point, observing that 'although the saxophone is considered by some critics to be best suited for mere "jazz" and useless for concert purposes, Mr Henton proved that there really is a "tone" in a saxophone, if played right. A violin has no sweeter sound than Mr Henton produced on his "sax".'[117] Such eulogies were a little ironic since Sousa was no fan of jazz, although he acknowledged its growing popularity and realised there was a market for it. Having apparently discontinued saxophone features in his concerts after Moeremans's departure in 1905, his decision to resurrect them in 1919, and to invite Henton to join the band, was in part an acknowledgement of the popularity of 'hot' music, and the much higher profile the saxophone had by then achieved as a result of its extensive use in that context.

Few of the soloists in the Sousa band did more to promote the saxophone as a concert instrument than Henton's successor, Jascha Gurewich (1896–1938). Like Henton, Gurewich was a highly accomplished player, but he left very few recordings that might underpin his posthumous reputation. Sousa, however, is reported to have told Gurewich that 'I have heard all the finest saxophone players of the past thirty years and the majority of them have played for me; but I have never heard anyone to equal you.' This may explain why, according to the same article – a two-page promotional spread in *Metronome* in 1927 – Gurewich was the highest-paid saxophonist ever employed by Sousa. And just as Henton had been described as the Paganini of the saxophone, so too was it noted that Gurewich 'plays the saxophone with the dexterity and expression that Kreisler has with the violin'.[118] Both Henton and Gurewich composed original pieces for the instrument, but whereas Henton's music tended to reproduce the musical miniatures that characterised much of the band work at that time (waltzes, theme with variations, etc.), Gurewich was more ambitious, sometimes drawing on formal models found in concert music. Gurewich undertook nationwide solo concert tours in the late 1920s, in which he performed much of his own material, either original compositions or arrangements. Although still working in film recordings and with dance companies in the early 1930s, little is known of his activities beyond this.

Rudy Wiedoeft

For all the achievements of those saxophone soloists allied to various professional bands of the 1910s and 20s, and the early jazz soloists working in other contexts, the most renowned saxophone player in America prior to 1930 was Rudolph Cornelius Wiedoeft (1893–1940). As Rudy Wiedoeft he achieved widespread recognition in the United States and beyond, largely on account of a virtuosic technique that, preserved through his many recordings, sounds as remarkable today as it did in his own time. Wiedoeft's importance for the history of the saxophone is in surprising contrast to the amount of detailed research undertaken on his life and work. But it is not too fanciful to divide that history into pre- and post-Wiedoeft periods, such was the impact he made, and such was the transformation in the social and musical identities pertaining to the saxophone over the course of his career. While he did not effect that transformation single-handedly, he played a significant role in it.

Wiedoeft was born into a musical family in Detroit on 3 January 1893. His parents, German immigrants, ran the Wiedoeft Family Orchestra, initially in Detroit and then in Los Angeles, playing in cafes and hotels. He subsequently worked as a clarinettist with a number of bands, including Porter's Catalina Island Band in San Francisco, where he was first clarinet in 1913. His initial – rather unsuccessful – acquaintance with the saxophone came as early as 1908, but he made a second attempt at mastering the instrument a few years afterwards, later claiming that in 1914 he 'took up the study of the saxophone seriously, practising from eight to ten hours a day.'[119]

In 1916 he arrived in New York as part of the pit band for a production entitled *Canary Cottage*. He appears to have made an immediate impact. One critic observed that 'Rudy's obbligatos [. . .] were so thrilling that he took more bows from the pit than the singer from the stage. His staccato was so fast and smooth that it required close attention to ascertain whether he was slurring or tonguing fast passages.'[120] Leaving the show, he put together his own group, the Frisco 'Jass' Band (the 'Jass' later became the more conventional 'Jazz', without the quotation marks) with whom he made his first recordings, for the Edison company, in May 1917. He made his first solo disc, playing one of his own compositions, *Valse Erica*, later the same year. After a brief period in various U.S. Marine bands towards the end of World War I, Wiedoeft resumed his civilian career, working in a variety of guises: as leader of the Master Saxophone Sextet; as part of groups such as the Wiedoeft-Wadsworth quartet of two saxophones, piano and percussion; as a contributor to a number of dance records, some under the name of Rudy Wiedoeft's Californians; as a soloist with orchestral accompaniment; and as a composer and arranger of light and classical repertoire for the saxophone.

Wiedoeft's extensive recording activity underpinned both his high profile at the time and his posthumous legacy. His recordings for a range of companies – among them Edison, Brunswick, Victor, Columbia – brought him to the attention of a wide audience, and eventually made him a well-known musical figure. Hubert Prior Vallée was so entranced by these recordings – to which he listened repeatedly – that his friends nicknamed him 'Rudy' in imitation of his idol; as Rudy Vallée (1901–86) he achieved considerable later success as a singer, saxophonist and radio star in his own right. Vallée writes in his autobiography that 'the beauty of Wiedoeft's tone, the terrific speed of his tonguing, his clean-cut execution all hit me with a thunderclap', and notwithstanding his somewhat awestruck attitude, such sentiments illustrate the impact the saxophone star made on contemporary audiences.[121]

Wiedoeft's assured control of the instrument is evident from his recordings. His sound is clean, full and warm, and coloured by a broad but consistent vibrato. His earliest recordings use less and narrower vibrato than later ones, perhaps because, like many of the time, his earliest aural models were players such as Lefebre, who used relatively little vibrato. His finger technique was remarkably crisp, and faster than any other player recorded in the late 1910s or for some time after; this was one reason why Wiedoeft made such a strong initial impact on those who heard him. What still sounds remarkable is Wiedoeft's exceptional articulation; it is the control of the tongue in relation to the speed of finger movement that quickly identifies a Wiedoeft

67.   Rudy Wiedoeft.

performance. For this reason, his observations on articulation and slap tonguing, in a method he wrote in 1927, are particularly interesting:

> Truthfully, the saxophone is unquestionably the most difficult wind instrument upon which to staccato rapidly. A rapid staccato is, more or less, a gift of nature, but any player with limited ability along this line can improve it by painstaking practice and study [...]. A very peculiar attack called 'slap-tongue' is almost essential in the playing of the lower tones in detached passages and in making a sforzando attack on these tones. This method may easily be abused and more sound of the impact of the tongue on the reed be heard than tone, making it too rough and obvious [...]. Slap-tonguing is especially effective for Oriental effects. It is not adapted to rapid staccato passages. In such cases the regular legitimate single-tonguing should be used.[122]

While the slap tonguing and 'oriental effects' hint at the comic saxophone style for which Wiedoeft was often known, other excerpts from the method illustrate his desire to be taken seriously, and his dismay at the often poor standards found among amateur players. He warns these aspiring performers against simply learning novelty techniques at the expense of getting the fundamentals correct, observing that 'too many amateur saxophonists start to play tunes and try to obtain weird and jazzy effects, believing that this will qualify them as players, without first mastering the real rudiments of saxophone playing: good tone, proper intonation, and thorough familiarity with all the scales.'[123]

Wiedoeft never considered himself by nature a jazz player; his own material has more affinity with ragtime in both structure and style, with piano accompaniments characterised by strong first and third beats and material frequently repeated in complete sections. He observed that it was 'with a spirit of unwillingness that I have made "jazz" records, or played this type of solo, but it is also true that it is what many people want to hear on the saxophone. Consequently I have endeavored to produce weird effects, such as glissando, tongue-flutter, "Oriental," etc., with the least possible sacrifice of the dignity of the instrument.'[124] Wiedoeft's characterisation of 'jazz' as being comprised largely of novelty effects illustrates the rather different meaning that was construed by many from the word at the time. In spite of his own ambivalence towards 'jazz', however, he became an important influence on a wide range of later jazz players, including Frankie Trumbauer – who, like Wiedoeft, also specialised on the C-melody sax – Lester Young, and even Charlie Parker, the latter being able to reproduce Wiedoeft solos as late as 1950.[125]

Wiedoeft's comment about not sacrificing the saxophone's dignity illustrates the tensions inhering between his public persona as pre-eminently a performer of light music and novelty techniques, and his own aspirations to be taken as a serious artist. He did not help himself in these aspirations, perhaps, by appending punning titles to some of his own compositions, such as *Sax-O-Phun* and *Saxophobia*. But other pieces such as *Valse Vanité* or *Valse Erica* demonstrate a compositional command of light classical miniatures that would influence later players such as Frankie Trumbauer and Jimmy Dorsey. Certainly Wiedoeft's musical intentions were genuine enough, and were further expressed in a column he contributed to *The Metronome* from 1925 to 1931. Although readers would frequently enquire how he produced his flashy novelty sounds Wiedoeft always responded that such effects had little intrinsic musical value and were best avoided. Elsewhere he argued in print for the value of radio as an educational medium, particularly for the dissemination of classical music.[126]

Wiedoeft's advocacy of the saxophone as a concert instrument further reinforces his historical significance. He gave a high profile concert at the prestigious Aeolian Hall in New York, on 17 April 1926, sponsored by The Instrument Manufacturers of America and broadcast nationally, which included arrangements of works by Bach and Tchaikovsky for saxophone quartet, as well as solos on the C-melody sax; it also comprised a work commissioned for the occasion from Willard Robison, for saxophone quartet, accompanied by the composer at the piano. A gushing review in *The Metronome* observed that the concert marked 'the first complete and satisfying appearance of the saxophone and saxophone ensemble in the legitimate concert field' and that the instrument was 'not only eminently suitable as a solo instrument but presents a family of instruments whose rendition of true classics not only requires no apology but permits a completeness of tone pictures and tone colouring of pleasing uniqueness'.[127] Wiedoeft made several classical recordings for the Columbia company in 1926, including Beethoven's *Minuet in G* and Tchaikovsky's *Melodie*, accompanied by the pianist Oscar Levant, with whom he also toured England the same year.

Wiedoeft's importance as a recording artist was reinforced by his association with a well-known touring group, the Eight Famous Victor Artists, whom he joined in 1922. He also took part, on 26 February 1925, in the one of the first electrically recorded musical performances, eventually issued on disc by the Victor company.[128] He made his last records for Victor in late 1927, and although listed as an exclusive Colombia artist in their 1928 and 1929 catalogues he seems to have made few if any recordings for the company in those years.[129] By then the hot jazz style for which Wiedoeft himself had provided some of the foundations was in the ascendancy, and his lighter more ragtime-influenced approach was out of fashion. As they were for the Brown Brothers and many other musicians of the time, the depressed 1930s were a difficult period. He might have found work in the radio orchestras, which generated much employment for good instrumentalists in New York around this time, but Wiedoeft was temperamentally unsuited to the work – believing it to be below his dignity – and unable to curb his natural soloistic tendencies in an appropriate fashion for section work.

Wiedoeft spent some time touring European capitals, where his music remained in vogue longer than in the United States. He lived in Paris for a year around 1930, prompting Henri Selmer, head of the eponymous instrument manufacturing company, to declare that 'I have never heard a saxophonist to equal Wiedoeft, and I doubt if there will be any to excel him, his staccato is so rapid, his execution so brilliant'.[130] Selmer's admiration led to Wiedoeft endorsing the company's saxophones in the early 1930s, no doubt to the disgruntlement of the Holton company in America, whose instruments Wiedoeft had similarly endorsed from 1927 (to the extent that one of their models had been even been named after him).

Back in North America, Wiedoeft's erstwhile fan Rudy Vallée had become a radio and film star in his own right, and his radio shows provided his former mentor with some continuing employment and exposure. Wiedoeft also made appearances on film, dressing up as a clown – recalling Tom Brown's trademark – in a Vitaphone short called *Darn Tootin'* in 1931, and he was also featured in a short talkie called *Rambling 'Round Radio Row* in 1932. But performance opportunities were becoming increasingly sporadic. A number of bizarre business ventures, including, possibly, some failed gold prospecting and oil drilling, served only to extend rather than ameliorate Wiedoeft's plight in the later 1930s. A fractious relationship with his wife, fuelled by excessive alcohol consumption, made Wiedoeft's home life miserable, and he would at times escape to the relative sanctity of Vallée's apartment in New York. He died in that city on 18 February 1940, of cirrhosis of the liver, doubtless a consequence of the hip flask that was his all-too-frequent companion.

It would be difficult to overstate Wiedoeft's contribution to the development and popularisation of the saxophone. He was an influential early figure in all the major genres where the instrument would later find a niche for itself during the course of the twentieth century: light popular and classical music, swing, and jazz. His technical facility set new standards for what might be achieved on the instrument. His numerous recordings not only reflected the saxophone's popularity at that time, but also provided aural models for those aspiring saxophonists who were the drivers of such popularity. His high profile ensured widespread dissemination of his pedagogic materials, and his insistence within these on the highest technical and musical standards served as a counterbalance to those who advocated the 'quick-and-easy' route to saxophone proficiency. Moreover, his advocacy of the saxophone as a serious concert instrument, underpinned by transcriptions, arrangements and commissions, while not unique in early twentieth-century America, achieved additional impact because of his national and international prominence.

The saxophone in the dance band

It was the inclusion of multiple saxophones in the dance bands of the 1920s that brought the instrument to its widest international audience. From this point on the saxophone would become iconically linked with American popular music, whether of the 'sweeter' variety produced by the large numbers of (often white) dance bands that serviced society functions and who could be heard extensively on the airways, or of those (often black) more jazz-oriented ensembles who were popular in the dance halls but less popular with segregation-minded radio programmers and record producers. And although it may have been a coincidence that America was swept by a dance craze over the same approximate time-scale as it was gripped by a saxophone craze, the latter was undoubtedly in part enhanced by the inclusion of saxophones in the bands supplying music for the former.

Although social dancing had grown significantly during 1910–13, the catalyst for the dance craze itself seems likely to have been the invention of the foxtrot around 1914. Variations on this basic step, as well as other dances, then followed: the quickstep, the tango, the charleston, and so forth. The famous dancing team of Irene and

Vernon Castle were influential in popularising this type of modern dance, and they also influenced the music that accompanied it. Nowhere was their impact more apparent than in their choice of James Reese Europe as musical director.

Europe and his fellow Washingtonian Will Marion Cook were important figures in the development of America's nascent dance scene in the 1910s. Both were well-educated, middle-class African Americans, with good musical training. In 1889 Cook – a violinist, composer and arranger – had formed an orchestra comprised entirely of African-American musicians, the instrumentation of which included a saxophone among other assorted string and brass/wind instruments. Elsie Hoffman was the saxophone player in the group, and she had performed a solo during a concert given by the orchestra at the Grand Army Hall on 26 September 1889; this may well have been the first concert solo given by an African American on the instrument.[131] Europe, also a violinist, pianist and composer, had moved to New York from Washington DC in 1903. In 1905 he was invited by the entertainer and impresario Ernest Hogan to join a group of some twenty musicians, singers and dancers called 'The Memphis Students' (notwithstanding that none were from Memphis and none were students).[132] This group, building on the minstrel tradition, would star Hogan himself and have music written by Cook. Among the various mandolins, guitars and banjos Cook also included a saxophone, and possibly other brass instruments. It may have been this sax/brass tinge to the sound that led the author and songwriter James Weldon Johnson later to describe the group as 'the first modern jazz band ever heard on a New York stage'.[133]

The saxophone became an important part of the characteristic sound Cook created for this band, and his approach greatly influenced Europe, not only when the latter assumed direction of the Students in December 1905, but also for those groups he would form later. In particular, Europe achieved widespread recognition for his Clef Club Orchestra, which played a significant date at Carnegie Hall on 2 May 1912, involving a 100-piece orchestra performing what was billed as a 'Concert of Negro music'.[134] The success of the event was such that it was repeated the following year, and while no saxophone appears to have been included in 1912, the 1913 event did involve John R. Burroughs on saxophone, and he also played in a tour given by the group later that year.[135] Shortly afterwards Europe was given a recording contract with Victor, and worked with a variety of dance groups of between six to twelve musicians. Although there are reports of saxophones in these groups there are none on the surviving recordings from this period. Nevertheless, a single saxophone remained as part of the Clef Club Orchestra even after Dan Kildare took over from Europe as musical director in 1914.[136]

Europe joined forces with Irene and Vernon Castle in late 1913, and the following year directed for them a band of 18 musicians on a tour around 30 cities in the United States. It appears likely that a saxophone remained part of Europe's instrumentation; Tom Fletcher, an African-American showbusiness stalwart, notes in his memoir that Europe was the first to add a saxophone to the dance orchestra during this tour with the Castles.[137] Europe's inventive scoring helped transform the earliest dance bands from small ensembles dominated by violin, piano and drums, with occasional banjo, to larger and more varied groups, which sometimes employed the saxophone. He was successful in part because of the general perception that his band played 'syncopated music', which formed the basis for many of the popular dance styles of the day. The musicians certainly played with enthusiasm and zest, often adding embellishments to the basic arrangements, which further enhanced this rhythmically vivacious music. But the innovations of Europe, Cook and others lay more in their imaginative arrangements, unusual ensemble scoring, and catchy compositions in an up-tempo, ragtime-influenced style. And Europe's persistent use of the saxophone in his ensembles would certainly have gone some way towards associating the instrument with dance music in the eyes and ears of those who were present.

Europe's band is only one of many routes by which the saxophone came into dance music in the mid 1910s. The influential African-American arranger Will Vodery similarly began to include alto and tenor saxophones in his scores from 1917 and possibly earlier.[138] Theatre orchestrations – the primary routes through which professional musicians of the time became acquainted with changes in musical style and instrumentation – also began to include parts for saxophones from about 1916. *Metronome,* for example, from its March 1916 issue, provided saxophone parts in the orchestrations it distributed with the publication. Noting that the saxophone had 'sprung into unusual prominence and popularity of late years, as a solo and ensemble instrument' the publication decided to add E♭ alto and B♭ tenor saxophone parts to its orchestral supplements, and full S/A/T/B alternatives for its band arrangements. The publication asked its readers in what keys they would prefer the saxophone parts to be provided, which elicited a series of exchanges over subsequent issues as to which instruments might be used in what contexts.[139]

Many other bandleaders were by then including at least one saxophone. W. C. Handy asserts that he first introduced the saxophone into the dance orchestra when he used one in a seven-piece group in Memphis in 1909; it was successful enough to have been used in two more of his groups, based on the same line-up.[140] The 'Hoosier Society Orchestra' at the Severn Hotel in Indianapolis had a six–piece band in 1915 that included a saxophone.[141] Bert Kelly, a cornettist and dance band leader working in Chicago, claims to have used a saxophone player by the name of Fred Miller, in Chicago in the spring of 1916.[142] The groundbreaking Joseph C. Smith orchestra added saxophonist Jack Wasserman for some of their sessions, possibly as early as 1917. A supplement published by the Victor company notes in the December 1917 issue that 'Joseph C. Smith and His Orchestra manage to produce a tone quality peculiar to themselves. It haunts you like the tone of a saxophone'.[143]

By the late 1910s that saxophone tone was coming to define modern dance music, and the instrument was increasingly found amongst those groups playing it. This dance music was more and more described as 'jazz', and it was during these years that the instrument became inextricably linked with this word. The chorus of Irving Berlin's 1917 song *Mr. Jazz Himself* begins: 'Shake hands with Mr. Jazz himself! / He took the saxophone from off the shelf', and this increasingly close association between jazz and the saxophone was iconically reinforced by the illustrations accompanying sheet music for 'jazz' numbers. Whereas many of the bands sketched in these pictures in the mid 1910s have no saxophone included, by the end of the decade the instrument was given increasing prominence, as evidenced by the covers of both

68. Sheet music covers of Irving Berlin's 'Shake Hands with Mr Jazz Himself' (1917) and Gene Quaw's 'Old Man Jazz' (1920), demonstrating the increasing visual prominence given to the saxophone in relation to the word jazz.

Berlin's song and Gene Quaw's *Old Man Jazz* (1920), the subtitle of which – 'An Eccentric Fox-Trot Song' – further demonstrates the semantic ambiguity surrounding the word jazz at this time (see ill. 68).

The instrument was increasingly being demanded by the record companies who were now central to the dissemination of what they advertised as 'jazz'. Even the Original Dixieland Jazz Band (ODJB), one of the most well known and frequently recorded white bands working in the New Orleans style, was persuaded by the record company Victor in 1920 to add saxophonist Benny Krueger (1889–1967) for a few sessions, augmenting their normal line-up of cornet, clarinet, trombone, piano and drums.[144] This was the first time a non-ODJB player had recorded with the group, and came about because this was how the record company felt that a dance group should by then be sounding (notwithstanding the rather tenuous connection between the saxophone and the New Orleans style the ODJB purported to purvey).

The rise of the saxophone section

While many of these examples demonstrate the addition of a single saxophone, multiple instruments soon became the norm, and the saxophone section became established as an identifiable component of dance music. The leader most often credited with developing a saxophone section in his band is the drummer Art Hickman. Based initially in California, Hickman has some claim to having introduced the word 'jazz' in relation to music, but his obviously dance-oriented style would not be designated with that term today, and he rejected the term in later life. He is significant, however, for having added, possibly as early as 1916,[145] two particular multi-instrumentalists to his band, both of whom were accomplished saxophone players.

In truth it is difficult to know for sure whether Hickman was the first to include several saxophone players in a dance band; he may simply have been reflecting an increasingly widespread trend. W. C. Handy, for example, recorded 15 titles for Columbia in September 1917, with a group billed as 'Handy's Orchestra of Memphis', in which several saxophones can be clearly distinguished, including a short two–bar solo break on the recording of *That 'Jazz' Dance*.[146] A month later he returned to the studio to make three test recordings with 'Handy's Saxophone Band' – the line-up of this group is unclear – but none of these recordings was issued; however, a picture from 1918 shows tenor saxophone player Nelson Kincaid as part of the band.[147] Similarly, a photograph of the Paul Whiteman band, from 1919, also shows two saxophone players, both holding tenors (although the photograph is clearly posed, leaving some doubt as to quite what instrumentation was in fact being used during performances).[148] Both Hickman and Whiteman were working in California in the late 1910s, and would have been aware of each other's work. But the players Hickman added to his band – Clyde Doerr (1894–1973)[149] and Bert Ralton (1900?–27) – both had strong musical personalities, and their playing began to establish a role for the saxophones in this context. The recordings they made with Hickman demonstrate that they seldom played together as a homogenous unit within the ensemble, taking instead a more expanded polyphonic role, in which soprano, alto and tenor saxes all contribute to a shifting contrapuntal texture, supported occasionally by Doerr's baritone; Hickman's 1919 recording of *Dance It Again With Me*, for example, contains a middle section saxophone feature in which a florid, arpeggiated alto line is set against the flowing tenor melody. Elsewhere the saxophone frequently replaced the trumpet on the melody line, an unusual way of scoring for the ensemble at the time.

This innovative approach to scoring is likely to have been the work of Ferdinand (Ferde) Grofé, a classically-trained pianist and string player who joined Hickman's band around 1915, but who moved in 1920 to work as pianist and arranger in Paul Whiteman's band. It was in this latter band that Grofé and Whiteman – also a classically-trained string player – between them developed the more homogenous saxophone section sound that would become so ubiquitous from the late 1920s. Whiteman was originally from Denver, Colorado. At the age of seventeen he was principal viola of the orchestra his father had founded in Denver, before moving to the San Francisco symphony orchestra some seven years later. Like Hickman he made his name as a bandleader in California before making a substantial international career based in New York. Whiteman's classical background begins to explain his later fondness for what became described as 'symphonic jazz', an early attempt at hybridising classical music and jazz, and his experience of working within the string section of a large orchestra is likely to have predisposed him – as bandleader and arranger – to conceive instrumentation in an analogous fashion to orchestral composers. Whiteman, and arrangers he worked with such as Grofé and Bill Challis, began to integrate the different band instruments in a more holistic fashion, using well-balanced block harmonies. Thus the various instrumental sub-groups of the band, particularly the brass and reeds, became seen as distinct units, not unlike the wind, brass or strings of a conventional symphony orchestra. However, whereas the saxophone family, then as now, only ever played a peripheral role in the symphony orchestra, it would soon become an essential and iconic component of dance and swing bands.

Some of Whiteman's earliest recordings reveal his use of the saxophone section as a more homogenous group than in Hickman's work.[150] While many of the very first recordings have only a pair of saxophones, tracks such as *Say it with Music* from August 1921 show a richer band sound overall, with three saxophones clearly identifiable as a distinct grouping.[151] Again, it is difficult to know whether Whiteman was genuinely blazing a trail, or simply aping instrumentation techniques he heard elsewhere. Certainly there was a great deal of flux in the way dance band forces were used at this time; for several years in the early 1920s many musician-arrangers were experimenting both with techniques of arrangement and the instrumental forces they might employ, and thus different sounds were evolving on an irregular basis. Quite what the level of Whiteman's innovation was in this respect we are unlikely to know for sure, but a saxophone section comprising two altos and a tenor – notwithstanding copious amounts of instrument doubling – was to become the standard dance band line-up for several years.

Whiteman was an enthusiastic supporter of the saxophone – perhaps not surprisingly given the financial success he enjoyed in part through promoting it – and described the instrument as the 'Caruso of the Jazz Orchestra'.[152] Not only did he include saxophones in his group from an early stage, but in the late 1930s, when he gave the various sections of his now famous orchestra the opportunity to shine as ensembles, he established the Paul Whiteman Sax Socktette. The Socktette eventually comprised nine saxophones (plus various doubles) together with two guitars, bass and drums. The group demonstrated how far removed Whiteman had become from his dance band origins. The success of the famous Aeolian Hall concert in 1924, in which he premiered George Gershwin's *Rhapsody in Blue* with the composer taking the solo piano part, had encouraged him to eschew actual dance performances and concentrate on producing a show band; the Socktette was the logical extension of that with regard to the saxophone section. The few recordings that were released, made from a session in 1939, demonstrate the remarkable collective virtuosity of the ensemble, as well the effectiveness of the homogenous saxophone family in a hot jazz context and the quality of the performers Whiteman was able to attract.[153] Although Whiteman was never the 'King of Jazz' that his publicity avowed, this did not prevent him from attracting some of the best jazz saxophone players, such as Frankie Trumbauer and Jimmy Dorsey, into his group; however, Whiteman's band was exceptionally successful, and he was able to offer better fees than most other bandleaders.

Over time the saxophone usurped the string instruments in the standard dance band formation. Obviously the instrument was substantially louder than the strings, and this was clearly a benefit in increasingly large dance halls, where the ability of the band to project its sound adequately was fundamental to an evening's success. Whiteman, for example, asserted that he had 'computed that one baritone saxophone is equal in sonorousness to a section of nine or ten cellos; that one alto saxophone equals sixteen first violins or twelve seconds; [and] that one tenor saxophone equals eight violas.'[154] Volume was also important in the recording studio. String instruments recorded very poorly under the acoustic recording process, and not until the advent

69. A montage of different dance bands published in *Metronome* in September 1923, showing the prevalence of saxophones by this time, and the varied line-ups involved.

of electrical recording in 1925 was the equipment sensitive enough to do them justice. In contrast, the greater volume of the saxophone worked well with such equipment, and this was a significant contributory factor in saxophones replacing the string section in these contexts. Nevertheless, many saxophone players at this time also played string instruments – indeed, many of them started as string players – and would change between the instruments as the occasion and orchestration demanded;

70.   The Paul Whiteman saxophone sextette, c. 1922.

in some cases their classically-oriented string training influenced their saxophone
playing, particularly in relation to vibrato and phrasing.

Volume was only one reason why saxophones were becoming increasingly important. In July 1923 Harry L. Alford, who had been producing arrangements for professional wind bands for many years, wrote enthusiastically in *Metronome* about the
possibilities the saxophone afforded, and asked whether it was any wonder that:

> an instrument that can play a sustained melody with the suavity and grace of a solo
> violin or cello, rapid figuration with the agility of a flute and yet 'carry' well
> enough to be heard clearly above the brass section (or blend with it if desired), has
> become popular? Add to these qualities the fact that it has a range of two octaves
> and a half, of practically uniform timbre, without noticeable breaks; and above all,
> that the performer can continue playing for long stretches without tiring, [and] its
> value in small combinations becomes obvious'.[155]

In September the same year *Metronome* also carried an article in which various
arrangers were asked to list their hypothetically ideal line-ups for dance and theatre
bands of different sizes; all arrangers stipulated at least one saxophone in every combination, rising to as many as four in the largest bands. One musical director and saxophonist, Charles Dornberger, went so far as to assert that the violin was no longer
essential in combinations of less than 12 players, and that 'the lingering popularity of

the lone fiddle is due entirely to so many leaders being primarily violinists and too dilatory to learn saxophone, which is a much better instrument.'[156]

Hickman, Whiteman and other bandleaders such as Jean Goldkette and saxophonist Isham Jones moved the dance band format into new territory over the 1920s and early 30s. Several saxophonists were also highly skilled and sought-after arrangers, notably Don Redman, who scored many of the pieces for the Fletcher Henderson Orchestra in the mid 1920s. Redman also refined the block scoring approach to the different instrumental groups within the dance bands. His arrangement for Henderson of *Copenhagen*, to give one example, recorded in 1924, clearly demonstrates this interplay of reed and brass trios.[157] Over time these brass trios developed into sections of trumpets and trombones, and saxophones began to dominate the reed group. *Copenhagen* shows Redman experimenting with different combinations of clarinets and saxophones as the piece progresses, further illustrating the important role played by the saxophone family in extending the timbral palette available to the arranger at this time.

As the 1930s progressed and the dance era turned into swing, so the smooth sound of the closely-knit saxophone section – whether playing unison lines or matched in close harmony – became internationally recognised. The bands themselves were growing in sophistication. Although the dance-oriented white bands of Benny Goodman, Glenn Miller and Artie Shaw, for example, had the greater commercial success at the time, the more jazz-inflected African-American bands of Duke Ellington (particularly), Jimmie Lunceford and Count Basie – each of whom allowed more space for their individual soloists to shine – have arguably enjoyed greater critical acclaim in posterity. As each group became increasingly successful so the bandleaders were able to support larger ensembles, and the individual sections expanded in proportion to each other. Four saxophones (2A/2T plus doubles) soon became common, as can be heard on many of Benny Goodman's early recordings, and by the end of the decade the regular addition of a baritone had brought the standard saxophone complement to five, usually comprising 2A/2T/B; this was matched by an expanded brass section of, perhaps, three trumpets and three trombones. This saxophone section instrumentation soon became *de rigueur* for bandleaders and arrangers of the day; it also established a hierarchical relationship between the 1st and 2nd alto and tenor players in the section, with the 1st players usually given any solo opportunities. Occasional doublings on soprano or bass, as well as various members of the clarinet family, further extended the available saxophone section palette. This not only increased the possibilities available to arrangers, it also demanded greater levels of craftsmanship and imagination to make the most of the resources available. Although the overall relationship between brass, reeds and rhythm section allowed considerable interplay of different ensemble timbres, it was the details of the reed scoring that offered arrangers the greatest flexibility and the greatest challenges. As Arthur Lange puts it in his classic *Arranging for the Modern Dance Orchestra* (1926), 'the saxophone individualises the American dance orchestra'[158] and Paul Erick went so far as to start his 1937 guide to dance band arranging by observing that 'because of its unusual amount of tone color, range and versatility, the saxophone section, from the arranger's point of view, is the most important section in the orchestra. This section of the dance orchestra compares in importance to the string section of the symphony orchestra.'[159]

The dance band saxophone section had long been constructed around E♭/B♭ saxophones, with the C-melody seldom making an appearance even at the height of its popularity, again underlining the point that it was largely seen as an instrument for amateurs rather than professionals (although Lange notes that in theory the instrument could replace either the B♭ tenor or the second E♭ alto).[160] Notwithstanding their essential homogeneity, the slightly different timbres of the saxophone family (plus other woodwinds) could be exploited to good effect, and arrangers became skilled at manipulating them. Glenn Miller experimented with a variety of reed combinations, for example. On the 1937 recording of *Sleepy Time Gal* the three-part voicing for one alto and two tenors has the melody in the lowest tenor voice; similarly *Time on My Hands* uses two altos and one tenor above the second tenor 'lead' line.[161] Miller eventually developed his idiosyncratic sound by doubling the melody line on solo clarinet and tenor saxophone, with the other four saxophones providing the harmony. Duke Ellington, whose masterly orchestration set new standards for big band writing, would sometimes score the distinctive sound of his baritone player Harry Carney playing the ninth (or higher) of the chord at the *bottom* of the harmonic formation, lending an ethereal quality to the texture.[162] Ellington's conceptualisation of the baritone line as being a distinctive entity was reinforced by the way in which he laid out his scores, which were usually written over four staves. The other four saxes were written on the first stave, at the top, with the baritone having a line to itself on the stave below, written an octave above its sounding pitch. Trumpets were put on a third stave and trombones on a fourth.[163]

Saxophone doubling and sectional skills

The growing size and importance of saxophone sections in the dance and swing bands from the 1920s onwards made increasingly complex demands on the players in them. In particular, the ability to play a variety of instruments, not only saxophones but clarinets, flutes and others, became a necessary skill for most professional saxophone players. This doubling on a range of instruments was of course common practice well before the 1920s. Circus and vaudeville musicians had long been multi-instrumentalists, and as Smith and Holmes had wryly observed as early as 1915, 'here in Chicago [. . .] if a flute, cornet or even a trap drummer is needed in any organisation, the first question asked is: "Can you double on the saxophone?" '[164] But by the 1920s expectations had risen, in line with levels of technical proficiency, and skilled doublers were in demand. Ernest Cutting, a respected arranger and conductor, noted in a 1923 *Metronome* article on instrumentation that saxophone players should be capable of playing the entire family of saxophones, as well as other woodwinds. 'Competition is keen', he went on to observe, 'but the ambitious fellow today is fully repaid for his efforts. Saxophone players especially cannot be too versatile. String bass players should also make a point of becoming efficient on bass saxophone or tuba. All this doubling is made necessary by the demand for color in dance music as in the classics.'[165] Harry L. Alford similarly noted that 'a saxophonist who doubles jazz clarinet for the "Blue" numbers is quite an asset; but there is an increasing demand for a saxophonist who can play either oboe, bass clarinet, or bassoon, and who has in addition a complete set of saxophones, from the infant sopranino down to the baritone.'[166]

Pictures of the time illustrate the significant numbers of instruments that saxophonists might be required to play. For the first performance of Gershwin's *Rhapsody in Blue*
in 1924, Whiteman's three reed players played no less than seventeen instruments
between them, and a year previously a Buescher advertisement had indicated his
players as doubling on 24 instruments. A later Whiteman soloist, the astonishingly
virtuosic Al Gallodoro (1913–2008), whom Jimmy Dorsey (1904–57) described as 'the
best saxophone player that ever lived',[167] became similarly renowned as a multi-
instrumentalist, equally adept on clarinet and bass clarinet, and at one stage recording
the Brahms clarinet quintet.[168]

Paul Whiteman lists his band playing at the Palais Royale in 1924 as including:

Gorman: E♭ saxophone [sopranino], B♭ saxophone [soprano], E♭ alto saxophone,
oboe, hecklophone [*sic*], B♭ clarinet, E♭ clarinet, alto clarinet, bass clarinet, octavin.

Strickaden: B♭ soprano saxophone, E♭ alto saxophone, B♭ tenor saxophone,
E♭ baritone saxophone, oboe, clarinet;

Byers: Flute, B♭ soprano saxophone, B♭ tenor saxophone, C soprano saxophone,
E♭ baritone.[169]

71. Paul Whiteman's band from c. 1923, taken from a Buescher advert. The accompanying text
indicates Hale Byers as playing three instruments, Donald Clarke as having nine, and Ross
Gorman twelve, although these do not all appear in this picture.

Being proficient in changing rapidly between these instruments, and quickly adopting the correct embouchure and fingering for each one, thus became part of an expanded skill set for dance band musicians (in addition to the need to own a good selection of instruments, mouthpieces, reeds, stands and so forth). But the most successful saxophonists were highly skilled musicians in other ways, particularly in terms of reading and transposing at sight, as well as providing short improvised solos when required. Ed Chenette wrote of Isham Jones's musicians in 1923 that 'nearly all of his programs are played from manuscript and very frequently the entire orchestra transposes a strain into another key instantly without rehearsal and without error. These numbers are full of double sharps, double flats, enharmonics, unnatural accents, weird effects, odd accompaniments, abrupt cadences, unusual progressions, the combination of which taxes the skill of these very competent musicians.'[170]

Saxophone players now also had to be sophisticated ensemble musicians, closely attuned to the playing of others in the section in respect of tuning, phrasing and articulation, much like the orchestral string player. The lead alto, in particular, began to take on a role similar to that of the leader of an orchestral string section, becoming a musical leader in terms of tuning, phrasing and dynamics. Players who became skilled in this soon attracted attention, not only from other musicians and bandleaders, but also occasionally in the press. A review of a Tommy Dorsey Orchestra recording in 1936, for example, praises the phrasing and consistency of Dorsey's lead alto player Hymie Shertzer (1909–77), and describes him as the finest lead saxophonist in the business, noting his more consistent approach than those 'many lead men [who] attach or release phrases or notes as is their want, hoping that the rest of the boys in the section will anticipate what's coming'.[171]

Such musical leadership skills are seldom detailed in saxophone methods, since they are often regarded as on-the-job training. But Ben Davis's 1932 *Comprehensive Course* does offer some help to the aspiring section player. Davis notes, for example, that 'in the first place there must be only one leader and the other two must adapt their playing to his in as many ways as possible' and that the second alto should 'study the [leader's] methods of tone production, and endeavour to match his own to them as much as possible'. Similarly the three players should be aware of producing similar styles of vibrato, although Davis does not recommend attempting matched vibrato – where all three lines undulate simultaneously – which he mistakenly considers impossible. There is more practical advice for the section player, much of which continues to hold true today: 'the sax team must all breathe in the same places in the music. Without this the team is doomed to failure'; and with respect to note values, he observes that 'some leaders like to hold notes over a shade, others to cut them off. Whatever the team leader's ideas are on this subject, the other two must copy him implicitly.' Finally Davis observes that 'If you *must* move your body in rhythm to the music, for goodness sake be unanimous about it. In any case, such movements, unless they are absolutely instinctive, look utterly absurd.'[172] Whatever one might now feel about the specifics of Davis's exhortations, they demonstrate that over the 1920s and 30s a particular skill set developed among dance and swing band saxophonists that required musical expertise of a kind, and to a level, not previously expected. There were a small number of other publications designed to help saxophonists develop these specialist skills, such as David Gornston's *Sax-Clarinet Doubling Studies* or *Sax Section Studies*, both published in 1937.[173]

For those willing to make the necessary investment to acquire such expertise, however, there were plenty of employment prospects. As early as 1915 a Buescher company advert had claimed – with a degree of corporate self-interest – that 'saxophone players secure more engagements, have more openings and more opportunities to make money than almost any other player'; the following year their saxophone adverts were titled as 'Buescher's Family of Money Makers'.[174] The Carl Fischer company was similarly urging performers to 'Make More Money: Double on the Saxophone' in its 1918 adverts.[175] As the dance craze snowballed over the ensuing years, establishing a need for more bands requiring more saxophone players, such opportunities grew exponentially. Moreover, the financial rewards for the players working in the best bands could be significant. In 1923 it was claimed that musicians working with Isham Jones were earning four times what they had previously earned playing in symphony orchestras,[176] and a year later Paul Whiteman similarly noted that 'each man in my orchestra makes from $65 to $300 a week all the year round while the best men in a big symphony orchestra are lucky if they earn $200 a week for six months of the year'.[177] Admittedly, bandleaders such as these were almost certainly paying the highest fees, and not all musicians would have been earning these kinds of sums. Nevertheless, the prospect of such rewards undoubtedly provoked assiduous practising on the part of many dance band saxophone aspirants.

Early saxophone recordings

Although the saxophone was developed nearly 40 years before Thomas Edison's invention of the phonograph in 1877, the instrument's rapidly increasing popularity from c. 1885 to c. 1930 coincided with the yet more rapid growth of recorded musical sound. Edison's wax cylinders, Emile Berliner's flat discs, and the 78-rpm shellac discs that superseded them both, all contributed to a technological innovation that profoundly changed the nature of musical performance. The portability and transferability of musical sound that we now take for granted was a liberating process for performers and listeners alike. The merchandising of performances by the emerging record companies allowed saxophonists and other musicians to benefit financially from the commercial exploitation of their recordings – although seldom to the extent that the companies themselves benefitted – as well as enabling them to hear the work of other performers

Nevertheless, the phonograph played little role in bringing the saxophone to a wider audience in the late nineteenth and very early twentieth centuries, since few people owned one of the new machines. Early costs of cylinders, discs and the machines on which to play them were prohibitive. Cylinder and disc manufacture was also laborious, and not until effective methods of mass duplication were developed around the turn of the century did the technology begin to offer viable possibilities. Thus, although saxophone players were making recordings from as early as 1890, not until the widespread success of recordings of the Brown Brothers from 1911 onwards, and particularly those made by Rudy Wiedoeft from 1918, might it reasonably be claimed that recording technology substantially impacted upon the dissemination of the saxophone.

The instrument presented particular problems for early recording engineers because the rudimentary recording equipment available to them struggled with the particularly rich overtone series the saxophone produced. The Columbia Company acknowledged as much in 1917 when it released recordings by the Saxo Sextette, noting in its catalogue that 'in all recording experience no instrument has presented the difficulties of the saxophone' before going on to boast that '[The] singular, dim, rich tone of the saxophone has at last, and we believe for the first time, been absolutely reproduced in all its fidelity on the initial records by the Saxo Sextette.'[178] This was marketing spin, since, as with all other instruments and voices, much better fidelity to the original sound was not properly achieved until the move from acoustic technology to electrically-enhanced recording in 1925. In fact, by the standards of many other instruments, the saxophone recorded tolerably well in the acoustic era, largely because it produced sufficient volume to make an impression on the somewhat insensitive recording equipment in use at the time. This was particularly true of the mid-range members of the family. The low tessitura of the bass saxophone presented special problems, although it was occasionally used to substitute for double basses, even in classical recordings: when Rachmaninov, for example, recorded his own Piano Concerto no. 2 for Victor in 1924 – the only acoustic recording by any artist of that work – a bass saxophone replaced the string basses.[179]

Various technical deficiencies and surface noise notwithstanding, recordings from around the turn of the century give valuable insights into how the saxophone was played at the time, and indeed earlier in the nineteenth century, since these pioneers were likely to have been replicating performance aesthetics they had been taught several years earlier, by teachers who were themselves building on traditions passed down over several decades. Thus recordings from the 1890s, for example, may offer tantalising glimpses into saxophone performance practice from the instrument's earliest days, particularly since many of the first soloists had received their musical training in Europe, and then transplanted these approaches to the United States.

Unsurprisingly, many early saxophone recordings were made by those who had already achieved musical prominence in the bands of Gilmore, Sousa and others. E. A. Lefebre may hold the title of the 'first recorded saxophonist', following a series of cylinders that he made for the US Phonograph company between 1890 and 1896, accompanied by Gilmore's band. The repertoire was typical of the light classical fare the band would have offered to audiences of the time. The seven cylinders recorded included Balfe's *Heart Bowed Down* and *Killarney* as well as a transcription of the *Intermezzo* from Mascagni's *Cavalleria Rusticana*.[180] In 1892 Lefebre's star pupil Bessie Mecklem (see ill. 51) appears to have made the first solo recordings, cutting a series of twelve cylinders for saxophone and piano on 23 April of that year for the Edison company.[181] These comprised various slow-paced popular tunes and waltzes, such as *Nightingale Song, Sweet Lullaby*, and the oddly out-of-season *Christmas Song*.

These were followed over the next decade by various other recordings. Moeremans recorded extensively for the Berliner company, and later for Victor, during the period 1896–1904. Again the repertory comprised light favourites, albeit of a rather more demanding type: Benedict's variations on *The Carnival of Venice*, or a fantasy on Foster's *Old Folks at Home*, demonstrated Moeremans's greater soloistic competence. Additionally, in 1904, Moeremans recorded one of his own compositions, an air and variations under the title *The Swell of the Day*. Moeremans also made a series of duet recordings with the flautist Frank Badollet on various dates from 1899–1900, and further duos with the clarinettist Jacques L. van Poucke. Eugene Coffin recorded a similar series of recordings for saxophone and band which were listed in the 1896 catalogue of the Columbia Company, and the saxophone section from Sousa's band made several recordings for Victor in 1902 and 1903. They also released one tune, *Annie Laurie*, on the Berliner label. Benne Henton recorded a number of cylinders and discs for the Victor and Edison companies between 1910 and 1918, including several versions of his own composition *Laverne*. Sousa's band provided probably the earliest recorded saxophone quartet. In August 1902 and September 1903 a quartet drawn from the band recorded for the Victor company arrangements of Mascagni's *Cavalleria Rusticana*, as well as *Dixie Girl* – a march by Lampe – and arrangements of works by Foster and Waldteufel, among others.[182]

What do these various recordings reveal about saxophone performance practice at the time? First, many of them are display vehicles, designed to show off the prowess of the individual soloist, and replicate the types of solo spots that such soloists would take during concerts given by the bands in which they often worked. Certain recordings, e.g. Moeremans' various versions of *Carnival of Venice* or Benne Henton's *Scenes That Are Brightest* (an Edison promotional disc issued in 1910), demonstrate the impressive finger technique that might be expected of the skilled instrumentalist; these recordings document the arrival of the saxophone virtuoso, rather than the more utilitarian performances given by circus or vaudeville musicians.[183] Technical skills are impressive in other ways: Benne Henton's 1916 version of his popular tune *Laverne*, backed by the Conway band, demonstrates his well-controlled use of the altissimo range in its final slow rising scale from g^3 to c^4.[184]

Even allowing for the limitations of the recording equipment, the saxophone, sound is more mellow and rounded than many with which we are now familiar; it remains remarkably homogenous throughout the registers, notwithstanding occasional discrepancies between adjacent notes, something that is implicit in the construction of many early wind instruments and which modern manufacturers have striven hard to overcome. The misalignment that we hear between soloist and band, and indeed within the bands themselves, while sounding today as rather ragged ensemble playing, would not have been heard as unusual by the listeners of the time; nor would the slightly unsteady rushing of the soloist relative to the accompaniment, or the shortening of certain note values to keep the soloist ahead of the ensemble. Similarly, the much more extensive use of rubato as an expressive device was in keeping with musical tastes of the time.

Vibrato is used more sparingly on the earliest recordings, and often not at all; when it is used it tends to be shallower and slightly faster than prevailing tastes today. This shallow vibrato remained the norm until the 1920s, and it was during the early jazz era that a slower and wider vibrato became established. One can hear the change quite distinctly between, for example, Rudy Wiedoeft's 1917 recording of his own *Valse*

Erica, in which his vibrato measures eight pulses per second, and his 1926 recording of Drdla's *Souvenir*, in which the vibrato is consistently around five pulses per second and is noticeably wider.[185]

Recordings by the Brown Brothers sound a little slow and somewhat mechanical when compared to James Reese Europe's recordings, for example, made around the same time, and they again sound rhythmically unsteady and slightly ragged to contemporary ears. But their rather more sedate approach was very popular at the time, and their records sold well. In 1917 Fred Brown put out four solo recordings with orchestral accompaniment (two of which had been recorded the previous year). These rather schmaltzy recordings, with the saxophone line underpinned by copious amounts of the string portamento that was still in fashion at the time, may well be the first recordings of solo saxophone with orchestra rather than band (although Wiedoeft issued the similarly saccharine *Valse Erica* with orchestral accompaniment the same year). Significantly, Fred Brown's saxophone vibrato here is noticeably more pronounced, and deeper, than other recordings of the time, and may indicate some alignment with the increasing use of vibrato among string players, particularly in these popular music contexts.

While these recordings now function as important historical documents, they provided for many aspiring saxophone players at the time important aural models of how the instrument *should* sound. This was particularly true of recordings by the Brown Brothers and, later, Wiedoeft, because of their popularity and the number of recordings they sold. In both these cases their relatively light and clear, well-rounded timbres, developed from band/classical models, set important precedents that others sought to imitate. Lester Young's brother Lee, a drummer in later life but a soprano saxophone player in the Young family band, recalled how Lester used to listen to Wiedoeft's records, practising six to seven hours a day, in order to emulate Wiedoeft's impressive articulation skills.[186] Recordings thus began to underpin autodidactic approaches to learning the saxophone in a range of contexts, at a time when formalised saxophone tuition was for many either unavailable, unaffordable, or simply unwanted.

Chapter 5

The saxophone in jazz

Early jazz

The word 'jazz' was probably initially used in African-American oral culture of the late nineteenth century as a synonym for sexual intercourse, and various suggestions have been put forward as to its etymology. It may have evolved from the word 'jasmine', which was used as a perfume in the red light district (known as Storyville) of New Orleans, Louisiana, where, it is often claimed, jazz originally developed. It may have derived from the Old Testament 'Jezebel', used at the time to designate a prostitute.[1] Thus, when the saxophone later became closely identified with the jazz tradition and its players, these earlier associations were to taint the instrument in the eyes of many. As the early saxophone pedagogue and performer Clay Smith wrote in *Etude* magazine in September 1924, 'if the truth were known about the origin of "jazz," it would never be mentioned in polite society'.[2] But the connection of both jazz and the saxophone with these nefarious activities is most likely overdone. While it is true that the important progenitors of the jazz tradition worked in the general area, only the pianists appear likely to have worked in the brothels themselves. New Orleans was a city in which music-making was widespread. Musicians might equally be employed in legitimate theatre or vaudeville contexts, in amusement parks or resorts on the shores of nearby Lake Pontchartrain, or in the community halls and saloons that held frequent dances.[3]

In this rich musical environment worked a number of the early figures who laid the foundations for what eventually became known as jazz. Cornettists such as Buddy Bolden, Joe 'King' Oliver and Bunk Johnson, or the pianist Ferdinand 'Jelly Roll' Morton, among others, have claimed – or had claims made on their behalf – to have been the 'father of jazz'. The veracity or otherwise of these claims is not important here, but what *is* significant is that none of these performers were saxophone players. Paradoxically, given its later centrality in this tradition, it is clear that the saxophone played little part in the early development of jazz.

This was largely because the instrument had only a peripheral role in the musical genres taken as precursors to jazz. Perhaps pre-eminent among these, in terms of its ultimate influence on jazz performance, was ragtime. Ragtime was largely the preserve of pianists, who developed a musical style based around particular 'striding' on-beat patterns in the left hand, played against heavily syncopated melodies in the right hand; it found its most articulate exponent in the now famous works of the pianist

Scott Joplin. The connections between the saxophone and ragtime have already been illustrated in Chapter 4, and while the instrument clearly played a significant part in the work of ragtime-influenced groups such as the Brown Brothers or the Musical Spillers, whatever musical impact 'ragging' may have had on early jazz players does not appear to have translated into the adoption of the saxophone as a preferred front-line instrument.

Another genre that contributed to the development of early jazz was the blues. Initially a vocal tradition that owed something to song styles brought by slaves from west Africa (quite how much is a matter of considerable speculation), the blues was related to a number of other African-American vocal traditions – field hollers, prison work songs, etc. – and was characterised melodically by the use of 'blue' notes, particularly on the third degree of the scale. This blue third could be either an ambiguous pitch, a 'bent' note lying somewhere between a major and minor third, or it might refer to a minor third used in contexts where the underlying harmony dictated that a major third would be expected. Other degrees of the scale such as the seventh or the fifth might be similarly treated. These vocalised, tonally ambiguous passages contributed to the mournful, introspective characteristics of many blues songs, and this was reinforced by song texts that described or alluded to themes that, in addition to revealing something of the oppression suffered by the southern blacks amongst whom they originated, have something of a timeless quality to them: the travails of romantic love, life on the road, the vagaries of fate, and so forth. These details relating to the blues tradition may appear unconnected to the saxophone's role in jazz, but it will be argued below that the blues roots of jazz in part account for the saxophone's later pre-eminence as a jazz instrument, and that the performance styles of the southern blues vocalists profoundly influenced a number of early jazz saxophone soloists.

Of the several genres that were melded into jazz, the brass band tradition probably had the greatest impact on early instrumentation. Brass bands were common throughout rural and small town areas of the United States in the second half of the nineteenth century, particularly among black communities. Local amateur groups provided musical accompaniments for a range of activities, such as funerals, church celebrations, street shows and parades. As the century progressed some bands were augmented by the inclusion of woodwind instruments. Taking their cue from well-established European military models, some of these bands were large, comprising up to 24 musicians. A typical line-up for these larger bands might include three to five each of trumpets, trombones and clarinets, a baritone and bass horn, perhaps one or two flutes and alto horns plus a snare and a bass drum.[4] Whereas by the turn of the century many of the professional white bands were already using saxophones, it was unusual for any of the amateur black bands of the South to include the instrument, and it was not really part of this tradition until later. Naturally there would have been occasional exceptions: the Holmes Band of Lutcher, fifty miles up the Mississippi river from New Orleans, may have incorporated saxophone players from around 1910, for example.[5]

In general these bands were small, perhaps numbering ten to twelve players, and smaller subsets yet of these musicians, sometimes joined by string players, would be employed for dances. From these smaller groups the preferred format of the first jazz groups evolved: a front line of cornet, trombone and clarinet, together with a rhythm section drawn from piano, banjo or guitar, with tuba or a string bass, and drums. In general, the cornet carried the melody, the trombone a counter-melody, and the clarinet, with its greater range and timbral contrast, weaved an obbligato line throughout the texture. Early photographs demonstrate the different variations of this instrumentation actually employed, as well as, usually, confirming the absence of any saxophones.

Gradually, however, the instrument began to feature more widely in the New Orleans musical landscape. Several African-American bands in the area are listed as having saxophonists in the period between 1913 and 1916. Sam Dutrey (1887–1941) is suggested in one source as being the first jazz musician to play the saxophone in New Orleans, some time before 1914.[6] Wilbur C. Sweatman, who worked with W. C. Handy around the turn of the century, released several sides with his 'Jass Band' in April 1917, in which his clarinet playing was backed by a saxophone quintet comprised of 2A/T/B/Bs. While the style and musical structures owe much to ragtime – and the instrumentation owes something to the popularity of the Brown Brothers at the time – Sweatman's occasionally improvisatory clarinet lines have led some to describe these as the first jazz recordings made by an African American.[7] Certainly Sweatman saw himself more as a jazz player, and his next group was in the style of a Dixieland jazz band, albeit without saxophones. If there is some ambivalence as to whether Sweatman's recordings count as jazz, then perhaps those made by Handy for Columbia in September of the same year would count as the first recordings by African American jazz players (see p. 171).

Why did the saxophone become increasingly attractive to these early jazz players? In later years the wide range of timbres of which the instrument is capable undoubtedly made it highly suited to the jazz idiom. The ability to create an idiosyncratic yet recognisable sound appealed to those many jazz soloists who were to follow, and whose conception of individual sound underpinned their creative aspirations; as Coleman Hawkins would later put it: 'the only thing nobody can steal from you is your sound: sound alone is important'.[8] But this emphasis on sonic individuality in jazz performance came rather later. In its earliest incarnations jazz was essentially a collective, ensemble-driven contrapuntal music, so the ability to create an individual sound on the saxophone is unlikely to have been a significant factor in its early adoption. Volume was another matter, however, and the ability to play loudly was clearly highly valued: part of the Buddy Bolden legend stems from the tremendous volume he is said to have achieved on his cornet.[9] In those unamplified days bands might well be working outdoors or in noisy dance halls; the acoustically efficient saxophone could compete in volume with the cornet and trombone in these environments, contributing to the overall volume of the band while at the same time blending with the other brass instruments. In tessitura also, both the alto and to a lesser extent the tenor saxophone could be seen as falling into an intermediate range between cornet and trombone, filling out the harmony while still allowing the clarinet to weave its obbligatos throughout the texture; this was perhaps particularly true of the C-melody saxophone adopted by several early players. As in other contexts, the instrument was robust enough to withstand a certain amount of rough treatment, and it was reasonably easy to learn, a particularly important point for players who would be largely, often exclusively, self-taught. And the saxophone, while not quite matching the clarinet in terms of musical dexterity, was certainly fluid enough not only to hold the melody line but also to contribute ornamental embellishments, as well as provide a counter melody when required.

Another reason for the appropriation of the saxophone by jazz players lies in the instrument's essentially vocal quality, and the relative ease with which the pitch of any given note can be manipulated or 'bent', thus imitating the flexibility of the human voice. Although not alone in this respect – string instruments and the trombone can slide between pitches with even greater ease – the saxophone appears often to be the instrument most frequently associated with the human voice; the warm, mellow sound produced on instruments of the time, unlike the brighter, edgier sounds more common today, would have further reinforced this association. Herein lies a connection with the blues tradition that, as noted above, was characterised by flexible and idiomatic forms of vocal delivery. For musicians who had the sounds of the blues firmly in their inner ears, the saxophone's vocal quality, and its capacity to imitate those blue vocal lines, would have appeared very attractive; indeed, the 'moaning' and 'wailing' sounds that distinguished the blues would later become iconic of the saxophone itself

72.   Fate Marable's New Orleans band on the *S.S. Capitol* in 1920, with sax players David Jones and Norman Brashear to the left of the youthful trumpeter Louis Armstrong.

(see pp. 338–40).[10] This being the case, however, it remains a minor enigma that the saxophone was not more readily adopted by early New Orleans jazz players, since it would appear to have been in many ways a very suitable instrument for them in relation to the sound ideals they pursued. As Ted Gioia points out, 'this obsession with sound gets to the heart of the New Orleans revolution in music [. . .]. Instead of aspiring to classical purity of tone, emulating an otherworldly perfection, the early jazz players strived to make their instruments sound like human voices, with all the variations, imperfections, and colorations that such a model entailed.'[11] And yet, despite the saxophone's relative lack of association with the aesthetics of classical music, and its timbral flexibility, it was not initially popular among the New Orleans players, as evidenced by the cornettist Bunk Johnson's observation that the instrument 'just runs up and down stairs with no place to go'.[12] By the late 1910s, however, with dance music in the ascendant, the saxophone was increasingly a part of the New Orleans musical landscape, not only on land but also on the riverboats that provided important and lucrative work for the musicians of the area (see ill. 72).

The first jazz soloists

Sidney Bechet

It was into the Creole community of New Orleans that Sidney Bechet (1897–1959), the first major jazz saxophone figure, was born, on 14 May 1897. It would be wrong to suggest that Bechet was one of the most influential figures in jazz history; his musical impact at the time was perhaps less significant than his subsequent fame might suggest, and the latter arises in part from a revival of interest in his work in France in the 1940s and 50s. But he is important in the present context for three reasons: he was one of the first truly modern saxophonists; his career is emblematic of the diasporic nature of New Orleans jazz after about 1915; and he established the jazz soloist as a cultural icon, and by association therefore, the saxophone, in much the same way that Louis Armstrong did for himself and the trumpet. Bechet is also important to historiographers of jazz because of the extensive autobiography he produced, *Treat it Gentle* (published in 1960, just after his death), which, although embellished and frequently inaccurate, remains an intriguing insider's view of the New Orleans tradition.

Bechet was born into a musical, middle-class Creole family. He received his first clarinet as a hand-me-down from his eldest brother Leonard, but he developed quickly on the instrument and began to establish a good local reputation. He had a temperamental character, and his clarinet lessons with teachers such as the renowned Tio dynasty and George Baquet appear to have been short lived. At some stage he was invited to join Bunk Johnson's Eagle Band, one of the preeminent local groups, but it wasn't until his 1916 departure for Chicago that he achieved national and later international attention.

Bechet's move north from New Orleans was part of a broader migration of early jazz musicians from the less welcoming southern states. Disenfranchised in many states after a key supreme court ruling, formally defined as inferior by segregation laws, and attracted by better economic prospects in the expanding urban centres of the north, between 1914 and 1920 more than half a million black Americans moved from the predominantly rural south to the urban north, an internal migration facilitated by the railroad lines. The three main destinations that were to become significant for the evolution of jazz, and by implication therefore, the development and dissemination of jazz saxophone playing, were Kansas City, New York and Chicago. It was to the last of these that many of the black and Creole New Orleans musicians were drawn, including Bechet; indeed, it is a paradox of so-called New Orleans jazz that much of it actually developed in Chicago.

Until about 1919 Bechet played exclusively on the clarinet, but during this year he was invited to join a tour to Europe with Will Marion Cook's Southern Syncopated Orchestra. The group's sojourn in London yielded two significant events. First, the noted Swiss conductor Ernest Ansermet heard Bechet's playing, after which he famously penned an article in the *Revue Romande* in which he described Bechet as 'an artist of genius';[13] second, Bechet acquired from a London dealer the instrument with which he was later to become closely identified: a soprano saxophone. Quite what made him turn to this relatively unfashionable member of the saxophone family is not clear, although there is a suggestion that he became interested in the saxophone generally after hearing a recording of the Brown Brothers' *Bull Frog Blues*, released in 1916.[14] Bechet himself dates his interest a little later, around 1918, while working in New York with the bandleader Tim Bryen:

> Tim had a regular clarinet player, named Kincaid; and this Kincaid, he had a curved soprano saxophone. I liked the tone of this saxophone very much, so full and rich. I'd tried one in Chicago when I was playing at the Pekin but I hadn't liked it, and I think there must have been something wrong with it. Well, I liked this one Kincaid had, and from that time I got more and more interested in the soprano saxophone.[15]

Bechet then relates how, in June 1919, he finally came to own one:

> And another thing I did when I got to London was to buy a straight soprano saxophone. I was walking around with Arthur Briggs when I saw one in the window of an instrument maker. We went in, and I ran through Whispering on it: this was the first number I played on it. I liked this saxophone as soon as that London instrument maker gave it to me, and Will Marion Cook, he liked it too [. . .]. This was a piece of good luck for me because it wasn't long after this before people started saying they didn't want clarinets in their bands no more. And there was I all set with my saxophone.[16]

Bechet's observation that it was the saxophone's tone that drew him to the instrument reinforces the idea that jazz players were attracted by the saxophone's timbral qualities and the relative ease with which these might be manipulated. Colour and texture were as important to New Orleans players as melody, harmony and rhythm. Bechet's own solos reflect this, with a range of different textures employed to colour the melodic line. Richard Hadlock, who was taught by Bechet, later recalled the instructions given to him in one lesson: 'I'm going to give you one note today [. . .]. See how many ways you can play that note – growl it, smear it, flat it, sharp it, do anything you want to it. That's how you express your feelings in this music.'[17] If Hadlock's recollection is accurate, it is unsurprising that Bechet found the saxophone and its tonal malleability well suited to his musical aspirations.

Changing from the clarinet to the louder and more penetrating soprano saxophone allowed Bechet to match the volume of the cornet and trombone in the traditional New Orleans front line. As already noted, New Orleans jazz performances were ensemble events in which improvisation was subsumed within a collective musical identity. Bechet and the trumpeter Louis Armstrong developed the art of the jazz solo, and this fundamentally changed both the structures of jazz and the musical conceptions of those who played it. From the 1920s the jazz soloist emerged as a quintessential figure within the tradition, analogous to the longer-established virtuosic soloists in classical music. Bechet's preference for the soprano saxophone instead of the clarinet, because of the greater timbral range and volume it afforded him as a soloist, is a significant marker of that changing jazz aesthetic.

Bechet's improvisations were characterised by rhythmic inventiveness. Whereas many players remained reasonably metrically consistent in their rhythmic subdivisions of the main beats of the bar, Bechet played more freely. His playing across the beats and his use of hemiola-like figures gave a very swingy feel to his improvisations, something that in its earliest incarnations was ahead of its time. His harmonic language, derived from his earlier clarinet training, is also significant. New Orleans clarinet players had to be more harmonically astute than cornettists and trombonists, because the arpeggiated patterns on which their solos were built demanded a more

Ex. 6. An extract from Sidney Bechet's 1939 recording of Gershwin's *Summertime*, showing the variety of different articulations and endeavouring also to communicate the flexibility of the saxophone line.

73.   Sidney Bechet and his clarinet-style saxophone posture in 1947.

sophisticated understanding of the underlying harmony than that required for the essentially melodic ornamentations that characterised the improvisations of other instruments. Bechet, perhaps realising that endless arpeggiations ultimately represented something of a creative dead end, combined his harmonic facility with an acute sense of melody, thus amalgamating these two dimensions of the improviser's art in a fashion that provided the groundwork for the next generation of saxophone soloists, and particularly Coleman Hawkins.

Bechet's style and technique has much more in common with the New Orleans clarinet tradition he grew up in than with other jazz saxophone players of the early 1920s. Notwithstanding his high profile as a soprano saxophone soloist, he played the saxophone much like he played the clarinet, maintaining a typical, even exaggerated, clarinet posture: head back, chin up, instrument held high, eyes looking ahead or even upwards; other players later developed more relaxed, chin down postures. In particular, his fast and wide vibrato – a performance characteristic that, once heard, immediately identifies a Bechet performance – was undoubtedly carried over from his

New Orleans-style clarinet playing. The clear relationship between Bechet's approach to the two instruments is underlined on a remarkable 1941 recording of *The Sheik of Araby*.[18] Made before magnetic tape facilitated multi-tracking, Bechet plays all the instruments on this recording himself: clarinet, soprano and tenor saxophones, piano, bass and drums. Each recording was played back while Bechet played along with it, thus superimposing the necessary instrumental lines one upon the other (although the drums are largely inaudible). The stylistic overlap between Bechet's clarinet and saxophone sounds is demonstrable, and lends further credence to the notion that he conceived the two instruments in very similar ways.

Bechet's early adoption of the saxophone notwithstanding, some would query whether he is fully deserving of a place in the jazz saxophone pantheon, precisely because in his hands the instrument appears largely to function as a clarinet substitute. And while his style was certainly distinctive, he was not as influential as he might have been, in part because he absented himself to Europe for long periods when major developments in jazz were taking place in the United States. For a short period in the 1930s he gave up playing, before being lured out of retirement by the bandleader Noble Sissle in 1938. During the late 1930s and early 40s there was a revival of interest in New Orleans-style jazz, and Bechet greatly benefited from this, finding himself once again in demand for performances and recordings. In 1949 he gave a well-received concert in Paris, and shortly afterwards moved permanently to France; he died in Paris on his birthday, 14 May 1959.

After Bechet

Bechet's advocacy of the soprano saxophone might have propelled that instrument to a more central position within jazz had he himself been more influential. But the soprano remained largely peripheral to what followed, and did not significantly resurface until the late 1950s and 1960s. Instead, the jazz saxophone baton passed to a different – and perhaps equally unlikely – member of the family, the C-melody saxophone. Despite the sometimes disdainful look given by professionals towards the instrument, the model's widespread popularity in the early 1920s led to several fine performers adopting it. Paul 'Stump' Evans (1904–28) played both alto and C-melody, and might have become more influential himself had he lived longer and played in bands other than those of King Oliver and Jelly Roll Morton, whose conservative New Orleans style waned during that decade. Evans had an excellent technique, influenced in part – as were many at the time – by novelty techniques such as slap tonguing and the virtuosic approaches developed by Rudy Wiedoeft.

The most renowned exponent on the C-melody instrument was Frankie Trumbauer (1901–56), whose work in the 1920s, particularly with the great cornettist Bix Beiderbecke, influenced a number of other saxophone players, notably Lester Young. Trumbauer's facility on the saxophone was exceptional for his time, and provides another indicator of the significance of Wiedoeft's impact on early jazz players; Trumbauer's influential 1927 recording of 'Trumbology' is particularly notable in this respect.[19] But it is Trumbauer's sound, a light, airy style contrasting notably with the heavier tenor sounds that predominated in the late 1920s and 30s, that is most

74. Frankie Trumbauer's *Modern Saxophone Solos* from c. 1927.

immediately noticeable today. Trumbauer's contribution to the development of the jazz solo is often overlooked, but, like Bechet, his most innovative work moved the music away from the harmonically-oriented arpeggiated solos that characterised New Orleans jazz, and towards the more horizontal/melodic formulations that followed. He also developed the formal structures of his solos, leading to a more narrative approach that again influenced other players; as Lester Young later recalled, 'Trumbauer always told a little story'.[20] Trumbauer was probably the most influential saxophonist of the 1920s after Wiedoeft, and the first truly significant saxophonist with regard to the creation of an identifiable jazz saxophone tradition. This influence was disseminated not only through his recordings, but also through various transcriptions of his solos, which began to provide a nascent jazz saxophone literature for those who were musically literate.

The bass saxophone also featured prominently in the 1920s, largely through its association with one particular player. Generally unwieldy and not given to florid solos in the manner of other saxophones, the bass was an infrequent visitor to jazz, being instead confined usually to marching bands or vaudeville acts such as the Brown Brothers. In early jazz groups the bass line was usually provided by E♭ tuba or B♭ sousaphone, until the later predominance of the string double bass. But in the hands of Adrian Rollini (1903–56) the bass saxophone achieved some recognition as a solo instrument. Rollini, a talented multi-instrumentalist who had recorded commercial piano rolls at the age of 16, briefly brought the instrument into the limelight in the 1920s and 30s, playing with various luminaries of the day, including Frankie

Trumbauer's orchestra. Rollini certainly managed to make the instrument swing, his infectious solos demonstrating his ability to extract a great deal of musical energy out of his unusual choice of instrument. More significantly, he changed perceptions of what could be achieved on the bass saxophone, developing its role away from simply delivering the onbeat 'ooms' of an 'oom-pah' style as found in the Brown Brothers' ragtime arrangements, and asserting a more equal voice for the instrument within jazz polyphony. Rollini thus demonstrated that jazz saxophone solos need not be confined to the more demonstrably agile smaller instruments, but could also be effective on the larger instruments. This re-conceptualisation of jazz saxophone practice would benefit later players such as Harry Carney and Gerry Mulligan, both baritone specialists.

Having fun was also part of Rollini's makeup, since he played and advocated a number of less serious instruments, including the 'goofus' and the 'hot fountain pen', before moving away from wind instruments and completing the latter part of his career as a vibraphone player.[21]

Jimmy Dorsey (1904–57) was an accomplished jazz player who influenced major figures such as Lester Young and Coleman Hawkins. His more innovative work in the 1920s was overshadowed by his subsequent success as a swing bandleader in the 1930s and 40s, both in his own name and with his trombonist brother Tommy in The Dorsey Brothers Orchestra. Hits such as *Oodles of Noodles* (1932) and his appearances in several films (including playing himself in the 1947 biopic *The Fabulous Dorsey Brothers*) made Jimmy Dorsey internationally recognised. Like Rudy Wiedoeft, Dorsey published a saxophone method, in 1940. It too offered basic technical instruction on the instrument, as well as some insights into the then fashionable but advanced techniques of double and triple tonguing. The method also offered an introduction to jazz improvisation, as well as basic instruction in the theory of jazz harmony, illustrated

75.   Promotional shot of Adrian Rollini and his bass saxophone in the 1920s.

through practical examples. That such practical and intellectual skills should be deemed to be essential for the neophyte saxophonist, and legitimated through being published in this kind of pedagogic text, demonstrates the significance that had by then become attached to jazz improvisation within American music-making as a whole, and saxophone playing in particular.

The swing era

Coleman Hawkins

The C-melody saxophone provides a link to the first indisputably great saxophone player of the jazz age: Coleman Hawkins (1904–69). Although he is usually remembered as a tenor player, and with good reason, Hawkins began his career on the C-melody instrument, again an indication of that model's prevalence in the United States in the 1910s and 20s. In later life Hawkins became a little evasive about the details of his early years and claimed that he had always played Bb tenor; several witnesses dispute this, asserting that they had seen him playing the C-melody.[22] Hawkins's evasiveness almost certainly stems from the frequent association of the C-melody instrument with amateur music-making. The achievements of Wiedoeft and Trumbauer notwithstanding, performance standards on the C-melody were often mediocre. It is also likely that Hawkins wished to underline his later status as 'father of the tenor saxophone', and saw no reason to associate himself with the by then unfashionable C-melody instrument, particularly since this would inevitably have been tainted by the novelty tricks and effects that Hawkins had himself long eschewed.

It would be difficult to over-estimate the importance of Hawkins's contribution to jazz in general, and jazz saxophone in particular. He was not the first jazz saxophone soloist; Hawkins himself acknowledged Stump Evans as well as Prince Robinson (1902–60) and Happy Caldwell (1903–78) as significant figures in their own right.[23] But their achievements pale by comparison with his. As the jazz historian Gunther Schuller puts it, 'Coleman Hawkins virtually invented the jazz saxophone, at least the tenor saxophone'.[24] Hawkins's later achievements are all the more significant because he had little by way of jazz saxophone tradition to build on, since in his formative years saxophone players were scarce and barely taken seriously. Hawkins himself later recalled that 'nobody paid saxophone any mind, the good ones couldn't improvise too much and some of the fellows used to play with those little bitty mouthpieces just like clarinet mouthpieces.'[25]

Hawkins learned both cello and piano at an early age, resulting in a strong grasp of music theory and notation; it also instilled in him a fondness for classical music, something that stayed with him and that led in turn to his unusually wide-ranging musical tastes. After schooling, and having experienced the itinerant musician's life supporting the singer Mamie Smith where he was billed as 'Saxophone Boy',[26] Hawkins moved to the Harlem area of New York. Again, the geography of jazz is significant: Chicago was the home of a type of hot jazz that built on the New Orleans style, but which gradually went out of fashion as the 1920s progressed. Although the

New York jazz scene developed slightly later than that of Chicago, the city attracted more innovative musicians and bandleaders, including Fletcher Henderson – whom Hawkins joined – and Duke Ellington. Both these bandleaders were experimenting with different textural and harmonic ideas, and they would eventually take jazz into the swing era. Hawkins and his saxophone were an important part of that changing jazz aesthetic

Hawkins appears to have switched permanently to the Bb tenor in 1922,[27] although like many reed players before and since he played other instruments as required; these included bass and baritone saxophones in his early years with the Henderson band, in order to provide a bass line that would otherwise be absent (Henderson having yet to accommodate a string or brass bass). Using relatively hard reeds Hawkins developed a large, powerful sound across the range of the instrument, establishing a benchmark in sound quality that was to dominate jazz tenor players for many years thereafter. It is tempting to speculate that Hawkins's early interests in the cello played some role in his later affinity with the tenor saxophone, since the tenor covers a similar range and, in Hawkins's hands at least, has a similarly warm, inviting sound. It is also possible that his approach to solo improvisations, in which vertical-harmonic conceptualisation goes hand in hand with horizontal-melodic inspiration, were similarly the result of a fusion between the melodic lines of the cello and the harmonic dispositions of the piano. Hawkins used vibrato extensively; it was not as fast or quite as wide as Bechet, but was still integral to his performance style. His articulation was always quite pronounced. Although he quickly dropped the slap tongue effects he and others had picked up from Wiedoeft, his tonguing remained hard, but it was used effectively to contour the melodic shape of his improvisations.

Although Hawkins's development of the tenor saxophone sound was important for other saxophone players, it was the inventiveness he brought to his improvisations, particularly in jazz ballads, that established his significance in the wider jazz world. His elaboration of melodic lines, often based around sequential figures and set against a sophisticated understanding of the underlying harmony, greatly influenced other soloists of the time. This approach perhaps reached its apotheosis in October 1939, when he recorded a version of Johnny Green's *Body and Soul* that became one the most influential saxophone solos in jazz, as well as a significant commercial success.[28] At a little over three minutes long, Hawkins's beautifully crafted phrases set new standards in terms of the formal cohesion and melodic inspiration that could be created within a single solo, as well as demonstrating the subtle variety of colours he was able to extract from the tenor saxophone. Although the track was recorded as an afterthought at that particular session – the wayward ensemble, tuning, and generally inconsequential roles played by the other musicians demonstrate that no proper arrangement had been prepared – it became Hawkins's signature tune, and he was obliged to play it hundreds of times thereafter, risking disappointment from those who had expected him simply to recreate the recorded improvisation with which they were so familiar.

Hawkins had spent the five years prior to recording *Body and Soul* in Europe. The original invitation for this had come from the English bandleader Jack Hylton, and during his time in London Hawkins was prevailed upon to produce three articles for

Ex. 7. Part of Coleman Hawkins's 1939 *Body and Soul* solo, demonstrating the importance of harmonic figurations in the development of his melodic lines.

Melody Maker magazine, published in 1934. These give interesting insights into his approach to saxophone technique and technology:

> The mouthpiece that I use is a metal one, specially made for me; I used to use a rubber one and found it pretty good. I prefer metal though; the lay is rigid and lasts forever and the tone seems to be stronger and firmer too. I find that a fairly stiffish reed suits me best, a shade on the hard side if anything. Most teachers advise you to insert about one third of the reed in your mouth when you blow. Perhaps they're right, but I hold less than that – under half an inch – in my mouth and I seem to manage! The actual grip of my upper teeth and lower lip is quite light and although you might think with such a little space to get hold of that I have to bite, it isn't so.[29]

In 1945 and 1948 Hawkins made further major contributions to the saxophone's place in jazz by recording two unaccompanied pieces for the instrument, titled *Hawk Variation* and *Picasso* respectively. Freed from the constraints of working with others, yet still imbued with his characteristic sequences and tonal variety, Hawkins produced work that still sounds modern today, and which laid the foundation for later unaccompanied saxophone performances by players such as Sonny Rollins and Ornette Coleman.

One notable aspect of Hawkins's career was its longevity. He came into jazz at a time when the New Orleans style still predominated and the saxophone was relatively peripheral; he was a towering figure during the swing era, but he was capable of adapting, albeit perhaps less successfully, to the new sounds of bebop that arrived in the early 1940s. And when cool jazz came along a decade later, Hawkins was still

76. Coleman Hawkins in 1947, with Miles Davies in the background.

there, no longer quite at the musical cutting edge perhaps – although never very far from it – but still internalising the new musical sounds he was hearing and using them to generate his own distinctive material. Hawkins continued to work right until his death in New York in 1969. As his biographer John Chilton observes, 'almost all of the recordings he made throughout a forty-five year period were outstanding examples of improvisation, but among them were masterpieces by which all jazz tenor saxophone solos will forever be judged.'[30]

Ellington, Carney and Hodges

As the 1920s progressed, jazz ensembles increasingly moved away from their small group roots and towards the big band combinations that would dominate the swing era of the 1930s. Fletcher Henderson's Orchestra, with Hawkins as his star soloist and another reed player, Don Redman (1900–60), as his influential arranger, was an important part of this development. Whereas New Orleans and Chicago jazz had relied on the contrapuntal effects generated by contrasting monophonic voices, within which extended solos had become increasingly embedded, the nascent big band sound developed by Henderson and then Duke Ellington and others relied on three instrumental groupings to provide textural variety: brass, reeds, and a rhythm section.

The development of the saxophone section within these was a significant part of the overall band sound, but it also provided a platform upon which many distinguished players could build their solos and make their reputations. Indeed, so important was the role of key saxophone soloists in the more jazz-oriented swing bands that their work came to be an integral component of each band's profile; in some cases the sonic identity of a band would change noticeably when prominent players moved on, or became unavailable for a particular session.

This rotation of individual players applied rather less to Duke Ellington's orchestra than to others, partly characterised as it was by the particular contributions of two iconic saxophonists, alto player Johnny Hodges (1906–70) and baritone player Harry Carney (1910–74), childhood friends who grew up in the same area of Boston. Perhaps more than any other band leader, Ellington valued the contribution made by

77. Harry Carney in 1941, with Russell Procope to his right.

his saxophonists both individually and collectively, and that esteem was rewarded by loyal commitments stretching over unusually long periods. Hodges was a member of the band from 1928 to 1970, except for a four year break in the 1950s. Carney was Ellington's confidant, often chauffeur, and an ever–present member of the band from the time he joined (aged 17) in 1927 to his death in 1974; his warm, rich yet penetrating baritone sound became the foundation for the Ellington orchestra as a whole for nearly half a century. Carney was for many years virtually the only baritone soloist in jazz, and was largely obliged to look elsewhere for his aural models. In later life he said of his baritone playing that he 'tried to make the upper register sound like Coleman Hawkins and the lower register sound like Adrian Rollini.'[31] Carney was one of the first jazz players to use circular breathing, a technique that was to become central to later performers such as Rahsaan Roland Kirk and Evan Parker. In 1973, towards the end of both their lives, Ellington again acknowledged the importance of Carney's work by building his 'Third Sacred Concert' very largely around the skills of his baritone player, and such was Carney's devotion to Ellington that when the latter died in 1974 Carney is reported to have said that 'with Duke gone I have nothing to live for.'[32] Four months later Carney himself died.

If Carney provided a secure bass for Ellington's harmonic innovations, Hodges proved to be the master of his melodic lines, especially in ballads. His work in the Ellington orchestra is particularly significant because of the standards he set as a lead alto player working within a saxophone section. He was as technically dexterous on the instrument as any of his contemporaries, but it is his later, more languorous, unhurried solos, often heard some way behind the beat and with a particular vocal quality reminiscent of the blues, that are most easily recognised. A Johnny Hodges solo is often characterised by extensive use of glissandi and portamenti, and these give a particularly liquid quality to his playing; by the 1940s Hodges's use of these techniques had turned them from the novelty effects of the 1910s and early 1920s into

Ex. 8. A transcription of one of the many versions of *I Got it Bad and That Ain't Good* recorded by Johnny Hodges, showing both the fluidity of his saxophone line and its rhythmic sophistication (taken from RCA Victor LPMLSP 3576, released 1966).

significant expressive gestures that were taken as central to jazz saxophone practice, and widely imitated by generations of later players.

While Hodges is best known as an alto player he was also a fine soprano saxophone player, having been influenced by, and taken lessons from, Sidney Bechet. Hodges also doubled on clarinet, but the preeminent multi-instrumentalist at this time was Benny Carter (1907–2003). His best alto solos of the late 1920s and 30s helped, along with Hodges, to define that instrument as a jazz voice. He also recorded several fine trumpet solos, and other recordings find him playing clarinet, tenor or soprano saxes, and even trombone.[33] And possibly his greatest claim to fame is as a composer and arranger, skills he began to develop while working with the Henderson band, before providing arrangements both for his own and Ellington's band, among many others.

78. Johnny Hodges in 1941, with Al Sears to his right.

Lester Young

Coleman Hawkins's achievements in the late 1920s and 1930s are counterpointed by a saxophonist of a rather different disposition: Lester Young (1909–59). Young was in many ways the antithesis to Hawkins. Where Hawkins developed a large, rumbustious sound with prominent vibrato, Young, particularly in the early part of his career, produced a lighter, airy tenor sound, coloured only occasionally with vibrato. Where Hawkins constructed solos that were chromatically complex, in which the horizontal line was closely interwoven against the underlying harmony, Young was given to more diatonic improvisations, sometimes less obviously situated on the harmonic changes and more extensively utilising the upper extensions of the chords: ninths, elevenths and thirteenths. Where Hawkins would fill the available soloing space with often unbroken melodic lines, pausing only to breathe, Young would deliberately introduce occasional gaps, spaces which allowed both his own and his audience's musical imagination time to reflect.

Young was born in Woodville, Mississippi. His parents divorced when he was 10, and when his authoritarian father Willis – known as Billy – remarried, to a musician, the new couple decided to form a family band: The Billy Young Jazz Band. Billy Young was a skilled multi-instrumentalist, and from him Lester learned violin, trumpet and drums. He had also learned the saxophone from a young age, joining many other members of his family who played the instrument, again an indication of the instrument's role in family music-making at that time (see ill. 113); he now decided that this would be his main instrument, later claiming that he 'just picked [it] up and just started playing it'.[34] Given the number of other saxophone players in his close family, however, and thus the immediate availability of at least rudimentary tuition, this claim appears unlikely. But it does underline the importance of autodidactic learning processes for many jazz players of the period.

Young is remembered primarily as a tenor player, although he also played alto, baritone and, in the early days, C-melody saxophone, all with some distinction. His brother Lee recalled that Lester's alto style was considerably more florid than his later tenor style, a point reinforced by Benny Carter: 'When I was on the road with McKinney's Cotton Pickers [. . .] we hit Minneapolis and somebody told us about a wonderful alto player in a local club. I went to hear [Lester] and was enraptured. It was the greatest thing I'd ever heard. He had a definition and a mastery that I don't think he ever felt necessary to display on the tenor.'[35] Young appears not even to have played the tenor a great deal until the age of 19. In 1928 he was touring with a group called the Bostonians, playing alto and baritone. Being unhappy with the tenor player in the band Young prevailed on the bandleader, Art Bronson, to buy him a tenor, which Young would play in the group. He later recalled that Bronson 'went to the music store, got me a tenor sax and we split. As soon as I got my mouth round it I knew it was for me. That alto was a little too high for me.'[36]

This comment on tessitura is intriguing; not that the alto was too high, but that it was 'a little' too high. What characterises Young's tenor saxophone sound is its lightness, and he tended to use the upper range of the tenor more than its earthier lower range. This stemmed in large part from his admiration of Frankie Trumbauer's playing on the C-melody saxophone, the latter being pitched a tone above the B♭ tenor and also having a lighter sound. Young, who was an admirer of Jimmy Dorsey as well as Trumbauer, felt torn between the styles of the two men: 'I had to make a decision between Frankie Trumbauer and Jimmy Dorsey [. . .] I wasn't sure which way I wanted to go [. . .] I tried to get the sound of a C-melody [saxophone] on a tenor'.[37] Young was constantly drawn back to the intermediate area between alto and tenor but, like Hawkins and many other professional saxophone players of the time, was unwilling to associate himself with the by then unfashionable C-melody instrument.

Another idiosyncrasy of Young's tenor saxophone playing is his extraordinary posture. With his head bent sharply to the right, the mouthpiece twisted accordingly and the saxophone itself pushed upwards on the right hand side, Young's stance looks uncomfortable if not improbable (see ill. 79). The posture may have originated from Lester imitating his father during the time when the Billy Young Band was working in a circus. To draw people's attention Billy Young would often hold his saxophone in an eccentric fashion (see p. 136); the young Lester may simply have got used to imitating him. But Lester also developed his own circus tricks, which might further explain his unconventional posture. Trumpeter Leonard Phillips, who played in the Billy Young band in the 1920s, later recalled that Lester put on an act during performances of *Tiger Rag*:

> He turned the mouthpiece around and played the horn upside down with the bell pointing straight to the floor. When he played that he took breaks. He would also put his left hand behind the back and the fingers at the bottom of his saxophone, and his right hand would be in front of him fingering the top end. He did that with all the bands at that time. He said that he couldn't put on a floor show, so he would just play an act.[38]

In 1933 Young settled in Kansas City, and again the geography of jazz explains something of its development. At this time Kansas City was economically prosperous – notwithstanding the general ravages of the Depression that permeated much of the rest of the country – because of the city's strengths in wheat and cattle trading and its advantageous central location. One by-product of this commercial success was that Kansas City, not unlike New Orleans some two decades previously, was replete with work opportunities for musicians. Nightclubs, cabarets, speakeasies and dance halls all provided potential employment, and the city administration's comfortable relationship with local gangsters – who controlled trade in illicit alcohol – ensured that the effects of Prohibition were never felt in the city. This drew in large numbers of musicians, particularly from the south-western states. In time a particular 'Kansas City' style of jazz developed. Elaborate orchestrations were reduced down to more transparent, riff-based charts, and a new rhythmic groove evolved, based on a more even four-in-a-bar feel, as opposed to the two strong and two weak beats that had characterised previous styles. Even the social climate was more easy going: whereas segregation was strictly enforced in southern states, and the beginnings of a ghetto culture were being established in the north, by the standards of the time Kansas City was less racially divided than many other cities. Many of the most

79. Lester Young and his idiosyncratic posture in the 1950s, with Mezz Mezzrow looking on.

significant jazz performers of the period were either born in or drawn to the city: bandleader and pianist William Basie (known as 'Count' from about 1935); saxophonists Herschel Evans (1909–39) and Ben Webster (1909–73), and later the young Charlie Parker, as well as pianist/composer Mary Lou Williams. Many other significant names played in the city at one time or another. All of this provided a fertile environment for Lester Young. The laid-back Kansas City style suited him, and gave him the space to develop extended solos. Here his mature style began to evolve.

Nurtured by his association with Count Basie, for whom he was tenor saxophone soloist for much of the period between 1934 and 1940, Young produced some of his best work.

Ironically, although Young was less of a progressive moderniser than Hawkins and his school, it was Young's improvisational style that arguably had the greater effect on subsequent players. Young took a more linear, horizontal approach to his improvisations, and was less concerned with overtly demonstrating the implications of the underlying harmony in his melodic phrases. He was fond of using the metaphor of storytelling to describe his approach to soloing, and several commentators have suggested that the roots of these devices – the emphasis on lyrical melodic constructions and the influence of oral narrative – have their roots in African traditions and the blues, albeit that in Young's case these have been infused by the musical traditions of the American Southwest, not the Southeast. Young also eschewed the more syncopated rhythmic patterns then fashionable – the dotted quaver (eighth note) and dotted semiquaver (sixteenth note) feel that characterised Hawkins's approach – preferring instead less rhythmic differentiation between consecutive notes of the same value (running quavers, for example); this gave his saxophone lines more of a triplet feel when heard over the underlying, evenly stressed, Kansas City-style rhythmic accompaniment.

Another innovation Young employed was the use of alternative ('false') fingerings for the same note. The orthodox fingering used for many notes on the saxophone can be modified by the substitution of other finger patterns; while these may not radically change the pitch of the note – they do alter it slightly – they often have a very different colour. Young may have been drawn to this technique as a way of mimicking

Ex. 9. An extract from Lester Young's 1956 solo on *There Will Never Be Another You*, showing the horizontal nature of his melodic conception, his generally understated approach, and his frequent preference for the higher register of the tenor saxophone.

speech patterns on the saxophone,[39] although it has become commonplace in contemporary music of all kinds. Equally unusual for the time was that Young used much less vibrato in his sound than many other players. He attacked notes cleanly, adding vibrato towards the end of a held note in order to colour or shape it, an aspect of his style that again demonstrates a debt to Trumbauer.

Young's interest in both the blues and the vocal nature of saxophone performance also helps explain the special relationship he enjoyed with the singer Billie Holiday. Although they met as early as 1934, they did not record together until 1937. Their relationship, although only platonic, became one of the most celebrated in jazz. The names they gave each other – 'Prez', short for president, in the case of Young, and 'Lady Day' for Holiday – became widely used, and the recordings they made together, although not especially successful at the time, have since come to be seen as jazz classics. Holiday was particularly appreciative of the vocal conception Young brought to his playing, observing that 'I always like to sing like a horn – a trumpet or tenor sax, and I think Lester is just the opposite. He likes to play like a voice [. . .] Lester sings with his horn. You can listen to him and can almost hear the words.'[40] Young himself was conscious of this close musical rapport, observing that 'Sometime[s] I sit down and listen to [the old records] myself, and they sound like two of the same voices, if you don't be careful, you know – or the same mind or something like that'.[41]

Young left Basie's band in 1940, rejoining it in 1942 after an ill-fated attempt at leading his own group. In 1944 he was drafted into the army, an uncomfortable experience for this mild-mannered, slightly introverted individual, which ended with him being courtmartialled and receiving a dishonourable discharge after a year's imprisonment. Although he was in demand as a performer and able to command good fees during the late 1940s and early 50s, his health, physical and mental, and his playing were all in slow decline. Heavy drinking was increasingly part of both the problem and the response. His sound had changed; the lighter, transparent tone of the thirties had become heavier and less idiosyncratic. He produced a final (televised) recording with Billie Holliday in 1957, the title of which – *Fine and Mellow* – was ironic in both their cases; but while the empathy between them is still evident, the music provides only an echo of their former glories. After an unsuccessful residency in Paris, Young developed internal bleeding on the flight home; he died in New York in January 1959.

Lester Young had a unique saxophone voice, and the consequences of his work continue to influence modern players. He was a major influence on the later bop and 'cool' approaches to jazz through his melodic construction and rhythmic flexibility, among other traits. He was also an emotionally complex individual who cultivated his own particular style of speech, an early form of jive talk.[42] He developed a number of affectations, bordering on effeminacy, including addressing individuals of both sexes as 'Lady'. He was something of a misfit, and in his later years observed to the pianist Horace Silver that 'I really don't think nobody really likes old Prez'.[43] Even his saxophone solos might be read as containing a certain ambiguity, introducing more feminine attributes of reflection and introspection as opposed to the masculine paradigms of power and straightforwardness that had previously predominated. None of this is to suggest any homosexual tendencies on Young's part, as others have erroneously implied. But it is to suggest that the quintessential Lester Young tenor saxophone sound, in its intermediate position between alto and tenor – the sound of an absent other? – can itself be read as indicative of Young's ambiguous and deeply sensitive persona.

The bop era

Charlie Parker

One of Lester Young's many legacies to jazz in general and the saxophone in particular arises through the influence he had upon possibly the most widely recognised saxophonist ever to have played the instrument: Charlie Parker (1920–55). It was Parker, together with trumpeter Dizzy Gillespie and pianist Thelonious Monk, who in the 1940s developed a new jazz language known as bebop (usually shortened simply to 'bop'), in which the saxophone played a central role, and which made such a profound impression on the evolution of the jazz tradition; it was Parker who established new levels of technical expertise on the saxophone, setting benchmarks as a jazz virtuoso against which others continue to be measured; and it was Parker who came to be – and in many ways continues to be – an iconic figure for aspiring saxophone players around the world. And this is all the more remarkable in light of the fact that his most significant recordings were made in a relatively brief period between about 1945 and 1953, and that he died in 1955 aged only 34.

Parker was born in Kansas City, Kansas, moving to the Missouri part of that same city when he was about seven.[44] His father had an early career working the black theatre circuit as a pianist and singer, and later worked as a railway chef. Parker Senior's frequent absences meant he was seldom part of Charlie's life, and he moved out of it altogether before his son was ten. Instead, it was Charlie's mother, religious and strongly maternalistic yet doting on her son and allowing him considerable licence, who was responsible for Parker's upbringing. At high school Parker had been allocated a baritone horn in the school band, an unsatisfactory arrangement in which, he later recalled, 'all I did was play *coop, coop – coop, coop'*.[45] But he soon became involved in the burgeoning jazz scene in Kansas City, having prevailed on his mother to purchase for him a used alto saxophone for the sum of $45.[46] In particular, he would go and listen to Lester Young, who became an important early influence. A friend later recalled that 'once, when we were talking about his beginnings in music, [Charlie] mentioned with a big grin "I used to stand outside the club in Kansas City where Lester Young played – I was only twelve at the time and couldn't go inside – and would listen for hours. Then I went and got an alto. I didn't get a tenor because I didn't want to copy Prez." '[47] Parker's recollections are often unreliable, and in fact Young was likely to have been only one of many players that he heard in Kansas City in the mid 1930s. But Parker did spend the summer of 1937 closely studying, and learning by rote, Lester Young solos on some recently released Count Basie recordings, and this was more likely to have been how he became so familiar with Young's music.[48]

The importance of aural tradition in jazz, and the significance of particular jazz saxophone lineages, has already been noted, particularly with respect to the transmission of sound ideals. But the point goes further than this, since jazz saxophone players also borrow from and build on melodic and harmonic figurations heard in the work of others. Of nobody is this more true than the young Charlie Parker in relation to Lester Young. The trumpeter Jerry Lloyd recalled that when Parker's reputation began to spread in the late 1930s, 'Benny Harris told me [. . .] "You know there's a saxophone player out in Kansas City who plays more horn than any other horn player you ever heard." To show me the way he sounded he put on a Lester Young record called "Shoe Shine Boy". He had a machine that could speed up the revolutions until the tenor sax sounded like an alto. "That's a rough idea of how he sounds." '[49] Similarly, if the 1940 recording made by the twenty-year-old Parker of *Lady Be Good* is slowed down, it bears considerable similarities to Lester Young's improvisations over the same tune in the mid 1930s.[50]

In the late 1930s Parker travelled briefly to Chicago and then to New York. He made relatively little impact at this time; indeed, he ended up washing dishes in one club, possibly so that he could listen to the jazz pianist Art Tatum, who sometimes played there. Around this time he acquired the nickname 'yardbird', usually abbreviated to 'bird', the sobriquet by which he later became universally known.[51] Returning to Kansas City he joined a band led by pianist Jay McShann, with whom he made his first commercial recordings in the early 1940s. These recordings, together with unofficial recordings of Parker's work at this time that gradually came to light after his death, demonstrate not only the musical sophistication he already possessed, but also the first green shoots of the bop language that was to follow.

Parker travelled back to New York with McShann's band, and for a while from late 1941 or early 1942 he made the city his base. He began working at the legendary Minton's club, with trumpeter Dizzy Gillespie, pianist Thelonious Monk, drummer Kenny Clarke and others. It was here that Parker and Gillespie – whom Parker would later describe as 'the other half of my heartbeat'[52] – forged a new jazz language. The Dadaistic description of this new style as 'bebop' was possibly taken from some of the improvised 'scat' vocables sung by Louis Armstrong on his 1927 tune *Hotter Than That*; but the term can also be construed onomatopoeically, as a linguistic analogue to the two-quaver 'doo–dat' trochaic rhythm which often marked the ends of certain phrases. The music was characterised by fast tempos and angular, fragmented solo lines; pieces displayed a much faster harmonic rhythm (the frequency with which chords changed), and the basic rhythmic unit was conceived as a quaver (eighth note) rather than a crotchet (quarter note). The bass played four notes to the bar rather than two, and the drums outlined a steady 'ten-to-ten' rhythm on the ride cymbal, with the foot-operated high-hat employed to mark out the second and fourth beats of the bar. The music became much more harmonically complex. Altered chords – flattened fifths, augmented sixths and so forth – became common, as did substitutions: using a Db7 chord where a G7 chord might have been expected in a cadence on C, for example. Piano 'comps' evolved, which sparsely outlined the harmonic framework while adding a further layer of rhythmic complexity. Improvised content was privileged over compositional form.

Many bop tunes were somewhat cursory compositions written over the harmonic structure of a well-known melody, which then simply provided convenient 'bookends' for the improvisations. Thus George Gershwin's *I Got Rhythm* became Gillespie and Parker's *Anthropology*, Morgan Lewis's *How High the Moon* became *Ornithology*, and so forth. But these compositional details were increasingly peripheral, since the tunes were only vehicles within which to display ever higher levels of individual virtuosity. The musical demands made of all players, especially saxophonists, now required greater technical skill and faster musical thought. Certain previous jazz staples such as the blues were retained, and Parker remained an excellent blues player, as one might expect of a musician brought up in Kansas City. But the blues phrases were seen through a modernist prism in which the speed and power with which they were played displayed them in a new light. If the term 'bebop' may be construed as Dadaist in its playful intent, it is the Futurists, with their emphasis on motion and velocity, and the sharp, angular lines of their pictures, who provide the more apt artistic comparison with the music itself.

The speed of that music provided a significant challenge to those saxophonists wishing to ape Parker's style, and in this respect his recordings took on increased significance, since they provided the opportunity for repeated listening and thus facilitated autodidactic progress. It was recording technology rather than live performance that by now offered the primary mechanism through which one saxophone player learned from another. Just as Parker had listened to recordings by Lester Young, so Young had learned from Trumbauer's discs; Young stated explicitly that 'in copying all [Trumbauer's] records, that's how I developed my sound.'[53] Tenor player Bud Freeman (1906–91) recalled in later life that in his youth he was 'learning more about jazz just through listening to records than I was occasioned to learn by going to the clubs, because in the nightclub atmosphere, your attention was not always on the music'.[54] The opportunity for repeated listening and, where necessary, to reduce the turntable speed and thus slow down the music, became particularly useful for those wishing to learn bop saxophone, because Parker's musical language was highly chromatic, and he played so fast.

Few other players in the 1940s could equal Parker in his ability not only to play a large number of notes per second, but also to organise them into coherent and musically satisfying phrases. As with most jazz saxophonists, Parker's improvisations were built on pre-conceived formulae and melodic patterns, some of which he inherited from swing forefathers.[55] Example 10 demonstrates this fast yet dense style. The fundamental characteristics of Parker's style are all here in these 32 bars, taken from a 1947 solo on *Donna Lee*: a fast metronome marking of crotchet = 240; the relatively abrupt beginnings and ends to phrases and their asymmetrical nature; the frequent use of chromatic lines; and the repetition of particular stock formulae throughout the improvisation.

While Parker's harmonic language was undoubtedly evolutionary, it was not perhaps as revolutionary as has sometimes been claimed. Part of the Parker mythology revolves around a statement credited to him, in which he claims that during a particular damascene moment he realised that 'by using the higher intervals of a chord and backing them with appropriately related changes' he could play the musical sounds he had been hearing in his head. Thomas Owens has shown, however, that these words were not originally uttered by Parker – they stem from an article written about

Ex. 10. An extract from Charlie Parker's solo on *Donna Lee*, recorded in 1947 (Savoy SJL 2201).

him in *Down Beat* in 1949 – nor are they an accurate reflection of his musical language. These 'higher intervals' – ninths, elevenths, thirteenths – were being used by other jazz improvisers well before Parker's time, and they do not characterise his style to a significant degree.[56]

A more fundamental characteristic of this style lies in the sound Parker made on the saxophone. While his outstanding finger technique might be seen as building on the foundations laid by earlier virtuosi such as Wiedoeft and Trumbauer, there is little in jazz saxophone lineage to presage the unique quality of his sound. Parker's alleged observation noted above that 'I didn't want to sound like Prez', if true, is an interesting insight into the tonal concepts he was already evolving during his teenage years in Kansas. Hawkins and Young on the tenor instrument had developed big, warm sounds, albeit that Young's was lighter. Bechet's soprano sound had been penetrating, certainly, but it was a sound conceived on the clarinet and then transferred to the saxophone, and heavily marked by vibrato. Wiedoeft's C-melody sound was warm, almost fuzzy, whereas Hodges's alto sound was liquescent, smooth and controlled. In contrast, Parker's sound was very bright, aggressive and edgy; even in his early recordings it is noticeably thinner than most. If previous saxophone sounds might be said to have asked the audience to listen, Parker's demanded it. Just as bop's harmonic developments brought modernism into the jazz language, so Parker's timbre brought the saxophone itself into the modern era. It had an uncompromising, almost harsh quality, a tone not previously conceived for the instrument. The sounds of those players who followed Parker were different and harder edged than those who preceded him, and the brighter, edgier saxophone sounds found in a variety of jazz genres today owe much to Parker's innovations in this area.[57]

Parker appears to have shown relatively little interest in the technology he employed to achieve this sound. He was generally unconcerned about which model of saxophone he played and would often use whatever instrument was available. In part this was because he became increasingly addicted to hard drugs and alcohol as his career progressed, and his instrument was frequently pawned to buy his next fix or drink. Tutty Clarkin, a club owner from Kansas City, recalls Parker's transition from his original $45 dollar instrument to a newer instrument:

> He had an old sax, made in Paris in 1898, that was like nothing. It had rubber bands and cellophane paper all over it, and the valves were always sticking and the pads always leaking. The reeds didn't make any difference. They were usually broken or chipped. He had to hold it sideways to make it blow [. . .]. I figured if Bird was great with a broken-down horn, he'd be sensational with a new one, so I threw his old sax into the snow and told him to meet me in front of the music store the next day. He was there on time, and I bought him a sax for $190. Bird cried and said, 'Man, I'll never be late again'. He didn't show for two days. Then I went looking for him. I found him where those cats hung out around 18th and Vine, but his new sax was in hock. I always took him back. You could tell: if the sax wasn't under Charlie's arm, it was in the pawn shop. He hocked it every week.[58]

Parker borrowed and played many different saxophones in his life, although he is often associated with the King Super 20 model, particularly since the King company produced one for him in 1947 on which his name was engraved. For at least part of his career he played a distinctive white mouthpiece (probably a Brilhart Tonalin Streamline); he also played on quite hard reeds. Such a set-up is likely to produce a greater proportion of upper partials (overtones) in the sound, and would have contributed in part to his characteristically hard, bright sound.

Another distinctive feature of Parker's playing is the relative absence of vibrato. Whereas vibrato had been an integral part of Coleman Hawkins's sound, and a coloration used extensively by Lester Young, it plays a much less significant role in Parker's style. In large part this is because longer notes occur only rarely in his improvisations; his dense use of rapid note patterns left little room for the static intervention of the held note. Where it is used, Parker's vibrato is both shallower and slightly slower than others.[59]

Parker was keen that bop should not be constrained by labels of one sort or another – he rejected the term bebop itself on many occasions – or by musical boundaries. He endeavoured to familiarise himself with current trends in contemporary classical music, and his conversations were occasionally laced with references to works by composers such as Schoenberg and Stravinsky. He met Wolpe and Varèse, requesting

80. Charlie Parker in 1947, with his characteristic white mouthpiece.

composition lessons from the latter. In the late 1940s and early 50s Parker made a number of recordings with string orchestra, and was delighted that the classical players took them seriously, though some jazz afficionados have subsequently queried their value, largely because of supposed weaknesses in Jimmy Caroll's arrangements. In 1949 Parker met the classical saxophone virtuoso Marcel Mule, in Paris. An amateur jazz fan who met Parker on several occasions later recalled that 'Bird was enormously impressed with this man's tone, attack, and intonation. Bird said he wished he could duplicate it'.[60] Parker was already familiar with the classical saxophone tradition, and had borrowed copies of Mule's recording of Ibert's *Concertino da camera*.[61]

Parker's demise is well documented. The use of hard drugs beginning in his teenage years, together with prodigious amounts of alcohol consumption, eventually took their toll even on his remarkable constitution. His demanding sexual appetite and destructive personality undoubtedly contributed to the difficulties he had in forming stable relationships with women, and his longer relationships, several of which were legitimised by marriage, failed to curb his dissolute lifestyle for any significant length of time. There were, of course, musical highpoints. His work in the mid 1940s with, among others, the young Miles Davis, ranks among some of the finest material recorded in jazz, and when Davis left at the end of 1948 Parker was able to put together a quintet with the trumpeter Red Rodney, which was launched at a club called *Birdland*, expressly designated so as to raise Parker's profile even further. His recorded work after 1950 is variable, with some of the better performances surfacing via the large number of unofficial recordings that have come to light in the half century since his death.

Eventually his nihilistic tendencies got the better of him. Thrown out by his last wife he spent his final years in a dour squat in Greenwich Village, close to the club named after him but in which his final appearance had ended in a very public slanging match with the pianist Bud Johnson. He was reduced to offering his services as a freelance soloist to anybody willing to risk booking him. He died in March 1955, in a friend's apartment in New York. The cause of death was given as a bleeding ulcer and pneumonia. More tellingly, however, the attending doctor estimated his age at between 50 and 60; Parker was in fact 34.[62]

Parker's early death undoubtedly underpins his iconic status as a jazz saxophonist, just as the early deaths of James Dean or Marilyn Monroe have underpinned their posthumous reputations as film stars. After he died, the legend 'Bird Lives' became a popular slogan for graffiti artists in New York; and, in the sense of his continuing influence on saxophone players as well as through the temporal dislocation that recorded music allows, this remains true. Parker is a pivotal figure in the development of the saxophone, particularly the alto saxophone, over the course of the twentieth century. He set new standards of individual virtuosity on the instrument as well as expanding the sonic possibilities it offered. In some ways he brought the saxophone into the modern era, with both his virtuosity and his sound providing the foundations for the instrument's use in a variety of genres after his death. And the bop language that he and Gillespie established was for some time the dominant language of jazz, and while it is now part of a more fragmented landscape of jazz idioms there are many for whom it remains a cornerstone of jazz improvisation. As saxophone player Jimmy Heath (b. 1926) later observed, 'we were in tune with whatever was happening with Bird and Diz. We knew that that was what we were supposed to do'.[63]

After Parker

Such was the impact of Parker's playing that those who followed were often caught up in the record companies' hype-driven search for 'the new Bird', and while this was true for none of them – since each retained a strong sense of their own musical individuality – it was certainly the case that they owed much to Parker's innovations. Perhaps the closest to Parker's own style was that of Sonny Stitt (1924–82), whose melodic formulas, phrasing and articulation resembled those of Parker. Stitt turned to baritone and, particularly, tenor saxophones in the late 1940s, possibly to distance himself from the association with Parker, and it is arguably the recordings he made on the tenor that provide his most notable contributions to the jazz canon. His fluid improvisational style, albeit still clearly indebted to Parker, contributed substantially to the domination of the bebop language at the time. Julian 'Cannonball' Adderley (1928–75) arrived in New York only a few months after Parker's death and made an immediate impact. He demonstrated a similar agility to Parker, but employed a richer, warmer sound and idiosyncratic improvisations that sounded less slavishly based on Parker's than were many others of the time. His swung quaver style tended to be slightly more fractured than Parker's smoother approach, and he made more use of detached articulation.[64] Phil Woods (b. 1931) became a significant bop player (although he did not start out as such), and his association with this style was furthered in the minds of many through his marriage to Parker's final partner Chan in 1957. But Woods's strong, smooth playing, together with a high level of funda-mental technical skills such as intonation control and sight reading, made him very popular as a session player, and for much of the 1950s and 60s he was a contributor to studio recordings made by a wide range of other artists. After spending time in Europe between 1968 and 1972 Woods returned to the US, but eschewed the session environment and instead led a variety of small ensembles, formats that provided convivial settings for his idiomatic use of the bop language; he also later composed works for saxophone quartet and a sonata for saxophone and piano that remain regularly heard in the concert hall.

Another significant player to emerge from the bop school was tenor player Sonny Rollins (b. 1930), whose longevity has kept him at the forefront of jazz saxophone playing for more than fifty years. Rollins was fortunate to have been brought up in New York in a rich jazz environment, and had worked with artists such as Thelonious Monk, Max Roach and Miles Davis before he reached twenty; his well-known album *Saxophone Colossus* (1956) can be taken as indicative of a position he has sustained in the jazz world over many years.[65] His tone is hard and occasionally rough but always distinctive, and he is also capable of great richness and warmth when playing ballads; emphatic attacks at the beginnings of certain phrases characterises some of his work. Taking his cue from Coleman Hawkins, Rollins has also made a feature of unaccompanied performances, in which his predilection for musical quotation can be given free reign. At the beginning of the twenty-first century Rollins continues to provide, with Woods, one of the few remaining direct saxophone connections with the original bop era.

Cool, modal and free

Birth of the Cool

It was somehow in keeping with those short bursts of intense, frenetic energy that so frequently characterised bop that no sooner had the style asserted itself than its star began to fade and a reaction set in, in the form of 'cool' jazz. Born out of a two-week residency in 1948 and refined in a few recording sessions over the next eighteen months, a nonet led by trumpeter Miles Davis produced the seminal album *Birth of the Cool*.[66] Rejecting both the astringent freneticism of bop and the large-scale sentimen-talism of swing bands, the album largely contained pieces in slow or moderate tempos played with quiet dynamics; it was the laid-back, spacious feel to the music that led it to be described as 'cool'. The instrumentation of the nonet was also atypical: four brass instruments including tuba and French horn, the normal rhythm section of piano, bass and drums, and two saxophones, alto and baritone. The omission of a tenor in a band of this size was unusual, given that the instrument had come to dominate so much of the jazz tradition until that point. The two saxophone players were Lee Konitz (b. 1927) on alto, and Gerry Mulligan (1927–96) on baritone.

These developments eventually led to a new sound-world being created for the saxophone in the 1950s, one which altered the perception of the instrument in the eyes and ears of the listening public. Now the brassy, forthright sounds of Hawkins and Parker became more mellow, recalling certain aspects of Lester Young's approach, and the energetic lines of the bop players were similarly transformed into rather more sinewy, lyrical improvisations. Whereas vibrato had been a significant component of most previous jazz players' style, it now became much less obvious: smooth, floating lines were a key component of the cool aesthetic. In addition to Konitz and Mulligan, saxophonists such as alto player Paul Desmond (1924–77) and tenor player Stan Getz (1927–91) evolved a new, relaxed and almost nonchalant dimension to the instrument's multi-faceted personality. If the saxophone had been seen only two decades previously as the epitome of hot jazz and frenetic dance styles, it was now transmuted into a quintessentially cool and easy-going instrument, as appropriate for the lounges and cocktail bars of the time as for the jazz club.

Konitz was undoubtedly influenced by Parker, but maintained a rather more ambiguous relationship with the bop language than did, for example, Sonny Stitt. Konitz's sound changed in the 1960s from the clear, vibratoless tone of the cool style to a richer, warmer version, in which the lower register of the alto began to resemble the sound of the tenor. Mulligan went on to became probably the most recognised baritone saxophone player of all time, demonstrating that even this large member of the saxophone family could be made to sound smooth and mellifluous. He was an accomplished arranger – providing several of the arrangements for the *Birth of the Cool* album – and it was perhaps this acute sense of harmony and orchestration that facilitated his well-crafted improvisations, in which he moved through the underlying harmonic changes with a simple yet irrefutable logic. Mulligan's baritone sound also became a cornerstone of West Coast jazz, a Californian-based version of 'cool' that outlasted its East Coast counterpart.

Paul Desmond created one of the most distinctive alto sounds in jazz, an ultra-light, sweet and slightly breathy tone which owed something to Konitz, particularly in the more weakly played notes at the top of the range; he is famously reported to have said that he wanted his saxophone 'to sound like a dry martini'. Desmond remained consistent with the cool principles throughout his career. He was not renowned for flashy technique, once observing self-deprecatingly that 'I tried practicing for a few weeks and ended up playing too fast'.[67] Desmond's role in the pianist Dave Brubeck's quartet brought him widespread recognition, particularly through his contribution to their 1959 album *Time Out*. Brubeck wrote everything on the album except one tune, composed by Desmond. That tune, *Take Five,* became a classic, crossing over into mainstream American popular music with unprecedented record sales: it is the best-selling jazz single of all time and remains one of the most widely recognised pieces of saxophone music (even though much of the original is in fact a drum solo) repeated in clubs, classrooms and busker's pitches around the world. The piece's simple sequences and infectious 5/4 rhythms continue to attract neophyte saxophonists, and many now take the piece as the embodiment of the cool aesthetic, and indeed late 1950s American culture more generally.

Stan Getz achieved similar levels of popular appeal through his fusion of cool jazz with Brazilian samba styles in the early 1960s, a form of musical hybridity that provided a precedent for many other types of 'world music' fusions in later years. Getz's tenor style arguably owed more to Lester Young than to bop, although he was certainly competent in that; but his light tenor sound, which in some ways resembled that of an alto, his sparing use of vibrato, and his slightly behind-the-beat style on ballads, were all reminiscent of the earlier tenor player. From the early sixties Getz developed a slight huskiness in that sound, something that continued to characterise his work, and which identifies a Stan Getz solo immediately for those who are familiar with it.

This cool style of saxophone playing was only one of several paths into which the jazz tradition fragmented in the post-bop era. Two other highly influential saxophone players charted different, albeit related, courses through the late 1950s and into the 1960s. The first, John Coltrane (1926–67), probably the most influential jazz saxophone player other than Parker, took tenor saxophone technique to new heights. The second, Ornette Coleman (b. 1950), is significant not only for his expansion of the saxophone's timbral palette, but also because of his radical rethinking of the jazz language as a whole.

John Coltrane

Coltrane's birth in Hamlet, North Carolina in 1926 – the same year as Miles Davis – made him only six years junior to Charlie Parker, but he and Davis ushered in a new generation of jazz players and styles. His father died of stomach cancer when he was only twelve and so, like Parker before him, Coltrane was raised largely by his mother. He immersed himself in music while at high school, and again like Parker, his first performances were as a horn player in the school band; but he soon switched to clarinet. Tuition from others came only occasionally, but his progress was aided in part by two personality traits that would stay with him for life: an obsession with practising, and an inquisitive autodidactic streak.

Coltrane developed an interest in the saxophone around 1940. He later recalled that, 'I chose the sax because Lester played it [. . .]. At the beginning I played the alto – I don't really know why, since I admired Lester Young at the time'.[68] This again indicates the importance of a jazz saxophone lineage in which Young has a key position. In 1943 the family moved to Philadelphia, at which point Coltrane acquired his own instrument for the first time, and in 1944 he began taking saxophone and theory lessons. These formal lessons enabled him to develop a strong technical background, both in relation to the saxophone and to music theory more generally. They also provoked an interest in contemporary classical music. Jimmy Heath, a close friend of Coltrane's at this time and himself a saxophonist, recalled that together they would listen avidly to Stravinsky, Shostakovich and others.[69] Although they did not consult the musical scores directly, they did familiarise themselves with pedagogical literature relating to the saxophone, particularly the books on harmonics by Ted Nash and Sigurd Rascher.[70] Coltrane was preoccupied with scale patterns throughout his life, and would later use extensively Nicolas Slonimsky's *Thesaurus of Scales and Melodic Patterns*; like Slonimsky, Coltrane was fascinated by the search for all possible scale patterns. Later still he would adapt for the saxophone exercises taken from piano pedagogues such as Czerny and Hanon, to provide himself with increasingly difficult technical material with which to sate his enormous appetite for practice. He also became interested in harps and their music, as a novel way of thinking about harmony. It was through these rigorous and often self-generated exercises that Coltrane developed an ability to practise and perform for sustained periods. He also achieved high levels of musical craftsmanship: he could sight read well, on clarinet as well as saxophone, and transpose between parts if the occasion demanded it.[71]

Philadelphia in the 1940s was a rather more convivial environment for a black, aspiring jazz saxophonist than many other places. Segregation was not as rigidly enforced as in the South (although it was still evident, and most bands were segregated), and there was a vibrant local music scene. It was sufficiently close to New York for a wide range of musicians to tour there, and thus Coltrane was able to hear a variety of other players and gain performing opportunities himself. His first major break came in 1948, when he played tenor sax for Eddie 'Cleanhead' Vinson's (1917–88) band, playing largely blues rather than jazz. Although Coltrane had considered himself an alto player, Vinson had insisted he play tenor in the group, and it was during this period that Coltrane developed a preference for the lower instrument. After nine months with Vinson, Coltrane moved to Dizzy Gillespie's big band, albeit on lead alto. It was a prestigious date but not without its frustrations; playing alto meant there were very few opportunities for solos, since these went to the tenor player, Paul Gonsalves (1920–74). But when the band eventually folded in 1950 he continued to work with Gillespie in a new quintet, reverting back to his now preferred tenor saxophone.

By now, Coltrane's mature sound and style were becoming evident. His sound on the tenor was large and forceful, and with a gritty and sometimes rasping edge that made it noticeably different from the tenor sax lineage of Hawkins and Young. Initially, however, it was not universally appreciated by those more used to the smoother sounds of earlier tenor players. The renowned jazz critic Whitney Balliett, writing in 1960 in the *New Yorker*, observed that 'Coltrane's tone is harsh, flat, querulous, and at times almost vindictive [. . .] [it] is bleaker than need be.'[72]

Coltrane's earlier recordings are characterised by medium fast vibrato and a certain amount of portamento, but from the mid 1950s the vibrato is noticeably slower and narrower. In ballads the hard-edged tone is often softened and more frequently coloured with additional vibrato. Like many saxophone players Coltrane was forever experimenting with different combinations of instruments, mouthpieces and reeds, in an attempt to produce his ideal sound. In Coltrane's case, however, this became something of an obsession, to the point where it is alleged he had his upper teeth filed into a slight curve so that they could better accommodate the shape of the mouthpiece.[73]

81. John Coltrane.

After his work with Gillespie, short tenures followed in the mid 1950s in bands led by alto saxophonists Earl Bostic (1913–65) and then Johnny Hodges. Undoubtedly Coltrane learned much from these two distinguished players. Bostic, although not a significant innovator as an improviser, had an outstanding saxophone technique. Coltrane later acknowledged that Bostic was 'a very gifted musician. He showed me a lot of things on my horn. He has fabulous technical facilities on his instrument and knows many a trick'.[74] The drummer Art Blakey also observed that 'if Coltrane played with Bostic, I know he learned a lot. Nobody knew more about the saxophone than Bostic [. . .]. Working with Earl Bostic is like attending a university of the saxophone'.[75] Bostic was particularly accomplished in the altissimo register of the saxophone, an area in which Coltrane had already developed an interest.

While Coltrane's reputation as a saxophone player continued to grow through the early 1950s, so too did his difficulties with heroin and alcohol. During his time with Hodges the heroin addiction became particularly problematic, and Hodges, himself unafflicted by such worries, felt obliged to let Coltrane go, probably in September 1954. This does not appear to have diminished Coltrane's respect for Hodges, for in 1961, when asked who his favourite musician was, he instantly replied, 'Johnny Hodges, the world's greatest saxophone player'.[76] Fortuitously for Coltrane, in 1955 Miles Davis asked him to join a quintet, and this was Coltrane's breakthrough. Davis was already a well-established jazz figure; by comparison Coltrane was still relatively unknown. But the latter's busy and fiery solos proved to be an excellent foil to Davis's more laconic and spacious improvising style. Unfortunately Coltrane's first stint with Davis ended in April 1957, when he was fired because of his continuing heroin problem.

The shock of being sacked by Davis appears to have been the spur Coltrane needed to beat his habit, and he soon gave up heroin and, for good measure, alcohol. He joined the pianist Thelonious Monk for a now legendary residency at the Five Spot in New York in 1957. Engaging with the sophisticated harmonic and rhythmic vocabulary of Monk's music challenged Coltrane to reach new heights. He later recalled that 'working with Monk brought me close to a musical architect of the highest order. I felt I learned from him in every way – through the senses, theoretically, technically. I would talk to Monk about musical problems and he would sit at the piano and show me the answers just by playing them.'[77]

It was also during this residency that the critic Ira Gitler coined the phrase 'sheets of sound' to describe the cascading runs of notes that Coltrane was using at this time. Although the description has been overused in relation to Coltrane's work in general, its original incarnation captures the sophisticated thinking that underpinned his improvisations at the time. These virtuosic runs were linear superimpositions of rapidly played scales derived from the underlying chords. As Coltrane himself explained:

> I was beginning to apply the three-on-one approach, and at that time the tendency was to play the entire scale of each chord. Therefore, they were usually played fast and sometimes sounded like glisses. I found there were a certain number of chord progressions to play in a given time, and sometimes what I played didn't work out in eighth notes, sixteenth notes, or triplets. I had to put the notes in uneven groups like fives and sevens in order to get them all in.[78]

In 1958, with his addiction problems behind him, a rejuvenated Coltrane was readily accepted back into the Miles Davis quintet, where he contributed to a number of recordings, notably *Milestones* in 1958 and *Kind of Blue* in 1959; the latter, very much in the cool aesthetic, would go on to become the biggest selling jazz album of all time.

Ex. 11. A short extract of John Coltrane's solo on *Straight, No Chaser* from the 1958 Miles Davis album *Milestones*, demonstrating the dense virtuosity of Coltrane's improvised lines and his rhythmic inventiveness.

Coltrane had already made two albums under his own name in 1957, but in 1960 he released *Giant Steps*, an influential album that became, as one commentator put it, 'the epitome of chord-based jazz material.'[79] The album's eponymous first track, based on a sequence of third-related chord changes played at high speed – although later takes released by the record label show that slower versions were also recorded – provided the kind of complex technical challenge that Coltrane relished, and many jazz players, saxophonists particularly, continue to regard the piece as a benchmark in terms of both the speed of harmonic thought required and the digital facility necessary to execute those thoughts.

‖: BMaj7 D7 | GMaj7 Bb7 | EbMaj7 | Am7 D7 |
| GMaj7 Bb7 | EbMaj7 F♯7 | BMaj7 | Fm7 Bb7 |
| EbMaj7 | Am7 D7 | GMaj7 | C♯m7 F♯7 |
| BMaj7 | Fm7 Bb7 | EbMaj7 | C♯m7 F♯7 :‖

Ex. 12. *Giant Steps* chord changes (untransposed).

If *Giant Steps* explored the limits of what it was possible to achieve within a chord sequence based on functional tonality – albeit a functionality significantly modified through chord substitutions – Davis and Coltrane had already signalled another approach in *Kind of Blue*. In this Davis and his collaborators took the music in the opposite direction from that implied by Coltrane in *Giant Steps*. Instead of basing the improvisations on pieces that had a fast harmonic rhythm, they instead used simplified structures, with long passages based largely upon one scale pattern; thus the classic *So What* from the album alternated passages only in D Dorian and E♭ Dorian, with improvised melodic lines staying relatively close to these scales. This became known – not entirely accurately – as 'modal' jazz, and it was a style Coltrane developed further in the early 1960s. Having left Davis he put together his own group, with McCoy Tyner (piano), Elvin Jones (drums) and Jimmy Garrison (bass); they would become one of the most renowned quartets in jazz.

Alongside his developing success Coltrane became increasingly interested in spiritual matters, and particularly with the Islamic religion. In late 1955 he married a Muslim convert, Juanita Naima Grubbs, who would be remembered in several of the titles Coltrane later gave to his compositions (his second wife, Alice, whom he married in 1963, would later take over the piano chair in the quartet). His engagement with the Islamic faith was only part of a growing interest in other cultures and their music, and, like a number of subsequent jazz players, Coltrane became particularly interested in the music of India. With its emphasis on improvisation using melodic modes over particular rhythmic cycles, classical Indian music has much in common with jazz, and Coltrane, particularly given his interest in the possibilities offered by different scales, drew much from his engagement with it.

Significantly, Coltrane's involvement in world music developed at around the same time as his interest in the soprano saxophone. Coltrane essentially reintroduced the soprano instrument to the jazz tradition; many of his listeners would have been unfamiliar with this particular saxophone before he began to use it. Coltrane himself was certainly aware of the Bechet legacy and of Hodges's work on the soprano (he later wondered whether 'I only play the soprano saxophone to stay in the lineage of Johnny Hodges – unconsciously, of course.')[80] He had also heard Steve Lacy (1934–2004), who was a soprano specialist, but in general the soprano saxophone in jazz was relatively unknown. The connection with world music comes from the sound Coltrane made on the instrument. Whereas his tenor sound was always strong and powerful, his soprano tone was much thinner and reedier. Coupled with his predilection for exotic scales, his tendency on the soprano to play florid melismatic lines, and the occasionally idiosyncratic intonation which the instrument itself sometimes engenders, Coltrane's soprano playing is frequently reminiscent of ethnic wind instruments elsewhere, particularly the Indian *shenai*, an oboe-like instrument. He largely kept his soprano repertoire separate from his tenor repertoire, notwithstanding that both instruments are pitched in B♭ and thus easily transferred between when conceptualising the underlying harmony. His most famous recording on soprano was a 1961 version of the Rodgers and Hammerstein tune *My Favourite Things*, which he always performed on soprano and never on tenor, whereas the opposite was true for the tune *Impressions*, released in 1963 and a now identified as a classic Coltrane tenor number.

The spiritual and pantheistic side of Coltrane's musical personality reached its apotheosis with the release of the album *A Love Supreme* in early 1964. It achieved extraordinary popular success: whereas Coltrane's albums would normally sell about 30,000 units – a very respectable figure in relation to other jazz releases – this album had sold half a million copies worldwide by 1970.[81] Conceived as a suite in four parts, its spiritual importance for Coltrane is immediately evidenced by the titles given to each part – Acknowledgment, Resolution, Pursuance, and Psalm – as well as by the liner notes in which Coltrane makes clear that the album is an offering to God. In the final section, Psalm, the saxophone line 'recites' a devotional text Coltrane had written, which was also reproduced in the liner notes. Lewis Porter has convincingly demonstrated how this text underlies Coltrane's performance at this point, and how the saxophone line can be read as an analogue of chant techniques used by black American preachers (see ex. 13).

Once again the connection between the saxophone and the human voice is explicit, and this vocal quality, together with the intense, visceral approach that Coltrane brings to the music, especially in his use of the altissimo register, adds to the sense of devotional communication and helps explain why the album appealed to listeners well beyond the normal jazz public.

A Love Supreme was followed in 1965 by the album *Ascension*, in which Coltrane's quartet was augmented to an eleven-piece band for a relatively free-form ensemble improvisation that he appears to have largely directed in the studio, rather than rehearsed in advance. By now Coltrane was increasingly at the boundaries of what was construed as jazz, and his late work baffled many of his fans. A quintet that included another equally adventurous and spiritually-enthused saxophonist, Pharaoh Sanders (b. 1940), and Coltrane's second wife Alice, was now playing something approaching free jazz, with no discernible rhythm to hold the music together. Coltrane himself was contributing virtuosic and dense musical lines, but it was not the style people wanted to hear. As Coltrane himself poignantly put it, 'everybody wants to hear what I've done. Nobody wants to hear what I'm doing.'[82] Unknown to many of these fans, however, and perhaps not even fully recognised by the man himself, Coltrane's health was failing. Tours and concerts began to be cancelled from November 1966, and he made his last brief appearance in April 1967. He died, aged forty, on 17 July the same year, from cancer of the liver. His death sent shock waves around the jazz world and beyond.

John Coltrane was one of the great saxophonists, and he achieved that greatness through intensive and sustained study of both the instrument and the musical possibilities it afforded. He enlarged the range of accepted saxophone techniques through his facility in the altissimo register, his use of multiphonics and false fingerings, and his virtuosity and control in all ranges and keys. He redefined the role of the soprano

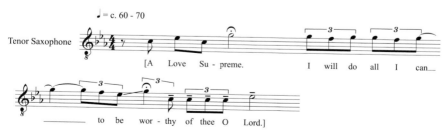

Ex. 13. Opening of 'Psalm' from *A Love Supreme* by John Coltrane, transcribed by Lewis Porter, demonstrating the devotional 'chant' of Coltrane's saxophone line.

saxophone in the jazz tradition. He broadened the jazz language through his use of asymmetrical note groups, his sophisticated system of chord substitutions, his adoption of different modes and scales, his engagement with world musics, and his later use of free structures and rhythms. In his final years the large numbers of discs he sold even succeeded in making avant-garde jazz temporarily popular. His musical legacy can be heard in a wide range of later players, many of whom have gone on to be influential figures in their own right. More curiously, his deeply spiritual nature led him posthumously to become a central figure for the One Mind Evolutionary Transitional Church of Christ in San Francisco, for which part of the Sunday ritual is based around the music and poem of *A Love Supreme;* stranger still, the church became part of the African Orthodox Church in 1982, and Coltrane was officially canonised as a saint. That such an eminent saxophonist should be embraced by a religious group in this way demonstrates the extent of the instrument's rehabilitation, following the frequently negative attributes with which it was imbued by other similar authorities earlier in the twentieth century. Yet such hagiography might well have embarrassed the shy, quiet young man from North Carolina, who would prefer, most probably, to be remembered for his music.

Ornette Coleman

Coltrane had brought the jazz tradition, and the saxophone that was by now such an important component of it, into new musical territory, one in which established harmonic, melodic and rhythmic frameworks were reviewed, modified, and in some cases overturned. But he acknowledged that he owed a considerable debt to probably the most controversial saxophonist of the late 1950s and 1960s, Ornette Coleman. Coltrane had taken some lessons with Coleman in the early 1960s, and spoke of him warmly: 'He's done a lot to open my eyes to what can be done . . . I feel indebted to him, myself. Because, actually, when he came along, I was so far in this thing ['Giant Steps' chords] I didn't know where I was going to go next. And I don't know if I would have thought about just abandoning the chord system or not. I probably would not have thought of that at all.' On another occasion in 1961 Coltrane recalled their rare performance together: 'I only played with him once in my life. I went to hear him in a club and he asked me to join him. We played two pieces – exactly twelve minutes – but I think this was definitely the most intense moment of my life!'[83] Their mutual respect is underlined by the fact that Coleman led one of the two quartets to play at Coltrane's funeral.

Although these two saxophonists worked in musically related areas in the 1960s, they got there by rather different paths. Coltrane was to some extent the product of a conventional musical education; notwithstanding his strong autodidactic streak he had taken lessons in music theory and on the saxophone. Coleman, by contrast, was almost entirely self-taught in both respects, and it was perhaps because of the unconventional route by which he arrived centre stage in the jazz tradition that he was able to challenge it in the way he did.

Born and raised in Fort Worth, Texas, Coleman was immersed in the State's blues-infused traditions of saxophone playing; and, for those who cared to listen carefully enough to Coleman's mature work, those blues inflections were never too far away.[84] Lacking opportunities for what might be described as 'conventional' music education, Coleman taught himself the fingerings for his first saxophone, a Conn alto, but he taught himself 'wrongly', not realising that the alto saxophone was a transposing instrument. This misunderstanding of musical rudiments only became apparent later, when Gunther Schuller endeavoured without success to teach Coleman the basics of music theory in 1960. The lessons were sufficiently traumatic that once Coleman – who was by then a well-known figure – realised his entire conception of music theory was at odds with convention, he became violently ill and discontinued the meetings. But as Schuller wrote the next year in the foreword to a book of Coleman transcriptions, 'it is precisely because Mr. Coleman was not "handicapped" by conventional music education that he has been able to make his unique contribution to contemporary music.'[85] Part of that unique contribution stemmed also from Coleman's idiosyncratic approach to tuning. This is not to assert that he played out of tune – although his later detractors were quick to suggest just that – but that his conception of tuning and tonality were simply unorthodox, something that he developed at an early age. He later observed that 'I realised that you could play sharp or flat in tune. That came very early in my saxophone interest. I used to play one note all day, and I used to try to find how many different sounds I could get out of the mouthpiece.'[86]

Coleman instead became part of the touring rhythm and blues circuit, having changed to tenor saxophone in the mid 1940s in order to work in this style; he stayed with the tenor for several years before returning to concentrate on the alto. He also familiarised himself in the 1940s with the bop style, jamming after hours with similarly inclined musicians. But even while assimilating these new developments Coleman was developing his own approach to jazz improvisation, one which eschewed rigid adherence to the harmonic implications of the underlying chord structures. He later recalled playing 'some standard theme like "Stardust," and it was my turn to solo on the chord changes of the tune. In that situation, it's like having to know the results of all the changes before you even play them, compacting them all in your mind. So once I did that, and once I had it all compacted in my head I just literally *removed* it all and just *played*.'[87]

Coleman's idiosyncratic approach was already setting him apart from many of the musicians he worked with, and he was outgrowing the limited musical opportunities available to him in Fort Worth. In 1953 he moved to Los Angeles, but here, too, his unorthodox jazz style found few friends. The sense of musical dislocation was reinforced in other ways. First, Coleman *looked* different. He had a beard and his long hair was straightened then curled in a particular style; he was regularly seen with homemade clothes and a long overcoat; and he acted differently from most musicians, with a quieter, more peaceful attitude than the overtly masculine positions adopted by many jazz players of the time.[88] Coleman's instrument also set him apart, since from 1954 he had been a keen advocate of the Grafton alto saxophone, which was white and made from plastic (see pp. 89–91). Having not been able to afford the Selmer saxophones that were the instruments of choice for many other players, he had opted for the cheaper Grafton as a means of acquiring a new instrument. In a 1961 interview he recalled that 'I didn't like it at first, but I figured it would be better to have a new horn anyway. Now I won't play any other. They're made in England, and I have to send for them. They're only good for a year the way I play them [. . .]. The notes from a plastic horn are purer. In addition, the keyboard is made flat, like a flute keyboard, whereas a regular keyboard is curved. On a flat keyboard, I can dig in more.'[89] Charlie Parker had also used a Grafton alto for a short time, but still the instrument was regarded by many professionals as something akin to a toy. Coupled with the pocket trumpet preferred by Coleman's long-time collaborator Don Cherry, there was no shortage of opportunity for those opposed to Coleman's style to denigrate him.

And denigrate him they did. The level of opposition to Coleman's playing, and the blatant, occasionally even violent, manner in which it was expressed is unparalleled in jazz. While in Los Angeles other musicians would leave the stage when it came to Coleman's turn to jam.[90] In 1959 he made his debut in New York, for what was intended to be a short season at the Five Spot club. Coleman divided the New York jazz fraternity like no other player, but the level of interest in his playing was good box office: such was the furore that greeted his planned residency of two weeks that it was extended by two months. The drummer Max Roach, having come to the Five Spot to hear what the fuss was about, was so incensed by what he heard that after the set he went over and punched Coleman on the mouth; Miles Davis observed that Coleman must be 'all screwed up inside.'[91] But others reacted more positively. The jazz critic Whitney Balliett noted that Coleman had 'forgotten more about Charlie Parker than most people have learned'. The journalist George Hoefer summed up the generally confused reactions to Coleman's playing in an oft-cited article in *Downbeat*: '"He'll change the entire course of jazz," "He's a fake," "He's a genius," "He swings like *Hell*," "I'm going home and listen to my Benny Goodman trios and quartets," "He's out, real far out," "I like him but I don't have any idea of what he's doing."'[92]

How did one saxophonist provoke such strong reactions? First, Coleman subverted conventions relating to jazz improvisation, in part by discarding the normal reliance on pre-arranged chord sequences ('changes') as the starting point for improvised creativity. As with much of his work, these apparently radical departures were underpinned by statements of profound simplicity: 'using changes already laid out gives you a place to start and lets the audience know what you're doing. I mean if they can whistle the song in your solo. But that means you're not playing all your own music, or all the music you're playing's not yours.'[93] Having rejected conventional approaches to harmony, Coleman instead focussed on melody, particularly through a form of motivic expansion and development, and through the use of unorthodox phrase lengths. In time his 'harmolodic' theory evolved, a philosophical approach to jazz improvisation that he claimed united melody, harmony and rhythm as one, and which could be applied beyond musical improvisation. In spite of his advocacy of this theory, it has not been widely influential. Coleman also had an unorthodox approach to tuning. He was always interested in non-tempered tuning systems, and felt that Western art music's increasing obsession with equal temperament and ensemble precision detracted from the expressive nature of the music; while such views can be found among some scholars and performers today, Coleman's advocacy of it was considerably ahead of its time. His recordings demonstrate how unconcerned he

82. Ornette Coleman, still performing in 2011.

and Don Cherry often were about endeavouring to play in tune, believing that such differences between them enriched their performances. Not everybody agreed. In the summer of 1959, for example, when Coleman attended the School of Jazz in Massachusetts, trombonist Bob Brookmeyer shouted at him 'Damn it, tune up!' before resigning from the faculty in protest at the attention being given to Coleman by others.[94]

But the most radical dimension of Coleman's playing was simply the way he sounded on the saxophone. More even than Coltrane, Coleman developed a saxophone style that recalled the human voice. Certainly there were blues licks, bop figures and identifiable motives, but these were accompanied by asymmetric phrases, the use of registral extremes as sound-generating (as opposed to pitch-generating) devices, as well as cries, wails, glissandi and other effects, all of which contributed to an improvisational style that went well beyond what was taken as the conventional jazz language of the time. Whereas other saxophonists used these extended techniques to colour and embellish the music, for Coleman they were the music. Balliett noted that hearing 'a blistering human-voice run [was] a shaking experience'.[95] It was the shock of hearing this visceral, intense and yet strangely human saxophone playing that so unsettled the audiences of the time.

The albums Coleman made in the early 1960s – among them *The Shape of Jazz to Come, Change of the Century* and *Free Jazz* – were jazz landmarks. It was this body of work that made such an impression on John Coltrane in his own explorations of freer forms of jazz in the 1960s. While two other jazz albums recorded in 1959 – Davis's *Kind of Blue* and Brubeck's *Time Out* – achieved substantial commercial success over the ensuing years, it is Coleman's prophetically titled *The Shape of Jazz to Come*, recorded the same year but not released until 1960, that has arguably had the greater lasting impact on the jazz tradition, despite not selling as many copies.[96] Later, the album title *Free Jazz* would be appropriated to describe an approach to jazz improvisation that eschewed conventional harmonic, rhythmic and melodic formulas, and instead produced more abstract and less structured performances.[97] Initially known simply as the New Thing, the description Free Jazz was appended later, and although Coleman provided the impetus for the genre he did not pursue it himself. Saxophonists such as Albert Ayler (1936–70) and Archie Shepp (b. 1937) – as well as other instrumentalists such as pianist Cecil Taylor (b. 1929) – would push the genre even further (see pp. 288–9).

The techniques Coleman developed and the sound world he mapped out now underpin the work of contemporary saxophonists in a range of contexts, and this is perhaps the most significant aspect of his legacy. By the mid 1960s his work, together with that of Coltrane, Ayler, Shepp and others, had taken the jazz saxophone into a world that in many ways overlapped with concurrent trends in contemporary art music: elevating the importance of timbre and texture while simultaneously de-emphasising melody and rhythm; overturning established musical forms and instead encouraging freer structures that increasingly moved the tradition away from the canon on which it had long been predicated; drawing on musical influences from other traditions and encouraging musical hybridity; and setting standards of individual hyper virtuosity in relation to instrumental technique that would continue to challenge saxophonists in subsequent years. A new identity for the saxophone had been forged, one that would allow the instrument to play a prominent role in a variety of musical genres in the post-war era. These more recent developments in jazz are outlined in Chapter 7. They are the continuation of what has been a long but closely-intertwined relationship between the saxophone and jazz, in which, from humble beginnings as little more than a substitute for the clarinet, the instrument has come to define the genre. And although there are many other instrumentalists – pianists, trumpeters, drummers, bassists and more – who have developed the musical and technical aspects of jazz, no other instrument has attracted such a large number of practitioners, nor supplied so many of the tradition's major innovators.

Chapter 6

The classical saxophone

The saxophone in the symphony hall and the opera house

The symphony orchestra has long had an ambivalent relationship with the saxophone. Although it was clearly part of Sax's initial expectations that the instrument should find a niche for itself in the orchestral context, such expectations have yet to be permanently fulfilled. Since the 1960s the saxophone has certainly been a more regular visitor to the symphony hall and the opera house, and prior to this there are a number of intriguing and often high-profile uses of the instrument in various works. But most composers have conceived the saxophone as offering an alternative tint within the symphonic palette, something to be used sparingly and for specific reasons, rather than as a colour that might be fully and frequently integrated within the overall picture.

Duke Ellington acknowledged something of this clash between the saxophone timbre and the orchestral sound world when he asked Maurice Peress to orchestrate his suite *Black, Brown and Beige* for orchestra in 1970. He initially observed to Peress that he didn't want to include saxophones in the orchestral scoring – notwithstanding that they formed an important component of his own band – because the orchestra 'had so many colors of its own'.[1] Peress's own view, however, was rather different, and he went on to score for the instrument in 'Come Sunday', later observing that 'I had come to the realisation that there were few solo voices in the symphonic family through which we sensed a sympathetic resonance with our own voice, nor any instruments that matched the tessitura of the alto saxophone. Besides, what other instrument could emerge so dramatically in the context of that inspired silence.'[2]

The same vocal quality appealed to Percy Grainger – an ardent fan of the saxophone – who wrote in the score to his wind band arrangement of English folks songs titled *Lincolnshire Posy* that, 'to my ears the saxophone is the most expressive of all wind instruments – the one closest to the human voice. And surely all musical instruments should be rated according to their tonal closeness to human kind's own voice!'[3] As in so many other contexts, it was the humanised, vocal nature of the saxophone timbre that was taken as the instrument's most notable characteristic, a quality that offered composers a different orchestral opportunity, one that was by definition distinctive and idiosyncratic, even non-conformist, within the more rationalised and hierarchical dispositions of the symphony orchestra.

Similar enthusiasm for the instrument was expressed by certain pedagogues. For example, in the revisions added to the second edition of his 1935 orchestration treatise Cecil Forsyth argued that while he felt the instrument fared poorly as a solo voice, it was too useful simply to be monopolised by the dance band. Forsyth believed the saxophone had much to offer in allowing the other wind instruments to bind:

> In the matter of solid chords – a thing every orchestrator must have when he wants them – the saxophones have great value. I don't know if anybody has ever heard the full wood-wind of a symphony orchestra playing spread harmony without strings or brass, and has been able to place his hand on his heart and declare that what he heard was satisfactory. I have not. The tone-colours of the individual instruments are too heterogeneous. Add four saxophones and you bind them together in a much more satisfactory mass [. . .]. And it will not sound like a chance family gathering of colour-specialists who are not on speaking terms with each other.[4]

Such positive sentiments towards the instrument have not always been widely shared, and others have considered the saxophone timbre to be an unwelcome addition to the orchestra, with the richness of its sound felt to mask the musical details of the other woodwinds. Walter Piston, for example, wrote in his influential 1955 orchestration treatise that 'the saxophone as played today cannot be used successfully in instrumental combinations';[5] Kent Wheeler Kennan similarly observed that although the instrument's often-heard 'blatant, "wailing" quality' was merely one style of playing, it appeared to him 'unlikely that the saxophone will ever become a regular member of the symphony orchestra'.[6]

Some of these more negative attitudes explain why the saxophone has found it difficult to make headway in symphonic music, and further reasons for this have already been detailed in Chapter 3. New works written for orchestras, especially in the nineteenth century, inevitably tended to replicate existing forces, and this orchestral heritage does not easily lend itself to accommodating new and unfamiliar sounds. This is not to suggest that the symphony orchestra is always an entirely fixed entity, merely that the saxophone is only occasionally employed as part of what Adam Carse has described as 'that shifting fringe of the orchestra which never is, and never has been quite stable, and is always open to extension at the whim of any composer, however insignificant'.[7]

Historically, since orchestras did not usually include saxophone players, composers wishing to write for the instrument feared that they might struggle to find a competent player when needed, and hard-pressed orchestral managers for long dissuaded composers for scoring for the instrument on the often spurious grounds that good players could not be found. Edward Elgar wished to include a saxophone quartet in his cantata *Caractacus* in 1898, but was dissuaded from doing so on the grounds that suitable players would be difficult to find and too expensive to rehearse. Elgar remained supportive of the instrument, however, declaring its tone to be 'beautiful and expressive and, if you wish, subdued', and observing that it would 'no doubt someday be established among us'.[8] Another English composer, William Walton, similarly complained of the difficulty of finding suitable players for those works of his which included a saxophone, especially his oratorio *Belshazzar's Feast*.[9] And while England may have demonstrated a particular paucity of skilled orchestral saxophonists in the decades either side of the turn of the twentieth century, the general principle of a lack of competent available performers, reinforcing an unwillingness in orchestral circles to adopt the instrument, held true more generally.

In other cases, when composers did score for the saxophone, they might indicate the part as *ad lib*, suggesting a somewhat peripheral or dispensable role for the instrument. Such is the case with Richard Strauss's *Symphonia Domestica* (1903), which includes parts for four saxophones. Strauss rather curiously calls for a C soprano, F alto, F baritone and C bass, none of which are likely to have been common at any time; indeed there is much debate about how many of the F/C family of saxophones were ever actually produced (see pp. 56–8); finding the required players and instruments would therefore have been doubly difficult. Whatever the arguments for and against the inclusion of saxophones in contemporary performances of this enormous work, Strauss's own practice when conducting it appears to have been to leave them out.[10]

Composers could circumvent the possible lack of a player or instrument by indicating an alternative instrument that might be substituted. Such is the case with perhaps the best known early orchestral solo for the saxophone, drawn from the incidental music for Daudet's play *L'Arlésienne*, and written in 1872 by the French composer Georges Bizet. Bizet's decision to score for the saxophone is all the more remarkable – notwithstanding his indication in the score that it might be substituted by the clarinet – since in the original production he was limited by financial constraints to just 26 musicians, 15 of whom were string players. It is possible that Bizet included the saxophone because he had just finished arranging a vocal score of Ambroise Thomas's *Hamlet*, where both alto and bass versions of the instrument are used.[11] But Bizet was obviously well attuned to the saxophone's particular qualities. In the original version of *L'Arlésienne* the instrument conveys the first hearing of the theme of 'L'Innocent', a peasant whose arrested development has led to this nickname, but whose mental faculties are miraculously restored by the shock of his own brother's suicide.[12] Winton Dean observes that 'the timbre of the saxophone gives a strangely haunting quality [that] suggests at once the fuddled brain and the hidden serenity of spirit'.[13]

Dean's description of the saxophone line as 'strangely haunting' draws attention to the fact that composers have frequently identified in the instrument's sound a sense of musical otherness, and have used it to connote particular states of mind or patterns of behaviour that are understood to be somehow unconventional. Another example is provided by the English composer Ralph Vaughan Williams, who scored for the saxophone in several works, notably in his Sixth (T) and Ninth (2A/T) Symphonies, and particularly in his 1930 piece *Job: A Masque for Dancing* (A). This last work, originally devised as a ballet but more frequently heard in the concert hall, was conceived as a response to a series of illustrations by the artist William Blake; these were in turn based on the Old Testament book of Job, but it is Blake's illustrations rather than the biblical text that provided the greater inspiration. Here the charlatan behaviour of

Ex. 14. The alto saxophone solo from 'The Dance of Job's Comforters' in Vaughan Williams's *Job* (1930).

one of Job's comforters, Eliphaz, who ostensibly comes to offer support but is in fact an emissary from Satan endeavouring to shake Job's faith in God, is represented through a sinuous and pleading alto saxophone solo, characterised by a series of descending major and minor thirds within a descending chromatic context. The musical content itself suggests the oleaginous qualities of the comforters. The musicologist Frank Howes infers from this that 'a drooping, pathetic minor third sounds sympathetic; so for that matter does a drooping major third, and either might suggest true sympathy, but place one against the other and harmonise in triads and you have complete ambiguity and double dealing'.[14] Conductors sometimes ask the saxophonist to emphasise the apparent sleaziness of this solo, presumably thinking – not necessarily correctly – that it was the sleaziness with which the saxophone is often associated that encouraged Vaughan Williams to score this material for the instrument. Little wonder, then, that a London reviewer remarked after an early performance of Vaughan Williams's Sixth symphony that 'in respectable music the saxophone usually stands for nastiness'.[15]

A similar link between musical sound and pictorial representation lies behind another well-known orchestral saxophone solo. In Ravel's orchestration of Mussorgsky's piano suite *Pictures at an Exhibition* (completed 1922), the fourth movement – 'The Old Castle' – is largely characterised by the *cantilena* melody line given to the alto saxophone. Mussorgsky's original, written in 1874, is programmatic in as much as it was a tribute to his artist friend Viktor Hartmann, and was intended to represent a walk around an exhibition of the latter's paintings mounted shortly after his sudden death in 1873. While some of Hartmann's works survive, the picture underpinning this movement appears to be lost, but an inscription given above Mussorgsky's score, taken from notes on the original exhibition made by its curator, describes it as 'a mediaeval castle before which stands a singing troubadour'.[16] It seems unlikely that Ravel ever saw the original picture, and he would have been relying on this inscription for his sense of what it might have contained. His thoughts on the subject are unrecorded, and we can only speculate on the degree to which he saw the singing troubadour as an isolated, perhaps melancholy figure, given the plaintive nature of the minor key melody. But again the saxophone is prominent here as a distinctive 'other' within the orchestra, the more so since it makes no further contribution to the work at any point.

Perhaps the most profound example of the saxophone timbre being used to suggest some form of psychological alterity is in Alban Berg's opera *Lulu.* Berg scored for the saxophone in two other late works: his concert aria *Der Wein* (1929) and his Violin Concerto (1935), in both of which it has a number of small solos; it also has a role in the *Lulu Suite* (1935), derived from the opera. *Lulu,* incomplete at the time of Berg's death in 1935, is undoubtedly one of the masterworks of twentieth-century musical theatre, although it has been plagued by controversies since its composition. The two plays from which the libretto was derived were regarded as obscene at the time of their publication; Berg's reworking of their themes retained the essential elements of Lulu's descent from reputable married woman to prostitute, whose associations with various men leads to their deaths, either by her or at the hands of others, until she is herself murdered in London by Jack the Ripper. The alto saxophone contributes effectively to a lush sound world created by Berg, one which is enriched through extensive use of the vibraphone and further enhanced by Berg's rather romantic approach to the twelve-note musical language he employed. The saxophone, in combination with the piano, often alludes to popular music styles in certain episodes, and this connection is reinforced by the use of two further saxophones in an offstage jazz band. But the instrument is also used, unusually for the time, as a fully integrated member of the orchestra. Different characters and their states of mind are under-pinned in the opera by different instrumental combinations, and thus the saxophone plays particular roles: it provides a voluptuous melody that is heard at the death of each of Lulu's victims, but it is also one of the instruments, along with the flute and the vibraphone, most commonly associated with Lulu in her role as coquette and temptress. Thus the saxophone's association with (wo)man's baser instincts in relation to sexual power and physical brutality serve once more to identify it as a musical other, when set against the normative implications of the conventional orchestral forces otherwise employed.

A different aspect of the saxophone's association with physical brutality and psychological trauma can be found in Benjamin Britten's opera *Billy Budd* (1951), set on a British naval ship in the late eighteenth century. Early in the opera an inexperi-enced sailor, the Novice, is punished for minor misdemeanours by twenty strokes of the whip. An expansive, mournful saxophone melody comments on this scene, as the Novice bemoans his fate, and the saxophone material returns later in the opera in relation to this theme of fateful suffering.[17]

The saxophone's role as a musical 'other' in the orchestra is reinforced through its frequent use in works connoting a sense of musical exoticism. At the turn of the twentieth century French composers in particular were fascinated by sounds that were deemed to be 'exotic', whether those of east or south-east Asia – as demonstrated by Debussy's well-documented interest in the sounds of the Indonesian gamelan, for example – or with contexts that might be closer to home, but exotic from the perspec-tive of the Parisian bourgeoisie: a rural peasant village, for example. In particular, a broadly construed 'Orient', taken to cover an area from Spain and Morocco in the west through to Persia, India and east Asia – provided the setting for many operas and ballets, as well as titles for symphonic and other programmatic works that offered stylised representations of what was taken to be music characteristic of these areas.

While other instruments in the orchestra – notably the oboe[18] – have more frequently been used by composers as orientalist signifiers, the saxophone, itself an exotic instrument within the symphony orchestra and one possessing a timbre that in many cases would have struck contemporary audiences as unusual in that context, provided in certain cases an ideal outlet for composers seeking to project exoticising musical gestures.

The saxophone's association with orientalist imagery has its roots in nineteenth-century works such as Massenet's *Le Roi de Lahore* (1877) and *Hérodiade* (1882). The romanticised version of Hindu heaven in act 3 of the former, for example, is characterised in part by the saxophone lines in the ritualistic exchanges between the spirit of King Alim and the god Indra. But perhaps the most well-known example of the exotic orchestral saxophone is Ravel's *Boléro* (1928). Originally conceived as a ballet set in Spain, at the first performance Ida Rubinstein danced the role of a flamenco dancer in a bar, surrounded by men whose admiration for her eventually turns into something more lustful. Ravel's appendage of the title *Boléro* was intended to evoke these exotic Spanish contexts, as was the constant repetition of a rhythmic ostinato in 3/4 time underneath a repeating quasi-vocal melody that deliberately – albeit loosely – resembles the traditional Spanish dance from which the piece takes its name. This repetition and the occasional syncopation of the melody are characteristic of Ravel's 'Spanish' works. The melody moves among different wind and brass instruments in the early stages of the piece, and is heard on both tenor and soprano saxophones (Ravel's original scoring, which split the latter solo between soprano and sopranino, has long been superfluous; the line is managed on the soprano with relative ease). Other unfamiliar orchestral timbres – oboe d'amore, E♭ clarinet, the high notes of the bassoon – provide similarly exotic sounds in what Ravel, a master of orchestral

Ex. 15. The second half of Ravel's *Boléro* melody (1928), played by both soprano and tenor saxophones.

technique, described as 'my very best orchestration'.[19] The long, melismatic melody is in two parts. The first is largely diatonic, and relatively conventional with respect to the harmony below. The second, which makes more use of flattened seconds, sevenths, ambiguous tonality and occasional glissandos, is rather less conventional and thus might be construed as particularly exotic. Almost inevitably, it is this second part which is given to both saxophones (see ex. 15).

In Puccini's opera *Turandot* (1926), set in Peking (Beijing) but with certain characters whose roots are in central Asia, the offstage saxophones employed in the Chorus of Boys in Act I function, as Mosco Carner observes, as 'important factors in heightening the impression of "instrumental exoticism"' in the opera as a whole.[20] And in Kodály's *Háry János* suite (1927), drawn from a Singspiel of the same name, the saxophone is heard as part of an orchestra characterised by the unfamiliar sound of the cimbalom. Here the exotic locale is provided by the rustic setting of the Hungarian village inn where Háry tells his tall tales of heroic derring-do. The alto saxophone contributes to only one movement, its doleful solo intended to provide ironic commentary on the defeat of Napoleon at the hands of the possibly fictional hero of the title. The irony is underpinned not only by the mournful and unusual timbre of the instrument in the ensemble, but also through the addition of faintly comedic sharpened sevenths and flat seconds in the melody line, underscored by sliding trombone figures (see ex. 16).

In a similar vein, several of the solo works for saxophone and orchestra composed in the early twentieth century also reference orientalist imagery. Charles Martin Loeffler's *Divertissement Espagnol* (1900) is one, but more well known is Debussy's *Rapsodie* (the genesis of which is dealt with in more detail below). The original commission, requested in 1901, called for a *Fantaisie* for saxophone, but by July 1903 this had evolved to become a *Rapsodie Arabe*. The work was not published until 1919, when it was described simply as *Rapsodie*. But a short score in Debussy's hand bears the title *Equisse d'une 'Rhapsodie Mauresque' pour orchestre et saxophone principal*, literally 'Sketch of a "Moorish Rhapsody" for Orchestra and Principal Saxophone'. This titular evocation of the Moorish cultures of North Africa and southern Spain, underpinned in part through the piece's melismatic saxophone line, further reinforces the exotic othering of the saxophone in the orchestral context.

If these images of geographic or social others provided orientalist settings for many composers in the late nineteenth and early twentieth centuries, the rise of jazz and dance music in the 1920s, and the frequent associations made between such music and

Ex. 16. The alto saxophone solo from Kodály's *Háry János* (1927).

Ex. 17. The opening bars of the solo alto saxophone line in Debussy's *Rapsodie* (1919), demonstrating the melismatic writing that lends the piece its 'oriental' flavour.

Africans and African-Americans, undoubtedly provided a rather different form of musical exoticism in the orchestral context. The rhythmic vitality, blue notes and novelty sounds, and especially the sheer physicality of jazz and dance music, all contributed to a form of music-making that, from the perspective of the formal, traditional and stylised symphony orchestra, appeared particularly foreign. Given the obvious association of the saxophone with jazz, many composers have utilised the instrument in the orchestra to draw on or allude to jazz and other popular musics, notwithstanding the irony that it was precisely this association between the saxophone and popular music – and the frequent valorisation of that music as cheap, worthless or dangerous – that in part militated against the instrument's inclusion in the symphony orchestra in the first place. Here again the instrument is an interloper; it is the most obvious indicator that the rarefied symphonic space has been intruded upon by these other musics. Appearing as a seditious conduit through which such musics enter the concert hall, it can be seen as both a constituent part of the orchestra yet simultaneously marginalised within it – a symphonic fifth columnist, perhaps.

Pieces employing the saxophone for its jazz or popular music associations are relatively commonplace in the orchestral and operatic repertoire. Probably the most-well known examples are in the works of George Gershwin. *Rhapsody in Blue*, originally composed for Paul Whiteman's band in 1924 and subsequently arranged for orchestra by Ferde Grofé in 1926, retains the 2A/T saxophone format that was often taken as the standard instrumentation for dance bands. While these are essential in the original band version written for Whiteman's 'experiment in modern music' concert in which the piece was first performed, the orchestral version published in 1942, building on Grofé's first (band) arrangement, overscores the saxophone parts (and the banjo), making much of their material redundant; this may indicate some reservations on the part of the publishers about the likely availability of saxophones, and/or predispositions towards them, in the traditional symphony orchestras at which this version of the work was aimed. The tone poem *An American in Paris* (1928) again uses three saxophones (ATB), and this three-saxophone dance-band line-up, with which Gershwin obviously felt comfortable given his Tin Pan Alley roots, also found its way into arguably his greatest achievement, the 1935 opera *Porgy and Bess*.

Gershwin's music arrived in the concert hall having come from the direction of popular music, but there were other composers who were sufficiently intrigued by the new sounds and rhythms of such music that they sought to integrate them within their own more classically-informed styles. By way of example, George Antheil (*A Jazz Symphony*, 1925), John Alden Carpenter (*Skyscrapers*, 1926), and Aaron Copland (*Piano Concerto*, 1926; *First Symphony*, 1928) all employed one or more saxophones in these works as a way of incorporating the idioms of this latest fashionable American music. Nevertheless, after this burst of enthusiasm in the 1920s, American composers only intermittently appropriated the sounds of jazz and its instruments until the 1950s, perhaps conscious that the jazz tradition was defined by an emphasis on individuality and improvisation, and these characteristics were not easily accommodated within a classical music tradition that had increasingly marginalised such traits. Again, then, the saxophone can be read as a signifier not only of musical sounds that were exotic within the concert hall, but of musical values and practices that were also deemed to be foreign.

The re-engagement of American concert music with the jazz tradition was arguably led by Leonard Bernstein, whose *Prelude, Fugue and Riffs* (1949) was first performed by clarinettist Benny Goodman and his band (having been originally written for Woody Herman). The saxophone has perhaps never been quite so at home in the concert hall than in Bernstein's idiomatic fusion of jazz, Broadway and classical music. The concert pieces he drew from successful shows such as *On the Town* (1944 – *Dance Episodes*, 1945) and *West Side Story* (1957 – *Symphonic Dances*, 1960), as well as that taken from his film score for *On The Waterfront* (1954 – *Symphonic Suite*, 1955), and other works such as his *Mass* (1971) and *1600 Pennsylvania Avenue* (1976), continue to provide a symphonic profile for the saxophone and its players, in addition often to demanding of them the doubling skills that are commonplace among the Broadway theatres in which some of the music itself originated.

If Bernstein ultimately demonstrated how the saxophone might be comfortably accommodated in the concert hall, for many composers outside of the United States in the first half of the twentieth century jazz remained unfamiliar, exciting and mysterious. Darius Milhaud's adoption of the saxophone for his ballet *La Création du monde* (1923) provides perhaps the best-known example of the curiosity provoked by this exotic music. Milhaud was unusually well informed about jazz and its improvisational foundations – at least by the standards of European composers of the time – having experienced something of it during a concert tour of the United States in the early 1920s, in which he spent several nights in Harlem, New York. Here he heard the musical comedy *Liza* by the African-American songwriter Maceo Pinkard, which, as he wrote a few years later, was scored for 'flute, a clarinet, two trumpets, a trombone, an assortment of percussion instruments all handled by one player, a piano, a string quartet in which the viola is replaced by a saxophone, and a double bass'.[21] This scoring very closely resembles that of *La Création*, and explains Milhaud's unusual decision to replace the viola with an alto saxophone, an instrument with which it shares a broadly similar if narrower range.

Milhaud reveals in his autobiography a fascination with an African-American saxophone player working in Paris in the 1920s, writing that he 'loved to listen to [the pianist's] playing, and to that of his partner, the negro Vance, who was an admirable saxophonist and banjo-player. Without any transition, these two would pass from fashionable ragtime and foxtrots to the most celebrated works of Bach.'[22] This interest in the image of the negro, while inevitably suffused with the prevailing attitudes of the time, led to the description of *La Création du monde* as a 'Ballet nègre'. In it Milhaud provides a pastiche of dance and jazz styles, with many syncopated rhythms and the widespread use of flattened thirds and sevenths. Indeed, the piece ends with a rising chromatic four-note figure on the saxophone that finishes on the seventh degree of the major scale, an unusual conclusion that denies the resolution to the tonic (see ex. 18). That this figure is played by the saxophone reinforces not only the stylistic alterity of the musical material itself, but also the saxophone's non-conformist role as an instrumental 'other' within the orchestra. Milhaud retained an interest in the saxophone in later life, scoring for it in a number of other orchestral works (*Le Carnaval de Londres*, 1937; Symphonies nos. 2 and 4, 1944 and 1947), as well as arranging his popular two-piano *Scaramouche* (1937) for saxophone and piano. In the early 1950s he became briefly interested in electronic music, and the one work resulting from this, *Étude poétique* (1954), also involved two saxophones.

Zeitopern, a musical genre that that was fashionable in Weimar Germany in the 1920s and early 30s, provides another important art music context in which the saxophone is used to reference jazz and hot dance music. *Zeitoper* – literally 'opera of the times' – was a term applied to particular music-theatre works by German composers that commented upon and reflected contemporary socio-political issues, and were often constructed around characters with a more relaxed approach to personal morals than was conventional for the time. Productions were frequently characterised by the incorporation of new technologies such as film or slide projection, the inclusion of which indicated a commitment to modernity and contemporary living. One of the most successful of these was Ernst Krenek's opera *Jonny spielt auf*, which, after its Leipzig premiere in 1927, received nearly 500 performances across Europe, before being staged in New York in 1929. The work evidences an extensive

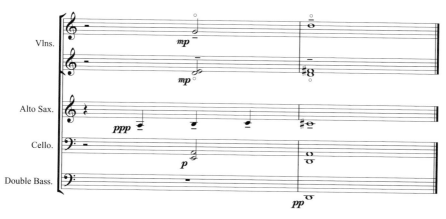

Ex. 18. The final gesture of Milhaud's *La Création du monde* (1923), with the saxophone finishing on the unresolved seventh degree of the scale.

German fascination with American culture during this period, and particularly with America's role as a beacon of modernity and freedom. The narrative is centred around the eponymous Jonny, an African-American bandleader and violinist, and in the finale the entire cast salute both Jonny and his country, and proclaim the redemptive qualities of popular music in general and 'jazz' in particular. Two saxophones (A/T), which can be seen as iconic of both American popular music and the modern, free-thinking capitalist values with which such music was associated, are heard in the on-stage jazz band. Although their roles are not especially musically significant – they have various prominent lines but play no other music beyond that heard periodically in the onstage band – their timbral and visual contributions help greatly in connoting the jazz tradition that is central to Krenek's opera.

Krenek's *Jonny* laid the foundations for *Zeitoper*, but was quickly followed by a number of similar works by other composers. While the essential elements of social commentary on contemporary living remained, the details inevitably changed. Paul Hindemith's *Neues vom Tage* (1929) was a satire on both the sensation-hungry media and the fragility of modern marital relationships; again the score is permeated with references to popular music, particularly in the final revue scene, where the alto saxophone figures prominently, along with the banjo and mandolin. Hindemith was well disposed towards the saxophone, scoring for it in a number of works during this period. An earlier opera *Cardillac* (1926), set in seventeenth-century Paris, and based on a story of a murderous goldsmith that is simultaneously both romantic and gruesome, calls for a tenor saxophone doubling clarinet; here it is the saxophone that characterises the central character throughout the opera, particularly in the first act when Cardillac is seen but not heard. Notwithstanding this prominent role, Hindemith's use of the saxophone timbre is paradoxical – perhaps deliberately so – in this otherwise rather neo–classical work.[23] Between these two works a one-act *Zeitoper* titled *Hin und zurück* (1928) had also given a prominent line to the alto saxophone, included as part of a small chamber ensemble of nine instruments that, although not specifically intended as a jazz ensemble, was probably designed to evoke the kind of pit band found in revue theatres of the time.

The composer whose work symbolises for many the music-theatre output of Weimar Germany is undoubtedly Kurt Weill. His collaboration with the playwright Bertholt Brecht resulted in a group of works (*Die Dreigroschenoper*, 1928; *Happy End*, 1929; *Aufstieg und Fall der Stadt Mahagonny*, 1930, among others) in which saxophones provide an important part of the musical texture. Indeed, in the smaller ensembles required for works such as *Die Dreigroschenoper (The Threepenny Opera)* and *Happy End*, the cabaret–style orchestration is to a significant degree characterised by Weill's adroit scoring for the saxophones. Much of Weill's theatrical output of this period cannot truthfully be described as *Zeitoper*, since his works function more as morality plays that argue against the decadence of certain aspects of modern society, rather than celebrating its achievements. Weill's use of the saxophone and his appropriation of popular entertainment styles was intended to denigrate the apparent vacuity of the society that craved them, whereas Krenek and Hindemith's *Zeitopern* celebrated modernity and the embracement of these new cultural trends.

This is not to suggest that Weill was implicitly opposed to either the saxophone or jazz. The banjoist and guitarist Michael Danzi recalls in his autobiography Weill's reaction to the improvising work of one of the saxophone players during rehearsals for the broadcast premiere of *Mahagonny* in 1930:

> The biggest surprise in the rehearsal came from Danny Polo, who had been told to improvise an American-style hot chorus, and later played a fine and soft, velvet-like solo on the baritone saxophone. He skilfully invented a driving hot chorus on this bulky instrument, and around Weill's involved harmonies, too. Kurt Weill just looked at Danny and told him 'I would love to write a hot suite in that idiom'.[24]

Unfortunately Weill was not to get the chance. His theatrical connections, Jewish ancestry and left-leaning politics meant that he quickly came to the attention of the growing fascist movement in 1930s Germany, and he left hastily in 1933, first to France, before settling in the United States in 1935. While he continued to include the saxophone in many of his later works, especially those written for the theatre, Weill was now endeavouring to become part of the American mainstream, and the instrument no longer denoted an unfamiliar music from elsewhere, nor characterised his style in quite the same way.

Arnold Schoenberg also left Berlin in 1933, again for France then America, having similarly suffered anti-Semitic discrimination. A few years earlier he had offered a different kind of commentary on the *Zeitoper* genre in his one-act opera *Von Heute auf Morgen* (1929). Schoenberg was dismissive of *Zeitopern* but intrigued by their commercial possibilities, and while his work borrows the familiar themes of lax personal conduct and marital discord it ultimately eschews a modern life of easy virtue and instead reaffirms constancy and fidelity based on love. This was the only work in which Schoenberg scored for the saxophone (one player doubling S/A and one playing Bs/T) – and undoubtedly its place in the score owes less to any passing fascination Schoenberg might have had with the instrument than with its ubiquitous adoption in the *Zeitopern* that he was endeavouring to satirise. Schoenberg and Krenek had fallen out in the late 1920s, arguing over the position and status of art music and the role of the composer; *Von Heute auf Morgen* was Schoenberg's final commentary on this disagreement between them, and there are several oblique references to Krenek's *Jonny* in the work.[25] But in Schoenberg's dodecaphonic landscape the saxophones play no music that might be construed as 'jazzy', although at one point the alto sax doubles a vocal line intended to be understood as a modern dance; but in general such associations are consciously eschewed – perhaps part of Schoenberg's ironic approach – and the bass in particular has some technically challenging material to play. It is sometimes suggested that Berg's use of the saxophone in his later works, particularly *Lulu*, may owe something to this work by Schoenberg.[26] But Berg had been curious about the saxophone for much of the 1920s, and *Lulu* offered him the opportunity to explore that curiosity.[27] *Lulu* can itself be seen as owing something to *Zeitoper* – with its use of silent film, allusion to popular music and characters of dubious morality – and it is this that links the two composers and their shared use of the saxophone, notwithstanding their own close personal and professional relationship.[28]

Russian composers have often demonstrated an interest in the saxophone, perhaps because of the high value they place on orchestration skills and the ability to deploy different orchestral colours effectively. Their interest in the instrument was enhanced not so much as a result of Glazunov's works for the saxophone – a concerto and a quartet written at the end of his life in the mid 1930s (see pp. 251–2) – but again because of its association with the jazz and dance music that were objects of fascination, and later official disdain, in the Soviet Union.

Prokofiev employed the saxophone in a number of works precisely because of its popular associations, and its place in his music is in some way emblematic of his own relationship with the Soviet State. After leaving Russia in 1918 he lived in the USA and Europe until 1936, but his career did not progress there as successfully as he hoped, and from the late 1920s he re-intensified his contacts with the Soviet Union. Perhaps in order to make his work appear more acceptable to the Soviet authorities, Prokofiev began to develop a lighter, more populist musical language, one that was intended to take its place alongside his more serious work. The orchestral suites Prokofiev fashioned from works such as *Lieutenant Kijé* and the incidental music for *Egyptian Nights*,[29] both from 1934 and including saxophones, mark the beginning of a period of about five years during which he composed primarily dramatic and programmatic music, in an attempt to develop what he described as a 'light with seriousness' style.[30] Prokofiev's frequent use of the quintessentially populist saxophone in many of these works, including the ballet *Romeo and Juliet* (1935–6), the film score *Alexander Nevsky* (1938, subsequently turned into a cantata) and the slightly later opera *Betrothal in a Monastery* (1940–41), provide evidence of his aspirations to suggest that he had found the common touch. This may well have been to reach out to the Russian masses; more pragmatically, it may also have been to cultivate good relations with Communist party *apparatchiks* in order to ingratiate himself with Russian officialdom.

Ex. 19. The short – and low – tenor saxophone solo in the 'Dance of the Knights' from Prokofiev's *Romeo and Juliet* (1935–6) (the saxophone appears here as written).

Prokofiev usually scored for the tenor saxophone, suggesting that he saw this member of the family – not unreasonably for the time – as being particularly emblematic of jazz and popular music. The instrument is used relatively sparingly but often soloistically in those works where it is employed, and Prokofiev frequently exploits the lower part of the instrument's range, as in the brief but well-known solo in the 'Dance of the Knights' from *Romeo and Juliet* (see ex. 19). Prokofiev's compatriots such as Shostakovich (*The Age of Gold,* 1930), Kabalevsky (Cello Concerto no. 2, 1964) and the Armenian composer Khachaturian (the ballet *Gayane,* 1942) have all also given prominent solos to various members of the saxophone family.

The idiosyncratic Brazilian composer Heitor Villa-Lobos used the saxophone extensively in his large and eclectic output. His synthesis of European art music techniques and reinterpretations of Brazilian music, and his unconventional approach to both musical form and orchestration, allowed him ample opportunity to include the instrument. Villa-Lobos was himself an enthusiastic saxophone player, and his studies in Paris in the 1920s may well have reinforced this enthusiasm, although he had been writing for the instrument long before he made his temporary home in the French capital. As early as 1904 he had scored for the saxophone in pieces for band, but from 1917 onwards saxophones were called for in a variety of orchestral and chamber works. His Symphony no. 4 (1919), for example, requires a full saxophone quartet, and several of his better-known *Bachianas Brasileiras* and *Chôros* series also use the saxophone prominently. His *Fantasia* (1948), originally conceived for solo soprano saxophone, string orchestra and three horns, remains one of the more popular solo concertos among saxophonists. Curiously, this *Fantasia* is written one tone higher in the manuscript than in the published version (see ill. 83). Although the piece was dedicated to Marcel Mule, for some unknown reason Mule was unenthusiastic about the work. It was instead premiered on 17 November 1951 by Waldemar Szilman, a friend of the composer, who didn't own a soprano saxophone. The piece was therefore played on the tenor instrument, and transposed down a tone at the request of the performer, so as to obviate certain passagework that went into the altissimo range of the instrument. The new key and the option of performing the piece on the tenor instead of the soprano were retained in the published score.

Naturally, not all of the saxophone's visits to the concert hall or the opera house fall into the general taxonomy outlined above. There are other examples, sometimes quite well known, of composers choosing the instrument for no apparent reason. The alto solo in Rachmaninov's *Symphonic Dances* (1940) provides a case in point. This was the only occasion that Rachmaninov used the instrument in his music, which might explain why he had to ask his friend, the American composer Robert Russell Bennett, how to score for it (and why the saxophone solo ended up being written with a key signature of seven sharps).[31] Nevertheless, although the saxophone could never be described as being commonplace on the concert platform, by the 1960s a sufficient corpus of orchestral material existed such that its appearance could be regarded as unusual, rather than extraordinary. From this point onwards the instrument became slowly more prevalent in new work written for symphonic and operatic orchestras, reflecting both stylistic changes within Western art music and a resurgence of interest in the instrument. These issues will be returned to in Chapter 7.

83. The first page of Villa-Lobos's *Fantasia* (1948), in its original key of F major, one tone higher than the published version.

Classical soloists and their repertoire

As already noted in Chapter 3, nineteenth-century composers such as Singelée and Demersseman, and soloists such as Wuille, Soualle and Lefebre, had all contributed to the development of an original saxophone repertoire that largely comprised small-scale compositions and arrangements which often functioned as display pieces. By the turn of the twentieth century this was a specialist but increasingly important area of saxophone activity, underpinned in part by the popularity of the soloists performing with professional bands in the USA; Lefebre, in particular, had published a wide range of transcriptions for the instrument. Nevertheless, the concert pieces available for the saxophone in the late-nineteenth century were classical or light classical miniatures, but as the twentieth century progressed a few individuals began to expand this concert repertoire, and their efforts deserve recognition because of the importance of their work in providing a different identity for the saxophone from that prevailing in popular contexts at this time. Yet it is one of the paradoxes of the development of the saxophone as a concert instrument that efforts to create this more substantial concert repertoire came not from those professional players who might have most benefited from it, but from an enthusiastic, determined – and most importantly, affluent – female amateur player based in Boston, Miss Elise Boyer Hall (1853–1924). Such was her early influence in this area that in 1925 Carl Engel observed that 'if a musicologist of the year 2000 should shake his head in wonder over the remarkable fact that every French composer of the twentieth century – Debussy [and] d'Indy not excepted – as well as [Charles] Martin Loeffler, wrote one composition for the saxophone, let him look to Boston and Mrs R. J. Hall for the answer'.[32]

Elise Boyer Hall and beyond

Elizabeth Boyer Swett Coolidge was born in Paris, in 1853. She spent much of her childhood in France and retained an interest in French language and culture throughout her life. She married an aspiring surgeon, Dr Richard J. Hall, in Boston in 1879, but they spent most of the 1880s in New York, where Dr Hall held various official positions and had a successful private practice. After suffering cocaine addiction – an unintended consequence of his research into the anaesthetic benefits of cocaine hydrochlorate – Richard Hall had a breakdown in 1888, and shortly afterwards the family moved to the healthier environment of Santa Barbara, a spa town in southern California. Here he developed a second successful private practice, before his unexpected and early death in 1897. At some stage in the mid–1890s Richard Hall appears to have suggested that his wife should take up a wind instrument, possibly in order to aid her recovery from typhoid fever.[33] A local labourer played, or at least

84. Elise Boyer Hall.

owned, a saxophone, and from these rudimentary beginnings Elise Hall began to develop her own skills on the instrument.

After Richard Hall's death his wife moved back to Boston. Clearly a woman of means, she helped found an Orchestral Club in Boston, the purpose of which was to provide orchestral experience for amateur musicians. Georges Longy, a French oboist with the Boston Symphony Orchestra from whom Elise Hall took saxophone lessons, was invited to advise and conduct the Club, thus reinforcing her own Francophile sympathies. From 1900 until 1911 the Club gave sporadic public concerts, the majority of which introduced new works that specifically included a saxophone, and/or arrangements of extant pieces for ensembles including saxophone. All the programmes demonstrated a bias towards French composers, and Elise Hall herself also gave several concerts in Paris, again largely devoted to contemporary French music.

The list of French composers whom Elise Hall approached to write new pieces for the saxophone, even though she was undoubtedly advised by Longy, is quite remarkable for an amateur musician based in the United States, and particularly one playing an instrument with very little concert tradition or repertoire to support it at that time. Composers such as Gabriel Grovlez (a 1915 *Suite*), André Caplet (*Impression d'Automne*, 1905?; and *Légende*, 1903) or Jean Huré (*Andante*, 1915, and *Concertstück*, date unknown), form only part of a group that includes more well-known names such as Vincent d'Indy (his *Choral varié* from 1903, premiered by Elise Hall in Paris in May 1904), Florent Schmitt (whose 1918 *Légende* is dedicated to Elise Hall) and Charles Martin Loeffler (*Rapsodie* [destroyed], *Divertissement Espagnol*, 1900; and *Ballade Carnavalesque*, 1903).[34] But undoubtedly the most significant composer to have been pursued by the redoubtable Mrs Hall was Claude Debussy, who composed his *Rapsodie* for alto saxophone and orchestra following a commission from her.

Debussy's apparent reluctance to complete the commission demonstrates the difficulties that players had in the early part of the century in getting the saxophone established as a concert instrument, as well as his own personal antipathy towards it. Although the piece was probably commissioned by Mrs Hall in 1901, in 1903, when she returned to Paris, Debussy had yet to begin work on it. In a letter to his wife that year he wrote scathingly of both the saxophone and his would-be patron, in terms that, more than a century later, appear faintly misogynistic:

> I do not know why 'the Saxophone Lady' appears to me like the Statue of the commandatore appeared to poor Don Juan! – Never will she suspect how much she bored me. Does it not appear indecent to you, a woman in love with a saxophone, whose lips suck at the wooden mouthpiece of this ridiculous instrument? – This must surely be an old mole who dresses like an umbrella.[35]

To his friend, the composer André Messager, Debussy similarly observed that:

> The tenacity of the Americans is proverbial [. . .]. The Saxophone lady landed in Paris at 58 Rue Cardinet, eight or ten days ago, and is inquiring about her piece. Of course I assured her that with the exception of Ramses II, it is the only subject

that occupies my thoughts. All the same, I have had to set to work on it. So here I am, searching desperately for novel combinations calculated to show off this aquatic instrument.[36]

Shortly after this Debussy's guilt appears to have got the better of him and he started work on the piece, as a letter to another friend in July 1903 reveals:

> Forgive me . . . for the last few days I am 'the-man-who-works-on-a-Fantasy-for-E♭-alto-saxophone' [. . .]. Since this fantasy was ordered, paid for, and eaten more than a year ago, does it not seem that I am late? At first it amused me very little, then I did not care enough about it to write you a detailed letter. The saxophone is an animal with a reed, about whose habits I know very little. Does it like the romantic sweetness of the clarinets, or the slightly coarse irony of the sarrusophone (or contra bassoon)? Finally I have made it murmur some melancholy phrases, beneath the rolling of the military drum. The saxophone, like the Grand-Duchess, should like the military [. . .] the whole work is entitled *Rapsodie Arabe*.[37]

As noted previously, the work was initially described as a *Rapsodie Mauresque*, although it is now more commonly known simply as *Rapsodie*. It had long been thought that the orchestration of the work was not by Debussy but was completed after his death by his friend and pupil Jean Roger-Ducasse in 1919. However, it was confirmed in the 1970s that the short score received by Elise Hall in Boston was not only in Debussy's hand, but did in fact contain quite explicit instructions regarding its entire orchestration; Roger-Ducasse was, to a significant degree, simply fleshing out instructions for the orchestration left by Debussy.[38] Most of the works commissioned by Elise Hall do not make virtuoso demands on the saxophonist, and the *Rapsodie* is no exception. The work itself is not a substantial piece. The saxophone line is prominent within the ensemble, but hardly concerto-like in the manner of other orchestral display vehicles, and this may well reflect the 'orchestral club' context for which it was commissioned, as well as Debussy's perplexity about how to deal with the instrument. Unfortunately Mrs Hall does not appear to have had the opportunity to perform the *Rapsodie*, and its first performance was given by Yves Mayeur in Paris in 1919.

Elise Hall's financial independence enabled her to pursue her interests in French music and the saxophone, and subsequent generations of saxophonists have benefited from the largesse of this amateur musician who commissioned such a range of composers. Were it not for her efforts, the creation of a solo repertory for the instrument during this period would have been much the poorer. In the 1920s and early 1930s the saxophone undoubtedly suffered in art music circles because of its notable success in popular music, and works such as the English composer Joseph Holbrooke's 1928 Concerto for alto saxophone and orchestra are very much the exception to this rule.

Nevertheless, some of the performers benefiting from the instrument's popular appeal, such as Rudy Wiedoeft, also endeavoured to promote its classical profile. Jascha Gurewich, an outstanding saxophone soloist with the Sousa band for a season (1920–1), composed a range of works for the instrument, including a fantasia for saxophone and piano (1924); a concerto for saxophone and orchestra (op. 102, 1925); and a sonata for saxophone and piano (1928). The concerto in particular remains part of standard saxophone repertoire. Gurewich hired New York City's Aeolian Hall, on 31 January 1926, for a formal saxophone recital. The Aeolian was a prestigious venue in the 1920s for classical music performance; Gurewich's performance was a small but significant assertion of the possibilities the saxophone afforded as a concert instrument. That particular concert programme consisted of original works by Gurewich (including his concerto), and transcriptions of pieces by composers such as Puccini, Verdi, Albeniz, Mendelssohn and others. Curiously, little more is known of Gurewich after this event. He disappeared from the limelight very quickly, and died in obscurity in 1938, at the age of 42.

Such pioneers were not only confined to the United States. In France performers such as François Combelle and Raymond Briard – both members of the *Garde républicaine* band – contributed compositions of their own as well as eliciting a small but continuing stream of solo pieces for the instrument from other minor French composers. But Elise Hall's commissioning of a repertoire for herself and her instrument remained an important example for classical saxophone players. Like Lefebre she was aware that, unlike most other instruments of the time, the saxophone did not have a core classical repertory for performers to acquaint themselves with. And the development of classical saxophone repertoire from the 1930s onwards was to a considerable degree focussed around a small group of performers who continued her pioneering spirit. Three names in particular demand individual attention: Marcel Mule, Sigurd Rascher, and Cecil Leeson.

Marcel Mule

The significance of Marcel Mule (1901–2001) within the classical saxophone tradition arises not only from his exceptional musical skill and the large amount of repertoire written for or transcribed by him, but also because of his position as Professor of Saxophone at the Paris Conservatoire, which was for several decades the leading centre of classical saxophone in the world. Born on 24 June 1901 in the small town of Aube (Orne) in Normandy, Mule was already playing the saxophone in a local band conducted by his father (also a saxophonist) by the age of eight. As a teenager he also learned violin and piano. After initially training to be a classroom teacher Mule was called up for military service, and moved to Paris in 1921. Initially assigned to the Fifth Infantry Regiment, his musical skills and band experience meant that he quickly became involved with the regimental band. Discovering that, in his words, 'my level in music was not at all inferior to my fellow soldiers'[39] he was stimulated to practise intensively, and soon made a reputation for himself in military circles as a skilled saxophonist. This brought him to the attention of François Combelle, the saxophone soloist with the band of the *Garde républicaine*, France's foremost military music ensemble. Entrance to the *Garde* was by competitive audition, and when a saxophone position became available in 1923 Mule came first out of the twelve players who competed for it. Six months later he succeeded Combelle as saxophone soloist with the band, a position he was to hold for the next thirteen years.

Just as military music had played an important role in the development of the saxophone in mid-nineteenth-century France, so too was it important in underpinning the expansion of classical repertory in the first part of the twentieth century, for it provided Combelle, Mule and others with a foundation around which to construct their musical careers. The profile Mule achieved as saxophone soloist with the band enabled him to give solo performances throughout Europe from as early as 1925, but his more influential solo work began in earnest in the mid 1930s, and in 1936 he finally left the *Garde* to pursue a solo career that lasted until his retirement in 1968.

Perhaps Mule's most profound impact on the development of twentieth-century classical saxophone playing was in establishing a coherent performance aesthetic, a playing style that was recognisably his own and which many other performers sought to emulate. Just as early popular music saxophone pioneers in America such as Wiedoeft, Trumbauer or Hawkins established benchmarks in their worlds, so too did Mule for classical saxophone players. He developed a warm, rounded tone that was consistent over the range of the instrument, and an exceptionally smooth legato that sought to minimise those timbral differences inherent in the instrument's design. Mule also introduced a more systematic approach to the use of vibrato, something he later suggested came about partly because of its use in the jazz and dance band tradition:

85. Marcel Mule.

At the point in time when the vibrato was used (1928–9), a school for classical saxophone did not exist. Strange as it may seem, jazz was important in two ways in establishing such a school. First of all, there was the influence upon me of the jazz player's use of vibrato with the saxophone [. . .]. In addition, however, there were many jazz performers who came to me for lessons during the twenties, and in later years [. . .] who, above all, wanted help in one particular area of their playing – tone quality! [. . .] Thus I spent years developing and refining my sonority and the use of vibrato.[40]

The suggestion that vibrato was not used at all in classical saxophone playing is not entirely consistent with the recorded evidence. But in developing his own sound Mule arrived at a deeper and more metrically consistent vibrato, an approach in which the pitch undulations become an integral part of the overall sound. This methodical approach was further replicated in some of his pedagogic material:

In my edition of the Ferling etudes almost every piece that is slow and lyrical has a marking of MM=72. I did this to allow the students the practice of playing four undulations per beat, giving them a general speed of ca. 288 undulations per minute, a speed which seemed to me ideal at that time [. . .]. In retrospect I feel that I made a mistake, that the marking should have been 76 rather than 72, giving a general speed of approximately 300 undulations per minute.[41]

It seems likely that these relatively high speeds were intended for pedagogic purposes, to facilitate and develop the control of vibrato, rather than to be uniformly applied in musical performance. Mule's own vibrato, while very pronounced, in fact ranges from approximately 180 to 250 undulations per minute, according to context.[42] In seeking to make his vibrato an integral part of his performance style, Mule was also influenced by other instrumentalists. He made clear his indebtedness to singers and string players, and his own training as a violinist undoubtedly informed his musical ideas.[43] Mule's almost single-handed creation of a French school of classical saxophone playing parallels the work of Paul Taffanel, the principal architect of the French Flute School, some 50 years earlier.[44] Mule would certainly have been aware of the increasing use of vibrato among Parisian flautists, a practice that had its origins at the Paris Conservatoire at the end of the nineteenth century. Thus the evolution of classical saxophone vibrato – something with which Mule was particularly identified with but which also began to characterise the performance styles of other players – can be traced to a number of different sources: its increasing use among string players of the period, and the transfer of this aesthetic from performers such as Mule who played both string and wind instruments; the recognition that other wind instrumentalists such as flautists were increasingly employing it; and the cross-fertilisation with a jazz saxophone tradition where it was already an established component of performance practice.

Mule's pedagogic influence was reinforced when he was invited to become Professor of Saxophone at the Conservatoire in 1942. The instrument had not been taught at the institution since the disbanding in 1870 of the saxophone class run by

Adolphe Sax. Given that in 1942 Paris was a city under German occupation it may appear a slightly unusual time in which to resurrect such a class, but both the Germans (for propaganda reasons) and the French (for the purpose of preserving national cultural identity) were keen that Paris's cultural life was sustained, and the re-establishment of the saxophone class at this time can be seen in this context.

The longevity of Mule's position at the Conservatoire – he remained there until his retirement in 1968 – and the close but hierarchical relationship between the national and regional conservatoires in France, meant that he profoundly affected the development of classical saxophone playing throughout the country; and because the French classical saxophone tradition was for several decades internationally pre-eminent, attracting a range of foreign visitors, Mule exerted a global pedagogic influence. His work was under-pinned by the considerable energy he put into developing suitable study materials. The adaptation of existing studies for other instruments – such as Ferling's 48 oboe studies (1840) mentioned above, for which Mule himself composed a further 12 studies in enhar-monic keys – was supplemented by extensive transcriptions of pieces from earlier eras.

But it was Mule's work in creating a dedicated repertoire for the classical saxo-phone that has provided his most significant legacy. The saxophone class at the Conservatoire required every year a *solo de concours*, a specially commissioned work which those completing their studies were (and are) required to perform. During his tenure the majority of these were dedicated to Mule, and many of them have become part of standard concert repertoire, such as Claude Pascal's *Sonatine* (1948), Alfred Desenclos's *Prélude, Cadence et Finale* (1956), and Roger Boutry's *Divertimento* (1964). Many other works now taken to be core repertory for concert saxophonists also came about because of Mule's patronage: Paul Bonneau's *Caprice en Forme de valse* (1950), various works by Eugène Bozza, Jean Francaix's *Cinq Danses exotiques* (1962), Paule Maurice's *Tableaux de Provence* (1948–55), and so forth.[45]

Mule's creation of new repertory also extended to the concerto form. On 16 November 1935 he premiered the Concerto in F, op. 65, for alto saxophone and orchestra, by Pierre Vellones; this was one of the earliest European performances of a saxophone concerto if one leaves aside the Debussy *Rapsodie*. A more well-known work, and one with which Mule became closely identified, was Ibert's *Concertino da camera* (1934), for alto saxophone and eleven instruments. This perennial favourite among classical saxophonists has a curious history. It was not commissioned by Mule, but by Sigurd Rascher, who gave the first performance of the complete work on 11 December 1935. Mule, however, claims to have performed the work on French radio prior to this date,[46] although Rascher had premiered the first movement alone on 2 May of that year. The exceptionally high altissimo notes – going up to ab4, a ninth above the conventional range of the alto sax – are certainly more characteristic of Rascher's technique than Mule's (see ex. 20). Whatever the truth of its performance history, Ibert's rhythmically vigorous style, the well-balanced contrapuntal interplay between soloist and the other instruments, and the challenging but idiomatic saxo-phone line have made the work one of the most well known and successful pieces for the instrument.

Mule was the single most influential figure in classical saxophone playing in the twentieth century, and his efforts in generating pedagogic material and new works for

Ex. 20. The short cadenza of Ibert's *Concertino da camera* (1934), showing the altissimo notes expected. An alternative is given for less adventurous players.

the saxophone – largely but not exclusively for the alto member of the family – came to provide a core classical French repertoire for aspiring performers. Nevertheless, it is reasonable to observe that there is a certain commonality of musical language running through the music of the composers with whom he most closely identified. The repertoire he stimulated may be differentiated to some degree by personal compositional style, but because Mule's commissions were very largely directed towards French composers who shared particular idioms, and who were geographically and chronologically related, there is less musical diversity in this core repertoire than might otherwise have been the case, and it fell to other saxophonists to bring to this repertoire a greater degree of stylistic variety.

Sigurd Rascher

The other major European saxophone player of the 1930s and beyond was Sigurd Rascher (1907–2001), whose work and career is often juxtaposed against Mule's, notwithstanding their rather different outlooks. Born in Elberfeld (now part of Wuppertal) in Germany on 15 May 1907, Rascher's early musical education centred around the clarinet, which he studied at the Stuttgart Musikhochschule. By the early 1930s he was based in Berlin, supplementing his teaching income by working in dance bands, but also playing in the Berlin Philharmonic Orchestra on saxophone, an instrument that he had taught himself to play. While working with the orchestra he met the German composer Edmund von Borck, who was persuaded to write what would be the first of many concertos dedicated to Rascher. The work was premiered in Hannover in October 1932, and subsequently heard also in Berlin in 1933, presented by the International Society for Contemporary Music (ISCM), where both the piece and its soloist made a considerable impact. One critic noted afterwards that the concerto was written 'with much dexterity, and makes skilful use of the possibilities of the saxophone. The solo part was played by Sigurd M. Rascher, an unsurpassed virtuoso of his instrument.'[47]

This was a catalyst for Rascher's career, and over the next few years he persuaded a number of high-profile composers to contribute works for the saxophone. Ibert's *Concertino da camera* has already been noted, but to it must be added Hindemith's *Konzertstück* (1933) for two altos, Glazunov's Concerto in E♭ (1934) for alto and string orchestra, Lars-Erik Larsson's Concerto (1934) – Rascher premiered these last two works on consecutive days in November 1934 – Eric Coates's *Saxo-rhapsody* (1936), and Frank Martin's *Ballade* (1938). That so many cornerstones of classical saxophone repertoire were commissioned and performed over this relatively short timescale is testament both to Rascher's industriousness and his awareness of composers likely to write idiomatically for the instrument. He was keen to keep abreast of contemporary compositional developments; a picture of him at the 1941 ISCM meeting in New York shows him among many of the compositional luminaries of the day, including Bela Bartók, Roger Sessions, Ernst Krenek, Benjamin Britten and Bohuslav Martinů, among others (see ill. 86).[48]

Rascher's large number of important commissions undoubtedly stemmed from a certain stubborn persistence. In March 1934 Glazunov wrote to a friend that he had started work on his concerto 'under the influence of attacks rather than requests' from Rascher.[49] Glazunov appears to have been pleased with the work, however, and in June that year he gave a description of it to the same friend:

86.   Sigurd Rascher and a group of composers at the 1941 ISCM in New York. Rascher is on the extreme right-hand end of the middle row (6). The composers include Béla Bartók (1), Roger Sessions (2), Ernst Krenek (3), Benjamin Britten (4), and Bohuslav Martinů (5).

I completed the *Concerto* for saxophone, both the score and clavier, and most likely I will hear performances within days by the Frenchman Mule and the Danish saxophonist Rascher. The concerto is written in Es-dur [E♭ major] and goes non–stop [. . .]. The form is very condensed, and the total time is no more than 18 min. The accompaniment is built on strings with much divis, which, in some point, will substitute [for the] missing wind section [. . .]. I did show my *Concerto* to Medtner [. . .] and Tcherepnine [. . .] and they approved of my work.[50]

Rascher's abilities brought him wide recognition in musical circles, but also unwelcome attention from the Nazi government that seized power in Germany in 1933. The Nazis regarded the saxophone as a degenerate instrument because of its associations with what they construed as 'negro' music, and saxophonists sometimes suffered under their regime (see pp. 320–6). Like many artists involved in Berlin's thriving cultural scene Rascher felt it expedient to leave the country, and moved to Copenhagen, where he taught saxophone at the Royal Danish Conservatory (hence Glazunov's description of him as 'Danish'); one year later he took on a similar position in Malmö, Sweden. He retained both posts until 1938. As with Mule in Paris, this pedagogic base allowed Rascher to develop his solo career, and with a growing repertoire of new works, and a rising reputation, he was busy on the European concert hall circuit for much of the 1930s. In 1939 Rascher made his American debut performing concertos with both the Boston Symphony and New York Philharmonic Orchestras. And as the war clouds gathered over Europe, Rascher decided to stay in the United States; he spent the rest of his life there, apart from the war years themselves when he was obliged to stay in Cuba (harvesting sugar cane) because of difficulties with immigration laws in relation to his German heritage.

After World War II Rascher resumed his concert career, as well as undertaking extensive teaching commitments at institutions such as the Juilliard School, and the Manhattan and Eastman Schools of Music. Through these he influenced a wide range of American and international saxophonists. Perhaps his most significant pedagogic legacy has been the book *Top Tones for the Saxophone*.[51] From his earliest days as a soloist Rascher had been keen to exploit the extended range of the saxophone above its theoretical top note of f♯³. He was initially alerted to the musical possibilities these offered by his teacher Gustav Bumcke (1876–1963), a saxophonist based in Berlin who also played a significant role in the development of the saxophone as a concert instrument. By devising a series of alternative fingerings to produce these high notes, Rascher achieved considerable facility in this range, something that was often reflected in the pieces written for him.

Rascher's commissioning activities ensured a steady flow of new works for the instrument. Nevertheless, like Mule and others of his generation, and notwithstanding his commitment to a range of different contemporary composers, Rascher rejected many aspects of modernism and the musical avant-garde. And in other ways, particularly in terms of his perspective on saxophones and saxophone sound, he looked backward as much as forward: he always endeavoured to stay close to what he conceived as an 'authentic' saxophone sound, based on Sax's original aspirations. Older instruments, particularly by Buescher, were often favoured over their modern counterparts, because of their particular tonal qualities, and Rascher designed and used mouthpieces that were closely modelled on Sax's originals. This commitment to a saxophonic version of historically-informed performance – at least in relation to what is sometimes construed as 'sonic authenticity' – might have been more influential had there been a greater corpus of early saxophone material on which it could be practiced. But the relative modernity of the instrument, and the limited musical insights that therefore accrue from adopting such approaches, has meant that the saxophone has remained relatively marginalised in the period performance movement that has been so influential in other contexts. Rascher's practice, while undoubtedly interesting, has ultimately proven to be idiosyncratic, rather than revolutionary, notwithstanding that it has continued to inform the practice of some of those associated with him, even in their commissioning of contemporary material.

Cecil Leeson

The third of the pioneering classical soloists, Cecil Leeson (1902–89), did not achieve as high an international profile as either Mule or Rascher, but his work in establishing the saxophone as a concert instrument is equally significant, particularly in the United States at a time when it was widely associated there with popular music. Born in North Dakota in December 1902, Leeson was a late starter on the saxophone, reaching the age of seventeen before he first took up the instrument. Nevertheless, he enrolled as a saxophone major only two years later at Dana's Musical Institute in Warren, Ohio, in 1921, (now part of Youngstown State University). Leeson initially played on a C-melody saxophone, before later realising that the alto offered more opportunities as a concert instrument, and, perhaps, also because of a growing realisation on his part of its identification with amateur musicians (nevertheless, it is illustrative of the widespread popularity of the C-melody instrument that it played a role not only in the early jazz tradition but also in the fledgling days of the American concert tradition). Leeson's performances at the Institute involved not only replicating the pieces already made popular by the professional wind band soloists and Rudy Wiedoeft, but also, doubtless because of the formal, classically-oriented setting in which he found himself, transcriptions of mainstream repertoire written for other instruments. Thus the now familiar mix of novelty originals, light classical miniatures and classical transcriptions furnished him with his first concert repertoire.

On leaving the Institute Leeson worked in various commercial groups in Detroit, before ending up back in Ohio, in Cleveland. Through fortuitous circumstances he was asked to undertake a series of live radio programmes, playing for 30 minutes every other week, for the radio station WHK. These started in the autumn of 1926 and lasted for nearly two years, and would later be followed by similar stints with KNX in Los Angeles (from 1930) and then CBS in New York (from 1935). Such broadcasts were highly significant. Radio was an important medium for disseminating music in 1920s and 30s America, and, despite the relatively small catchment areas of the more local stations, Leeson's broadcasts provided a very different style of saxophone playing from the jazz and dance saxophone sounds to which American ears had become accustomed. Wiedoeft had previously argued for the importance of radio for the

87.   Cecil Leeson.

dissemination of classical music, now Leeson demonstrated it. Furthermore, the advertising associated with such programmes also meant that Leeson's name and image, and the concept of the saxophone as a recital instrument, were also promoted by such broadcasts.

Both this advertising and Leeson's performances helped to counter widely-held views of the saxophone as a lightweight novelty instrument. This 'new' approach to saxophone performance was not lost on critics and commentators, who frequently juxtaposed descriptions of his playing alongside references to the instrument's rather different uses elsewhere, while also demonstrating some sympathy for his aspirations to define a new role for the instrument. A writer in the *Hollywood News* observed, for example, that 'in Leeson's capable hands, the saxophone [is] no longer the blatant jazz instrument of popular conception, but an instrument of really beautiful tone color [. . .]. If there were other saxophonists who could play as Leeson does, the saxophone would speedily make its appearance in the symphony orchestra.'[52] Similarly, an advertisement for King Saxophones quoted a letter from the composer and bandmaster Edwin Franko Goldman to Leeson, asserting that 'in your hands the saxophone is a dignified and worthwhile musical instrument [. . .]. If we had more players of your type the saxophone would soon occupy in the musical firmament the place it deserves.'[53]

Like Mule and Rascher, Leeson was of necessity an enthusiastic commissioner of original works for the instrument. He was aided in this through his association with a young American composer, Paul Creston, who had been assigned to him as an accompanist by the National Music League, an organisation devoted to developing the careers of young artists. Creston was an excellent accompanist, and the two artists formed a partnership that lasted – intermittently – from 1934 to 1939. Their friendship resulted in several works that are now core repertoire for saxophonists: a Suite (1935) for saxophone and piano; a Sonata (1939) for the same combination (probably now the single most frequently performed recital work in the saxophone repertoire); and a Concerto (1941).[54] Together they gave, on 5 February 1937, the first performance by a saxophonist at New York's illustrious Town Hall, with a programme that included the US premiere of Glazunov's concerto, albeit with piano accompaniment rather than full orchestra.

Such was Leeson's eminence from the mid 1930s that he was soon being offered concerto opportunities. The full US orchestral premiere of the Glazunov concerto, for example, was given during a concert with the Rochester Philharmonic on 13 January 1938, conducted by José Iturbi. This was the first time the saxophone had been given a solo role in such a high-profile concert setting, and its appearance at the front of the orchestral platform was sufficiently unusual that Iturbi felt it necessary to make clear before the performance that Leeson was not a vaudeville act but a serious artist.[55]

Leeson commissioned many other pieces over the course of his career, from composers as diverse as Edvard Moritz, who wrote two sonatas (1938, 1940) and a work for saxophone and string quartet (1940); Burnet Tuthill, who also composed several sonatas (1939, 1968) and a concerto (1965);[56] and Leon Stein, who completed five works for Leeson, including several for unusual chamber combinations. Leeson also requested concertos from several composers who were unwilling or unable to respond. Paul Whiteman's arranger Ferde Grofé, a fine composer in his own right, promised to write a work, even sketching out a theme for a concerto in D, but was unable to find the time to complete the piece. Percy Grainger, on the other hand, dismissed the request outright, on the grounds that he was against putting one instrument ahead of any other, because he was 'an Australian and a socialist'.[57]

Leeson's concertising was prolific by the standards of the time, but he also undertook pedagogic work on occasion, partly through commitment to the instrument and partly through economic necessity. As early as 1930 he had joined the faculty at the Hollywood Conservatory of Music and remained there for several years; he also initiated saxophone instruction at the National Music Camp at Interlochen, Michigan, from 1937. In later life he was appointed as Professor of Saxophone at Northwestern (1955–61) and Ball State Universities (1961–77). Like Wiedoeft before him, he also published a series of articles in *Metronome* in the mid-1930s, aimed at providing guidance for aspiring saxophonists. The titles of these articles – for example, 'Some Factors in Saxophone Tone Production', 'Mastering Saxophone Vibrato' – demonstrate their essentially didactic and pragmatic nature. Leeson's interest in the fundamental issue of saxophone tone was further illustrated in a doctoral thesis on the subject he completed in 1955.[58]

Leeson's style of saxophone performance established in the United States a school of classical saxophone playing that differed from the European model largely built around Mule's work in Paris. Leeson's sound was a little brighter and 'brassier', perhaps because of the inevitable influence of popular music styles around him, and his vibrato tended to be slightly shallower and faster than his European peers. There was also a rhythmic vivaciousness to his playing which is again characteristic of the American school of classical saxophone playing as a whole, albeit that in part it arises from the compositional styles of many of the key works written by American composers for Leeson and the instrument.

A prediction offered in *The Musician* of 1934 that Leeson was 'an artistic pioneer [. . .] blazing a trail over which it is probable a line of new saxophone virtuosi will follow' has proved to be entirely correct.[59]

Later soloists

While Hall, Mule, Rascher and Leeson pioneered a concert tradition for the saxophone, many others followed their lead, and in some cases overlapped with them. Any selection of names is inevitably arbitrary, but listing some of them here evidences how widespread the classical saxophone concert tradition became from its relatively humble beginnings in the early 1930s, through to a more established international network of soloists and pedagogues by the late 1970s.

In the United States Laurence (Larry) Teal (1905–84) was a prolific performer and teacher on a range of woodwind instruments; he held positions with the Detroit Symphony Orchestra both as a bass clarinettist and, later, as a flautist. His appointment as Professor of Saxophone at the University of Michigan in 1953 was an important step in establishing saxophone tuition among the elite American universities, and he subsequently organised the first doctoral programme in saxophone in the United States. His book *The Art of Saxophone Playing* (1963) remains an important pedagogic text, and he is also the dedicatee of composer Bernhard Heiden's well-known Sonata (1937). Vincent Abato (1920–2008) was a saxophonist and clarinettist who influenced a wide range of pupils through his work as Professor of Saxophone at the Juilliard School in New York. He made many early classical saxophone recordings, including first recordings of Creston's sonata and concerto pieces. Frederick Hemke (b. 1935) was the first American to study with Mule in Paris, in 1955–6 (where he was awarded a *premier prix*), and he has contributed greatly to the development of a classical saxophone infrastructure in the United States, not only through his performances but also through his extensive pedagogy, in part pursued through a long career on the staff of Northwestern University, which he joined in 1962. His doctoral dissertation on *The Early History of the Saxophone* (1975) remains a key text, and he has done much to encourage saxophone scholarship in the United States. Eugene Rousseau (b. 1932) is a similarly renowned American performer and teacher, whose long incumbency as Professor of Saxophone at Indiana University (1964–2000) attracted a range of international students and visiting artists. Kenneth Douse (1906–83) was perhaps the most outstanding saxophonist to work in a military context, and was soloist with the Marine Band until

1950, before working as both violinist and saxophonist in the National Symphony Orchestra from the 1950s.

Many of Mule's students have gone on to develop the classical saxophone in France, none more so than Jean-Marie Londeix (b. 1932), who has been based since 1970 at the regional Conservatoire in Bordeaux, an institution that has attracted a large number of international students. Londeix has also stimulated a considerable range of new concert music, from composers as diverse as Edison Denisov, Conrad Beck, Ryo Noda and Henri Tomasi. Again Londeix's pedagogic material has been important, and his work as a founder of the Association des Saxophonistes de France and of the World Saxophone Congress has contributed much to saxophone scholarship and performance around the world.[60] François Daneels (b. 1921) has performed the role in Belgium that Mule undertook in France, creating the first class specifically dedicated to the saxophone at the Royal Conservatory in Brussels in 1954; prior to this the instrument had been taught within the institution by clarinettists.[61] Like Mule and Rascher, Daneels has had an extensive international career. His list of commissions in a variety of genres includes fellow Belgian composers Jean Absil, Marcel Poot, and Henri Pousseur, as well as French composers such as Pierre-Max Dubois.

The saxophone and chamber music

Saxophone chamber groups

The most significant and successful area of saxophone chamber music-making has been in relation to ensembles composed entirely of saxophones. It was always Adolphe Sax's expectation that such groups would and should evolve, and that the homogeneity the instrument brought to the military band and elsewhere could be exploited independently. As early as 1844 Léon Escudier had written that 'there could actually be a quartet of saxophones [. . .] this is a new world opening up for instrumental art'.[62] Several of Sax's Parisian allies provided works for saxophone groups, some of which were published by Sax himself. As already noted in Chapter 3, in 1844 Georges Kastner had offered a *Grand Sextuor* for six saxophones (S/2A/T/B/Bs) as part of his first saxophone method; Jean-Baptiste Singelée (1812–75) contributed two early S/A/T/B quartets, in 1858 and 1864; and Jérôme Savari (1819–1870) composed a range of works in the early 1860s, for various combinations of saxophones from quartet to octet.

Subsequently, interest in independent saxophone groups went into something of a decline in Europe, mirroring the trajectory of the instrument itself. In contrast, however, towards the end of the nineteenth century the saxophone quartet medium became increasingly popular in the United States, initially through the activities of professional soloists such as E. A. Lefebre but then across a greater cross-section of American musicians (see pp. 139–40). Much of the repertoire for these groups consisted again of light classical transcriptions or popular pieces: the Waldteufel waltz transcription and an arrangement of the song *Annie Laurie* recorded for Victor in 1902 by The American Quartette – drawn from Sousa's band – is indicative of the repertoire that many such groups were performing at this time. These performances were important in demonstrating the viability of saxophone ensembles, in developing ensemble musical skills among saxophonists, and in providing aural models for others to follow; in this sense they too are an important part of the classical saxophone quartet heritage.

Notwithstanding the trailblazing efforts of many of these groups, it was arguably a quartet drawn from a different band that established the saxophone quartet as a serious concert force in the twentieth century. On 2 December 1928 Le Quatuor de la Musique de la Garde Républicaine gave its first concert in La Rochelle, France. Established by Marcel Mule on soprano, with his colleagues René Chaligné (alto), Hippolyte Poimboeuf (tenor) and Georges Chauvet (baritone), the Quartet underwent several changes of name over the course of the next forty years: when Mule left the Garde in 1936 it became known as Le Quatuor de Saxophones de Paris, and then in 1951 the Marcel Mule Quartet, in order to capitalise on its leader's growing reputation. The group also underwent various changes in personnel prior to its disbandment in 1967, just before Mule's retirement.

Just as Mule had established a classical French repertoire for the saxophone as a solo instrument, so too did his quartet stimulate the creation of a – largely French – classical repertoire for saxophone quartet. Composers such as Robert Clérisse (*Cache-Cache*, 1930), Alexander Glazunov (Quartet op. 109, 1932), Eugène Bozza (*Andante et Scherzo*, 1938), Florent Schmitt (Quartet op. 102, 1941) and Claude Pascal (Quartet, 1961), among many others, generated a range of pieces that sought to exploit the particular characteristics of the ensemble. This French repertoire provided for many years the bedrock of classical quartet playing in Europe and beyond; it was largely also characterised by the same idiomatic constraints that have already been noted in relation to solo repertoire. Notwithstanding the importance of this classical French repertory for saxophonists and their ensembles, one has only to compare this saxophone quartet repertoire with string quartets by Shostakovich or Bartók (to name but two), composed over a similar timescale, to realise the musical gulf that exists between the different genres. There are, of course, some fine works, and saxophonists will cherish their favourites, but few if any works for saxophone quartet could be said to be familiar to the wider public, unlike, perhaps, the Glazunov or Ibert concertos.

Thus, although Mule's quartet was the pre-eminent saxophone group of its time, its major legacy was perhaps not so much the repertoire it generated but its demonstration of the saxophone quartet as a viable medium that could be taken seriously as a concert ensemble. The group also reached new heights in saxophone ensemble performance, transferring into the ensemble domain the standards that Mule had established in his solo work: timbral homogeneity and rhythmic precision became the hallmarks of the ensemble, together with a collective virtuosity that was unusual among saxophone groups of the period. A further significant aspect of the group's legacy has been its impact on those ensembles that have followed, which have similarly sought both to continue generating new material as well as developing performance standards. Sigurd Rascher's name again comes to the fore, since the Sigurd Rascher Quartet, formed in 1969 with his daughter Carina Rascher on soprano, quickly established itself on the concert circuit. Continuing Rascher's preference for older saxophones and his aspirations for a type of sonic authenticity, the quartet developed a particularly distinctive sound and has commissioned works from

88. The Marcel
Mule Saxophone
Quartet.

a wide range of composers. François Daneels formed the Quatuor Belge de
Saxophones in 1953, and commissioned a large number of (principally Belgian)
composers to write for the group. The New York Saxophone Quartet was formed in
1959 and the Chicago Saxophone Quartet in 1968; both continue today, albeit with
changed personnel, and are part of a now thriving North American saxophone quartet
scene. In Britain the Michael Krein Quartet was established in 1941, with Krein
(1908–66) himself contributing a certain amount of light material to their repertoire.
As elsewhere, this pioneering work laid the foundations for a significant number of
later British groups, starting with the London Saxophone Quartet in 1969.

Composers often enjoy writing for saxophone quartet because it offers many of
the challenges and advantages of writing for string quartet without the anxiety of influence – as Harold Bloom described it – that arises from a significant historical lineage.
In particular, the timbral homogeneity achieved by four saxophones parallels to a
considerable degree the homogeneity offered by the string quartet medium, although it
is fair to observe that, for most listeners, the saxophone quartet does not carry the same
emotional range or depth as does the string quartet. In Europe the preferred

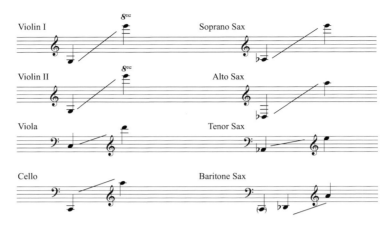

Ex. 21. A comparison of the ranges covered by a saxophone quartet (S/A/T/B) and a string quartet (the upper ranges of the string instruments are approximate and do not include notes achievable with harmonic fingerings).

instrumentation for classical saxophone quartets has usually been S/A/T/B, whereas in the United States the 2A/T/B formation has sometimes been employed, particularly in the first part of the twentieth century (Lefebre's later quartet and the American Quartette both used this combination). This 2A/T/B formation, which might be seen as the direct equivalent of the string quartet (2 violins, viola, cello), offers particular homogeneity, whereas the more distinctive nature of the soprano line in the S/A/T/B disposition facilitates a slightly greater timbral range, as well as a wider range of available pitches within the instruments' normal ranges. Modern baritones fitted with a low a° key sound as low as the cello's lowest note C, although the saxophone quartet does not have the same range and flexibility above the treble stave as a string quartet has, even with the use of the altissimo registers; nor do the ranges of individual saxophones compare favourably with the much greater ranges of their string equivalents (see ex. 21).

With either line-up homophonic passages are relatively easily scored, without the difficulties of instrumental balance presented by the very different timbres of a mixed woodwind quintet, for example; yet the different tessituras and timbres of the individual saxophones are distinct enough to facilitate clarity in contrapuntal passages. Today the S/A/T/B ensemble is most commonly found worldwide, although composers often manipulate this basic formation, sometimes by asking performers to double on other saxophones to create unusual groupings, in order to maximise the available timbral variety.

Mixed ensembles

Many of the reasons that have hindered the saxophone's widespread adoption in symphonic and operatic genres apply equally to its relatively slow incursion into mixed chamber ensembles. The instrument's distinctive timbre, its tendency to mask other instruments if not sensitively scored, the pejorative associations sometimes construed upon it, and the inevitable conservative momentum generated by ensembles with dispositions settled in the eighteenth and nineteenth centuries, have all made composers sometimes reticent about including the saxophone in chamber music contexts. In some cases the difficulty of balancing its greater volume against softer instruments has also been an issue. Charles Koechlin, in his 1937 septet for wind quintet, cor anglais and alto saxophone, made a point of asking that the tone of the saxophone be matched with that of the other wind instruments, doubtless because he was only too keenly aware of these problems of balance.[63] Stravinsky held similar views. Although he intended the instrumentation of *The Soldier's Tale* (1918) to evoke a prototypical jazz ensemble, he used the bassoon instead of the saxophone because he felt the latter to be 'more turbid and penetrating' than the former, and thought that the saxophone worked better in orchestral combinations (not that, in Stravinsky's case, this was ever put into practice).[64] The instrument's association with jazz and popular music meant that, as elsewhere, it was either avoided by those composers who felt such associations might taint the otherwise serious nature of their endeavours, or it was used precisely to allude to those popular musics in which the instrument was most commonly found.

A number of examples serve to illustrate these points. An explicit association with the popular music styles of the 1920s arises in William Walton's settings of Edith Sitwell's poems in *Façade* (1922). Here Walton assimilates tangos, foxtrots, charlestons and other fashionable jazz-tinged dance music of the time. Walton was influenced by both Stravinsky's *Histoire* and Schoenberg's *Pierrot lunaire* in his sublimation of popular styles into an art music context; the small ensemble for the work comprises flute, clarinet, trumpet, cello, percussion and alto saxophone, as well as a reciter of Sitwell's texts. The first version of the work was performed privately in 1922 and contained no saxophone, but the instrument was added for the first public performance the following year, as Walton increasingly 'pepped up' his score to reflect the popular music styles of the day.

Stefan Wolpe's 1950 Quartet uses a tenor saxophone – with trumpet, percussion and piano – to create a jazz-influenced surface that belies a complex structure infused by Wolpe's serially-based musical language. Though Wolpe had taught composition to a number of jazz-oriented composers, he did not set out to write a jazz piece *per se*, but, given his socialist sympathies, endeavoured instead to allude through this instrumentation to the populist nature of both jazz and the saxophone. The piece was written as a celebration of the founding of the People's Republic of China, and Wolpe wrote to his publisher that he felt it to be one of his best 'Kampfmusiken' (music for the struggle), something he could only admit privately, given the influence of Senator McCarthy's anti-communist sentiments in the USA at this time.[65]

The tenor instrument is also used in one of the better-known examples of chamber music involving the saxophone, Webern's Quartet op. 22 (1932) for saxophone, clarinet, violin and piano. Why Webern should have chosen to incorporate the saxophone in this group is not clear, particularly since the original inspiration for the work arose during walking tours of the Carinthian Alps, far from the dance-band influenced urban centres of Weimar Germany where the instrument was more normally found. While writing the piece, however, Webern observed in a letter to Berg that he had 'made the discovery that, basically, the instruments become more and more immaterial to me',[66] and it is possible that the saxophone, with its particularly strong extra-musical associations, was chosen to demonstrate just how disassociated and 'immaterial' Webern conceived the instruments to be. It is also possible that Berg's use of the saxophone in his works of this period influenced Webern's choice of instruments (Webern also used the alto saxophone in two later choral works, *Das Augenlicht* in 1935 and the Cantata no. 2 in 1943). The quartet was originally conceived as a concerto for violin, clarinet, horn, piano and string orchestra, and Webern's sketches reveal associations between some of the musical material and the natural landscapes through which he walked; they also reveal plans for a third movement – probably to be heard before the other two – that was never completed.[67] Webern's delicate musical pointillism is not especially well suited to the tenor instrument, which can easily overshadow the others in this piece, and the control required of the player makes this a particularly challenging work in the saxophone's chamber music repertoire.

Unsurprisingly, much chamber music involving the saxophone in the early decades of the twentieth century emanated from composers who had shown some sympathy to the instrument in other works. Joseph Holbrooke's obscure Serenade Op. 61b (c. 1915), which includes five saxophones, was penned by a composer who also wrote a concerto and a sonata for the instrument. Villa-Lobos's enthusiasm for the saxophone was manifested in a number of chamber works, including the *Sexteto mistico* (1917) for flute, oboe, guitar, celesta, harp and saxophone, and the Quartet (1921) for flute, celesta, harp, alto saxophone and female voices (the latter sparingly used). The unusual instrumentation is typical of Villa-Lobos's idiosyncratic approach, as are the flowing, fantasy-like musical forms. But the pieces are effective because the instruments complement each other well, and the composer creates an idiomatic sound world that accommodates the saxophone's distinctive timbre; the ear is not predisposed to hear it as a strange interloper added to an otherwise familiar ensemble such as a wind quintet or string quartet, but rather as an equal voice in a mixed if somewhat 'exotic' instrumental group. The similarly unusual scoring of Hindemith's Trio (1928) for viola, tenor saxophone (or heckelphone) and piano may have arisen in part from Hindemith's own work as a professional viola player, and the growing interest of his brother Rudolf in jazz and the saxophone.[68]

Development of chamber repertoire was also inevitably stimulated by those early soloists noted previously, who were actively seeking to enlarge performance opportunities for themselves. André Caplet's *Légende* (1903) for 2 flutes, oboe, clarinet, alto saxophone and double bass, and Henry Woollett's *Octuor No.1* (1909) for oboe, clarinet, alto saxophone and string quintet, can both be attributed to the patronage of Elise Hall. Indeed, one Boston newspaper observed in 1905 that 'if the saxophone ever gains recognition as an instrument for chamber concerts, it will be largely due to Mrs Hall'.[69] Henri Tomasi's interest in the saxophone stemmed from his friendship with Marcel Mule, for whom he wrote several solo pieces prior to *Printemps* (1963) for wind quintet and alto saxophone. The latter work was in fact dedicated to a wind sextet from Dijon, France, and is one of a number of pieces commissioned for this instrumentation; Pierre-Max Dubois's *Sinfonia da camera* (1964) is another. Sigurd Rascher commissioned a similar sextet from Walter S. Hartley in 1960. Rascher's industrious generation of new material involving the saxophone produced numerous chamber works over the years: the trio for violin, saxophone and piano (1935) from Edmund von Borck, whose concerto Rascher had played frequently in the early 1930s, and a quartet for saxophone and string trio from Werner Wolf Glaser (1950) provide but two examples. Cecil Leeson demonstrated similar energies, and was also sufficiently intrigued by the 'woodwind quintet plus saxophone' formula to commission an inventive and effective example from Leon Stein in 1958.

But the saxophone's use in mixed chamber ensembles inevitably pales into insignificance against its widespread employment in other contexts, and it remains the case that classical saxophonists have diverted most of their energy into developing repertoire for the essentially homogenous saxophone quartet rather than exploring the obvious heterogeneity of mixed chamber groups. This relative paucity of material may also indicate some dissatisfaction on the part of both composers and performers with the results achieved when saxophones are employed in this fashion. Nevertheless, those works that do include the instrument not only provide valuable – if scarce – opportunities for saxophonists to engage in a broader range of chamber music-making, they also further legitimise the instrument in the eyes of those who seek such legitimation through participation in Western concert genres of one kind or another.

Chapter 7

Modernism and postmodernism

Globalisation and music technology

Since the 1970s there has been a significant resurgence of interest in the saxophone. It is now one of the most frequently heard and widely recognised musical instruments, and used in an exceptionally broad range of musical contexts. In part this success may be attributed to changes in musical styles, notably a significant expansion of Western popular music, often underpinned by developments in studio technology. But the instrument has also notably benefited from globalisation and the proliferation of mass media, which have made it more widely recognised by and available to musicians around the world. It has become a quintessentially postmodern instrument – 'postmodern' used here to allude to musical plurality and the cultural consequences of globalisation – and its versatility and timbral flexibility have made it adaptable for a range of musical uses. Whether conforming to the strictures of symphony orchestra performance, competing with the hard-edged sound of an amplified rock band, or finding its place among less familiar instruments in a non-Western context, saxophone players have been able to manipulate the instrument's fundamental characteristics to suit the occasion; a sound for all reasons, as it were. All this has made greater demands on the players themselves, and professional saxophonists especially are now expected to be competent in a broad range of musical styles, in order to make themselves as potentially employable as possible.

Other characteristics have proved important in this global dissemination: the comparative simplicity of the fingering and the speed with which a performer can achieve basic competence; the ease with which pitches can be modified in performance; the instrument's robustness, acoustic efficiency and reasonable cost of manufacture and therefore purchase price; in fact, all those qualities that underpinned the saxophone craze of the 1910s and 20s have again contributed to the instrument's more recent popularity in the late twentieth and early twenty-first centuries. And, just as the saxophone helped to democratise popular music performance in the 1920s, so too has it been central to more recent tendencies in the West towards anti-egalitarian music-making; in popular music particularly, the de-emphasising of acute specialisation and extensive formal training has increased the attractiveness of the saxophone, as it has other instruments such as the electric guitar and the synthesiser.

These changing musical demands have inevitably led to developments in saxophone technology, although, as noted in Chapter 2, the fundamentals of saxophone design have been largely unchanged since the 1950s and the instrument remains remarkably similar to its nineteenth-century antecedents. But the need for saxophone players to compete with electronic instruments, and the premium thus put on bright, edgy sounds in many contemporary commercial contexts, has meant that manufacturers have endeavoured to supply instruments that accommodate these needs. Bore sizes have occasionally been modified, crook dimensions sometimes altered, and various types of lacquer employed (or omitted) in order to make the acoustic saxophone as powerful an instrument as possible.

Instruments made by the French company Selmer were dominant from the mid 1950s to the 1970s, largely because of the extraordinary popularity of their Mark VI model, which has now achieved something of a mythical status. This model's intonation and projection were deemed by many to be superior to other instruments, and its keywork was felt to be especially ergonomic (although the basic disposition of the keys was unremarkable). Unusually, the alto version was often equipped with an extension to low a°, a feature that was not retained by other manufacturers, or by Selmer itself on later models. But many companies subsequently based their keywork design on the Mark VI principles. In the last decades of the twentieth century newer manufacturers, especially Japanese companies such as Yamaha and Yanigasawa, also

89. An alto version of Selmer's famous Mark VI model. The three keycups on the bell of the instrument evidence the extension down to low a°.

brought out popular designs, often with similarly ergonomically efficient keywork. More recently, some Chinese manufacturers have sought to emulate successful earlier designs; benefiting from lower labour and manufacturing costs has enabled them to produce notably cheaper instruments, some of which have also been of sufficient quality to take others by surprise.

Mouthpiece design evolved particularly from the 1970s, with many players working in commercial contexts preferring metal mouthpieces to the ebonite varieties, again in the belief that this gives the instrument more power and the saxophone sound more edge. The variety of mouthpieces now available – each of which utilises different chamber shapes, tip openings, lays and baffle profiles – is testament to the many different contexts in which performers work, and the wide range of different sounds the instrument is now expected to produce (see ill. 2).

The saxophone has also been significantly involved in the electronic enhancement of instrumental sound. Saxophone players often find themselves working in the studio environments where such work originates, and technological innovation has also arisen from the need to develop new repertoire for an instrument that has comparatively little classical music heritage. One of the first electrical modifications to the basic saxophone sound was the Varitone attachment, produced in 1965 by Selmer in Paris in association with the Electro-Voice company (see ill. 90). Undoubtedly influenced by similar technology applied to the electric guitar, the Varitone unit allowed the saxophone player to alter volume and tone; it also facilitated the addition of echo, tremolo and a sub-octave synthesised tone to the basic acoustic sound. A small control box was mounted on the saxophone near the right-hand key guard, where it might be easily operated during performance; turning the unit off returned the instrument to its normal acoustic state. The signal for the unit was provided by a microphone fitted to the neck of the instrument. The output from the Varitone was fed into a preamp, amplifier and speaker contained in a separate unit.

What now appears as a relatively primitive form of signal modification was innovative for its time, and attracted the attention of a number of performers, especially jazz players. Cannonball Adderley used it in the late 1960s (on 'Gumba Gumba' from his 1968 *Accent on Africa* album, for example),[1] and Sonny Stitt also made several recordings utilising the unit. Perhaps the most well-known example comes from Eddie Harris, whose 1967 album *The Electrifying Eddie Harris* demonstrated how the unit could be employed in a musically satisfying fashion in the context of his laid-back early funk/groove style.[2] John Coltrane was given a Varitone attachment and endorsed it commercially, although he does not appear to have used it either in performance or recordings.[3] But the unit did not achieve widespread success and was eventually discontinued. It did, however, presage a period in the early 1970s when saxophonists, particularly those working in studio contexts, began to experiment with treatments of the basic saxophone sound, building on the possibilities offered by the Varitone unit by adding studio effects such as ring modulation, delay, chorus and more.

Although the Varitone unit preserved the essential feel and performance characteristics of the saxophone, the next generation of technologically enhanced 'saxophones' had a rather more ambiguous relationship with the instrument. Wind controllers such as the Lyricon, from the early 1970s, or Yamaha's Wx series and the Akai Electronic

90. LP cover for a record demonstrating the possibilities of Selmer's Varitone unit, showing how the unit itself could be controlled by the performer.

Wind Instrument (EWI), all developed over the course of the 1980s but still occasionally found today, work on broadly similar principles. They rely on converting wind pressure information into synthesiser control data. Thus, while the performer blows down the instrument and moves his or her fingers over a key or pad system that, being Boehm-oriented, loosely resembles a saxophone, the instrument makes no sound itself; it is only used to control other electronic units which can thus be programmed with an enormous array of synthesised sounds. Breath pressure and changes in embouchure tension can all be converted into controlling data, meaning that the performer can transfer a certain amount of saxophone performance technique onto these new instruments. Different articulations are also registered electronically, in order to replicate as closely as possible the response given by an acoustic instrument.[4]

Nevertheless, such instruments are only tenuously linked with the saxophone; they bear no acoustic relationship to it and might equally be mastered by other wind instrumentalists or musicians with other specialisms. But they have been used with some success by saxophone players keen to explore a wider range of timbral possibilities than the acoustic instrument itself allows. Michael Brecker (1949–2009) was probably the most well-known exponent of such instruments, and his EWI version of Ellington's *In a Sentimental Mood*, on the album *Magnetic* (1986) from the group Steps Ahead, is often cited as an effective musical example.[5] A number of art-music composers have also made use of these instruments, notably Morton Subotnick in *In Two Worlds* (1987), where the soloist changes between saxophone and wind controller during the course of the piece.

The Synthophone, developed by Martin Hurni in Switzerland in the early 1980s, works on similar principles. Again the instrument produces no acoustic sound but, significantly, it is housed within the body of a real – albeit specially adapted – saxophone, and its tactile interface therefore closely resembles the instrument on which it is modelled; it feels like a real saxophone because it is one, even though it doesn't necessarily have to sound like one, because it is again being used to control other units.[6]

Although wind controllers have had some success they remain a niche market, and their popularity has waned since the early 1990s. Many performers find that, for all the possibilities they offer, their comparative lack of physical response or subtlety, when compared with a conventional acoustic instrument, is less satisfactory (pianists often make similar observations about electric pianos). This is mitigated to some degree by the significant range of sounds available. But the complex interface between the human body and an acoustic instrument provides for many players sufficient challenges and variety in itself, and many performers find wind controllers replicate this experience inadequately. Even Brecker observed of the EWI that 'it's a kind of half toy, half real instrument [. . .]. It's not an acoustic instrument and does not and will not replace the saxophone.'[7]

Hybrid instruments such as the Metasaxophone developed by Matthew Burtner in the United States endeavour to combine the best of both worlds, and offer intriguing possibilities for the future. The Metasaxophone, constructed from a conventional Selmer tenor model, employs a series of micro switches attached to its keypads, which register whether the key is open or closed. These switches provide MIDI information that can be used to control other MIDI devices; they are also pressure sensitive, allowing different information to be sent and therefore different expressive parameters to be explored. A motion sensor in the bell tracks the movement of the instrument, which provides further information that can be used in performance. But the instrument retains full saxophone functionality and can be played as a normal saxophone. It also has an embedded microphone system that can amplify the acoustic sound, making it an electric saxophone, as it were. Thus the instrument can operate on three levels simultaneously: as a normal acoustic saxophone, as an amplified version of the same, and as a sophisticated MIDI wind controller (see ill. 91).[8]

Given this close association between the saxophone and various forms of music technology, it is unsurprising that the instrument is often found in the world of electroacoustic composition. The preeminent saxophonist in this area is the Frenchman Daniel Kientzy (b. 1951), whose work over three decades – much of it based at IRCAM in Paris[9] – has generated a large number of contemporary pieces. Early

91. The Metasaxophone.

examples of this genre, such as Milton Babbitt's *Images* (1979), Jonty Harrison's *EQ* (1980), Gilles Racot's *Exultitudes* (1985), or Jean Claude Risset's *Voilements* (1987), all examine various aspects of the inter-relationship between the saxophone and the prerecorded sounds that were stored on tape when they were first composed. But whereas in such pieces the tape effectively becomes an unchanging 'accompanist', later trends have been towards more interactive relationships between the performer and the technology. Composers have become interested in exploring real-time transformations of the saxophone sound, with the rich harmonic spectrum of the instrument lending itself particularly well to these kinds of treatments. In some cases, by means of careful programming and pitch-tracking software, a computer can follow and respond to the live sound produced by the saxophonist; in effect, the performer 'plays' the computer as well as the saxophone.

Extended techniques

The electronic treatments described above represent one way in which the basic saxophone sound has been manipulated, but, like other instrumentalists, saxophonists have since the 1960s also developed a number of extended acoustic techniques that generate a range of 'unconventional' sounds. So integral to contemporary saxophone performance practice are some of these techniques that some explication of them is necessary here.

The use of the altissimo register – the range beyond the conventional written top f³ or f♯³ of the instrument – has long been part of saxophone technique, and the possibilities offered by this extension were acknowledged in Adolphe Sax's time. The saxophone is, usually, a monophonic instrument, capable of producing only one note at a time; this single note, however, comprises not only a fundamental tone but also a rich series of other related tones, and the altissimo notes are derived from this overtone series. As early as 1926 Gustave Bumcke formalised an approach to this in his *Saxophon Schule*,[10] but it was really Sigurd Rascher who developed the best-known method with his *Top Tones for Saxophone* (1941). Rascher supplied an extensive chart that demonstrated how, by use of different fingerings and a modified embouchure, players could extend the range at the top of the instrument by as much as two octaves or more (later writers have suggested slightly different approaches). Some facility in this part of the saxophone tessitura is now seen is essential for players working in both classical and popular musics. The brief cadenza in Ibert's *Concertino* (1934) represents an early mainstream application of the altissimo register (see ex. 20); Edison Denisov's Sonata for alto saxophone and cello (1995) is a rather more challenging example that demonstrates how competent modern soloists are now expected to be in this range (see ex. 22).

A first step for many saxophone players in mastering the altissimo register is to finger the low bb° of the instrument, that is, its lowest note with all keys closed, and then to manipulate the jaws and throat in order to force out the upper harmonics of that particular harmonic series (bb¹, f², bb², d³ etc.); this is very similar to a brass player using embouchure changes to produce different notes on an instrument such as a trombone, without changing slide position (in some avant-garde works even this technique has been employed, with the saxophone player taking the mouthpiece off the instrument and blowing it like a trumpet).

This overtone series can be exploited in other ways. With a combination of special fingerings and embouchure modification the saxophone can produce multiphonics:

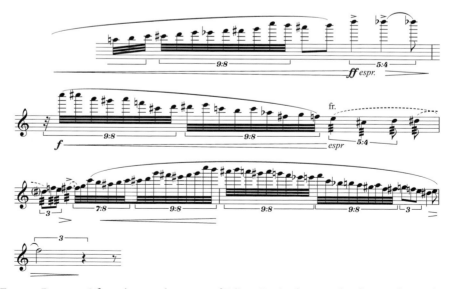

Ex. 22. Bars 41–46 from the saxophone part of Edison Denisov's *Sonata for Alto Saxophone and Cello* (1995), third movement.

'chords' comprising more than one note, thus producing a polyphonic instrument; the technique is common to all woodwind instruments but is particularly effective on the saxophone. The special fingerings encourage different parts of the air column to vibrate at different frequencies, resulting in several pitches being heard simultaneously. Some multiphonics can be loud and raucous, others are more subtle. Most are discordant – usually involving microtones – but with care some concords can be produced. Multiphonics can be used in various ways. The louder, more intense types can induce tension or an element of noise into a melodic line, whether in a composed piece or an improvised solo; softer multiphonics are more atmospheric and can be variously inflected by skilled players for different purposes. Daniel Kientzy has produced a comprehensive list of multiphonic fingerings for saxophones (see ill. 92), although such fingerings are not always transferable from one player to another, or from one make of saxophone to another.[11]

Another technique that generates inharmonicity in the instrument is the saxophone growl. This is produced by simultaneously singing or growling in the throat while playing. The technique appears to have been introduced by brass players in the 1920s, in Ellington's creation of what was described as the 'jungle sound' in some of the

92. A page from Daniel Kientzy's *Les Sons multiples aux saxophones* (1982), tabulating fingerings for producing different multiphonics.

arrangements for his band, but it has often been used by saxophone players, particularly in rock music, because it lends a distorted element to the sound that matches the distortion sometimes found in amplified instruments such as the electric guitar; the playing of Clarence Clemons (1942–2011) with rock singer Bruce Springsteen provides one example. The technique has also been employed elsewhere as a means of adding colour and heightening tension. Composers sometimes stipulate the pitches that might be sung while playing, thus setting up a polyphonic texture between the sung note and the played note (see ill. 93).

One consequence of the saxophone's conical bore, especially for the smaller instruments, is that the very lowest notes can be difficult to play quietly. A different manipulation of the overtone series – known as subtoning – endeavours to overcome this. Here the reed is prevented from vibrating normally, so that the higher overtones are reduced and the lower ones predominate. The saxophone, generally a rather loud instrument, can be made to sound surprisingly soft with this technique, and it is often heard from jazz players, particularly tenor players, when playing the lower notes of the instrument in ballads. It is achieved in one of two ways: either by pulling back and compressing the lower lip, drawing the jaw away from the instrument, or by lightly placing the tongue on the reed. The technique is not only used in contemporary works such as Betsy Jolas's *Episode quatrième* (1983) for solo tenor, but can be useful in standard repertoire, such as 'Lullaby for Jumbo' from William Walton's *Façade* (1922), which has a long, low line for the alto saxophone that would otherwise overpower the other instruments involved.

Vibrato has been an important part of saxophone technique from early in the twentieth century. Saxophone vibrato is usually produced through jaw movement rather than the changes in diaphragm pressure that are more characteristic of flute vibrato (although this latter approach has occasionally been employed and is sometimes requested by contemporary composers). Saxophone pitch can be altered considerably by varying jaw pressure; as a general principle, the shorter the air column being used to produce the note, the more pronounced will be the pitch change. Extending this technique across a wider pitch range produces the swoops and glissandos between notes that are so characteristic of saxophone performance in many genres, and which reinforce the instrument's essentially vocal quality. By gradually adjusting the tension in the embouchure and sometimes combining this with a slower, 'sliding' movement of the keypads, the pitch can be made to change smoothly from one note to the next, reminiscent of the sliding portamento of a string player. Again the effect is more pronounced, and easier to produce, with shorter than longer air columns. The technique was common among early jazz clarinettists, and was probably transferred onto the saxophone as the latter instrument became increasingly employed in jazz contexts. The work of Johnny Hodges as lead alto with the Ellington band is an iconic example of this technique (see ex. 8), as is the playing of Tom Scott for the 1976 film soundtrack to *Taxi Driver*.

A different form of pitch manipulation can be achieved through the use of microtones, that is, intervals smaller than the conventional semitones of the tempered Western scale. These are particularly effective on the saxophone, and can often be more readily perceived by an audience than when played on other instruments. They are normally achieved by the use of unorthodox fingerings – although embouchure modification can also be employed – such as closing some of the toneholes on the instrument that normally lie open when producing a note, or overblowing an orthodox fingering to produce one of its natural harmonics. In both cases the harmonic or altered note will be different in both pitch and most likely timbre from the orthodox fingered version it replaces, and this difference can be fruitfully exploited in both improvised and composed work. The fingerings used to produce these notes are often known among saxophone players as 'false' fingerings.[12] Microtones can usually be generated on the instrument for all pitches above c#[1]; the very lowest notes are more problematic.

A variety of extended articulation techniques are also now commonplace, and again some of these have their roots in the novelty techniques of the 1920s. Slap tonguing, so beloved of the Brown Brothers, Rudy Wiedoeft, and bass saxophone players such as Adrian Rollini, brings a particularly percussive element to a saxophone line. The effect, which is produced by the player creating a slight vacuum between the reed and the tongue before suddenly withdrawing the latter with a clicking motion, can be done 'dry', with very little pitch heard, or 'wet', with more of the pitch heard after the attack. Although possible on all saxophones it is increasingly effective with larger reeds, and hence larger instruments, and also with lower notes, where the longer bore length acts as a more effective acoustic resonator for the initial plosive attack.

The facility with double and triple tonguing heard from certain players of the 1920s and 30s is seldom emulated today, but the techniques themselves remain important. One way of generating this effect is to interpolate a 'ku' sound made in the throat between the 'tu' sounds produced by the tongue; double tonguing thus produces a 'tu-ku-tu-ku' action, while triple tonguing requires 'tu-ku-tu tu-ku-tu' pattern (or some variation thereof). The difficulty lies not so much with the tongue-throat pattern but with matching it accurately against rapid fingerwork. Other types of articulation include ram tonguing, where the note is forcefully stopped with the tongue, and flutter tonguing, in which the tongue is rolled rapidly against the palette, thus disturbing the flow of air as it enters the mouthpiece. Skilled players can increase or reduce the amount of flutter in the sound, and can move smoothly from full flutter tongue to none at all.

Circular breathing is common to a range of traditional and modern wind instruments. This enables a wind player to produce a continuous melodic line, unbroken by the need to draw breath. On all instruments the basic principle is the same: a small reservoir of air is stored in the cheeks and then expelled by the cheek muscles through the mouth while the player inhales through the nose. Many jazz saxophone players employ this approach; for some, such as Rahsaan Roland Kirk (1935–77) or Evan Parker (b. 1944), both of whom construct lengthy and complex unbroken solos that combine circular breathing with other extended techniques, it is an important component of their improvising style.

The size of most saxophones ensures that the instrument is also effective as a percussion resource, since its large body acts as an efficient resonator: the relatively large key pads ensure that key clicks – slapping a key pad against the saxophone body

93. The first page of Karlheinz Stockhausen's *Entführung* (2006) for soprano saxophone, pre-recorded sounds and electronics. The score calls for a combination of various extended saxophone techniques, including singing while playing, lip glisses, fluttertonguing, and exaggerated vibrato.

with or without blowing – can be fruitfully exploited. This is especially true of the lowest notes of the larger instruments, which make a quite substantial sound. The pitch of the key slap can often be inferred by an audience, particularly if the sound is amplified. The body of the instrument can also be used to amplify breath sounds. Blowing through the saxophone without allowing the reed to vibrate properly results in air sounds with very little pitch, although the amount of pitch heard can be altered by careful control of the embouchure. A rapid mix of pitched and unpitched sounds, with different quantities of air in the sound, can give a slightly skittish or nervous effect to the music.

The saxophone's capacity to produce a wide range of these different sound effects has underpinned its emergence as a particularly modern instrument, and these extended techniques are now common in many of the contexts in which the instrument is used. This is in some ways ironic, since many of these techniques build on the novelty effects that contributed significantly to the instrument's poor reputation in the 1920s, and against which performers such as Wiedoeft or Smith and Holmes frequently railed. In the last few decades, however, this extended sound palette has been welcomed as a valuable addition to the language of contemporary music, and it has significantly enhanced the saxophone's reputation as an essential contributor to musical modernism.

Contemporary classical music

Although the saxophone struggled to be taken seriously as a concert instrument for much of the first half of the twentieth century, the work of performers such as Mule, Rascher and Leeson provided a secure foundation for the instrument's increasing involvement in what can broadly be described as 'classical' music. The instrument continues to be uncommon in the symphony orchestra – albeit less than previously – because of that institution's reliance on a core repertory of works around fixed instrumentation that does not include the saxophone. But in many other contexts the presence of one or more saxophones now seldom provokes comment. Concertos, sonatas, quartets and many other works are abundant, such that a recent listing of saxophone concert material runs to some 18,000 separate pieces.[13] Saxophonists have remained adept transcribers, adapting many pieces written for other instruments so as to provide variety within their own concert programmes; this is particularly the case where there is some overlap in instrumental tessitura, as is the case with the soprano saxophone and the oboe, or the baritone saxophone and the bassoon. This expansion in repertoire has been stimulated by a large number of distinguished players drawn from more recent generations. Any selection of names is inevitably arbitrary, but performers such as Paul Cohen, James Houlik, Trent Kynaston, Kenneth Radnofsky, John Sampen, Donald Sinta and James Stoltie (USA), Claude Delangle, Jean–Yves Fourmeau and Daniel Kientzy (France), John Harle (UK), Iwan Roth (Switzerland), Paul Brodie (Canada), Arata Sakaguchi and Nobuyu Sugawa (Japan), are just some of those who have contributed to the global development of classical saxophone repertoire since the 1970s.[14] The work of John Harle (b. 1956) in bringing the classical saxophone to a wider audience, and in generating a substantial amount of new

94. The British saxophonist John Harle.

repertoire for the instrument, is particularly noteworthy. He is the most widely recorded classical saxophonist of the late twentieth and early twenty-first centuries, and the eclectic range of music he has generated for the instrument, from composers as diverse as Birtwistle, Nyman, Rorem, Torke and others, is emblematic of the diversity of styles with which the saxophone and its players are now engaged.

Harle's work represents one dimension of a now thriving classical saxophone scene that is particularly manifested through the increasing number of concertos written for the instrument. Although the alto saxophone has numerical superiority in this genre, there are many works for soprano, tenor, and more recently baritone, accompanied by orchestra or ensemble. In a few cases the relative ease with which performers can change from one saxophone to another has also been exploited: for example, the Russian composer Edison Denisov's *Concerto piccolo* (1977) for one saxophonist and six percussionists, or *Points d'or* (1982) by the French composer Betsy Jolas for saxophonist and mixed ensemble, both require the soloist to play a complete set of S/A/T/B instruments. Spanish composer Luis De Pablo's *Une Couleur* (1988) goes even further, requiring the soloist to play six instruments from sopranino down to contrabass, omitting the alto.

But the conventional concerto disposition of a single player with one instrument has yielded a significant number of works since the 1970s. This can again be partly explained by the needs of concert saxophonists to generate repertoire for themselves, ensuring that most saxophonists are engaged with contemporary music-making to an extent not always required of other instrumentalists. Some saxophonists have been involved in large-scale collaborative ventures for commissioning new material, whereby a consortium of performers collectively funds a new work and gives simultaneous worldwide premieres of the work.[15]

It is too soon to tell which of all this new material might in future assume the status of core repertoire, but certain pieces have already been widely acclaimed; to give just three examples: Robert Muczynski's Concerto for Alto Saxophone and Orchestra (1981) was nominated for the Pulitzer Prize in Music in 1982; Donald Martino's Concerto for Alto Saxophone and Orchestra (1987) arose from a consortium commission by John Sampen, James Forger and Kenneth Radnofsky, with the latter giving the premiere; Mark-Anthony Turnage's *Your Rockaby* (1994) successfully subsumes references to the saxophone's jazz heritage within Turnage's own striking orchestral language. All three works have been widely performed and recorded. Occasionally the saxophone shares the solo spotlight with others, building on the well-established classical tradition of the double concerto. Works by both Robin Holloway – for clarinet, saxophone and two chamber orchestras (1988) – and Michael Nyman – for alto saxophone (doubling soprano), cello and orchestra (1997) – can be seen as part of this tradition; the rather different musical language of Harrison Birtwistle's *Panic* (1995), for alto saxophone, jazz drummer and an orchestra dominated by wind, brass and percussion, also belongs in this group.

One contemporary musical style that has achieved considerable popular appeal since the 1970s, and that has utilised saxophones extensively, is so-called 'minimal' music. The founding fathers of minimalism – Steve Reich, Terry Riley, Philip Glass and LaMonte Young – have all written for the saxophone, and both Riley and Young also perform on the instrument. It is unsurprising that the saxophone should have found a niche for itself in this field, since the early roots of minimalism owe more to various non-Western musics, jazz, and rock music than to the Western art tradition. Initially less drawn to regular classical ensembles such as the symphony orchestra or the string quartet, these composers utilised a range of less conventional forces, including non-Western instruments, synthesisers, and other music technology. The saxophone provided them with a modern, flexible, and timbrally distinctive voice; it lacked overt historical and cultural associations with the Western art tradition but was instead more closely identified with those popular traditions on which the early minimalists drew.[16] And in Jon Gibson (b. 1940), a saxophonist-composer who worked in California, then from 1966 in New York, they found a collaborator who was both a skilled and committed advocate of the progressive music they were producing.

Thus the saxophone featured in a number of contexts: as an unaccompanied instrument (for example Glass's *Gradus*, 1968, and *Melodies*, 1995); as a quartet (Glass's Concerto for Saxophone Quartet and Orchestra, 1995; and the quartet arrangement of Reich's *New York Counterpoint*, 1999); and as a constituent part of various ensembles that coalesced around the composers themselves. Steve Reich's 1968 *Reed Phase* was originally intended as a work specifically for saxophone, and carried the title *Saxophone Phase*;[17] Riley and Young also performed extensively on the instrument in many of their often partly or wholly improvised performances; in Young's case, as he became increasingly interested in 'just' intonation, he also attempted to make his sopranino saxophone sound more like an Indian *shenai*, and spent some time trying to fix a double reed to it.[18] While these 'minimalist' composers were seen in the 1970s as avant-garde and therefore lying beyond the mainstream, the subsequent popularity of their work, both in the concert hall and on film and video, has brought them to a much wider audience. The saxophone has benefitted from this later exposure, while simultaneously providing such composers with an important instrumental sound that usefully bridges the classical and popular musical styles on which they draw.

A number of what might be conceived as 'post-minimal' composers have continued to give the saxophone important roles in their music. While sometimes retaining a degree of the musical repetition that marked early minimalism, their musical language more explicitly draws on rhythmic and timbral aspects of popular music; again the saxophone has proved to be a comfortable natural fit in ensembles that might also employ electric guitars, keyboards or drum kit. This is particularly true of the Dutch composer Louis Andriessen and some of his pupils such as British composers Steve Martland and Graham Fitkin. Andriessen's *Hout* (1991) for a quartet involving tenor saxophone, or the challenging saxophone quartet arrangement of his *Facing Death* (1993, originally for string quartet), based on the bop style of Charlie Parker, are idiomatically well suited to the saxophone, while again explicitly drawing on the instrument's jazz and rock heritage. Andriessen's influence, combined with the popularity of the instrument in Holland and consequently a significant number of skilled performers, has led to a corpus of saxophone works by Dutch composers that is surprisingly large relative to the size of Holland's population.[19]

Like Andriessen, Michael Nyman may also be conceived as broadly a post-minimal composer. Nyman's success as a film composer has greatly increased his international profile, and this has brought further attention to the saxophone, for which he frequently scores. His saxophone concerto, *Where the Bee Dances* (1991), not only references his score for Peter Greenaway's film *Prospero's Books*, but also betrays its minimalist roots in the extensive use of a repeating four-chord sequence, which provides material for both the saxophone's longer melodies and its more rhythmically urgent phrases. This work joins others such as the double concerto noted previously, the saxophone quartet *Songs for Tony* (1993), a Concerto for Saxophone Quartet and Orchestra (2001), as well as several other works in which the saxophone has a central role.

The saxophone's timbral flexibility, rhythmic agility and stylistic affinity with various popular musics have enticed many other composers in the postmodern era to draw on these associations in their work. In the middle movement of Michael Torke's Saxophone Concerto (1993), for example, the lyrical saxophone melody over rich string harmonies has its roots, according to the composer, in a 1991 album – *Unforgettable* – by the pop singer Natalie Cole. The busier rhythmic patterns of the outer movements are more reminiscent of the same composer's piece for saxophone quartet, *July* (1995), in which the compositional impulse similarly sprang from the reworking and rescoring of a rhythmic groove first heard in a pop song; the original song is unheard in the composition, but its rhythmic vitality and drive remains in the use of both layered and interlocking semiquaver rhythms. A well-known example of this kind of crossover is the jazz player Phil Woods's Sonata for Alto Saxophone and Piano (1980), the blues-inflected phrases and improvised passages of which have become a popular concert work for saxophonists. Pianist Keith Jarrett's suite *Luminessence* (1974) for saxophone and string orchestra was written in the early years of his now well-established collaboration with Norwegian jazz player Jan Garbarek (b. 1947). Film composer Michael Kamen's more deliberately commercial Concerto for Saxophone (1991) was written for the jazz-funk player David Sanborn, and combines Kamen's film-score rooted harmonic language with soaring melodies for the alto saxophone.

Given the eponymous dedicatee of Richard Rodney Bennett's *Concerto for Stan Getz* (1990),[20] the fusing of certain aspects of an idiomatic jazz language with Bennett's own serially-informed style was perhaps to be expected. The syncopated repetition of a single note at the saxophone's first entry may well be a covert reference to some of Getz's very successful 1960 *bossa nova* recordings. Similarly, both Franco Donatoni's *Hot* (1989), for tenor saxophone (doubling sopranino) and small ensemble, or the now classic Sonata for Alto Saxophone and Piano (1970) by Edison Denisov, draw to some degree on jazz sound worlds refracted through the lens of the composer's own personal language.

Many of these works are fully notated, but several also provide space for the performer to improvise, an understandable compositional choice since composers know that many saxophonists have this skill. This mix of notated passages interspersed with spaces for improvisation was common in music of the seventeenth and eighteenth centuries, although improvisation became less central to Western art music as the nineteenth century progressed, with concerto cadenzas, for example, increasingly written out by composers. It is ironic, therefore, that it is the saxophone, an instrument with very little heritage as a soloist on the concert platform, that is in some works returning to that mix of pre-composed and spontaneous performance that was for long characteristic of this concert tradition.

For other composers the saxophone's associations with popular music have been less important, and some of the major figures in twentieth-century classical music composition have approached the instrument simply on its own terms. Karlheinz Stockhausen's *In Freundschaft* (1977) exists in versions for several instruments, including saxophone, in addition to other works for the instrument such as *Entführung* (2006) shown above (ill. 93). Luciano Berio used the instrument in a number of ensemble pieces, but concert saxophonists will be more familiar with the two transcriptions of his sequenza series: *Sequenza IXb* (1981) for alto saxophone, adapted from the clarinet sequenza (1980), and *Sequenza VIIb* (1995) for soprano saxophone, based on the oboe sequenza (1969). The latter is especially challenging in its detailed application of extended techniques, particularly in its use of altered (false) fingerings that supply timbrally differentiated versions of the same pitch. As with other sequenzas, *IXb* is also used as the basis for another work, *Chemins VII* (1996), in which it is given an orchestral accompaniment. Given the significance often accorded to Berio's *Sequenza* series within a tradition of twentieth-century writing for solo instruments, it is both curious and unfortunate that no original work for the saxophone was included. *Tre Pezzi* (1956), by the idiosyncratic Italian composer Giacinto Scelsi, is written for soprano or tenor saxophone. The scrupulous attention to dynamics, coupled with asymmetric phrasing and quasi-modal writing, reinforces for some the saxophone's supposed ethnic qualities. Elliott Carter's *Canonic Suite* (1939, rev. 1981), Iannis Xenakis's *XAS* (1987), and John Cage's *Four⁵* (1991), all for saxophone quartet, provide further evidence of the willingness of some of the twentieth century's most eminent composers to create new works for the instrument. Xenakis's work in particular, from a composer known for his emphasis on timbral manipulation, demonstrates the tonal variety that can be achieved from the otherwise comparatively homogenous saxophone quartet genre.

Although the soprano and alto instruments are the most frequent visitors to the concert stage, the tenor saxophone has an increasing solo repertoire, reflected in, for example, concertos by Morton Gould (*Diversions*, 1990) or Russell Peck (*The Upward Stream*, 1985) in addition to the Bennett concerto intended for Stan Getz already noted. As interest in the saxophone continues to grow, so too does the number of performers specialising in the baritone instrument, thus contributing to further repertoire expansion: Sofia Gubaidulina's Duo Sonata For Two Baritone Saxophones (1977), Werner Wolf Glaser's Concerto for Baritone Saxophone and Orchestra (1992) or Mauricio Kagel's *Burleske* (2000) for mixed choir and solo baritone sax, provide just three examples of this trend. Even the less familiar members of the saxophone family have occasionally been called upon by composers: Horacio Vaggione's *Thema* (1985) for amplified bass saxophone and tape, for example, makes extensive use of that instrument's potential as a sound-generating resource, employing a variety of extended techniques to complement the studio-generated sounds on the tape. Vaggione's use of the bass instrument is indicative of the fact that the more 'exotic' saxophones – sopranino, bass, contrabass – are more often found in the experimental fringes of contemporary music-making than they are in whatever might be taken to be the mainstream.

Classical composers are more willing to score for the instrument in the postmodern orchestra. The timbral palette of the orchestra has continued to evolve over the course of the late-twentieth and twenty-first centuries, and the saxophone now sounds less 'exotic' in this context. Indeed, it is now rare to find a composer who has *not* scored for the saxophone at some point, with most of those already mentioned having included the instrument in one or more of their ensemble scores. To these names, by way of a few further examples, might also be added Pierre Boulez (e.g. *Domaines*, 1968–9; *Rituel*, 1974–5; and the two alto saxophones in his *Improvisation I* from *Pli Selon Pli*, 1957–62); Hans Werner Henze (in many works, including his well-known opera *The Bassarids*, 1964–5 rev.1992: *Nachtstücke und Arien*, 1957; and several symphonies); Michael Tippett (whose 1988 opera *New Year* calls for three saxophones); and David Del Tredici (whose various orchestral works from the late 1960s and 70s based on Lewis Caroll's *Alice* stories frequently utilise two soprano saxophones as part of a 'folk group').

The saxophone's long connection with military band and other wind-dominated ensembles, and the prevalence of many skilled saxophone players working in these contexts, has led to a number of contemporary works for wind band and saxophone soloist. This genre has its roots in the display pieces performed by the bands of Jullien,

Gilmore and others in the nineteenth century, as well as in the work of soloists such as Combelle and Mule in their time with the Parisian Garde républicaine. The tradition was continued by composers such as: Paul Creston, whose 1941 Concerto is scored for alto saxophone with orchestra or band; Karel Husa, whose 1967 Concerto for alto and wind ensemble was premiered by Sigurd Rascher; and Ross Lee Finney, whose 1974 Concerto for alto and wind band was composed to mark the retirement of distinguished American performer Larry Teal. More recent additions include *Distant Variations* (1997) for saxophone quartet and wind band by John Casken; the Concerto for alto saxophone and wind ensemble (1999) by David Maslanka, who has also composed several other works featuring the saxophone – including a duet with marimba (1998) – that demonstrate his rhythmically vital style; and Graham Fitkin's *Game Show* (1998), again a work that shows off the saxophone's inherent suitability for precisely articulated, rhythmically oriented music. The genre remains popular with saxophone soloists because many of them develop their ensemble experience in these wind band contexts, particularly in the United States. Nevertheless, such pieces remain something of a niche market, with only limited broader popular appeal.

Pedagogy and large ensembles

The rising popularity of the saxophone in the last few decades has greatly increased the demand for expert tuition from skilled, authoritative practitioners, and many professional saxophonists now find that a portion of their time is given over to teaching of some kind, as with other instrumentalists. The institutionalised nature of classical saxophone teaching is longest established in France and Belgium, as evidenced by the appointment of Marcel Mule to the Paris Conservatoire in 1942, and François Daneels to the Royal Brussels Conservatoire in 1954; in each case these appointments led to the creation of similar posts held by other distinguished saxophonists at regional conservatoires. Other countries have followed suit. In the United States, Larry Teal's appointment as Professor of Saxophone at the University of Michigan in 1953 (succeeded by Donald Sinta in 1974) was followed by others such as Cecil Leeson at Northwestern University (1955 – succeeded by Frederick Hemke in 1962) and Eugene Rousseau at Indiana (1964); many similar appointments followed, and the United States now has an extensive network of classical saxophone pedagogy in its universities and colleges. In Britain, Walter Lear was professor of saxophone at Trinity College of Music for more than 50 years, while Michael Krein held a similar position at the Guildhall School of Music and Drama, after which he was succeeded by Stephen Trier in 1966; the latter also taught at the Royal College of Music from 1970. Elsewhere, Clive Amadio was Professor of Clarinet and Saxophone at the Sydney Conservatorium of Music from 1941. In the last decades of the twentieth century the saxophone has thus largely left behind the disreputable image it acquired in the 1920s, and its appearance in many centres of learning around the world, with approved syllabuses and examination processes to match, confers upon it a legitimacy that now parallels other instruments.

This developing pedagogic infrastructure has inevitably led to a considerable expansion of educational literature. The relatively few methods available at the turn of the twentieth century, admittedly augmented by a range of material of variable quality during the saxophone craze of the 1910s and 20s, have now been supplemented by a much greater number of modern publications. As with other instruments, these comprise a wide range of methods, study books, specially commissioned material, and so forth; there is now only slightly less material available for saxophone students than there is for those studying the perennially popular, and much longer established, flute and clarinet.[21] Some of this material – such as Marcel Mule's edition of 48 studies by Ferling, Bozza's *12 Études Caprices* or studies by Guy Lacour – has achieved something of a canonic status within classical saxophone teaching, certainly in Europe. Modern teachers and students are not obliged, therefore, to provide self–generated literature and extensive transcriptions as were their predecessors (though some still choose to do so). Furthermore, the very large range of elementary material available suggests a significant market for it, which in turn demonstrates the continuing widespread popularity of the instrument among beginners.

Just as the saxophone has become more legitimated within educational establishments so too has jazz, and the institutionalisation of jazz saxophone teaching now also exists within a structured pedagogic framework. This is particularly the case in the United States, where formal jazz education has been part of the educational landscape since the establishment of the Schillinger House of Music (now Berklee College of Music) in Boston in 1945, and the dance band programme at the University of North Texas in 1947. Over the following decades a range of American institutions developed first undergraduate and then graduate programmes in jazz, leading to specialist jazz saxophone professors being appointed to positions analogous to their classical counterparts.

Jazz saxophone is, by the nature of the craft, less dependent on published literature to sustain it than its classical equivalent; nevertheless, jazz players now also have significant amounts of printed material available to them. Methods that teach both saxophone basics and rudiments of theory aimed specifically at aspiring jazz players are common. The hegemony of the – often bop-derived – chord-scale language, where neophyte improvisers learn a range of scales deemed appropriate to use over given chord sequences, has ensured a large range of publications that endeavour to provide saxophonists with such information. Some of this literature is generic for many instruments, but there is much aimed specifically at saxophone players. Numerous collections of jazz studies – sometimes titled as 'etudes' in a further act of cultural legitimation – are now available, as well as specialist volumes on, for example, jazz tone production. Especially popular are those books that transcribe and dissect the solos of the saxophone greats, allowing later generations of players sometimes to bypass the aural approach to learning material (an approach over which earlier players often had no choice). Collections of solos by Lester Young, Coleman Hawkins and many others remain of interest for those who wish to engage with jazz history as practitioners, but it is the music of Charlie Parker – particularly the various versions of the *Charlie Parker Omnibook* – and John Coltrane that appears perennially in demand. Such pedagogic material now sits alongside the recordings made by these players in the ongoing construction of the jazz saxophone canon. And the autodidactic streak that has always characterised jazz education is now reinforced for the saxophone and other jazz instruments by the popularity of 'play along' publications, where a pre-recorded accompaniment provides the student with rhythmic and harmonic support against which they then practice improvisation. The Jamey Abersold series is perhaps the most well-known example of this approach.

This growth in saxophone pedagogy has inevitably increased the number of saxophone players seeking performance opportunities, not only as soloists but also collectively, resulting in an upsurge in the number of saxophone ensembles. This is particularly true of saxophone quartets, a medium that has seen a significant growth in interest – reflected in the regular annual commissioning of new works – since the 1970s. Whereas the quartets established by Mule, Daneels or Rascher were notable in part because of their unfamiliarity, now professional quartets are common throughout Europe and North America, and anywhere else where a sufficient pedagogic framework exists to produce a sufficient number of skilled players.[22] Such quartets provide modern outlets for those long-held personality traits that require saxophonists, often through necessity, to arrange and commission new material. But in many cases they also provide important performance opportunities for aspiring professionals seeking to bridge the gap between the end of their formal training and a fully-fledged career.

In educational contexts particularly, it is the resurgence of large-scale saxophone ensembles, sometimes now described as saxophone choirs, that is especially notice-able. The situation is reminiscent of the United States in the 1920s, at the height of the saxophone craze, when many companies or municipal authorities wished to support a large saxophone ensemble (albeit not on the same scale). Now it is often educational institutions which run such groups, in order to provide the collective

95. The contemporary French saxophone ensemble Urban Sax.

performance opportunities that might otherwise be denied the many saxophone students they recruit. These groups may number anything from six to fifty players, with varying instrumentation according to circumstance – the well respected twelve-piece ensemble at the Paris Conservatoire is presently based around Sn/2S/3A/3T/2B/Bs – and they are supported by a range of commercial publications, in addition to bespoke arrangements.

The revival of interest in large saxophone ensembles is not only confined to educational contexts. Jean-Marie Londeix established his Ensemble International de Saxophones de Bordeaux as early as 1977. This group of twelve professionals generated, either by commission or arrangement, an original repertoire for itself, and its success provided a model for similar groups around the world.[23] Perhaps the most extraordinary group of this type is the French ensemble Urban Sax. Originating as a group of eight players for a festival in the south of France in 1973, the ensemble now comprises more than thirty saxophonists. Clothed in outlandish costumes, this large collection of saxophonists create intriguing visual spectacles that involve not only playing various saxophones, but also theatrical elements that seek to integrate topography, architecture and music into a contemporary, urban Wagneresque music drama (see ill. 95).

One further aspect of the institutionalisation of saxophone teaching and performance has been the parallel creation of international organisations that exist to support the work of saxophonists. These are often, but not exclusively, driven by classical rather than jazz players, because it is the classical players who more frequently have institutional bases around which such organisations can be built. The World Saxophone Congress, a performance-led, international meeting of saxophonists, was founded in 1969 and continues to attract saxophonists from around the globe to its triennial gatherings. The North American Saxophone Alliance (NASA), which acts as an umbrella organisation for saxophonists in the United States and publishes the annual *Saxophone Symposium*, was founded in 1976. In France, A.SAX (Association des Saxophonistes) was created in 1997 from the merging of two extant organisations: l'AsSaFra (Association des Saxophonistes de France, founded in 1971) and APES (Association pour l'Essor du Saxophone, founded in 1983). It also has an annual publication, *Les Cahiers du Saxophone*. Similar associations include the Clarinet and Saxophone Society of Great Britain (founded 1976), and the Queensland Clarinet and Saxophone Society in Australia (founded c. 1980). Such organisations are both reflective of and contributors to the increasingly inter-connected global framework that supports saxophone pedagogy and performance, and further evidence the more formalised and professional frameworks that now support the instrument.

Jazz

From the late 1960s jazz has expanded both musically and geographically, and stylistic fragmentation has become the norm. Trends are more difficult to discern, and many players now work in multiple musical contexts, adapting to the different aesthetic demands made in each. Again the saxophone's inherent flexibility supports these stylistic crossovers, with performers becoming skilled at manipulating their sound and technique to suit their musical aspirations. While alto and tenor saxophones have continued to dominate, other members of the family have become more conspicuous; the soprano – post-Coltrane – has became particularly widely employed; the baritone is also common, though to a lesser degree. These different jazz styles have greatly expanded the range of timbres taken to be 'the saxophone sound'. Instead of being conduits through which to express specific harmonic or melodic ideas, jazz wind instruments in general – and the saxophone is by far the pre-eminent jazz wind instrument – have become sound generators, capable of producing and/or imitating sounds well beyond those previously accepted as part of the jazz performance aesthetic. As with players working in art music genres, saxophonists have drawn considerably on the range of extended saxophone techniques outlined previously. As the jazz writer Jeff Pressing puts it, 'the cries of animals, the screechings of machines, the susurrations of the natural elements, the conversational twitterings of evoked harmonics and the gorgeous jazz ballad tone [are] now all equally possible.'[24]

Despite this stylistic fragmentation, the bop language established by Charlie Parker has continued to play a role; arguably it has become something of a 'classic' jazz language in that it is often learned by aspiring soloists during their formative years and, as noted above, comprises an essential part of many jazz curricula and pedagogic texts. Here the saxophone is an explicitly virtuoso instrument, the hallmarks of the bop player being rapid finger technique and the skill to think creatively over fast-moving harmonic sequences (although sensitively performed ballads remain important). While the bop style receded in the late 1960s and 70s, players such as Phil Woods (b. 1931) and Dexter Gordon (1923–90) continued to play in this fashion. The late 1980s and 90s saw something of a bop revival, with players such as Joe Lovano (b. 1952), Joshua Redman (b. 1969) and Courtney Pine (b. 1964) demonstrating that there was still an appetite and an audience for an updated take on this style. Although Lovano's approach is the most firmly rooted in an acoustic 'authentic' bop tradition, players such as Redman and Pine have melded their bop roots – and sounds – with more technology-driven popular styles. Redman's first two recordings – *Joshua Redman* and *Wish* (both 1993) – sold a quarter of a million copies between them, demonstrating the widespread appeal at the time of this modern twist on bop saxophone playing.

The bop revival was to some extent stimulated by the trumpeter Wynton Marsalis and his saxophonist brother Branford (b. 1960), and the latter provides a good example of the disparate fields in which many modern saxophone players are now engaged. Marsalis's background is in mainstream, bop-influenced jazz, but he reached a wider audience during the 1980s as a featured soloist with the rock star Sting, particularly on the albums *Dream of the Blue Turtles* (1985) and *Nothing Like the Sun* (1987). His wispy soprano playing on 'Englishman in New York' from the latter album is heard both solo and as a counterpoint to the vocal line, and the success of this track promoted the sound of the soprano saxophone – and Marsalis's playing – to a large global audience. Marsalis has also recorded an album of classical French repertoire (*Creation*, 2001),[25] which includes performances of Ibert's *Concertino da camera* and Milhaud's *Scaramouche*. Thus, while the musical ground he has covered is particularly wide, his work serves to illustrate the adaptability now expected of contemporary saxophonists, and the exceptionally high international profile some of them have achieved.

If the bop revivalists have to some extent looked back to the Parker school for their primary inspiration, many others, particularly tenor players, have built on foundations mapped out by John Coltrane. Of none is this more true than Michael Brecker, whose technical command of the tenor saxophone, as well as his stylishly idiosyncratic playing, made him one of the most influential saxophonists of the late twentieth and early twenty-first centuries. Brecker's work as a session player in New York initially obscured his contributions as a jazz sideman, but his collaborations with composer-pianist Horace Silver in the late 1960s and early 70s demonstrated an exceptional ability to construct well-crafted saxophone solos in a variety of musical contexts. This, coupled with an impressive technical control over the entire range of the instrument, embracing the altissimo register, multiphonics and other extended techniques, and a distinctive tenor sound that is both velvety in ballads and bright and hard-hitting in more up-tempo numbers, means Brecker's playing is quickly recognisable. It was widely imitated during the 1990s particularly, spawning a school of post-Coltrane,

96. Michael Brecker, one of the most influential jazz saxophone players in the late twentieth century and beyond.

Brecker-inspired tenor players that serves to underline the continuing importance of aural tradition among jazz saxophone players, now reinforced by the high profile of artists such as Brecker, and the dissemination of their work through a variety of mass media.

Brecker formed The Brecker Brothers in 1974 (with his trumpeter brother Randy), before moving on to another band, Steps Ahead, in the early 1980s. With both these bands Brecker contributed to the evolution of a hybrid genre often described as jazz-rock.[26] Although the roots of this lie in the late 1960s work of improvising rock groups such as Cream, or Blood, Sweat and Tears, its starting point is often taken to be Miles Davis's 1969 *Bitches Brew*.[27] This influential album produced a form of jazz that drew extensively from the rhythmic patterns and improvisational approach of rock musicians – in this early instance particularly from guitarist Jimi Hendrix – and which, as it developed, came to rely increasingly on studio production techniques more common in pop and rock music.

This interventionist, studio-oriented perspective on jazz production, different from the more traditional recording approach that sought simply to capture or replicate acoustic performances, had significant consequences for the perception and production of saxophone sound and technique. The generally brighter sounds and crisp attacks obtainable from synthesisers and electric guitars, and the greater volumes at which fusion groups frequently work, have encouraged saxophone players working in these contexts to attach a similar premium to incisive articulation, bright, edgy saxophone timbres, and increasing reliance on amplification. The studio manipulation of saxophone sounds to match these other instruments, and their increased electronic treatment by way of added reverb, equalisation, octave dividers and other techniques, has also led to a changed perception more widely about how a saxophone should or might sound. Thus many players who made reputations for themselves in this area evolved very different types of saxophone sounds from their acoustically minded forefathers, and conceived their own saxophone sound in very different ways, often in negotiation with engineers and producers. And to reproduce in live performance a sound that has been partly created in the studio often therefore requires recourse to the studio technology that initially helped to generate it.

The saxophonist on *Bitches Brew* had been Wayne Shorter (b. 1933), but when Davis's new direction appeared to leave less space for significant saxophone contributions Shorter left this group and formed his own group with pianist Joe Zawinul. This band, Weather Report, were to become one of the defining groups of the jazz-rock field. Although their first album, the eponymous *Weather Report* (1971),[28] was a purely acoustic release, the subsequent fourteen albums demonstrated increasing and imaginative use of studio technology to provide a balance between preconceived material and jazz improvisation.

Although initially known as a tenor player, Shorter had used the soprano during much of his time with Weather Report, bringing that instrument to a wider audience even than Coltrane had done. Shorter's adoption of the instrument was indicative of the soprano becoming more widely used and familiar in jazz, and for some players an equal of the alto or tenor. In this respect Shorter was also building on the work of Steve Lacy (1934–2004), a soprano specialist who had worked in free jazz with pianist

Cecil Taylor in the late 1950s, but whose wide-ranging career included periods with Gil Evans, Thelonious Monk, and in the 1980s work with Japanese and Indian musicians. Lacy became widely identified with the soprano instrument (a point underlined by his 1995 publication *Findings: MY Experience with the Soprano Saxophone*),[29] and although he had initially been inspired to take up the soprano after hearing Sydney Bechet play, Lacy's own often sparse and vibrato-less style was in many ways the antithesis of the New Orleans player.

If Brecker had appeared for some the quintessential jazz-rock tenor player during the 1980s and 90s, he was matched in that respect by David Sanborn (b. 1945) for those specialising in the alto. Commercially very successful, Sanborn's rasping yet smooth alto sound has, like Brecker's tenor sound, been much imitated. Having grown up in Missouri it was almost inevitable that he should be influenced by the blues, and there is a particularly vocal quality to his playing in the jazz-rock/funk musical language he employs. This is reinforced by his characteristic split high notes, a trademark Sanborn technique reminiscent of a vocal cry or scream, used at key points to increase tension in his solos. The technique might be seen as harking back to the wailing of early blues singers, or the previous manifestation of that deep South vocality in the Texas tenor style of tenor players Illinois Jacquet or Arnett Cobb (see below), now transposed onto the alto instrument.

The possibilities offered by jazz-rock fusions and electric amplification also interested the ever innovative Ornette Coleman in the 1970s. His band Prime Time, formed in 1975 with an unusual line-up of two guitarists, two drummers, two bassists, and Coleman himself on saxophone, violin and trumpet, produced a mixture of jazz, funk and rock that came as a surprise to those who were familiar with Coleman's earlier forays into more radical forms of jazz improvisation or his compositions for classical ensembles. Coleman continued his 'harmolodic' explorations during the 1980s and 90s, and eventually achieved wide recognition as one of the most important and influential jazz saxophonists of his time.

Albert Ayler (1936–70), whose life was cut tragically short by his presumed suicide, also developed free jazz saxophone playing in the 1960s with an approach in which growls, honks and squeals proliferated. His visceral tenor saxophone style, underpinned by a wide, raucous sound and a slow, almost excessive vibrato, was made possible in part through his use of very hard, plastic-covered reeds. Archie Shepp (b. 1937) and Pharaoh Sanders (b. 1940) both built on Ayler's initial explorations, particularly in relation to the use of the saxophone's altissimo register, which, in its inherent flexibility between pitch centres as well as its occasional instability, again plays on the instrument's essentially vocal nature.

This free jazz saxophone tradition was continued by players such as Anthony Braxton (b. 1945) and John Zorn (b. 1953). Both have pursued approaches in which a wide range of musical sources have been melded into individual improvisational/compositional languages, and both occupy a middle ground between jazz and avant-garde art music, and bring an intellectual quality to their work. Braxton, who specialises in less familiar saxophones and is often heard on sopranino and contrabass instruments, is particularly known for unaccompanied performances that use a wide range of extended techniques (see ill. 97). Zorn's wide-ranging work, influenced by

97. Anthony Braxton playing contrabass saxophone.

Braxton, demonstrates the increasing difficulty – or fruitlessness – of applying labels to artists working in these avant-garde areas. His pieces draw on genres as disparate as punk rock, klezmer, mainstream jazz, reggae and so forth. But both Braxton and Zorn continue to see themselves as connected to the jazz tradition, as demonstrated by albums that rework the music of earlier yet equally idiosyncratic jazz masters: in Braxton's case his *Six Monk's Compositions* (1987), based on the music of the pianist Thelonious Monk, and in Zorn's case his rather more tangential tribute to the work of free jazz patriarch Ornette Coleman, in *Spy vs. Spy* (1999).

Rahsaan Roland Kirk (1936–77) was a particularly idiosyncratic jazz saxophonist (see ill. 98). Kirk was renowned as a multi-instrumentalist, playing solos on flute and clarinet as well as saxophones. Unlike most multi-instrumentalists, however, he did not restrict himself to playing one instrument at a time, but instead learned to play up to three saxophones simultaneously. With one instrument functioning as a drone and with keywork modifications made to the other two, Kirk was able to play in three-part harmony with himself. He also somehow managed to use circular breathing at the same time, allowing him to construct extended solos on the three instruments. Kirk was notable for using two unusual saxophones, in addition to his normal tenor. He modified a King Saxello by adding to it a slightly larger bell, then described the

98. Multi-instrumentalist Rahsaan Roland Kirk in 1972.

instrument as a 'manzello'; he similarly used the term 'stritch' to describe a straight Buescher E♭ alto.[30] Kirk also incorporated slide whistles, sirens and other irregular instruments into his performances; yet he was no novelty act, but a serious and inventive soloist with a remarkable ear who was unusually competent in many disparate styles, from Dixieland to free jazz.

Although jazz is quintessentially a North American cultural form, its fragmentation and development in the later twentieth century has broadened its geographical base, and many renowned jazz saxophone players have flourished outside of the United States, especially in Europe. This is true of both mainstream and more avant-garde styles. For example, the British saxophonist Evan Parker (b. 1944) – well known on European jazz circuits if less so in the United States – has over many years developed an innovative and idiosyncratic approach to free improvisation, particularly on the soprano saxophone. His unaccompanied work is especially striking. By extensively using circular breathing Parker constructs solos that may last 30 minutes or more, and through a complex use of alternative fingerings, multiphonics and overtones, as well as rapid changes between registers, he is able to create a sustained web of near-polyphonic textures. He also employs an unorthodox tonguing technique, moving the tongue vertically in the mouth, rather than back and forth against the hard palette as in the conventional *tu-tu* or *tu-ku* style.

The Norwegian Jan Garbarek (b. 1947) is a major figure in European jazz. Although initially an avant-garde player in the manner of Albert Ayler, in the mid 1970s Garbarek moved into a more mainstream, post-bop language, noted particularly through his work with the pianist Keith Jarrett and underpinned via a long-standing association with the German record label ECM. Although elements of his earlier, more dissonant solos occasionally resurface, Garbarek's playing is now characterised by its lyricism and his incorporation of traditional folk melodies, particularly from his native Norway. These folk music associations are reinforced through a modal rather than chromatic improvisational language, and Garbarek's long, sometimes mournful melodies have also prompted comparison with traditional vocal styles elsewhere: funerary laments such as Celtic keening, perhaps, or even the Islamic call to prayer. These resonances with traditional music are quite consciously fostered, and encourage those who have heard Garbarek's playing to invest in the saxophone something of an 'ethnic' quality, thus recalling similar traits in John Coltrane's later work.

Garbarek unexpectedly achieved significant commercial success in 1993, when the album *Officium* became an international best seller.[31] This crossover disc was unusual in that it used medieval and renaissance vocal music sung by an early music group – The Hilliard Ensemble – as a basis for Garbarek's melodic improvisations. Since cathedral-style resonance and temporal spaciousness were already hallmarks of Garbarek's playing, the combination with the vocal group was more sympathetic than it might first appear. This ethereality has become a hallmark of the record label ECM more generally, and it could be argued that the slightly austere yet still emotionally intense approach to performance that characterises some of the saxophone playing on this highly successful label – and of which Garbarek is the most notable proponent – has acted as a counterweight to the more overtly virtuosic saxophone styles common in other parts of the jazz landscape.

While few would describe *Officium* as jazz *per se*, the album provides further indication of the saxophone's timbral and generic flexibility in the postmodern musical world, and the unusual crossover formation of classical vocal group and solo improvising saxophonist also demonstrates the wide variety of ensembles within which improvising saxophone players may find themselves. Along with the various fusion ensembles, free jazz innovators, large and small combos, big bands and others, the jazz tradition has evolved considerably in terms of the instrumentation deployed in its name. Notwithstanding that the conventional bop quartet of piano, sax, bass and drums can still be found, this line-up no longer occupies the central importance for jazz players that it once did, and there are many different ensembles that provide jazz saxophone players with contexts for their work.

This is further evidenced by the rise of the jazz saxophone quartet. Whereas the quartet medium is long established among classical players, it is a more recent development in jazz, although it might be argued that it is an extension of the saxophone section in the swing band. But swing band arrangements usually emphasise – through their often homophonic saxophone writing – the inherent homogeneity of the saxophone family, and while this characteristic also surfaces in independent jazz quartets, the musical roles within such groups are frequently more diverse, since the group must provide solo line, harmonic accompaniment and rhythmic energy without recourse to other musicians. Polyphony is thus inherently more common, and there is more reliance on the baritone instrument to provide the rhythmic drive, in the absence of a conventional rhythm section.

The Hollywood Saxophone Quartet, a group comprising session musicians from the Hollywood area who worked together during the 1940s and 50s, provided one step on the road to a fully independent jazz saxophone quartet.[32] With an S/A/T/B line-up they drew on swing-style arrangements of standard repertoire from arrangers such as Lennie Niehaus (b. 1929)[33] and others; the group also played some of the classical saxophone quartet repertoire. Although several of the swing tracks they recorded added a rhythm section to the group, there were many arrangements for four saxophones alone. In this they preceded groups such as the New York Saxophone Quartet (founded 1959), similarly comprised of top session players,[34] and particularly the World Saxophone Quartet (WSQ, founded 1976; see ill. 99). The latter demonstrated a rather more hard-edged approach, aligning the jazz quartet medium with a contemporary jazz aesthetic, largely involving original compositions and extensive solos for all four players, rather than as a vehicle for cover versions (although their 1991 album *Plays Duke Ellington* remains a notable and successful exception). The WSQ's line-up (2A/T/B) illustrates the overlap with swing band instrumentation (conventionally 2A/2T/B), although they do employ other instruments, particularly a soprano on the top line. This 2A/T/B line-up also parallels the two violin/viola/cello disposition of a conventional string quartet, but a greater resonance with the string quartet tradition arises from all four players having equal roles in the music, thus evoking a sense of 'chamber jazz'. The founders of the group – Oliver Lake (b. 1944) and Julius Hemphill (1938–95) on alto, David Murray (b. 1955), tenor, and Hamiet Bluiett (b. 1940), baritone – were all strong soloists in their own right; thus the WSQ functioned from the beginning as a forum in which their solo skills could be heard within the context of an undifferentiated saxophone group rather than the heterogeneous tonal diversity offered by most other jazz ensembles. Bluiett's baritone playing provided the aggressive, edgy bass line that drove the group, and this approach provided a model for others, such as the 29th Street Saxophone Quartet (founded 1982), similarly driven by the baritone line of Jim Hartog (b. 1950). In both cases the variety of articulations employed by the baritone players are quite deliberately reminiscent of, and serve to replace, the bass drum of the missing kit player or the percussive action of a pizzicato string bass.

The Rova Saxophone Quartet further illustrates the diverse styles of music-making now undertaken by modern saxophone quartets. Formed in 1977 their work explores an intermediate area between contemporary jazz, free improvisation, and composed art music. In addition to their own compositions and their work with composers such as Terry Riley, they sometimes augment the basic saxophone quartet with additional instruments, as in their recreation of John Coltrane's influential work *Ascension* (1997). Their background in free improvisation leads them to draw extensively on extended techniques, and through this, and their use of all the members of the saxophone family, they demonstrate the unusually wide timbral palette that four unaccompanied saxophones are in fact able to generate.

Rock and pop

For all the artistic significance attached to the work done by jazz and classical saxophonists, the instrument reaches its widest global audience in the fields of rock and pop music. Many jazz players – Michael Brecker, Branford Marsalis, Phil Woods and

99.   The World Saxophone Quartet.

others – have contributed to the work of rock and pop artists while themselves retaining a predominantly jazz profile. But the saxophone's historical involvement in these genres stems less from its centrality in the adjacent jazz tradition with which this music sometimes overlaps, and more from its parallel involvement in early rhythm and blues, and then rock and roll, in the 1940s and 50s.

The point at which rhythm and blues became rock and roll is a matter of dispute beyond the present volume. Nevertheless, the saxophone was an important constituent of both styles, and it can reasonably be argued that early rock and roll actually owes more to the saxophone than it does to the electric guitar, notwithstanding that the latter would eventually supplant the former in the instrumental solos that characterised it.

Rhythm and blues evolved out of the blues-based big bands that began to achieve commercial success in the early 1940s. The famous wailing tenor solos of Illinois Jacquet (1922–2004) on both the 1942 disc of *Flying Home* with the Lionel Hampton big band, and in 1944 as part of the Los Angeles *Jazz at the Philharmonic* series, are iconic recordings that some take to be the start of a saxophone led rhythm and blues tradition. This 'honking and screaming' style, in which a fat tenor saxophone sound was allied to low honks and high screams as well as other forms of textural and pitch manipulation, also characterised the playing of others from Texas, such as King Curtis (1934–71) and Arnett Cobb (1918–89). It is particularly associated with Big Jay

McNeely (b. 1927), who combined it with highly theatrical solos involving 'walking the bar' (literally walking along the bar of a small club to enthuse the audience; see ill. 116). These southern-bred rhythm and blues saxophone players drew heavily on the performances of blues singers, and the saxophone's essentially voice-like characteristics once again made it ideally suited to this playing style.

Many saxophone players were significant figures in these rhythm and blues and early rock and roll styles, but their work, and their names, are less well known now, perhaps because of the perceived ephemerality with which much pop music is often endowed, in contradistinction to jazz, which is frequently invested with greater artistic kudos and thus seen as more worthy of preservation. But the importance of these players in raising the profile and popularity of the saxophone deserves acknowledgement. For example, Louis Jordan (1908–75) was both a singer and a saxophone player, whose growling alto solos (though he played all the saxes) characterised many of the enormous number of hits he had in the 1940s and 50s, often with his group The Tympany Five. Jordan's high-energy, infectious form of jump blues was an important bridge between the swing era and early rock and roll. Another significant early rhythm and blues saxophonist was Jackie Brenston (1930–79), who worked as part of Ike Turner's band and made a substantial contribution to Turner's early hit *Rocket 88* (1951), a disc identified by some as being the first rock and roll record.

Both Jordan and Brenston were significant influences on Bill Haley and the Comets, whose long-standing saxophone player Rudy Pompilli[35] (1926–76) was an important contributor to both the music and the onstage showmanship of the group. He also appeared with them in several films, and his performance of 'Rudy's Rock' in the 1956 film *Rock Around the Clock*, which involves extensive physical exuberance and raucous saxophone riffs ending on a high squeal, undoubtedly reinforced for many the association of the saxophone with early rock and roll music, and the supposed depravities that some sought to invest in both. Such was his perceived influence on rock and roll saxophone playing that an album released in 1975 was titled *Rudy's Rock – The Sax that Changed the World*.[36] But this epithet might have been applied to other players at the time, such as King Curtis whose growling tenor sound graced numerous records in the late 1950s and 60s, particularly his well-known solo on *Yakety Yak*

100. Rudy Pompilli in action with Bill Haley and the Comets in 1963.

(1958) by The Coasters;[37] Curtis had several solo instrumental hits in the 1960s, as well as providing saxophone contributions for soul stars such as Aretha Franklin.

The solos on these records were less technically demanding than the bop style then fashionable in jazz, but the rasping, 'dirty' saxophone sound with which they were performed quickly became a significant component of both rhythm and blues and rock and roll, and part of the sonic identity of this new youthful music. Just as the saxophone had been pivotal to the youth-driven dance band counterculture of the 1920s, so too was it central to the music accompanying the rise of the similarly rebellious teenager in the 1950s and early 1960s.

As the 1960s progressed the rock and pop music landscape also became more fragmented, although the saxophone was still central to certain genres: Maceo Parker (b. 1943) made significant contributions to James Brown's success for many years in the 1960s and 70s, at the beginning of a long career that made him one of the most important funk saxophonists; Junior Walker (1931–95) provided both vocals and tenor saxophone solos with his group the All Stars, and their soul-filled groove became a mainstay of the Motown label during its heyday around the same time. Yet in general the instrument played a less prominent role, having lost ground in both the careful studio arrangements underpinning the work of groups such as the Beatles, and the increasing role given to the electric guitar in more rock-oriented groups such as the Rolling Stones.[38] Nor did the instrument feature significantly in the album-driven work of major 1970s supergroups such as Led Zeppelin, Yes, or King Crimson and similar.[39] But towards the end of that decade a number of singles appeared in which the saxophone did feature prominently, and its high profile in certain key recordings in the late 1970s and early 1980s contributed significantly to what can now be construed as a second saxophone craze, one which began around this time and which has led to the instrument's current popularity.

Two recordings from the late 1970s stand out in this respect, if only because they demonstrate the two most common ways in which the saxophone has been used in pop music. Billy Joel's *Just the Way You Are* (1977) features a lyrical sixteen-bar solo from alto player Phil Woods that remains a classic of the genre. Carefully constructed from bluesy figures that lead from one verse into the next, and delivered with swooping glissandos that match Joel's vocal delivery – again reinforcing the point that it is the quasi-vocal nature of much saxophone playing that leads to its success – Woods's solo made a substantial contribution to a record that went on to win two Grammy awards in 1978. That same year Gerry Rafferty released the single *Baker Street*, which opens with a rasping eight-bar alto solo that both introduces the piece and is repeated several times as the song progresses; played by Raphael Ravenscroft it provides the hook to the record, instantly identifying the song from the first few bars, and firmly placing the saxophone in the ears of the very many people who bought and listened to the record.

Through the 1980s a number of hit records repeated one or other of these formulas, and the saxophone regained something of its earlier prominence. By way of further examples: more extended solos were recorded by Wesley McGoogan on Hazel O'Connor's *Will You* (1981), Stuart Matthewman on Sade's *Smooth Operator* (1984), and, as noted above, Branford Marsalis on Sting's *Englishman in New York* (1987). The repeating hook was heard on tracks such as George Michael's *Careless Whisper* (1984, alto played by Steve Gregory) or Dire Straits's *Your Latest Trick* (1985, tenor solo by Michael Brecker).[40]

The saxophone's popularity was further enhanced during this period by the development of the music video, which visually reinforced the instrument's sonic identity. Although such videos became increasingly common through the 1970s, the genre came into its own in 1981 with the launch of the American network MTV, a channel dedicated entirely to music videos. The visual aspects of popular music performance had always been important, now they became crucial. The saxophone benefited from its association with a range of telegenic musicians – male and female – who were seen to be playing the latest, trendiest music, and filmed using rapid cuts between images for up-tempo numbers or *noir*-ish lighting and camera angles for ballads.

This telegenicity undoubtedly helped launch the career of Candy Dulfer (b. 1969), whose stylish good looks and soft funk saxophone playing have been commercially very successful since her debut album *Saxuality* was released in 1990 (see ill. 115). The album was launched because of the success of her contribution to the soundtrack to a Dutch film *De Kassière* (The Cashier), from which the 1989 hit single *Lily Was Here* was taken. Dulfer's pentatonically-based approach to what has been called 'smooth jazz' built on the similar earlier work of Grover Washington Jr. (1943–99), who was popular during the 1970s and 80s. But the success of both is considerably overshadowed by

101.   Kenny G.

Kenneth Gorelick (b. 1956) – better known by his stage name Kenny G. – who is undoubtedly the most commercially profitable saxophone player of all time (ill. 101). His various albums, notably the breakthrough *Duotones* (1986), are again based on a 'smooth jazz' formula in which his wispy, breathy soprano saxophone sound is heard against soft funk rhythms or slow ballad accompaniments. Gorelick, who also performs on alto and tenor, is more an embellisher of melodies than an out-and-out improviser, but there is no doubting the success of his formula. His 1992 album *Breathless* has sold more than 15 million copies worldwide to date, and overall his album sales exceed 70 million.[41] Gorelick is a contentious figure among saxophonists themselves – and indeed other musicians – since his commercial success and 'easy listening' approach make him a soft target for those who believe that an imagined 'authentic' tradition resides in a more robust, earthier and perhaps overtly masculine context. They may also be envious of the fact that, in the early twenty-first century, when many millions of people around the world think of the saxophone, they think of Kenny G.

The rise of soul and funk during the 1960s was accompanied by increased scoring for wind instruments, and by the late 1960s the horn section – a small group of wind instruments that provides rhythmic punctuation and short instrumental interludes as required – had become an integral component of many rock and pop bands. Horn section instrumentation is flexible, and can involve any combination of trumpets, trombones and saxophones, and even occasionally tuba or French horn. One popular combination is a trio of trumpet, tenor saxophone and trombone, but the alto saxophone features regularly, and a combination of trumpet and two saxophones is also common. As the sophistication of horn section writing has evolved so the musical craftsmanship that originally developed in the saxophone sections of the swing bands has been taken a stage further. Close attention to phrasing, articulation and tight, well-tuned ensemble playing, as well as the production of a bright individual and collective sound, have become essential. Studio technology has also been employed to make the horn section sound as tight and crisp as possible. Several horn sections made names for themselves beyond the groups with which they were originally associated. The Tower of Power used a five-horn ensemble of two trumpets, two tenors and a baritone sax in their highly influential line-up from the early 1970s onwards. Groups such as The Ohio Players, Kool and the Gang, The Commodores, and Chicago, were all very dependent on their horn sections for their commercial success. Another well-known section were the Phoenix Horns, led by saxophonists Andrew Woolfolk (b. 1950) and Don Myrick (194093), who joined Earth, Wind and Fire in 1975; they also appeared regularly for Phil Collins, Genesis and others during the 1980s. Again the saxophone played an integral role in defining the sounds and musical textures of these popular music styles, and the sonic and visual profile given to the instrument in these contexts has further contributed to its recent popularity and global identity.

The saxophone on the world stage

As the twentieth century unfolded so the saxophone's global penetration increased well beyond those Euro-American environments with which it was initially identified, and the instrument is now found in music emanating from a large range of different cultures. Although empirical evidence is hard to come by, it is reasonable to speculate that this widespread diffusion is rivalled by few other instruments, with the possible exceptions of the clarinet, violin and guitar. Certainly the saxophone has become one of the most recognised musical instruments in the world, and although this global dissemination has an historical dimension that goes beyond the loosely post-1960s focus of this chapter, a few case studies are considered here because the broader engagement with different forms of global music-making in part characterises musical postmodernism as a whole.

The most important conduit for the global distribution of the saxophone in the late nineteenth and early twentieth centuries was undoubtedly the military band. As these bands travelled in support of the colonial administrations overseen by various European powers, so the indigenous populations in these areas became increasingly familiar with their music and instrumentation. In India, for example, beginning in the early nineteenth century, this led to the creation of related 'Westernised' ensembles by those local rulers who could afford to sustain them.[42] Indian musicians thus needed to learn the new European instruments their employers wished to hear. Hereditary musicians learned these new instruments in order to increase and sustain their position, and they were joined by other musicians who were trained directly by British bandsmen or British-trained Indian musicians. Thus performers of the traditional *nagaswaram* – a large oboe-type instrument – started to learn the clarinet. As the latter became increasingly prevalent it began to usurp traditional instruments, a pattern that the saxophone would later repeat in a variety of contexts. In the late nineteenth century, private Indian bands began to emerge, servicing a growing preference for wedding and other processional music, and the clarinet retained its important position within these, often played by the bandleader. These players were already proficient on the 13- and 14-key Albert system clarinets that were common in India at the time, and it was therefore a relatively easy progression from these to the saxophone. During the first decades of the twentieth century saxophones were increasingly included in such bands, and these changes can be heard on early recordings. Discs made in 1911 by The Madras Corporation Band, for example, show the ensemble to consist of clarinets, brass instruments, bagpipes and assorted percussion, but recordings from 1933 show an expanded instrumentation, now including two alto saxophones, which then appear to have become permanent fixtures in the group.[43]

The interest of these musicians in the saxophone would have been reinforced by the instrument's preeminent role at this time in dance music and jazz. Such was the international popularity of this music – globally disseminated through recordings and broadcasting – that, even in the early 1920s, dance bands were in demand in many parts of the world, and the music they played would in some cases be imitated by local musicians. Cities such as Bombay and Calcutta (now Mumbai and Kolkata) were part of an extensive circuit in south and south-east Asia for which touring dance bands would provide music in upmarket hotels, usually for expatriate Americans and Europeans rather than the local population. Some local musicians were intrigued by this new music and sought to emulate it as a possible source of income. For example, in Goa, a small state of west India that has long connections with Europe through its lengthy status as a Portuguese colony, local musicians led dance bands from as early as the 1930s. A Goan saxophone player named Paul Gonsalves recorded with Indian swing bands in the 1930s and 40s.[44] After Indian independence in 1947 a reaction against Western values set in, and jazz on the Indian subcontinent went into temporary decline. But in the 1950s another Goan saxophone player – Braz Gonsalves – became one of the first Indians to play modern jazz. He went on to be a major name on the Indian jazz scene for several decades, with whom a number of jazz luminaries played during tours of India.[45]

The saxophone has also had some impact on Indian classical music, even though the instrument's equally-tempered scale is not always easily aligned with an Indian tuning system that extensively uses microtones. But the Carnatic tradition of southern India, particularly, has seen a number of wind players adopting the saxophone in preference to more traditional instruments. The most renowned of these is perhaps Kadri Gopalnath (b. 1949). Like many others, Gopalnath started as a *nagaswaram* player. He changed to the alto saxophone as a teenager, but found that he had to modify the instrument in order for it to work effectively in the Indian context. Since Carnatic music is usually confined to a range of around two octaves (following the normal range of the human voice), Gopalnath removed some of the keys at the extremes of the instrument that he didn't use; he also replaced the connecting rods with strong rubber cords, and exchanged the leather keypads for felt, convex equivalents. All this mitigates the snappy, percussive nature of the saxophone action. Combined with a performance style that emphasises rapid melismas and portamentos, and a timbre that is warm rather than penetrating, the saxophone can sound surprisingly idiomatic in this context, and once again it is the vocal nature of its sound that

102. The Indian saxophone player Kadri Gopalnath.

appears to underpin its success. One drawback, however, is that the modal range is relatively limited: Gopalnath is nearly always working in concert B♭.[46]

Both jazz and Indian classical music are characterised by forms of improvisation that use particular melodic modes over given rhythmic cycles. This natural affinity has led to several collaborations between musicians working in these fields – another characteristic of musical postmodernism. Drawing on Indian music became quite fashionable among jazz musicians in the 1960s, when saxophone players such as Bud Shank (1926–2009) and John Coltrane used Indian themes and principles of improvisation in their work. The particular timbral qualities of the saxophone also facilitated such approaches. The soprano saxophone, especially, has sometimes attracted commentary for the perceived 'ethnic' sound qualities with which it is sometimes invested, as has already been noted in relation to players such as Coltrane and Garbarek.

The interrelationship between colonial expansion and Euro-American popular music also aided the saxophone's penetration into certain parts of Africa, particularly through the numerous African styles that began to fuse Western popular music with local traditions, such as township jive in South Africa, *chimurenga* in Zimbabwe, *rai* in north Africa, and so forth. Highlife music, found in certain countries of west Africa such as Nigeria, Liberia, and especially Ghana, provides a specific example. Highlife similarly arose from the hybridisation of Western musical genres fused by local musicians with their own indigenous styles. Three particular streams evolved: a 'palm wine' style arising in coastal areas, in which the music and instruments of foreign sailors were adopted; the *adaha* style adapted from brass band music played by military bands in the coastal forts (although these were largely brass bands some are likely to have included saxophones, and would have been one of the ways the instrument became familiar on the African continent); and a third stream based on dance orchestras that were already common in the area from the 1920s; the first dance orchestra in Ghana, for example, was established in Accra as early as 1914.[47] This third stream, playing waltzes, polkas, Latin dances and the like, provided music for the black elite in expensive clubs and hotels. Eventually the musicians also began to produce polished versions of local music, which the poorer blacks, congregating outside the clubs because they could not afford to participate, named 'Highlife'. During World War II, when many British and American troops were stationed in west Africa, these local musicians, in collaboration with some of those musicians temporarily stationed there, began to provide the swing music that the comparatively wealthy servicemen wished to hear. E. T. Mensah, a saxophone and trumpet player who became well known in Ghanaian music after the Second World War, relates that a Scottish saxophone player by the name of Sergeant Jack Leopard established during the war the 'Black and White Spots' – a mixed swing band of African and white musicians; this inevitably led to the transfer of musical ideas and practices: Mensah observes that 'it was Sergeant Leopard who taught us the correct methods of intonation, vibrato, tonguing and breath control, which contributed to place us above the average standard in town'.[48] Mensah had already learned the basics of saxophone technique while at school in the 1930s, suggesting that it was during this period that the saxophone became more available to black musicians in the area: 'My elder brother, Yebuah Mensah, star saxophonist, roped me in. He was one of the first in the country to handle a sax. Mr Lamptey bought it for him'.[49] Lamptey was the teacher who directed the school orchestra, and this group went on to become the Accra Rhythmic Orchestra; the instrumentation, a clear imitation of American swing band models, consisted of five saxophones, two trumpets, one trombone and a sousaphone, plus string bass, guitar and percussion.

Another local swing band demonstrated similar cross-cultural roots: The Tempos was formed by a Ghanaian pianist Adolf Doku and an English engineer and saxophone player by the name of Arthur Leonard Harriman. Doku later recalled that 'Harriman was a good saxophone player, having played with several European bands in Britain before coming out to west Africa. He once met me at a private party, where I was playing the piano, and asked if I would allow him to play his saxophone with me at that party [...] and soon we were playing dance music to which the guests danced. After this we [...] decided to include a drummer and trumpeter to the team. We drafted in two members of the armed forces who were in the Gold Coast at the time.'[50] After the war the foreign troops left, and although many of these swing bands folded, The Tempos survived, now with a fully African membership. Led first by tenor saxophonist Joe Kelly and later by E. T. Mensah, the band became one of the most important west African highlife dance groups of the 1950s, creating a highlife style

103. Ghanaian saxophone players E.T. Mensah (right) and J. A. Mallet in the 1937 Accra Rhythmic Orchestra.

with a swing touch to it, and Mensah's laid-back saxophone playing became widely influential in west Africa as a whole.[51]

Kwela, a riff-based musical genre closely associated with South African townships in the 1950s and 60s, provides another example of musical globalisation. It arose from young musicians aspiring to emulate the swing style of the American big bands heard in films and on radio and disc, albeit necessarily using the more limited musical means available to them. Pennywhistles (end-blown flutes), played at an unorthodox slanting angle to the mouth, were used to imitate the blue notes, chromaticisms and smears heard in the swing players' solos. Given the central role played by the saxophone in the bands that were being imitated, the instrument's subsequent displacement of the pennywhistle might now be seen as almost inevitable. The 1958 recording by Spokes Mashiyane of *Big Joe Special* is often viewed as the beginning of the end of traditional flute-dominated kwela and the start of its transformation into what became known as Sax Jive.[52] The commercial success of Mashiyane's recording ensured that those record producers driving the popularity of kwela music in the late 1950s were keen to find saxophone players able to offer similar performances. Most pennywhistlers were happy to change to the new instrument, provided they could somehow acquire one. The saxophone offered more musical possibilities than its rather limited predecessor, but also, and perhaps more significantly, it connoted for both players and audience a more sophisticated, urban and pan-tribal identity that satisfyingly contradicted conventional apartheid conceptions of black, rural back-wardness. In part, therefore, the commodification of kwela music, and the high profile it achieved through the widespread exposure offered by mass media, was again enhanced through its eventual association with the saxophone, an instrument so frequently seen – as will become clearer in Chapter 8 – as a symbol of internationali-sation and modernity.

These African examples demonstrate explicitly how the saxophone became caught up in a web of transnational cultural flows that led to its increasing dissemination around the globe: overseas postings for Western military musicians provided musical models that might be emulated, musical instruments that might be adopted, and on occasion collaborations with local musicians through which different cultural and musical concepts might be exchanged. Reinforced by the increasing availability of Western dance music propagated via rapidly expanding mass media conduits, hybrid musical styles evolved in which the saxophone can now be seen not only as an agent of cultural change, but an icon of it also.

In other contexts, rather than being part of a process of stylistic hybridisation, the saxophone has been accommodated as a new voice within existing forms of music-making, sometimes usurping traditional instruments in the process (as with the Indian *nagaswaram*). Such trends have not always been welcomed, and the saxophone, perhaps precisely because of its internationalist and modernist associations, has often been seen as an unwelcome interloper. The folklorist Leonidas Dodson's 1947 observation, in rela-tion to the instrumental folk music of south-western Pennsylvania, that 'the music of fiddle and flute will not endure the onslaught of the saxophone', is just one example of the threats sometimes perceived to exist when traditional musical styles are transformed through the acculturative influence of newer instruments such as the saxophone.[53]

These issues relating to innovation, authenticity and the saxophone are clearly played out in the case of the 'orquesta típica' found among the people of the Mantaro Valley in the Peruvian Central Andes.[54] These ensembles – traditionally consisting of indigenous instruments such as the *quena* (an end-notched flute), together with instruments demonstrating Spanish colonial influence, such as the Andean harp and the violin – provide dance and processional music for festivals and dramas throughout the region. The inclusion of clarinets in these groups from the 1910s, and then saxophones, possibly from as early as the 1920s,[55] are embedded within a local discourse about what constitutes the 'true' tradition of the orquesta típica. As Raul Romero points out, older generations saw saxophones as having been almost forcibly introduced into the ensemble, and felt those groups that relied on clarinets rather than saxophones produced an ensemble sound that was truer to the tradition, despite clarinets having themselves replaced traditional instruments such as the *quena*. Thus the arguments for and against the inclusion of saxophones were part of a long tradition of changing instrumentation, and represented a process of social negotiation about what constituted an 'authentic' musical past. In one particular town, Huaripampa, the celebration of the Fiesta of the Tunantada (Epiphany) is marked by the specific exclusion of saxophones from any orquesta típica providing music for the celebration; on one occasion the association staging the festival agreed to pay the wages of the saxophone players who had arrived with an orquesta only if they left the town, so that they could not possibly take part in the festival.[56]

Inevitably, it was the younger generations in the Mantaro valley who were most keen on introducing the saxophones, not only because of the instrument's modernist connotations but also because of the different timbre and greater power it lent to the ensemble. Saxophones allowed the orquesta to, as the local musicians put it, 'sound

104. An orquesta típica from the town of Huanchar, Peru, in 1985.

more', implying not only greater volume but also a greater density of sound. It was the richer sound of the saxophone, as opposed to the thinner timbres of the clarinet or violin, that made it desirable in this context: the richer the sound of the orquesta from one particular locale, the more prestige accrued to the people who identified with that group, and particularly the committee who organised it. For several decades the standard saxophone section in the orquesta consisted of 2A/T, not unlike dance bands elsewhere. From the 1960s, however, as the pressure to 'sound more' grew, so increasing numbers of saxophones were added, so that today it is not uncommon to find eight saxophones involved: 4A/2T/2B.[57]

The saxophone's identity as a modern, international instrument can also be seen in the Dominican Republic, where it takes a central role in several forms of the internationally recognised Latin style known as merengue. Because merengue is a globally significant form of Latin music, it might be thought that the saxophone's inclusion arises once again through the influence of swing and jazz. While these have had some impact on merengue from the 1930s, the saxophone could be found as part of this style – even in rural areas – as early as the 1910s, some time before the United States' influence on the country was really felt.[58] It is not clear how the saxophone would have found its way there at such an early stage, but it is likely that military garrison bands again played a role in its dissemination. In the early twentieth century the *merengue típico cibaeño* (Cibao-style folk merengue), an African-Hispanic riff-based dance form, was the preferred social dance in the countryside and lower-class urban neighbourhoods, performed by a quartet of *tambora* (a double-headed drum), *güira* (metal scraper), button accordion and alto saxophone. Pedro 'Cacú' Lora and Avelino Vásquez are likely to have been the architects of the original merengue saxophone style.[59] The instrument has remained at the heart of merengue performance, particularly since the use of swing-band style saxophone sections, albeit still often using riff-based arrangements, have come to accompany many later iconic figures of the tradition such as Johnny Ventura. Deborah Pacini Hernández contrasts the position of the dominant saxophone-oriented merengue tradition with that of another genre, the increasingly marginalised guitar-oriented *bachata*. She sees the opposition of these two genres as representative of a class struggle, with one class deliberately trying to dominate the other. In the minds of some local musicians, she argues, 'the poor and dispossessed metaphorically become one instrument – the guitar – while the more affluent metaphorically become the saxophone.'[60] This again reinforces the view taken here that – in addition to its physical and performance characteristics – it is the saxophone's identity as a particularly modern instrument and a symbol of material wealth that makes it attractive to many musicians around the globe.

This brief review of the saxophone's place on the world stage by no means fully covers the enormous penetration the instrument has now achieved in global music-making, and there are numerous other examples in which the saxophone has become a significant voice that might equally have been advanced: in the more modern updating of the Algerian *rai* tradition during the 1960s; in some of the crossovers between jazz and flamenco in *nuevo flamenco* in Spain; in the Jewish Klezmer tradition, whether in the Middle East, Europe, or in and around New York; in the so-called 'wedding music' of Bulgaria, partly established by the Bulgarian saxophonist Yuri Yunakov in collaboration with the clarinettist Ivo Papasov; in both Mexico's *tejano* (Tex-Mex) and *norteño* (regional) styles of popular music, as well as in Argentinean tango; and so forth. While the specific reasons for the instrument's adoption inevitably vary from one situation to another, the inherent hybridity of many of these styles is somehow appropriate in relation to the saxophone, given the instrument's own essentially hybrid brass/wind nature. But it is once again its timbral flexibility, its capacity to produce and manipulate so many different types of sound, its comparative robustness and simplicity, and its frequently iconic status as a marker of innovation and modernity, that ultimately accounts for much of the instrument's success in being assimilated into such a disparate range of musical styles and contexts.

Chapter 8

The saxophone as symbol and icon

Modernity and the making of America

The saxophone was developed to address specific problems that Adolphe Sax had identified among low wind instruments, and his solution to these was made possible in part because of nineteenth-century advances in engineering – particularly in the manipulation of sheet metal such as brass – and through increased understanding of acoustics and the musical possibilities such understandings afforded. From its inception, therefore, the instrument has been identified with modernity, innovation, and a sense of exploration and enquiry, and this reputation has in many ways remained with it since. These characteristics were explicitly promoted in the nineteenth century by Jullien and others in their popular concerts in Paris, London, New York and beyond, in which musical novelty was combined with astute showmanship for commercial gain. Here the instrument's unusual morphology and its unfamiliar timbre were harnessed to great effect, imprinting the saxophone in the minds of the audience as something new and exotic. The responses of these audiences were not unrelated, perhaps, to similar responses arising from the wonder and astonishment with which they would have greeted circuses, international exhibitions and freak shows, where they would also have been presented with unfamiliar shapes, sizes and sounds from a wide range of animate and inanimate objects that lay outside their customary realm of experience. The response of one London critic on first hearing the instrument in 1852 that it bristled with keys and appeared to be 'a musical monster, neither fish nor flesh' is suggestive of just such a mindset.[1]

In part to counter any notion of frivolity or ephemerality attaching to the saxophone, Sax and his supporters argued at length for its serious qualities and its inclusion in art music genres. In truth its penetration in these areas was achieved only slowly, except for a small number of operas, although it quickly became a regular part of the military band instrumentarium. It was considered a serious enough instrument to be played in church and at funerals. The saxophone was included as part of military band ensembles, for example, in two religious masses performed in Paris in 1867, one of which was in Notre Dame.[2] And a saxophone quartet played the Funeral March from Beethoven's *Eroica* Symphony at Rossini's funeral in 1868, a fact noted in the *RGMP* at the time, and an appropriate tribute to one of Sax's longstanding supporters.[3]

This mix of the saxophone being seen as both a novel, unfamiliar instrument in some contexts, while simultaneously promoted as a worthy and legitimate contributor to others, continued in the United States in the late nineteenth century. Circuses and vaudeville circuits provided ample opportunity for the unfamiliar sound and shape of the instrument to be exploited, and the relative ease with which multi-instrumentalists could achieve some level of basic competence on the instrument further accelerated its acceptance in these environments. Equally, the touring activities of the professional bands of Gilmore and Sousa, and the work of early concert artists such as Elise Hall, established a concert base for the saxophone, in which the instrument was used both as a soloist and as a contributor to ensembles performing classical or light classical arrangements. But by the early twentieth century, as the saxophone craze in the United States began in earnest, these more 'legitimate' activities were overshadowed in the public consciousness by the image of the saxophone as a fun – and funny – novelty, an instrument that was easy to play, not to be taken too seriously, and from which one could extract all sorts of novelty sound effects. This transformation was noted by commentators such as Henry F. Gilbert, who in 1922 observed that 'it has remained for jazz to exploit [the saxophone]. And this has been done in a way to make the angels weep (with laughter). Originally an instrument having a richly pathetic and lyrical tone quality, it has been made to perform all sorts of ridiculous stunts, amounting to an indecent exposure of all its worst qualities. It is as if a grave and dignified person were forced to play the part of a clown at the circus.'[4]

While this image of a lightweight novelty was the despair of those who sought a more serious profile for the instrument, the populist egalitarianism that the saxophone came to represent has, with hindsight, a more significant historical resonance. For this was the period in which America itself was forging its modern identity, an identity that would sustain it throughout a twentieth century that, from many perspectives, it came to dominate. And although the saxophone may have begun life as a European instrument, by the 1920s it was very clearly perceived as an American one, partly through the saxophone craze in which the USA was by then immersed, but also because of the instrument's close identification with those styles of American popular music that were by now being rapidly disseminated throughout the world. As such, the saxophone can be seen to denote the particular qualities that Caucasian Americans (at least) saw themselves as espousing: a democratic, inclusive, egalitarian society driven by the free market. This was a nation founded on the basis that if you worked hard enough you could succeed, you could do it for yourself, without necessarily needing to rely on others. The saxophone was attractive for precisely the same reasons. Anybody, it seemed, could play the saxophone if they put some work into it, just as they could make something of themselves if they took the same attitude in life. The saxophone wasn't weighed down by centuries of tradition, or enmeshed within the class-oriented structures prevailing in European art music. It was an instrument you could teach yourself, with minimal reliance on others, and without the need, apparently, for extensive specialist education. It appealed to and could be played by all classes and ethnicities. It represented something of a fresh start, a new way of doing things, not unlike America itself for many of its newly immigrant population. Perhaps it was a little loud at times, and it didn't always sound pretty, but it got the job done and provided a little fun along the way. Although rooted in the Old World it was not unduly constrained by such associations. Just as America could modify or eschew European systems of governance or economics, so too could it establish its own forms of music-making and refashion the Old World's instrumentarium. All of this contributed to the image of a modern, innovatory, 'can do' twentieth-century America; the saxophone provided the soundtrack to the American dream. Even later in the century, when the United States identified new frontiers to be conquered in outer space, the saxophone continued to play a symbolic role: it was the first musical instrument to be taken into orbit, by astronaut Ron McNair on the space shuttle *Challenger* in February 1984 (see ill. 105).[5]

Clay Smith, one of those who endeavoured to promote the saxophone as a serious instrument in the early 1900s, also viewed it as quintessentially American, noting that it 'has been perfected and improved in America until it is really more of an American instrument than anything else',[6] and a picture of a Sioux Indian Chief playing a saxophone in *Metronome* in 1924 ran under the caption 'A 100 per cent American who loves America's National Instrument'.[7] Smith also saw the instrument as emblematic of America's growing economic stature,[8] and this identification of the saxophone with successful commercial enterprise is prescient of an explicit later association between the instrument and American capitalism. Both at home and abroad the saxophone became symbolic of North America's increasing wealth and economic power. A cartoon in *Life* magazine from December 1925 shows President Calvin Coolidge, playing the saxophone – engraved with the word 'Praise' – to provide a musical accompaniment for a dancer whose dress is inscribed with the words 'Big Business' (see ill. 106). Also in 1925 the *Boston Post* observed that 'the only music typically American is that made by the mocking-bird, the saxophone, and the cash register'.[9] Perhaps it is no coincidence that the temporary demise of American capitalism in the 1929 stock market crash also marked the end of the country's initial infatuation with the saxophone.

Although they were emulated by musicians around the world, the big bands of the 1930s and 1940s remained quintessentially American musical icons whose sonic

105. Ron McNair playing the saxophone on the space shuttle *Challenger* in 1984.

106. A cartoon of the otherwise reticent American President Calvin Coolidge serenading the dancer of 'Big Business' with a saxophone engraved with the word 'praise'. Published in *Life*, December 1925.

identity was to a significant degree defined by the smooth homogeneity of their saxophone sections. After America's entry into World War II these big bands and their saxophones could be seen as evidence not only of corporate America's economic power, but also as a reminder of its military and political strength. America was assuming a role for itself as the world's policeman, and the policeman's preferred form of musical entertainment, or so it seemed, involved the big band and the saxophone. Underpinned by radio broadcasts, gramophone discs and films, as well as by the touring activities of the bands themselves, the big band sound served not only as a reminder of the capacity of the United States to influence lives in parts of the world far beyond its own geographical boundaries, it also played an important role in boosting morale at home and for American troops abroad. Glenn Miller's band is most often thought of in this respect, partly because Miller himself signed up for active duty in 1942 and photographs of him in military uniform abound, and partly because of the shock caused by his sudden disappearance on a flight from England to France in 1944. His saxophone-dominated recordings of tunes such as *In the Mood* and *Moonlight Serenade* (both 1939) connote for many people America's involvement in the war, as well as the difficulties, deprivations and occasional diversions of everyday life during it.

Throughout the 1940s and 50s the growing dominance of the Hollywood film industry continued to impact on public perception of the saxophone, particularly since the widely-held view of jazz as being somehow anti-authoritarian was now reinforced by the music's appropriation for certain film scores, to the great delight of a newly-discovered and headstrong breed of American: the teenager. Films such as *The Wild One* (1953) or *Rebel Without a Cause* (1955), starring Marlon Brando and James Dean respectively, used up-tempo, saxophone-infused swing cues to enhance the often edgy, rebellious nature of their plots and protagonists.

A different part of the 1950s jazz landscape gave a new aspect to the saxophone's profile. Cool jazz had become very trendy, and the players and instruments associated with it were increasingly seen as style icons. Cool jazz started with a small group of relatively young players, among them saxophonists such as Gerry Mulligan, Lee Konitz and Stan Getz, who not only wanted their music to sound good, they also wanted to look good. Sharp suits and expensive shoes were *de rigueur* for these new trend setters, and the visual and sonic chic with which they were associated charac-terised several films, notably those by French New Wave directors such as Louis Malle's *Ascenseur pour l'échafaud* (*Lift to the Scaffold*, 1958) – for which Miles Davis and a small combo including saxophonist Barney Wilen improvised the soundtrack – or Jean-Luc Goddard's *À bout de souffle* (*Breathless*, 1960). The saxophone featured in all these, and the instrument's participation at the forefront of musical and cinematic innovation during this period further enhanced its reputation as cool, trendy and youthful. Many later film scores would exploit this 'urban cool' aspect of the saxo-phone's persona, notably Henry Mancini's 1963 score for *The Pink Panther* and Bernard Herrmann's title track for Martin Scorsese's 1976 *Taxi Driver*. Perhaps more tellingly, the instrument featured significantly on screen in a number of successful films set in urban environments; for example, Scorsese's *New York, New York* (1977), in which Robert de Niro's anguished tenor saxophonist slowly falls in love with Liza Minnelli's equally troubled singer (see ill. 107), or Bertrand Tavernier's *Round Midnight* (1986), in which real life saxophonist Dexter Gordon this time plays the tenor man in a factually-based tale set in Paris.

By the last decades of the twentieth century the saxophone was widely seen as a cool accessory, not only an object of aspiration but also a marker of material wealth and achievement, characteristics that went well beyond its function as a musical instru-ment. This transformation from musical novelty to hip accessory was reinforced through the instrument's widespread use in advertising. The saxophone appeared as an incidental prop in adverts for furniture, drinks, different clothing ranges, vehicles, cigarettes, and so forth; for example, in the 1980s Kool menthol cigarettes were adver-tised in front of a jazz saxophone player with the tag line 'There's only one way to play it'.[10] The subliminal message here and elsewhere endeavoured to connect the

107. A poster advertising the cool urban saxophone player Robert de Niro falling in love with Liza Minnelli in *New York, New York*.

product with the chic materialism taken to be connoted by the saxophone: 'you must have this product because it is cool, funky and modern, just like the saxophone'. President Bill Clinton similarly generated a certain amount of popular political appeal through his well publicised skills on the instrument.

Throughout the twentieth century, therefore, the saxophone and its players were cast in a variety of roles within modern American culture, sometimes in the background but often centre stage. And while these associations with a constantly evolving but complex American identity might reasonably have resulted in a very positive image for the saxophone, this was not always the case, either in the United States or further afield. For much of the first half of the twentieth century, particularly, the instrument suffered a poor reputation in many quarters, tarnished by its association with increasingly negative responses to American popular music in general and jazz in particular. This anti-saxophone sentiment, and by implication the negative qualities imputed to the instrument as a cultural symbol, manifested itself in a variety of areas, of which three will be considered in more depth here: the perception of the saxophone as a depraved instrument in the eyes and ears of those for whom dance music and jazz represented a threat to public morality; the association of the instrument with black jazz musicians for those ideologically aligned to white supremacy; and the role of the instrument as a symbol of North American capitalism and democracy for those opposed to the United States as a political entity.

Mad, bad and dangerous to blow

The saxophone's close association with dance music and jazz in the first half of the twentieth century has been without question the single most important reason for its present widespread familiarity. But for much of the 1920s and 30s particularly, and for many years thereafter, the instrument suffered because of this. The arrival of these new styles was accompanied by an outraged response from the moral majority (as is so often the case in the development of Western popular music – consider also rock and roll, punk, hip-hop, etc.), who saw in them evidence of every kind of youthful dissolution. The opposition to what was construed as 'jazz' was especially fierce. By way of example, in 1925 the editor of *Etude* magazine observed that 'we know that in its sinister aspects, jazz is doing a vast amount of harm to young minds and bodies not yet developed to resist evil temptations. Perhaps this is the explanation of America's enormous crime rate at the present.'[11] Such sentiments were widely expressed in musical publications of the 1920s through to the 1940s, and more occasionally beyond.

What were taken at the time to be somewhat lascivious dance styles or, in the case of jazz clubs, the identification of a nascent counter culture seemingly involving drug consumption, promiscuity and other ills, inevitably resulted in a backlash against the musicians promulgating such music and the instruments they played. The saxophone suffered particularly in this respect. Whereas the trumpet, trombone, double bass or piano were all established, 'legitimate' instruments with a strong classical background, and could thus perhaps be viewed as only temporarily errant when found in more degenerate contexts, the saxophone had no such heritage to call upon. And since the unfamiliar sound and shape of this relatively new instrument took a dominant role in many of the musical proceedings, it could clearly be identified as the principal miscreant, at whose door much of the blame for this decadent musical behaviour could be laid.

Consequently, a series of profoundly negative views of the saxophone arose, which can be loosely divided into two related categories. In the first was a conservative musical establishment, long dominant in Europe particularly, whose belief in the essential 'decency' or merit of the Western art music canon was set against the worthlessness of what they described as 'jazz'. Their assertions were also driven by a conviction – usually unstated – that competence, and therefore musical value, could only come through extensive technical training and acquaintance with the master-works of the classical tradition itself. The saxophone and its players seldom fulfilled these requirements. The second category comprised those who appropriated for themselves the role of moral guardian, and were thus less concerned with the implications for Western musical culture than for the welfare of society as a whole. For this group it was what they perceived as the essentially sinful or evil nature of dance music and jazz that was most troubling, and in their view the principal architect of such depravity was again the saxophone.

Unsurprisingly, it was the admonishments of the social moralists, fearing the downfall of society as they knew it, that were particularly severe. The dance craze of the 1910s had led to the rise of a number of explicit and sexually suggestive dance moves – the turkey trot, the bunny hop and others – that outraged the more conservative members of American society. Thus in 1922 *Jacob's Orchestral Monthly* observed that 'something has got to give. There is a wave of protest against the immoralities, the indecencies, the suggestiveness, the savage wrigglings which evil-minded or merely ignorant dancers interpolate in this dancing and this wave is being surely directed [. . .] against the music for this sort of dancing, against the musicians who produce it and against the instruments from which it is produced, with the saxophone heading the list as the worst offender of them all'.[12] Similar fears of moral subversion, with even more blame directed at the saxophone, were evident in an article titled 'The Saxophone: Siren of Satan', which appeared in the *San Francisco Chronicle* in 1917:

Listening to the profane music [of a café ragtime band] and noting the deplorable effect which these pagan strains and lawless rhythms produced in the dancers, I was prompted to analyze this appeal. Soon I became convinced that nothing was so much to blame as the saxophone, an instrument which seems to lead all the others in the dance music of the modern cabaret. Obviously, the saxophone as an instrument is capable of producing pure, healthy music, and it can be employed in strictly legitimate fashion, but there can be no doubt of its immorality in the cabaret. In accompanying a dance it is so played that it preys upon the passions and emotions. It becomes patently suggestive, instinctly animal-like. No other musical instrument can be so immoral [. . .]. The saxophone is guttural, savage, panting and low in its appeal. It achieves a peculiar whining, creeping mysterious sound. As cabaret musicians play it a call insinuating and reckless comes from it – a call that possesses some strange psychologic power over the young dance devotees of America. The broken tempo in which it croons dance music is without principle or dignity [. . .]. The abstract immorality of the saxophone [. . .] is but an example of the power that gilded sin has for the moment over thoughtless minds [. . .]. Some severe action must sooner or later be taken upon the matter of our dance music and measures enforced prohibiting the use of the saxophone in this connection or compelling musicians to play it in another fashion.[13]

When a special committee was appointed in 1924 by New York's Woman's City Club to investigate the city's dance halls, it too noted that the 'devilish combination' of the saxophone and snare drum provoked 'grotesque and barbarous' performances on the part of the dancers.[14] A similar view was espoused by a contributor to *Music and Letters* in 1929, who observed that 'if the saxophone and the brass band are instruments of Satan it is our business to rout Satan with his own inventions and win over jazz and brass bands to our idea of righteousness'.[15]

Such views may have been disseminated within the print media, but they were also found well beyond them. A few years previously, in 1914, the Vatican had condemned the instrument, forbidding it to be played in church, an edict that would have surprised the saxophone players at Rossini's funeral only a half century previously.

The religious establishment was still suspicious of the instrument as late as 1948 in Worcester, England, when a performance of Vaughan Williams's *Job* had to be given without the movement containing the prominent alto saxophone solo, because the church authorities refused to allow the profane saxophone inside the church where the performance was due to take place.[16] And inevitably, when moral turpitude looms, it is the honour of their young women that societies frequently deem to be most at risk. In his book on music censorship in America, Eric Nuzum notes that 'when the saxophone was popularised in the 1920s, critics called it the "devil's flute" and thought that its low, seductive tones would cause young girls to behave immorally'.[17] At least one Washington D.C. policewoman in 1925 similarly believed that 'any music played on the saxophone is immoral'.[18]

The musical establishment in England was a little less vitriolic in its disdain for the saxophone, if often more snooty. Disparagement of the instrument was frequently embedded in negative appraisals of what was taken to be 'jazz'. One reviewer commented that the defining characteristics of jazz were to 'eliminate all grades of tone but three, play your melodies so that they sound like that greasy-pole, the saxophone, and cultivate slickness to the *n*th degree. "Horrible", shudders the musician.'[19] Another observed that 'much [modern dance music] seems to me to have a touch of foulness, and I believe this effect can be traced to the persistent tremolo and portamento, and to the vile animalistic noises produced by the wind instruments, especially the saxophone.'[20] Even in contexts more closely allied to 'legitimate' classical performances the saxophone was not immune from this kind of criticism. A review of one of Rudy Wiedoeft's recordings noted that 'he does dexterous things with a Beethoven Minuet and his own "Valse Manzanetta," without being able to make us forget the fatal tendency of the instrument to snivel';[21] while a 1936 performance by Sigurd Rascher of Ibert's *Concertino da camera* was deemed to be 'an attempt to obtain recognition in good society for that disreputable instrument'.[22]

A similarly disparaging if more entertaining view was offered by the editor of the London *Times* in May 1933. While absolving Adolphe Sax himself from any blame for the subsequent uses to which his invention had been put, the editor, prompted by a report of a gala held (somewhat belatedly) in Sax's honour in Paris the previous month, wondered how it was that:

> by combining a reed mouthpiece and a conical bore a man could work so much mischief [. . .]. [The saxophone] has, we read, 'affinities with the harmonium' – a harmonium, surely, perverted from its usual pious office into some shocking black-magical mystery. Berlioz found in it 'vague analogies with the timbre of 'cello, clarinet, and cor anglais, with, however, a brazen tinge' – a musical fellow, in fact, to Alice's drink, which 'had a sort of mixed flavour of cherry-tart, custard, pine-apple, roast turkey, toffee, and hot buttered toast'. Of such an instrument nothing can drown the noise. It defies a whole orchestra, and the din of a ballroom is as silence before it. It is at once penetrating and languorous, aggressive and cajoling. It mopes and yearns with all the reticence of a film-star. It is blatant and slimy; it is honey powdered with cayenne pepper [. . .]. It is as sentimental as a green suburban girl with a 'crush' on a matinée idol, and as delicate as an income-tax

form or a Customs officer on a cold, wet morning. And it is very easy to play – so much easier than the clarinet or the bassoon that, without extraordinary versatility, the players can pick it up to crow or yearn a bit, and then pop it down again while they snatch up a violin or hammer on a xylophone.[23]

Historical perspective now allows us to see such comments as very much of their place and time. But they are indicative of strongly felt views among certain Western moralists and intellectuals in the 1920s and 30s, who saw the saxophone as emblematic of a changing world in which long-cherished cultural values were being reassessed, political alliances renegotiated, and global economic power redistributed. Such widespread change inevitably provoked feelings of insecurity and perhaps frustration among some, as old certainties were fractured and new dispositions arose. The saxophone, with its unusual shape, distinctive timbre and occasionally raucous emissions, provided for many a convenient target upon which antipathetic ridicule could be heaped, thus helping to express and possibly alleviate those underlying fears and insecurities that the rapidly changing times engendered.

Ethnicity, jazz, and the saxophone

The ethnic tensions that so characterised North American culture around the turn of the twentieth century and beyond, particularly though not exclusively in the southern states, inevitably had an impact on the work of saxophonists and the manner in which the instrument itself was disseminated. While patterns can be difficult to identify – not least because the marginalisation of the African-American community during this period has ensured that we have less detailed information than we do for white musicians and their contexts – it seems likely that the saxophone was more common among white musicians and the groups in which they played than among black musicians, at least up to the mid 1910s. This does not necessarily demonstrate musical preference, but is more likely a consequence of the more limited opportunities available to black musicians at the time. Nineteenth-century circuses, for example, employed almost exclusively white musicians, and although from the late 1880s they began to employ blacks, such changes came slowly.[24] In these contexts the saxophone, initially at least, would have been played more by whites than blacks. Examples of saxophone-playing vaudevillians of both colours can be found, but again, until some years into the twentieth century, most of these performers were white. The professional bands such as those of Gilmore and Sousa were also white ensembles; all the saxophonists within them, and the soloists that arose from them, were white.

Inevitably, New Orleans presented a rather different picture. At the turn of the twentieth century the city was a notable melting pot of different ethnic backgrounds and cultural practices: a well-preserved Afro-Caribbean culture in large part sustained by emancipated slaves and their descendents, who were becoming increasingly urbanised as the burgeoning American railway system facilitated travel to urban areas from rural districts; a white European culture, originally predicated upon French and Spanish colonists but swollen by more recent immigration from countries such as Italy and Ireland; and a Creole culture of mixed race Africans and Europeans, whose relationship with the other two groups was complicated by their intermediate and thus frequently marginalised position. Yet, as noted in Chapter 5, the saxophone played only a peripheral role in this New Orleans tradition, and by the time the instrument had become more widely accepted New Orleans jazz was in decline, and hot jazz and early swing were in the ascendency. The exponents of these latter styles took to the instrument in increasing numbers, however, regardless of their ethnic background, and by the mid 1920s the saxophone was an essential component of nearly all bands working in the jazz tradition. And notwithstanding the extensive empirical evidence that both white and black jazz players used the instrument, over time, both inside but especially outside of the United States, the saxophone in general, and the tenor saxophone in particular, became closely identified with African-American jazz musicians.

The association of the saxophone with dark-skinned performers – or whites masquerading as them – considerably predates the jazz tradition. The activities of one of the first saxophone soloists, Soualle, in mid-nineteenth century Europe and beyond, included dressing up in exotic costumes and passing off the instrument as the 'turcophone'. Impresarios such as Jullien and Alfred Mellon also introduced the instrument to their audiences via similarly dressed 'Turkish' performers (see pp. 113–16). And the instrument's involvement with various works of musical exoticism – notably Debussy's *Rapsodie* – could all be seen as further connecting the saxophone with images of non-Caucasian performers and contexts in the mid to late nineteenth century.

Such associations continued in the United States, particularly in relation to the minstrel tradition. Here the stereotypical lampooning of 'negro' caricatures provided the basis for what is now seen as a rather pernicious form of entertainment, notwithstanding its widespread popularity at the time. A core element of minstrelsy was the blacking-up – colouring the face through the use of burnt cork – of white entertainers, who would then act out what were taken to be African-American stereotypes, be it a rural farm worker or a city dandy. (Such caricatures were usually predicated on inaccurate and insulting notions that African Americans were by nature uneducated and thus stupid, and often spoke pretentiously.)[25] The banjo – often seen as connoting rural backwardness – was the quintessential minstrel instrument, and the saxophone was seldom heard in these contexts. However, Tom Brown's later adoption of a black-face persona in the Brown Brothers' shows served to perpetuate the legacy of the minstrel tradition, and the attitudes towards African Americans it denoted, during those years of the 1910s and early 20s when the Brown Brothers achieved their greatest successes (see ill. 59). Thus the later identification of the saxophone in some quarters as an instrument associated with non-white musicians, and specifically African Americans, has a rather more complex and longstanding historical legacy than is initially apparent.

The point is significant because the antipathy demonstrated by whites towards dark-skinned 'others' has a long and inglorious tradition in both Europe and America. In European literature, for example, whether in Dante's *Inferno*, where 'Maometto' – Mohammed – is found in one of the circles closest to Hell, or in Shakespeare's *Othello*, whose eponymous Moorish principal is subject to considerable racist abuse for his love of the white Desdemona, such characters were subliminally viewed as bestial figures, imbued with sexual voracity, physical strength or magical powers. Edward Said describes these preconceptions as 'a form of paranoia', underlining the European fearfulness implicit in such representations of these 'exotic' others.[26] Similarly, many of the so-called 'Coon' songs that were central to the minstrel tradition in North America perpetuated equally negative images of African Americans. The historian James Dormon notes that such songs promoted blacks as 'not only ignorant and indolent, but also devoid of honesty or personal honour, given to drunkenness and gambling, utterly without ambition, sensuous, libidinous, even lascivious [. . .]. Blacks were not only the simple-minded comic buffoons of the minstrel tradition; they were also potentially dangerous.'[27] The saxophone's implicit association with such negative stereotypes inevitably contributed towards those negative constructions that began to surround the instrument itself.

As African Americans became increasingly conscious both of their own cultural heritage and its difference from the dominant Euro-American paradigms, so they rejected and fought against these stereotypes. Jazz in general, and the saxophone in particular, can be seen as cultural mechanisms by which resistance was offered and change sought. Initially, such change was slow in coming, notwithstanding the jazz migrations that encompassed the larger cities of the north as well as those of the south and west United States. Burton W. Peretti notes that 'the spirit of progress and racial pride that animated both the black migration and black music up to the mid-twenties became tempered by a growing awareness of the severe limits placed on black advancement across the nation'.[28] But jazz, notwithstanding its appropriation by certain white bands and the white-dominated recording industry, gradually became recognised as an essentially African-American tradition, one in which 'black players exercised a kind of leadership in America that has rarely been permitted or acknowledged'.[29]

As the tradition evolved so the image of the African-American saxophone player became increasingly iconic of it, both for African Americans themselves and for the world at large. In his 1922 novel *The Beautiful and Damned*, F. Scott Fitzgerald writes of one character that 'he liked "Johnston's Gardens" where they danced, where a tragic negro made yearning, aching music on a saxophone until the garish hall became an enchanted jungle of barbaric rhythms and smoky laughter'.[30] Fitzgerald is of course guilty of perpetuating precisely those exoticist stereotypes – through his 'jungle of barbaric rhythms' – against which writers such as Said would later caution, but his words provide a useful example of the close identification made by many between the saxophone and American dance music and jazz as played by black musicians.

The tenor saxophone, in particular, became seen as a quintessentially African-American instrument. As Ornette Coleman would later put it, 'the tenor is a rhythm instrument, and the best statements Negroes have made, of what their soul is, have been on tenor saxophone. Now you think about it and you'll see I'm right. The tenor's got that thing, that honk, you can get to people with it. Sometimes you can be playing that tenor and I'm telling you, the people want to jump across the rail.'[31] But while Coleman is implicitly looking backwards, recalling an African aesthetic in which rhythm and timbre ('that honk') are prioritised over melody, others viewed the African-American saxophone player as a more forward-looking icon. Donna Cassidy draws attention to a 1934 painting by the African-American painter Aaron Douglas, titled *Aspects of Negro Life: Song of the Towers*, which contains a black saxophonist at its centre.[32] Behind him is silhouetted the Statue of Liberty, whose pose he mimics. Cassidy suggests that the saxophone figure symbolised for Douglas a sense of cultural achievement by African Americans, as well as an association between jazz and democracy as constituent elements of American identity. Such associations were also imbued with, in Douglas's own words, 'anxiety and yearning from the soul of the Negro people',[33] a reference to the continuing marginalisation of African Americans within the wider American community. Thus the picture can be read as representing what W. E. B. Du Bois termed the 'double consciousness' of the African American, through which the individual strove to accommodate a distinctive African heritage within a modern American identity. As Du Bois put it (in 1903), the African American 'simply wishe[d] to make it possible for a man to be both a Negro and an American',[34] and thus the black saxophone player can be seen as symbolic of this struggle to reconcile the heritage of the past with aspirations for the future.

By the 1940s, bop in particular could be seen as a progressive, modern music, created by African-American musicians increasingly confident of their cultural identity. Bop fulfilled the symbolic role of allowing African Americans to develop a more contemporary music, one that rejected primitivist notions and musical frameworks

108. Aaron Douglas's 1934 painting *Aspects of Negro Life: Song of the Towers*, with a black tenor saxophone player foregrounded against the Statue of Liberty.

implied by or derived from the blues. Instead they endeavoured to project through their music a collective identity that was partly founded upon social and cultural resistance to white hegemony, in the increasingly anti-segregationist attitudes that developed from the 1950s onwards.[35] For example, Nicholas Gebhardt reads Charlie Parker's 'chaotic genius' and 'instinctive spontaneity' as evidence of his role as a key figure in asserting the creative power of the individual in the face of post-war American militarism, anti-communism, organised labour and big business, particularly in as much as this contributed to the creation of black self-consciousness.[36]

The African-American saxophone player became increasingly symbolic of twentieth-century American musical culture as a whole. Gebhardt notes the novelist John Clellon Holmes's observation that the 'quintessential American artist was the black jazz musician',[37] but a more recent example is provided by the cover of the 2001 *Garland Encyclopaedia of World Music*, whose third volume, devoted to the United States and Canada, is adorned only by a picture of a black tenor saxophone player (ill. 109).

By the late 1930s, therefore, a complex set of associations had enveloped the saxophone as an American musical symbol. On the one hand it was taken as representative

109. The cover of volume 3 of the *Garland Encyclopaedia of World Music*, with a black tenor saxophone player iconically representing the music of the USA and Canada.

of Euro-American commercial enterprise, modernity and innovation, traits that were reinforced through the increasingly global hegemonic success of American popular music (notwithstanding the latter's dissemination by both white and black musicians); this music was in turn often represented by the saxophone that played such an important role within it. Yet, on the other hand, the saxophone came to be seen as closely identified with an African-American culture that was increasingly self-conscious and aware of its marginalisation within American culture as a whole. Such identification was viewed positively by many African Americans themselves, who felt the instrument's modernist associations connoted a more progressive image than that offered by the banjo and the blues, but negatively by those seeking material with which to support their own rather more racist agendas.

The saxophone and the politics of sound

If images of black saxophone players were celebrated by African Americans as positive expressions of collective identity and social progress, others used them in rather more pernicious ways, aligning themselves with that inglorious tradition of viewing non-whites in general, and Africans in particular, as animalistic, threatening, or potentially destructive. Sir Henry Coward, a renowned chorus master who was one of the most outspoken critics of jazz in England in the 1920s, warned against 'this gigantic black man striding over the world with a banjo in one hand and a saxophone in the other, disintegrating the British Empire'.[38] The English painter John Bulloch Souter exhibited his work *The Breakdown* at the Royal Academy in 1926, which created something of a minor scandal. *The Times* noted that it represented 'a nude lady dancing to the tune of a saxophone played by a nigger who is seated on the head of a fallen colossal statue'. The paper observed that the statue may have been intended to represent Britannia, but that it was 'not true that any civilization worth a cent has succumbed to the saxophone'.[39] The *Monthly Musical Record* observed some months later that the picture was 'a protest against the widespread influence in Western countries of primitive rhythms in music and dancing, which we broadly designate jazz.'[40]

England may have been particularly culpable in this respect, but such opinions were disconcertingly widespread in Europe between the two World Wars, where the legacies of nineteenth-century colonialism, combined in several cases with the rise of fascism, produced attitudes that promoted nationalist orthodoxy while denigrating those construed as political or cultural others. The dark-skinned outsider provided a convenient target for those seeking individuals deemed to exemplify values alien to any given national culture, or scapegoats on which to project collective psychotic anxieties; Africans and African Americans were especially victimised, imputed with negative traits such as backwardness, dirtiness, and/or sexual voracity.

This was certainly true of Germany in the 1920s and 30s, with the rise of National Socialism and the subsequent coming to power of the Nazi party in 1933. Prior to this period the saxophone had made little headway in Germany, and had been little used either by art music composers or in military bands. But in the 1920s, with the arrival of American dance music and indeed a widespread interest throughout Germany with many aspects of American commerce and culture, the saxophone became much more widely known. For Germans this 'American' instrument denoted modernity and innovation, and thus hope for the future of a resurgent German nation, following the defeat and traumatic aftermath of the First World War. German musicians began to learn the instrument, and various German 'jazz' bands were formed, with their leaders, for reasons of commercial expediency, often Americanising their otherwise Germanic names.[41] In truth the music they produced was more an amalgam of folk, light classical and other popular tunes, with a judicious sprinkling of syncopated rhythms and ragtime styles, rather than anything resembling jazz or American dance music proper. However the allusion to the American jazz band was reinforced through the instrumentation of such groups, which included a drum kit and often two or three saxophones, usually scored in close harmony.

More 'authentic' hot dance and swing music, and later jazz, was supplied by visiting American and British groups. But with racism and xenophobia on the increase such bands were often targeted for protests or censorship if they contained black or Jewish musicians. The English bandleader Jack Hylton, who became very successful in Germany in the early 1930s, left behind in Holland the great jazz saxophonist Coleman Hawkins during the band's tour of Germany in 1935, because of the negative publicity and unwelcome attention that would have resulted from his inclusion (although this did not prevent Hylton from receiving later similar attention from the Nazi authorities on account of the Jewish members of his band).[42]

Black musicians were rare in Germany during the 1920s and 30s. Even recordings of black American jazz players such as Louis Armstrong or Duke Ellington appear to have been unavailable in Germany until about 1930.[43] In 1924 the 'Nigger-Jazz-Band' had performed in Berlin, with another eleven-piece all-black group performing there the following year. This latter group was arguably the first 'big band' to be heard in Germany, yet when the Sam Wooding Orchestra played in Germany in 1931, it was the last time an all-black group would be heard there for eighteen years.[44] Nevertheless, Europeans in general and Germans in particular construed jazz as essentially music made by blacks. Although the paucity of black musicians meant this was largely a cultural construct rather than being empirically grounded, it remained a powerful driver of German sentiment and a principal reason for the negativity demonstrated towards jazz and the saxophone by the Nazis and their sympathisers.

The German attribution of negative characteristics to Africans and African Americans had been further reinforced in the early 1920s, after the country's defeat in World War I, through the stationing in certain parts of Germany of black soldiers from French colonies in North Africa and elsewhere. Many Germans saw this as an affront to white German culture, and a threat that was imbued with sexual as well as racial menace. Therefore, as cultural historian Marc A. Weiner eloquently puts it, 'American jazz became the acoustical sign of the transplanted black and thus it could designate both America as the foreign and victorious New World divorced from European traditions and, at the same time, Africa as the purportedly uncivilised Dark Continent from which the feared black was seen to challenge Europe's racial and national hegemony.'[45] And the quintessential signifier of jazz's difference was undoubtedly the instrument with which it was most closely associated: the saxophone.

110.   An expressionist photograph from c. 1926 by Yva (Else Neuländer-Simon) of a black
saxophone player surrounded by white dancers, titled *Charleston.*

Weiner goes on to illustrate how these tropes of 'Otherness' are embedded within
a range of contemporary German literature, notably in Hermann Hesse's famous novel
Steppenwolf (1927). Here the central character, Harry Haller, explores the liberating
world of jazz-infused nightclubs, among which he meets Pablo, a saxophone player.
This 'beautiful exotic demigod of love' of Creole descent devotes himself to hedon-
istic pursuits. At one point in the novel Pablo declares that 'when I take hold of
my mouthpiece and play a lively shimmy [dance], it will give people pleasure. It gets
into their legs and into their blood.'[46] This conflation of signifiers – the saxophone,
the dark-skinned foreigner, the ascendance of physical pleasure over intellectual
control – exemplifies precisely those traits widely identified as characterising black
jazz musicians that contributed to the negative perception of the saxophone in
Germany at this time.

German *Zeitopern* of the twenties and thirties further reinforced such associations in
the minds of the German public, particularly through the eponymous Jonny in
perhaps the most well-known example of the genre, Krenek's opera *Jonny spielt auf*
(1927) (see also pp. 237–8). Although Jonny, a black American bandleader, plays the
violin in the opera, he was associated with the saxophone in a variety of ways: most
obviously through the advertisements and score cover for the work, where he is
pictured with a saxophone, but also because the music associated with him is

characterised by saxophones, and he carries a saxophone in his first entry onto the stage. In Max Brand's *Maschinist Hopkins* (1929) – a work that was immensely popular until the rise of fascism (which it parodies) prevented further performances – a night-club scene includes a song performed by six black musicians, three playing banjo and three on the saxophone. The character of Jonny resurfaces in the operetta *Blume von Hawaii* (1931) by Paul Abraham, a Hungarian Jewish composer whose work in Germany was quickly proscribed once the Nazis took control. At one point in the opera Abraham's Jonny sings, 'Black face, woolly hair, big saxophone. Don't you recognise me from the bar? [. . .] I'm just a Nigger and no white man will give me his hand. But the ladies find me exciting, fascinating!'[47] Such explicit racial and sexual allusions would not have been lost on audiences of the time, and again reinforced the associations between the saxophone and the potentially threatening black.

These images again provoked strong reactions in certain quarters against jazz in general and the saxophone in particular. When in 1927 the Hoch Conservatory in Frankfurt announced that it would offer jazz instruction the following year, on several instruments including the saxophone, it caused a storm of protest. One writer could not believe that such barbarism would be taught in a German institution. Others, including the staunchly conservative but well-known composer Hans Pfitzner, suggested that jazz was implicitly anti-German.[48] Pfitzner had previously made known his views on both jazz and the saxophone in the introduction to a polemical text titled *The New Aesthetic of Musical Impotence* published in 1926. There he had asserted that:

One is astonished by the amazing virtuosity of the saxophonist who, lit by white light, tackles his racing rhythms with sovereign confidence [. . .] a type of art risen into eminence from the café and the variety show: soulless; lacking in depth and content; distant from the realm of the beautiful; distant from our experience; teasing the ears and laughter; sensation; deafness; meanness conveyed by sound. The public is downright fascinated [. . .] by this soulless American machinism that I find unspeakably repellent.[49]

Pfitzner's views were often articulated in extreme language, but they were shared by many who subscribed to the National Socialist ideology. Thus when the Nazis took power in 1933 life became difficult for German saxophonists. Many players sold their instruments or refused to play them. Nazi storm troopers would knock the saxophones out of the mouths of dance-band players, and local SS branches occasionally prohib-ited use of the instrument.[50] The (non-Jewish) virtuoso Sigurd Rascher felt sufficiently threatened that he moved to Denmark in 1933, then to America. Yet the Nazis had a confused relationship with the saxophone. On the one hand they saw it as symbolic of those qualities antithetical to their racist and nationalist agenda, but on the other they were conscious of the instrument's European heritage, its usefulness in military contexts – it was even introduced into the Music Corps of the *Luftwaffe* in 1940[51] – and its commercial importance for certain German instrument manufacturers.

The latter group had suffered particularly after 1933, as people turned away from the saxophone, and they had appealed to the new government for assistance.

Ideological aspirations were thus complicated by economic expediency, and this led to inconsistent and contradictory pronouncements typical of intensely bureaucratic totalitarian regimes. In September 1933 a press release titled 'Rescuing the Honour of the Saxophone' was circulated, which observed that:

> As a result of the petition of May 10, 1933, the Economics Ministry has been in contact with the Reich Administration in order to avoid a boycott of the saxophone, which could result from the ban on so-called Negro music. The Reichs Ministry for Education and Propaganda answered that the saxophone bears no responsibility for Negro music. It is an invention of Adolf Sax, born November 6, 1814, and is mainly used in military music [. . .]. As with all other instruments, one can play good music with the saxophone. A ban on Negro music is no obstacle to continued use of the saxophone. A pertinent newspaper notice to this effect will be released.[52]

The Germanic spelling of Sax's name, rather than the correct French orthography of Adolphe, arose from a propagandist attempt to claim Sax as having German heritage, an endeavour that was quickly found to be unsustainable and that was corrected by later Nazi writers.

But the saxophone continued to function as a symbol of racial difference, and was consistently imputed with negative values. Perhaps the most well-known example of this is the appropriation of the original poster for Krenek's *Jonny spielt auf*, published in 1927, for the *Entartete Musik* exhibition in Düsseldorf in 1938. The description *Entartete Musik*, or 'Degenerate Music', was coined following the widespread success of the *Entartete Kunst* (Degenerate Art) exhibition the previous year, and this musical imitation was organised largely at the behest of a particular individual, Hans Severus Ziegler. It comprised portraits of various composers, including Schoenberg, Webern, Hindemith, Krenek and Weill, accompanied by derogatory slogans that attacked the character and racial origin of those on display; scores and theoretical treatises by the same composers were similarly disparaged. In parallel with the exhibition Ziegler published an inflammatory pamphlet designed to further discredit those involved. The cover for this comprised a modified version of the cover of the piano reduction of Krenek's opera. Whereas the original featured a slightly comical blackface actor 'playing' a 'saxophone' and adorned with a large flower on his lapel, now a 'negro' caricature was employed, again playing the saxophone, but with the flower replaced – somewhat incongruously – by a Jewish six-pointed star, an indication of the Nazi's ongoing but largely unsuccessful attempts to align jazz not only with African Americans but with Jews also.

This conflation of racist signifiers in the *Entartete Musik* image – the black performer, the Jewish star, the saxophone – appears now faintly absurd, although its message would have been clear to Ziegler's contemporaries, who would have understood the deeper meanings implied by its cartoon-like caricature. Although not officially sanctioned by the Nazi Propaganda Ministry, the picture would have reinforced for many the image of the saxophone as a disreputable and potentially threatening instrument, if found in the wrong hands.

111.   *Left:* Poster for the 1938 *Entartete Musik* exhibition, defaming various German-Jewish composers. *Right:* The sheet music cover for 'Leb wohl mein Schatz', the 'jazziest' aria in Krenek's *Jonny spielt auf,* published in 1927, the year of the opera's premiere. The latter image demonstrates the inspiration for the former.

The original 1938 *Entartete Musik* exhibition was reconstructed in 1988 in Düsseldorf, as an example of the manner in which music and musicians can become embroiled in political ideologies.[53] The original image was also reproduced as part of the advertisement for this reconstruction, although it was now set against a silhouette of the head of the composer Anton Bruckner, a Nazi favourite. Thus another layer of meaning accrues to the saxophone in this context. Now rehabilitated in German culture, the instrument signifies a newly invigorated Germany. The paradoxical juxtaposition of the saxophone, the racist caricature and the image of the quintessentially Austro-German composer Bruckner is deeply suggestive of a country endeavouring to reconcile its troubled recent past with its less contentious heritage as significant force in European musical culture, as it looks towards an increasingly multicultural future.

Another aspect of the saxophone that troubled several Nazi writers was the instrument's role in jazz improvisation. One commentator observed, for example, that 'the "breaking" of the melody, which [. . .] is generally deliberate, being explained as "variation on the given theme," is unnecessary'. Another noted that 'continuous improvisation on the part of individual artists is no longer permitted. It should be the aim of the modern saxophonist to play the written notes as if he were improvising.'[54] Such spontaneity and creative individuality sat uncomfortably with a Nazi ideology in which subservience to the party and collective discipline were highly valued. Certainly this appears to have been the case in another totalitarian regime that also persecuted the saxophone and its players, the Soviet Union under Stalin in the 1950s and 60s.

In some ways the position of the saxophone and jazz in the Soviet Union mirrors that of Nazi Germany. What was regarded as 'degenerate' under the Nazis was seen as 'decadent' by the Soviets. The principles of spontaneity, physicality and individualism that jazz appeared to promote were just as anathema to a repressive Communist ideology as they were to National Socialism. And the iconic association of jazz with capitalist values and the commercial expansion of the United States served only to emphasise cultural difference. Again the saxophone was held to be the ultimate symbol of jazz values; as the writer Frederick Starr puts it, for the Soviet authorities 'the saxophone *was* jazz, its wail of abandon symbolising the free style of life with which jazz was associated.'[55]

Initially the instrument was not as widespread in the Soviet Union as it was in Europe. Although dance music and what was construed as jazz were heard in Russia from the early 1920s, the dissemination of these styles was impeded by a lack of available instruments. One player later recalled that in 1931 there were only three saxophonists in Moscow and that he had himself needed to travel to Kiev to purchase an old military-band instrument at an inflated price. The shortage of available instruments continued for decades. Even as late as 1966 an aspiring Siberian player had travelled into central Asia to acquire a good instrument (made by Selmer) from a village bandsman near Tashkent, into whose hands it had somehow fallen.[56]

However, the relative difficulty in procuring instruments and the slow dissemination of the music itself appear not to have dampened the Soviet authorities' persecution of jazz and those who played it. In 1929, when Krenek's *Jonny spielt auf* was performed in Moscow, proletarian ideologues succeeded in closing the show and then launched a campaign to ban saxophones from the Soviet Union. Although this first attempt to proscribe the saxophone was unsuccessful, when the campaign against jazz and the saxophone became particularly acute in the Stalinist purges after World War II a second attempt did briefly succeed.[57] Many jazz and light-music players were arrested, imprisoned or exiled. Saxophonists, obviously identified as specialising in the instrument most closely associated with the officially despised jazz tradition, were particularly persecuted. In 1949–50 all the saxophonists in the Radio Committee Orchestra were summarily fired. On a particular day in 1949, every saxophonist in Moscow was ordered to bring his instrument and identity card to the office of the State Variety Music Agency. Their instruments were confiscated, even though in many cases they had been imported and made available to the musicians by the government itself. Identity cards were amended to remove all references to the saxophone. One player was miraculously transformed into a bassoonist, despite never having held a bassoon. Another suddenly became an oboist. Saxophone tuition in conservatories was halted, and even classical works containing the instrument, such as Prokofiev's *Lieutenant Kijé*, were banned.[58]

The determined persecution of jazz and its players by the Soviet authorities had the unintended effect of transforming them into something resembling cultural martyrs;

jazz became a symbol of resistance and non-conformity in the face of the State's heavy-handed authoritarianism. By association, the saxophone also became a symbol of such resistance and of what was taken to be an ideologically dangerous individualism that was otherwise frequently circumscribed. It is noticeable that after Stalin's death in 1953, and the cultural thaw that emerged under Khrushchev, Soviet jazz players began to develop their improvisation skills much more extensively than previously; not only because they could now engage with the improvisation-dependent styles such as bop that had emerged in the past decades and from which they had been shielded, but also because they were able to make statements of individual creative freedom that they felt they had been long denied. From the late 1950s onwards the saxophone became increasingly unfettered, and although jazz and the saxophone were not to achieve the same freedoms in Russia as in the West until the post-communist era, the instrument would never again be proscribed as it was in Stalin's time.

The gendered saxophone

Another aspect of the symbolic nature of musical instruments lies in their capacity to be endowed with gendered meanings. This gendering of instruments may arise in several ways: from the social practice of music-making, that is, whether an instrument is played by or seen as more appropriate for men or women; from the morphology of the instrument and the degree to which it may be taken to represent male or female bodies; or through the iconographic representation of the instrument and the manner and contexts in which it is depicted. The saxophone appears to be particularly rich in several of these respects.

With regard to the social practice of music-making, there is little evidence of women playing the saxophone in nineteenth-century Europe. Given that the instrument was used largely by the military, and also given the importance attached by Victorian society to a type of feminine domesticity in which the piano played the central role, it seems very unlikely that the saxophone was played much by women at this time. Adolphe Sax's brother, Alphonse, promoted a group of female brass players in the 1860s, partly on the grounds that playing brass instruments would be good for their health; but this group appears not to have included saxophones. There were distinct social prejudices against women playing wind instruments at this time: an attempt to organise an all-female orchestra in Vienna, for example, often needed male players to complete the wind and brass sections.[59] Alphonse Sax was himself the subject of a certain amount of ridicule for his attempts to promote female brass players, as demonstrated in an image from *Le Boulevard* in 1862 in which he is dressed as a ballerina, but with a beard, moustache and breasts, stockily built and carrying a saxhorn.[60] The satirical image relies in part for its impact on what was taken at the time to be a faintly ridiculous notion that women might play brasswind instruments. Such attitudes towards women playing the saxophone appear to have continued in Europe, and particularly France, for some considerable time. It is noticeable that the roll call of Marcel Mule's saxophone classes at the Paris Conservatoire between 1942 and 1967 contains only two female names, neither of which appears to be French.[61]

112. An 1862 caricature of Alphonse Sax (Adolphe's brother), arising from his aspirations to encourage women to play brasswind instruments.

But the identification of the saxophone as an instrument predominantly for male use was not continued once it had arrived in the United States, where female saxophonists appear to have been long established. The examples of Louise Linden and Bessie Meeklens, both nineteenth-century female students of E. A. Lefebre, have already been noted. Similarly, Elise Hall's work as a soloist and commissioner of works for the instrument, while unusual for its time, is another example of more widespread acceptance of the saxophone's suitability for female performers (notwithstanding the observation in 1905 by one of her contemporaries that on one occasion she had 'played the saxophone solo with a skill fairly astounding to those who appreciate the fact that this is essentially a masculine instrument').[62] Hall was originally advised by her doctor (and husband) to take up the saxophone to improve her lungs after illness, a fact that provides a curious historical resonance with Alphonse Sax's similar exhortations some 40 years earlier.

Nevertheless, professional musical activity in the United States in the late nineteenth and early twentieth centuries remained largely male dominated, and in general women on both sides of the colour divide were discouraged from playing instruments conventionally seen as masculine. As Mario A. Charles notes in his biography of jazz trumpeter Valada Snow, in the 1920s 'society discouraged ladies from playing masculine instruments such as the trombone, trumpet, cornet, saxophone, or any other wind instrument'.[63] This sense of discouragement, and of the saxophone being seen as an inappropriate instrument for women, is underlined by an article in the jazz magazine *Downbeat*, written as late as 1951, in which the wife of a jazz player of the time observes that 'girls who want to be musicians should stick to instruments such as piano, violin, harp, or even accordion – any instrument that the playing of which doesn't detract from their feminine appeal'.[64] When Bert Etta Davis auditioned for the famed Prairie View Collegians in 1940, in competition with a long list of male players, she was prevented from taking the place awarded to her not by the male bandleader or any dissatisfied male saxophonist, but by the College's Dean of Women, who regarded the participation of a woman student in such a context as unacceptable.[65] Women who played instruments normally ascribed to men not only risked not being taken seriously, but also of being seen as sexually profligate.[66] Yet it is clear that there were more women playing saxophone in the early decades of the twentieth century than were playing trumpet, trombone or drums, and the instrument – because of its obvious adoption by members of both sexes – already begins to demonstrate at this time a rather more ambiguous set of gender associations.

This was particularly true in the more utilitarian contexts of the circus bands and vaudeville, where the social niceties of appropriate female behaviour were often mitigated by the need to earn a living in a manner that required public display; women working on stage, or in allied contexts, were thus viewed more negatively than their counterparts elsewhere. Nevertheless, such contexts provided opportunities for many women to play the saxophone. An engaging picture of the women in the Billy Young family band from some time in the early twentieth century shows a youthful Lester Young seated in front of his sister Irma – who would go on to be a fine jazz soloist in her own right – with their mother and two aunts, all holding saxophones (see ill. 113).

During the saxophone craze of the 1910s and 20s all-female saxophone quartets such as the Darling Four and the Schuster Sisters became increasingly common, as, eventually, did larger troupes of female saxophone players, such as the one put together by Rudy Wiedoeft in 1928 to support his own vaudeville show, which toured under the headline of his 'Saxophobia Idea'. Undoubtedly the novelty of such all-female groups further enhanced the novelty value of the saxophone itself. In one sense these groups might be taken as evidence of female musical independence, and it is certainly true that such ensembles provided outlets for female musicians at a time when professional musical performance was still very male dominated. But many, such as Wiedoeft's troupe or Burt Earle's 'Twenty Saxophone Girls' (see ill. 61) were clearly under the direction of those men who were controlling the vaudeville and other circuits in which they worked, and were being used to provide a mix of glamour and novelty, rather than demonstrating genuine female emancipation.

Over the same time scale all-female dance and swing bands began to emerge, partly in response to the difficulty women experienced in gaining entry to the more widespread male-dominated ensembles. This created both opportunity and demand for professional female saxophone players. While some of these bands contained skilful

113. The Young family band in the mid-1910s, with Irma Young seated just above Lester. Their mother stands in the middle, with two cousins on either side.

players and produced good music, others were put together at the behest of promoters and agents keen to cash in on their novelty value and their looks, what Linda Dahl describes as a 'Look, Ma, no hands' approach.[67] The Ingenues provide an example of the first type. A group of between fifteen and twenty versatile instrumentalists, they were successful enough to have made a short Vitaphone film in 1928, *The Band Beautiful*, a title doubtless intended to allude to their photogenic qualities. But these were very competent musicians, who each doubled on between five to seven instruments, covering not only the normal swing band instrumentation, but also accordions, banjos, strings, bassoon, percussion and more besides. A 1935 publicity photograph shows the Ingenues somewhat incongruously serenading a lasso-wielding cowboy on the steps of San Diego's Fine Arts Gallery, their matching hairstyles nicely offset by the full complement of saxophones on display (see ill. 114).

Female musicians often achieved higher profiles – and were offered more work – during the Second World War, when the military duties of men overseas allowed more opportunities for the women left behind. Perhaps the best known all-female band was The International Sweethearts of Rhythm, formed in 1939 in Mississippi, with an ethnically diverse line-up – hence the 'International' in their title – that continued in

114. The Ingenues and a cowboy in San Diego, 1935.

various permutations until the mid 1950s, and with a saxophone section comprising the normal swing band disposition of 2A/2T/B.

The masculine domination of jazz, and the largely male-oriented representation of it, has tended to marginalise the activities of female jazz soloists, and although these were not common in the early jazz years, by the 1980s such soloists and groups were increasingly widespread. And in the 1990s the first international female saxophone superstar emerged: Candy Dulfer's polished and popular formula of 'smooth' jazz found a worldwide audience; perhaps inevitably, her photogenic looks have been capitalised on by various record companies to promote her work in a similar manner to the promotion of female saxophonists of earlier years (see ill. 115).

Today the saxophone – at least in the West – appears to be largely gender-neutral in terms of the social practice of music-making, and various studies done by psychologists on the sexual stereotyping of particular instruments, for example, reinforce this view. One 1978 study, undertaken in North Carolina, suggested that the saxophone, along with the cello, was broadly conceived as gender neutral both by young children, in terms of their perceptions of the sound of the instrument, and by their parents, in terms of their aspirations for what instruments they might wish their child to play.[68] Similarly, a 2005 study of school music tuition across the United Kingdom showed that whereas the flute and clarinet were consistently more popular among girls, and the trumpet more popular among boys, the saxophone was evenly divided among the

115.   Candy Dulfer and her saxophone in a tiger-ish pose.

two sexes, at all school levels, again suggesting it to be perceived as largely gender-neutral in the educational context.[69]

The shape of musical instruments also allows them to be endowed with gendered characteristics. Wind and brass instruments such as flutes or trumpets are frequently seen as male because of their phallic associations, whereas instruments such as the violin or harp might be conceived as female, both on account of their feminine, curvaceous shape and the 'sweeter' sounds they are deemed to produce. In the West these distinctions can be traced back to ancient Greece, where the *aulos* or double reedpipe was conceived by writers such as Plato and Aristotle as being devoted to the pursuit of pleasure, and wind instruments were identified as being played by satyrs. By contrast, the *kythara* or lyre – a form of harp – was associated with harmonious contemplation and moderation. Thus the priapic Dionysian ecstasy of wind instruments was set against the Apollonian restraint represented by the strings. This distinction was continued through the Middle Ages and beyond when, for example, the bagpipes were often symbolically taken in art and literature to represent human depravation in general and sexual lust in particular. Such associations persist today, as demonstrated by the semantic overlap in the English language between the use of the word 'horn' to describe a range of wind instruments such as trumpets, trombones and saxophones, and the colloquial use of the term 'horny' to describe sexual arousal.

As a wind instrument one might expect the saxophone to be characterised as essentially masculine, with the soprano saxophone, in particular, seen as a fundamentally phallic symbol like the trumpet. Certainly the instrument can be played in such a way as to emphasise its phallic associations, as demonstrated by the theatrical performance postures of certain 'honkers and screamers', such as Big Jay McNeely, in the 1950s (see ill. 116). The sexual suggestiveness is enhanced by the saxophone being played between the legs – rather than to the side of the body – not dissimilar to the manner in which Jimi Hendrix would later use the electric guitar.

But from another perspective the saxophone can also be seen as something of an ambiguous or hermaphrodite instrument, since the integral curves of the S-shaped models allude to more feminine characteristics – not unlike the curves of the violin family. Furthermore, the bell end, with its flared opening held at the level of the hips and parallel to the groin, appears more suggestive of female genitalia than the male phallus, adding yet another layer of ambiguity. The German sociologist Theodor Adorno also viewed the saxophone as being sexually ambivalent, although in his view this ambiguity arose because the saxophone was made of metal but played like a woodwind instrument, and was thus less easily construed as either masculine or feminine.[70]

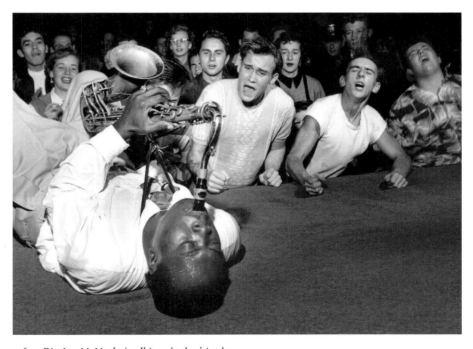

116. Big Jay McNeely 'walking the bar' in the 1950s.

117.   Berlin showgirls in 1927.

These gender connotations have long been reinforced through iconographic representation. The adroit but often gratuitous inclusion of the instrument in images
designed to be sexually stimulating appears frequently to use the saxophone to allude
to feminine physiology or, at least, to sexually provocative availability. As early as the
1920s such suggestiveness could be quite obvious, as is the case with the backdrop to
the 1927 Berlin showgirls shown in ill.117 (it seems likely that this image has some
connection with Krenek's *Jonny spielt auf*, premiered that year). The sole blackface male
actor on stage, and the defensive gesture of the female dancer with her faux saxophone, also resonate with points made above in relation to the supposed sexual threat
of the black saxophone player.
     Such images can be found in many contexts. Illustration 118 shows a British
cigarette card from the late 1930s or early 40s. The sexual suggestiveness of the
young woman is reinforced through her association with the saxophone and, by
implication, its salacious reputation. Perched on top of her 'rock', 'Valerie' entices the
viewer towards her with the promise of her beguiling saxophone playing; her imagined saxophone sound functions as a sexual invitation, just as the singing sirens of
ancient Greek myths lured sailors towards them. The model, whose sexually provocative embouchure would appear to demonstrate little previous familiarity on her
part with the instrument, is described on the reverse of the card as being a member
of The Revudeville Girls. These were a part of the mildly licentious show put on
at the Windmill Theatre London in the 1930s and 40s – captured in the film
Mrs Henderson Presents (2005) – in which nude actresses appeared as statues on
stage. The accompanying text on the reverse of the card reinforces the model's
suggestive pose.

118. 'Valerie', a member of London's Windmill Theatre Revudeville Girls.

The text on the reverse of the card states:

> Here we see 'Valerie', the youngest member of the Revudeville show-girls appearing at the famous Windmill Theatre in London, her own birthplace. 'Valerie' is only 16 years old, is dark-haired with merry dark eyes, and has a slender, beautifully proportioned figure. She is very fond of outdoor pursuits, particularly of riding.

By the 1970s the association between the saxophone and sex was increasingly explicit, as evidenced, for example, by the work of Italian saxophone players Gil Ventura and Fausto Papetti (1923–99). Both players released numerous albums of cover versions of well-known songs, arranged in an 'easy listening' style that was very fashionable at the time. In both cases their album covers were characterised by artfully photographed but overt female nudity; occasionally the saxophone itself would be shown, but more often than not the album design would simply feature the word 'sax' prominently, the lexical substitution requiring very little decoding on the part of the potential purchaser (see ill. 119).

In our now more permissive times this symbolic reinforcement of sexual suggestiveness through the inclusion of a saxophone is commonplace. Numerous images on CDs, television or the internet, or adverts for products unrelated to music, incorporate attractive and sometimes scantily-clad women, reinforcing the implicit correlation between the image of the saxophone and sexual allure. Even the promotional video for Candy Dulfer's punningly titled album *Saxuality* (1990) explicitly played on this theme, interspersing images of Dulfer and her band with clips of couples in passionate embraces, underscored by lines such as 'Everybody needs a little bit – S-A-X'.

That moanin' saxophone sound

Ultimately it is perhaps the changing sounds of the saxophone that provide its most powerful symbolic attributes. The manner in which the instrument's sound can be manipulated, its rich overtone spectrum and its peculiarly vocal qualities have been recurring themes in this book, and it is appropriate to conclude with some further thoughts on this particularly nebulous area.

Although music is obviously central to musicology, any discussion on the nature of sound itself is often challenging, in part because we have no dedicated lexicon to describe sound and must frequently resort to metaphors. Musical notation is very poor at communicating information about timbre – whereas it is quite good at

119. A typically suggestive Gil Ventura LP cover from 1974.

communicating information about pitch and rhythm – which means that discussions about the nature of musical sound are further marginalised in musicological discourse. This disadvantages the saxophone, since it means that its most fundamental and distinctive attribute lies beyond those areas that scholars most frequently discuss.

Yet musical timbre is particularly suggestive, and can be meaningful in ways that may lie beyond, or contradict, those meanings construed upon specific melodic or rhythmic patterns. Vocal timbre is especially meaningful. The sociologist John Shepherd, for example, has suggested that different vocal timbres can be read as projecting different gender locations or images, with the rasping tones of overtly masculine 'cock rock' clearly distinguishable from the 'rich, resonating sound' of the 'woman as nurturer', or the more hard-edged female head tones of the 'woman as sex object'.[71] Shepherd also characterises the ideology underlying Western art music as insisting on a 'standardised purity (which students are carefully taught to achieve) [and which] has in turn resulted in the unexamined assumption that timbre in "classical" music is a neutral and largely unimportant element, having little to do with the expressive quality of the music'.[72] Shepherd goes on to reject this assumption.

Given the vocal nature of the saxophone sound, therefore, it is unsurprising that so much significance should be attached to it, and much of what Shepherd writes about vocal timbre could be mapped onto the saxophone. The timbres of heavy rock music, characterised not only by vocal rasp but also by distorted guitar sounds, have been emulated by saxophone players in these contexts, who have similarly sought to develop edgy, piercing, saxophone sounds. While this undoubtedly arises partly from sonic expediency – endeavouring to complement or compete with the similar sounds of fellow musicians – it can also be seen as projecting an essentially masculine, penetrating, aggressive image, one which may be further reinforced by the sexually suggestive nature of the saxophone shape, as noted above, and the performance gestures of the players.

Other types of sound could be subject to different interpretations. Perhaps the softer, smoother 'cool' sounds of players such as Paul Desmond or Gerry Mulligan could be heard as connoting a sense of support or security, of accommodation rather than conquest; these warmer, more resonant sounds resemble a deeper '(wo)man as comforter' ideal, one which projects the more feminine attributes of the saxophone's hermaphrodite personality. The classical saxophone sound does indeed generally demand purity, a disassociation from the edgier sounds of the instrument in other contexts, and one which more easily conforms to those notions of transparency and clarity that frequently prevail in Western art music. Here the instrument leaves behind its populist associations by eschewing those timbres that characterise its participation elsewhere. As Shepherd rightly asserts, this more neutral tone is not entirely devoid of timbral connotations; it signals conformity or 'legitimacy', an aspiration to be accepted as part of the longstanding tradition of classical music.

Another aspect of tonal variation relates to the different qualities of sound produced by early African-American saxophone players when compared with their white counterparts. Jazz players such as Frankie Trumbauer, Rudy Wiedoeft and Jimmy Dorsey played in the 1920s and 30s with a smooth, clean and focussed sound, derived in part from their classical training and their efforts to establish the saxophone as a serious instrument. Wiedoeft went as far in his method to assert the need for a 'beautiful, even, clear tone'.[73] However, African-American players such as Sidney Bechet and (especially) Coleman Hawkins developed performance aesthetics that consciously fostered grittier, rougher saxophone sounds. This trend was later taken further in the so-called 'honking and screaming' of the southern rhythm-and-blues players such as Illinois Jacquet and Big Jay McNeely.

These more raucous, 'dirtier' saxophone sounds produced by black players might be taken as evidence of an African musical aesthetic resurfacing in African-American saxophone playing. In African music timbral and textural variety are arguably more significant as structural devices than in the Euro-American traditions. Doug Miller suggests that the popularity of the saxophone in African-American popular music arose because 'as an instrument it appeared to offer black musicians the ability to sustain African musical concepts in the areas of sound quality, technique and delivery style'.[74] The importance of vocalisation in African music could also be transferred, albeit in a restricted sense, to the saxophone. Thus the instrument functioned as an extension of African oral tradition and 'came to substitute for and/or complement the voice in Afro-American musical performance'.[75] Clyde Taylor, writing in 1982, similarly observes that the 'hums, chants and sighs [...] followed by screams and piercing keening, roars, hollering, screeches, and then pants, and lyrical obbligatos' of certain black jazz vocal performers represented the 'fundamental cries of human existence. These are expressive sounds that instruments can only imperfectly emulate [...] most noticeably in the growling, screeching saxophones of the last thirty years'.[76] For both writers, therefore, the saxophone's vocal qualities, as used by black jazz performers, reinforce a musical association with particular African performance aesthetics. Such readings also resonate with Henry Louis Gates's notion of 'Signifyin(g)'. Gates, drawing on African-American literature, argues that whereas white writers signify objects or ideas through their use of signs, black writers focus attention on the sound of a text rather than just its literal meaning. 'Signifyin(g)' therefore explains how African-American artists confront culturally dominant aesthetic forms while simultaneously participating in those modes of artistic creation by which such forms are produced.[77] Transplanted to the world of hot dance music and swing, the characteristic 'gritty' saxophone sound produced by early black players can be read as articulating difference through 'signifyin(g)' upon the cleaner, more transparent sounds made by those white players working in the same domains, but who were drawing at least in part on traditional European sound ideals.

The connection with the human voice is perhaps most closely realised in what is variously termed the saxophone 'wail' or 'moan', a kind of portamento achieved through embouchure manipulation and sometimes a sliding effect with the saxophone keys. Strictly speaking this is an aspect of pitch manipulation rather than timbre, but combined with timbral variation this idiomatic flexibility provokes frequent comparisons with the modulations of the human voice, and makes the saxophone for many an especially evocative instrument. The technique was evidently a component of saxophone performance from early in the twentieth century, and probably evolved from the comedic requirements of circus and vaudeville in the United States. By the mid 1910s it was a key part of the saxophone's sonic identity, as demonstrated in numerous recordings. 'That Moaning Saxophone Rag', for example, was the first major hit for the Brown Brothers in 1914 and undoubtedly cemented the relationship between the saxophone and 'moaning' in the eyes and ears of many (see ill. 120). In 1915 Euday Louis Bowman composed his famous 'Twelfth Street Rag' which contains the line 'when the slide trombone and the moaning saxophone begin to play', thus conflating two obviously similar sounds. And the lyrics of Earl Carroll's 1916 song 'When you hear Jackson moan on his saxophone' went on to assert that 'there's something in the tone that makes you feel at home', a sentiment that was not necessarily shared by all during the subsequent saxophone craze, when 'moaning' and other novelty effects became too prevalent for some tastes. But by the end of that decade the notion that the saxophone was an instrument that moaned was very widely held.

'Moaning' in English has a broader semantic field than is first apparent. When we moan we may indulge only in verbal behaviour: moaning about how we are treated, or how bad the weather is. But intense moaning is often also accompanied by physical behaviour. Moaning, groaning, are frequently reinforced by drooping shoulders, facial gestures, and other non-verbal, embodied behaviour that emphasises our sense of grievance or discontent. This point is significant because describing the saxophone as moaning – or wailing – implicitly alludes to this sense of physicality; the instrument's sound becomes symbolic of physical behaviour, not just a conduit for musical interaction. Moaning and wailing are rather animal (particularly the human animal) types of sound. Moaning connotes embodiment, and thus there is a sense in which the saxophone, almost anthropomorphically, is construed as having a physical presence precisely because it moans.

120. Sheet music cover of 'That Moaning Saxophone Rag' by the Brown Brothers, from 1913.

However, as with the caricatures of African Americans noted previously, this unconscious association of the saxophone with basic, instinctive human traits, particularly those pertaining to physicality and sensuality, were conceived as negative attributes in the minds of some in the 1920s. Among the early indignant opposition to jazz and dance music, the instrument's ability to moan was often perceived to be an unwelcome if widespread characteristic. The point was made explicitly by one commentator in 1921 who observed that 'those moaning saxophones [. . .] and the rest of the instruments with their broken, jerky rhythm make a purely sensual appeal [. . .]. Jazz is the very foundation of salacious dancing.'[78] The conflation of quasi-human moaning and potentially destabilising physicality could not be clearer.

As the Blues tradition became more widely recognised so the saxophone wail was invested with different meanings. The instrument was already increasingly associated with African Americans, and so the wail of the Blues began to overlap with the wail of the saxophone. But this was a wail of pain and resentment, part of the protest of African Americans at their social marginalisation and tragic history, the 'anxiety and yearning from the soul of the Negro people' that Aaron Douglas had described (see p. 318). F. Scott Fitzgerald again neatly encapsulates this imagery in his 1925 novel *The Great Gatsby*, in which he writes that 'all night the saxophones wailed the hopeless comment of the Beal Street Blues'.[79] The saxophone was not initially part of that curious melange of work hollers, prison songs and traditional west African music from which the Blues tradition may have evolved. But once both the instrument and the genre became seen as musical icons of African-American culture, so the moaning of one became inextricably entwined with the wailing of the other. It is both ironic and yet somehow appropriate that a sound that began as a comedic effect in, among other places, blackface minstrelsy, should become transplanted and subsequently perceived as an expression of pain and rage against precisely those caricatures and lampoons that such minstrelsy sought to promote.

Although moaning and wailing are both highly emotive and embodied actions, they are not only associated with pain or yearning. Ecstatic moaning, of the kind that accompanies physical intimacy and particularly lovemaking, is also a deeply sugges-tive sound that has been taken by many often to be connoted by the saxophone. This association between the sound of the saxophone and the sexual act – reinforced by the quasi-homophonic relationship between the words 'sax' and 'sex' – is both wide-spread and long established. Nowhere is this association more explicit than in film and television, where an on-screen sexual encounter, or the implication of one taking place off-screen, is almost inevitably underscored by a saxophone solo, particularly one involving a saxophone moan. The conductor and pianist André Previn, who had an extensive early career as a film music composer, is reputed to have observed that 'if I hear another slurping alto saxophone solo in a bedroom scene I'm going to throw up'.[80]

A few examples will suffice to demonstrate the ubiquitous nature of this approach to film scoring (although attentive listening to many film or television scores would reveal countless others): in the film *Baby Face*, as early as 1933, Barbara Stanwyck plays a women from a somewhat sordid background who sleeps her way to wealth and security in a Wall Street bank. Each rise through the business hierarchy, and hence corporate lover, is accompanied by a particular rising saxophone phrase. In 1951 America's Catholic Legion of Decency (a group formed to provide moral comment on film content) famously objected to Elia Kazan's film adaptation of Tennessee Williams's play *A Streetcar Named Desire*. A scene in which the husband Stanley (played by Marlon Brando) carries his wife (Kim Hunter) towards their bedroom after a brutal argument was originally underscored by composer Alex North with a saxophone solo. But the scene offended the Legion, who declared it to be a violation of common decency. Conscious of the damage their condemnation might cause at the box office, various cuts were made to the film. But in this particular scene, the League was placated when North altered the scoring, changing the saxophone cue to one played by the French horn; the visual images remained unchanged. When the film was released on DVD in 1993 the original saxophone cue was reinstated.[81] *Casino Royale*, the 1967 James Bond spoof, has both Peter Sellers and David Niven in the Bond role, and an improbable number of beautiful women parading on screen, many supposedly on their way to Bond's bedroom; the score is thus replete with moaning saxophone solos. More recently the film *Mrs Henderson Presents* (2005) told the story of London's Windmill Theatre in the 1930s and 40s. The theatre's owner, Mrs Henderson, caused some trembling of the stiff upper lips of the British Establishment by having naked females as part of the theatre's revue (hence the attraction of 'Valerie' in ill. 118). In the film the moment when the stage actresses are first required to disrobe in rehearsals is again underscored by a prominent saxophone solo. Nor is this association between the moaning saxophone and the sexual act confined to Hollywood. In India, Bollywood films have also long borrowed this Hollywood cliché in their scores, and used a bluesy saxophone cue to accompany a female character who is deemed to be in some way unvirtuous.[82]

The association between sex and the saxophone goes beyond the latter's 'moaning' qualities, however, and for some it is the very timbre of the instrument that connotes sexual engagement. The following passage from Ernest Ansermat's 1961 book *Les Fondements de la musique dans la conscience humaine* explicitly illustrates this connection:

> The only new instrument which has come into the family since the classic era is the saxophone, which even then appears only occasionally due to the exaggerated 'affective' quality of its timbre. The sensual and phallic nature of this timbre predestined the saxophone to the music of pleasure: in jazz, the melody of the tenor-saxophone spans the syncopations without faltering, as the phallus spans the spasms of the coitus, and with the same physical reality.[83]

Timbral associations, like much else in music, are socially constructed. Timbres that are taken as meaningful in one context may be understood very differently in another. Nevertheless, it is clear that certain saxophone timbres are now widely taken to connote ideas about sexual activity. Yet one wonders what particular saxophone sound Ansermet had in mind when he wrote these words, since, as observed frequently here, it is the saxophone's essential quality as a sonic chameleon, and its ability to produce a wide range of timbres, that characterise the instrument. Discovering which particular saxophone timbres might be especially construed as sexually provocative – breathy, or rasping, or edgy? – might provide an interesting avenue for further research.

It is perhaps this difficulty in establishing the true identity of the saxophone as a musical instrument that continues to underpin our fascination with it. And this fascination is enhanced by the saxophone's ongoing image as slightly rebellious, non-conformist and unconventional, not unlike the electric guitar. Such non-conformism might, even now, be taken as an implicit threat to the established musical order, since the instrument's propensity to bend notes, to depart from musical conventions, can be read as signifying a break with such conventions. If, as some have argued, the five-line musical stave and the system of highly rationalised functional tonality that it represents can be read as codifying the normal social relations of industrialised Western society,[84] then it might equally be suggested that the bending of notes and the unstable saxophone wail are threatening precisely because they confront this comfortable, rationalised musical existence. The saxophone is potentially destabilising because it subverts and challenges the musical frameworks underpinning those contexts in which it is most usually found. This is in addition to the quasi-human properties the instrument implicitly exudes through the voice-like qualities of its rich sound spectrum. The sound of the saxophone remains both immediately identifiable and, simultaneously, unclassifiable, because of the variety of timbres it can produce and the wide range of contexts in which it is found. Ultimately, as an ambiguous hybrid between the woodwind and brass families, the instrument resists comfortable accommodation within even the most fundamental categories through which we conceptualise music in Western culture, again challenging those basic taxonomies we use to understand our world.

The saxophone, one of the most successful and widely recognised musical symbols of the twentieth century and beyond, remains both a profoundly beguiling yet also disconcerting musical instrument.

Appendix
Adolphe Sax's 1846 saxophone patent

Specification filed in support of the application for a patent of fifteen years by Mr Antoine Joseph (called Adolphe) Sax, manufacturer of musical instruments living in Paris at rue neuve St Georges no. 10, address for service care of M Perpigna, lawyer, 10 rue neuve St Augustin, for a new System of Wind Instruments called Saxophones.

Explanation

One knows that, in general, wind instruments are either too loud or too soft in sonority. It is particularly in the basses where one or the other of these faults is most appreciable. The ophicleide, for example, which reinforces the trombones, produces a sound by nature so disagreeable that one is obliged to banish it from closed rooms, for lack of being able to modify the timbre. The bassoon, on the contrary, makes a sound so feeble that one cannot use it except to fill out the accompaniment. And for particular loud orchestration effects it is perfectly useless. Note that this last instrument is the only one which blends with string instruments.

It is only the brasswind instruments that give the most satisfying effect in the open air. Also a wind group composed of these instruments is the only orchestral combination that has the power to be used in such circumstances.

As for string instruments, everybody knows that, in the open air, their effect is useless because of the feebleness of their sound. This makes them nearly impossible to use in such conditions.

Struck by these various drawbacks, I have sought a way to remedy this by creating an instrument which, by the character of its voice, can blend with string instruments, but which possesses greater strength and intensity than these. This instrument is the Saxophone. Better than any other, the Saxophone can finely modify its sounds to give them the qualities just mentioned and to preserve a perfect evenness throughout its range. I have made it from brass in the shape of a parabolic cone. The saxophone has a single reed mouthpiece with a very flared interior which tapers to the part that fits the body of the instrument.

Description and nomenclature of the various individuals of the saxophone family

No. 1 Saxophone in E♭ tenor all closed. B in E♭ makes D in C

No. 2 Saxophone in C, descending to B♭ in its pitch. The same instrument could also be made in B♭ and consequently would descend to A♭, made by B♭ in its pitch.

No. 3 Saxophone in G contrabass. One could also make this in A♭

No. 4 Saxophone in C bourdon. One could also make this in B♭ (one tone lower)

Saxophone numbers 5, 6, 7 and 8 are in the same pitches as those preceding but one octave higher.

Fingerings

No. 1 The fingering of this model partly follows that of the flute and the clarinet. One can apply to the rest all possible fingerings and uses.

All closed D in C.[1]

1. Key of C open.[2] – 2 C# – 3 D – 4 D# – 5 E – 6 F. – 7 F#. – 8 G. – 9 G#. – 10 A. – 11 A#. – 12 B. – 13 C. – 14 C#. – 15 D – 16 octave key for the first part of the instrument – 17 D# – 18 E – 19 F – 20 octave key for the second part of the instrument.

No. 2 All closed B♭ – 1 B – 2 C[3] – 3 C# – 4 D – 5 D# – 6 E – 7 F – 8 F# – 9 G – 10 G# – 11 A – 12 A# – 13 B – 14 C – 15 C# – 16 D – 17 D# – 18 chromatic octave key for the first fifth of the instrument – 19 octave key for one part of the following notes – 20 octave key for the rest of the following notes, in other words to produce the highest sounds of the instrument.

Description of the Mouthpiece

No. 9. Bass saxophone mouthpiece. The other mouthpieces are in the same proportions. One can in each case make them a little smaller or larger as desired.

Made in Paris 20th March 1846. Approved with two words deleted.

Adolphe Sax

---

[1] i.e. when all keys are closed, the resulting b° sounds d°, because the instrument is pitched in E♭.
[2] i.e. this is the low b° key which, when open, gives the note c[1].
[3] The original text has a sharp sign added here, which is clearly an error.

Ministère
de
l'Agriculture et du Commerce.

Durée quinze ans.

N° 3226

Loi du 5 juillet 1844.

Extrait.

Art. 32.

Sera déchu de tous ses droits :

1° Le breveté qui n'aura pas acquitté son annuité avant le commencement de chacune des années de la durée de son brevet ;

2° Le breveté qui n'aura pas mis en exploitation sa découverte ou invention en France dans le délai de deux ans, à dater du jour de la signature du brevet, ou qui aura cessé de l'exploiter pendant deux années consécutives, à moins que, dans l'un ou l'autre cas, il ne justifie des causes de son inaction ;

3° Le breveté qui aura introduit en France des objets fabriqués en pays étrangers et semblables à ceux qui sont garantis par son brevet.

Art. 33.

Quiconque, dans des enseignes, annonces, prospectus, affiches, marques ou estampilles, prendra la qualité de breveté sans posséder un brevet délivré conformément aux lois, ou après l'expiration d'un brevet antérieur, ou qui, étant breveté, mentionnera sa qualité de breveté ou son brevet sans y ajouter ces mots : sans garantie du Gouvernement, sera puni d'une amende de 50 francs à 1,000 francs. En cas de récidive, l'amende pourra être portée au double.

Brevet d'Invention

sans garantie du Gouvernement.

Le Ministre Secrétaire d'État au Département de l'Agriculture et du Commerce,

Vu la loi du 5 juillet 1844 ;

Vu le procès-verbal dressé le 21 mars 1846, à 12 heures 20 minutes, au Secrétariat général de la Préfecture du département de la Seine et constatant le dépôt fait par le sieur Sax dit Adolphe d'une demande de brevet d'Invention de quinze années, pour un système d'instrumens à vent, dits Saxophones.

Attendu la régularité de la demande,

Arrête ce qui suit :

Article premier.

Il est délivré au sieur Sax, Antoine Joseph dit Adolphe, fabricant d'instrumens de musique, à Paris, rue neuve Saint Georges n° 10 à ses risques et périls, sans examen préalable, et sans garantie, soit de la réalité, de la nouveauté ou du mérite de l'invention, soit de la fidélité ou de l'exactitude de la description, un brevet d'Invention de quinze années, qui ont commencé à courir le 21 mars 1846 pour un système d'instrumens à vent, dits Saxophones.

Article deuxième.

Le présent arrêté, qui constitue le brevet d'Invention, est délivré au sieur Sax dit Adolphe pour lui servir de titre.

A cet arrêté demeurera joint le duplicata certifié de la description et du dessin déposés à l'appui de la demande, et dont la conformité avec l'expédition originale a été dûment reconnue.

Paris, le vingt deux Juin mil huit cent quarante-six.

Le Ministre Secrétaire d'État de l'Agriculture et du Commerce.

Pour le Ministre et par délégation.
Le Conseiller d'État Secrétaire général,

Mémoire descriptif déposé à l'appui de la demande d'un Brevet d'invention de quinze ans par Mr Antoine Joseph (dit Adolphe) Sax fabricant d'instruments de musique demeurant à Paris rue neuve St Georges N° 10 ~~à Paris~~ & élisant domicile à l'effet des présentes chez Mr Perpigna Avocat 10 rue neuve St Augustin pour un nouveau Système d'instruments à vent dits Saxophones.

Exposé

Original.

On sait que, en général les instruments à vent sont ou trop durs ou trop mous comme sonorité ; c'est particulièrement dans les basses que l'un ou l'autre de ces défauts est le plus sensible. L'Ophicléide, par exemple, qui renforce les trombones, produit un son d'une nature si désagréable qu'on est obligé de le bannir des salles fermées ; faute d'en pouvoir modifier le timbre. Le basson, au contraire, rend un son si faible qu'on ne peut l'employer que pour des parties de remplissage & d'accompagnement ; ou encore pour des effets particuliers d'orchestration dans les Forte, il est parfaitement inutile. Il faut remarquer que ce dernier instrument est le seul qui se marie avec les instruments à cordes.

Il n'y a que les instruments à vent en cuivre dont l'effet soit satisfaisant en plein air ; aussi l'harmonie composée de ces instruments est-elle la seule combinaison d'orchestre qu'on puisse employer dans de pareilles circonstances.

Quant aux instruments à cordes, tout le monde sait que, en plein air, leur effet est nul à cause de la faiblesse du timbre ; ce qui rend leur emploi presque impossible dans de semblables conditions.

Frappé de ces divers inconvénients j'ai cherché le moyen d'y remédier en créant un instrument qui, par le caractère de sa <u>voix</u>, pût se

rapprocher du instruments à cordes, mais qui
possédât plus de force & d'intensité que ces
derniers. Cet instrument c'est le Saxophone
Mieux qu'aucun autre le Saxophone est
susceptible de modifier ses Sons à fin de leur
donner les qualités qui viennent d'être mentionné
& de leur conserver une égalité parfaite dans
toute leur étendue : Je l'ai fait de cuivre
et en forme de cône parabolique. Le
Saxophone a pour embouchure un bec à
anche simple dont l'intérieur très évasé
va en se rétrécissant à la partie qui vient
s'adapter au corps de l'instrument. ————
—— Description & nomenclature du divers
individus de la famille des Saxophones. ——

N⁰ 1. Saxophone en mi♭ ténor tout fermé :
si en mi♭ fait ré♮ en ut. ————
N⁰ 2 Saxophone en ut, descendant en si♭ dans
son ton. ————
Le même instrument se fait aussi en si♭ &
descend par conséquent en la qui fait si♭ dans
le même ton. ————
N⁰ 3 Saxophone en sol contrebasse ; on peut aussi
le faire en la♭ ————
N⁰ 4 Saxophone en ut Bourdon, on peut
aussi le faire en si♭ (un ton plus bas) ————
Les Saxophones N⁰ 5, 6, 7 & 8 sont dans les
mêmes tons que les précédents à l'octave supérieure ————
———————— Doigtés. ————————
N⁰ 1. Le doigté d'ce modèle participe de la
flûte & de la clarinette, on peut au reste lui
appliquer tous les doigtés possibles & en usage
Tout fermé ré♮ en ut. ————
1. Clef d'ut ouverte. — 2 ut # — 3 ré — 4 ré # —
5 mi — 6 fa. — 7 fa #. 8 sol. — 9 sol #. 10 la. —
11 la #. 12 si. — 13 ut. — 14 ut #. 15 ré —
16 clef pour octavier la première partie de
l'instrument — 17 ré # — 18 mi — 19 fa — 20 clef pour
octavier la seconde partie de l'instrument. ——

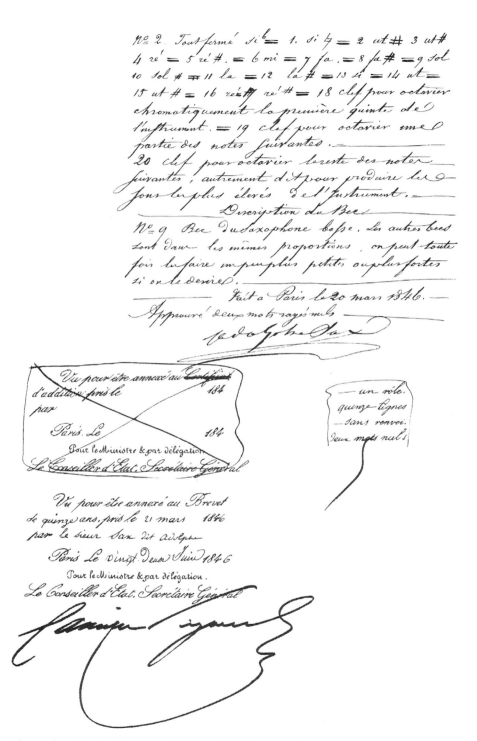

Nᵒ 2. Tout fermé si♭ = 1. si ♮ = 2 ut ♯ 3 ut ♯
4 ré' = 5 ré ♯. = 6 mi = 7 fa. = 8 fa ♯ = 9 sol
10 sol ♯ = 11 la = 12 la ♯ = 13 si = 14 ut =
15 ut ♯ = 16 ré ♯ ♯ ré' ♯ = 18 clef pour octavier
chromatiquement la première quinte de
l'instrument. = 19 clef pour octavier une
partie des notes suivantes.
20 clef pour octavier le reste des notes
suivantes, autrement d'A pour produire les
sons les plus élevés de l'instrument.
                Description du Bec
Nᵒ 9 Bec du saxophone basse. Les autres becs
sont dans les mêmes proportions, on peut toute
fois les faire un peu plus petites ou plus fortes
si on le désire.
                Fait à Paris le 20 mars 1846.
Approuvé deux mots rayés nuls
                Adolphe Sax

Vu pour être annexé au Certificat
d'addition pris le   184
par
Paris Le   184
        Pour le Ministre & par délégation
Le Conseiller d'Etat. Secrétaire Général

— un rôle.
quinze lignes
— sans renvoi.
Deux mots nuls

Vu pour être annexé au Brevet
de quinze ans, pris le 21 mars   1846
par le sieur Sax dit Adolphe
    Paris Le vingt Deux Juin 1846
        Pour le Ministre & par délégation.
Le Conseiller d'Etat. Secrétaire Général

The saxophone patent sketches are reproduced on p.49 of the present volume.

Notes

Preface

1. Kool 1987; Ventzke, Raumberger et al. 1987; Dullat 1999.
2. Haine 1980; Horwood 1980.

Introduction

1. Comettant 1867, p. 717.
2. Hoeprich 2008, p. 92.
3. Cokken 1846, p. 4, Kastner 1846, p. 26. The relevant passage in Kastner's method notes that 'Il faut naturellement jouer l'anche en dessous, c'est-à-dire portant sur la lèvre inférieure'.
4. Kastner 1846, p. 27.
5. 'La lèvre supérieure enveloppe le bec sans que le contact des dents nuise à la qualité du son.' Cokken 1846, p. 4.
6. Mayeur 1867, p. 3.
7. 'Saxophone Questions', *The Metronome*, 15 July 1925, p. 24.
8. Vereecken 1917, p. 2.
9. See Levinsky 1997, pp. 122–3.
10. Davis 1932, pp. 40–2, original emphasis.
11. Howe 2003, pp. 101–2.
12. Sax did not invent the idea of curved keypads, since they can be found on a number of clarinets made in first half of the eighteenth century. See Rice 2003, p. 217, n. 7.

Chapter 1 The life and times of Adolphe Sax

1. Fétis 1866–8, pp. 411–12.
2. Belgian patent no. 134, 'Perfectionnement dans la construction du cor', 23 June 1825.
3. Comettant 1860, pp. 4–5.
4. Fétis 1866–8, p. 413.
5. Comettant 1860, p. 6.
6. Haine 1980, p. 45.
7. Quoted in Haine 1980, p.46.
8. See Fétis 1866–8, vol. 7, p.413, and Haine 1980, p. 46.
9. For more on Sax and the bass clarinet, see Hoeprich 2008, pp. 265–6.
10. *Journal des débats*, 12 June 1842, p. 3.
11. Haine 1980, p. 52.
12. See Kastner 1848, p. 235 and Comettant 1860, p. 10.
13. The revised edition of François-Joseph Fétis's *Biographie universelle des musiciens et bibliographie générale de la musique* was published by Firmin-Didot between 1866 and 1868. The biography of Sax is in vol. 7 of this eight-volume work, on pp. 413–23.
14. *Revue et Gazette des Théâtres*, 3 December 1843. See also Kastner 1848, p. 244.
15. *RGMP*, 11 March 1841, p. 159.

16. French patent number 15213, 'Système d'instruments d'harmonie à trous ou à clefs donnant plus de justesse et plus d'intensité aux sons', granted 21 June 1843.
17. According to Pontécoulant in *La France musicale*, 9 June 1844, p. 182.
18. French patent number 15364, 'Système d'instruments chromatiques', 17 August 1843.
19. French patent number 2306, 22 November 1845.
20. Addendum to French patent number 8351, 30 June 1852.
21. French patent number 24698, 7 November 1855.
22. French patent number 56610, 16 February 1863.
23. French patent number 72010, 24 August 1866.
24. See Horwood 1980, p. 123.
25. These are listed in Haine 1980, pp. 190–203.
26. *RGMP*, 3 December 1843, p. 445.
27. Comettant 1860, p. 53.
28. Berlioz 2002, pp. 452–3.
29. Berlioz 2002, p. 329.
30. Wieprecht's initial misgivings about Sax's work appear to have been on the basis of misinformation published in the *Leipziger illustrierte Zeitung* on 31 August 1844. This contained sketches of four instruments that were wrongly described. On this basis Wieprecht accused Sax of copying designs that were already current in Germany. The two men met in Bonn a year later, in a meeting arranged by Liszt, on the occasion of the 75th anniversary of Beethoven's birth. Sax had the opportunity to demonstrate some of his instruments to Wieprecht (although not the saxophone). Reports of this meeting vary, but Wieprecht's response was at best lukewarm, and a number of literary exchanges ensued between the two men over the next few years. For further details, see Hemke 1975, pp. 109–25.
31. *L'Illustration*, 17 June 1845, p. 227, quoted with translation in Hemke 1975, p. 192.
32. Hemke 1975, p. 194.
33. Kastner 1848, p. 252.
34. *RGMP*, 28 September 1845, p. 316.
35. *Journal des débats*, 1 April 1845, p. 2.
36. Carafa (albeit attributed as 'Caraffa') had written one of the letters published in the *Revue et Gazette des Théâtres* on 3 December 1843, in which he offered Sax 'my sincere compliments on your interesting instruments which, with your talent and the perfectionism you bring, are called to rendering a great service to instrumental music'. Some of this letter is reproduced in Kastner 1848, p. 244.
37. *RGMP*, 27 April 1845, p. 134.
38. Kastner 1848, pp. 265–6.
39. Kastner 1848, p. 265.
40. *La France musicale*, 27 April 1845, p. 133.
41. Quoted in Horwood 1980, p. 64.
42. *L'Illustration*, 17 June 1845, quoted in Hemke 1975, pp. 204–5.
43. *La Quotidienne*, 11 May 1845, p. 1.
44. Hemke 1975, p. 203.
45. *RGMP*, 21 September 1845, p. 309.
46. *RGMP*, 1 November 1846, p. 352. Cokken's name is found with various orthographies, including 'Koeken' and 'Kocken'.
47. *RGMP*, 29 August 1847, p. 288.
48. Buffet Crampon was established by Jean-Louis Buffet sometime between 1839 and 1844. Buffet himself was one of the signatories to a letter opposing Adolphe Sax written to the war ministry in 1845. The company has been based in Mantes La Ville, France, since 1850, notwithstanding various developments and associations with other companies (such as being incorporated as part of the Boosey and Hawkes group between 1981 and 2003). The Besson company was founded by Gustave Auguste Besson in c.1837. Besson was also caught up in several legal battles with Sax, and was obliged to escape to London to avoid paying Sax damages. Although largely associated with brass instruments, a London branch of the company was advertising saxophones for sale in the mid 1890s. See Waterhouse 1993, p. 30.
49. 'Halary' was in fact a *nom de plume* established by Jean-Hilaire Asté and was continued by several makers who took over the business during the course of the nineteenth century, notably Jean-Louis Antoine and Jules-Léon Antoine. Pierre Louis Gautrot was the principal architect behind

the campaign to discredit and oppose Sax. The company which bears his name was formed in 1845 via a merger with his brother-in-law Auguste Guichard's existing company. His son-in-law renamed the company as Couesnon & Cie. in 1888. From 1911 to 1925 it was one of the largest companies of its kind in the world, but has declined since. It continues to exist on a much smaller scale in Château Thierry, a small town some 85 kilometres north-east of Paris. Raoux was one of oldest Parisian instrument manufacturers, with a reputation stretching back to the late seventeenth century. The company was particularly renowned for their hand horns. The business was sold by Marcel-Auguste Raoux to J. C. Labbaye in 1857, apparently because he became disillusioned in his various battles with Sax.

50. See Comettant 1860, p. 220 and Pontécoulant 1861, p. 349. The organisation sometimes named in this respect is L'Association Générale Des Ouvriers en Instruments de Musique (The General Association of Musical Instrument Workers). However, this was in part a protective organisation for its members, rather like a trade union, and in any case was not formed until 1865. See Haine 1985, p. 286.

51. Haine 1980, p. 123.

52. Horwood 1980, p. 74.

53. Quoted in Hemke 1975, p. 139.

54. See also Appendix and pp. 48–62.

55. Comettant 1860, p. 220.

56. Pontécoulant 1861, p. 286.

57. See Hemke 1975, p. 146.

58. Jardin and Tudesq 1983, p. 195.

59. Comettant 1860, pp. 319–23.

60. As listed in Haine 1980, p. 107. In fact the cavalry ensembles were still destined to retain some of Sax's instruments, but not under the name 'saxhorn', recalling the arguments that had long been advanced as to whether Sax could genuinely claim this as an invention. One of the decrees issued by the provisional government ordered that 'the names given to certain instruments will be replaced by their proper names'. See Haine 1991, p. 109.

61. *RGMP*, 3 September, 1848 p. 272.

62. Horwood suggests that in June 1848 Sax himself took up arms against 'the insurgents', i.e. those opposed to the monarchy. The support Sax had received from the King might well have inclined him towards a monarchist viewpoint, but there is little evidence elsewhere that he actually fought for it. The long-established music critic of *The Times* (in London) does note in his memoirs an occasion when Sax was arrested by soldiers, although this appears to be a case of mistaken identity. See Horwood 1980, p. 82, and Davison 1912, p. 129.

63. Quoted with translation in Hemke 1975, p. 158.

64. *RGMP*, 25 August 1850, p.285. Rivet was fined 400 francs and required to pay Sax the same amount in damages.

65. Haine 1980, p. 167.

66. *La France musicale*, 12 March 1848, p. 79.

67. The others having been Cavaillé-Coll, an organ manufacturer, and one of Sax's wind instrument competitors, Raoux.

68. Hemke 1975, p. 221.

69. This list is from the *Journal militaire officiel*, 1854 no. 59, p. 292, reproduced in Haine 1980, p. 112. Comettant, however, has a total of 56 players in this ensemble (1860, p. 426.) The discrepancy appears to be over whether the list included a side drum or not.

70. Adolphe Sax's brother Joseph Edouard died in September 1852, aged 27; two of his sisters, Marie-Josephine and Marie-Louise-Adèle, died in November and December 1852, aged 21 and 20 respectively. See Haine 1980, p. 17.

71. The Belgian patent for this piano, dated 17 March 1848, was in fact in the name of Joseph-Edouard Sax, another of Charles's sons. But the French patent taken out in 1852 to allow the piano to be imported into France was signed by the father, Charles-Joseph. Haine 1980, pp. 194–5.

72. Haine 1980, p. 34.

73. French patent no. 29431, granted 27 December 1856. Further evidence of Alphonse's desire to distinguish himself from his brother may be inferred from his description of this as 'Système *saxalphomnitonique*'.

74. Ellis 1999, p. 224.

75. Alphonse Sax self published a book advocating his views on this in 1865. For an appraisal of his work with female brass groups at this time, see Ellis 1999.
76. Horwood 1980, p. 125.
77. Horwood 1980, p. 99.
78. See Haine 1980, pp. 19–21.
79. Sax's original address of 10 rue Neuve-Saint-Georges was later renumbered as 50 rue Saint-Georges, probably when the street was renamed in 1846 (my thanks to Nigel Simeone for this information). The building where Sax's business was located retains this number today.
80. The first child died on 10 May 1856, and Sax's sister died on 17 May of the same year. It is probable that the child had already been buried before Sax's plot could accommodate her. However, since the second child was not buried here it seems unlikely, for whatever reason, that Sax wished to accommodate either.
81. Price 1987, p. 121.
82. *Journal des débats*, 17 December 1847, p. 1.
83. In fact Horwood suggests that Sax was against this change of pitch, and thus did not benefit from its introduction, although he gives no source for these observations (1980, p. 114.). This seems unlikely. It is improbable that Sax would have stood by and watched his competitors profit, even if he himself was ideologically opposed to the new pitch. It is conceivable, however, that Sax's tools and equipment were configured to produce instruments at non-standard pitches, and that he either lacked the resources or the will to change them.
84. See also Haine 1980, pp. 164–9.
85. Haine 1980, p. 156.
86. Quoted in Haine 1980, p. 160.
87. Sax recalled these incidents in some detail in his 'Appeal to the Public' written in 1887 and published in *La Musique des familles*, 21 April 1887, pp. 215–16, and 28 April 1886, pp. 223–4.
88. Wagner 2007, p. 513.
89. Hemke 1975, p. 248.
90. Quoted in Rorive 2004, pp. 205–6.
91. See Haine 1980, p. 117. Rorive (2004, p. 205.) further asserts that the classes in the basement of the conservatoire were given under the name of 'l'Ecole de musique militaire de Paris'.
92. Macdonald 2002, p. 301.
93. Rorive 2004, p. 207.
94. 'Appeal to the Public' quoted in Deans 1980, p. 177.
95. Sax's brass instruments were, in general, constructed without plating or gilding, although he did plate and gild certain instruments for exhibition display.
96. The collection had in fact been offered complete for the sum of 40,000 francs, but this was not raised; hence the subsequent auction. See Haine 1980, p. 132.
97. See Haine 1980, p. 161.
98. Haine 1980, p. 133.
99. See also note 87.
100. See Deans 1980, pp. 171–9, from which this translation is taken.
101. Prod'homme 1935, p. 464.
102. François-Édouard Millet de Marcilly married Sax's youngest daughter, Adèle-Marie. He was a sculptor who executed a bust of his father-in-law towards the end of the nineteenth century; the bust is now in the Musée de la musique, Paris.
103. Sax's burial place can be found in the first line of the fifth division, tomb number 2 on Avenue Montebello in Montmartre cemetery.
104. *The Times*, 10 February 1894, p. 5.
105. Quoted in Horwood 1980, p. 147. The cartoon is reproduced in Shafer 1950, unpaginated.
106. *The Times*, 1 May 1933, p. 15. See above, pp. 314–15, for the editor's entertaining observations on the saxophone itself.

Chapter 2   *The saxophone family*

1. Patent no. 3226, 'Système d'instruments à vents, dits saxophones', granted 22 June 1846, p. 2.
2. Belgian patent no. 2256, 'Nouvelle combinaison de cylindres applicables aux ophicléides et aux autres instruments de basse', 8 August 1842.
3. See Haine and de Keyser 1980, p. 250.

4. *RGMP*, 13 March 1842, p. 99.
5. *RGMP*, 10 September 1843, p. 316.
6. *Musical World*, 3 June 1841, pp. 366–7.
7. For a more positive appraisal of the ophicleide's qualities and historical significance, see Herbert 2006, pp. 200–3.
8. Many writers have thought similarly, among them Carse 1939, p. 176, Baines 1967, p. 142, and Horwood 1980, pp. 31–2.
9. *RGMP*, 13 March 1842, p. 99.
10. See Haine 1985, p. 89.
11. Hemke 1975, p. 13.
12. Marcuse 1975, pp. 654–7.
13. Hemke 1975, p. 2.
14. Carse 1939, p. 176 and Wood c. 1833. For more information on the history of the alto fagotto see Rendall 1932.
15. Kool notes that Constant Pierre claimed in an 1890 publication that Victor Mahillon showed an alto fagotto to Sax at some stage. Given Pierre's antipathy to Sax, however, this claim needs to be treated with caution. See Kool 1987, p. 205.
16. It is peculiar that Kool describes the bore as being slightly conical when it appears demonstrably cylindrical, something his own playing of the instrument confirmed. See Kool 1987, pp. 202–4.
17. For detailed descriptions of Desfontenelles's bass clarinet and Wieprecht and Skorra's bathyphon or contra-bass clarinet, see Rice 2009a, pp. 328–32.
18. Curiously, the credit for this revised tárogató is more often given to Schunda, whereas it was Stowasser who appears to have played the greater role. See Falvy 1997, p. 365–6.
19. Maurice Hamel, *Notes complémentaires sur Adolphe Sax* (Archives of H. et A. Selmer, Paris, 1925), p. 38, quoted in Hemke 1975, p. 10.
20. Jobard 1842, p. 154.
21. See also McBride 1982, p. 114.
22. Quoted in Haine 1980, p. 52.
23. Haine 1980, p. 52.
24. 'Réponse à M. Sax père' in *La Belgique musicale*, 8ème année, 1847, no. 9 p. 2. Quoted in Haine 1980, p. 52.
25. Kastner 1848, p. 233.
26. *RGMP*, 12 June 1842, p. 245.
27. *La France musicale*, 12 June 1842, p. 218.
28. Berlioz: 'Instrumen[t]s de Musique: M. Ad. Sax', *Journal des débats*, 12 June 1842, p. 3.
29. Quoted with translation in Hemke 1975. Howe (2003b, pp. 109–10) follows Hemke in dating this letter as 14 January 1842. But some years later, in a review of legal proceedings in which Sax was then involved, the *RGMP* states that the letter was dated 14 June 1842 (see *RGMP*, 23 May 1847, pp. 172–3). This June date appears more plausible, since Sax was clearly in Paris at this time, demonstrating his instruments both publicly and privately, and it coincides with much else that was being written and published about the saxophone at that time.
30. See Reginald Morley-Pegge and Philip Bate, 'Ophicleide', *Grove Dictionary of Music and Musicians*, 6th edition (1980), vol. 13, p. 652.
31. *RGMP*, 10 September 1843, p. 316.
32. See Howe 2003b, p. 113.
33. *La France musicale*, 27 August 1843, p. 278.
34. *La France musicale*, 7 January 1844, p. 432.
35. Kastner 1844, p. 39.
36. Haine 1980, p. 123.
37. This letter from Charles Finck dated 14 October 1844 was included as part of sales brochure ('prospectus de vente') circulated by Sax c. 1850; see also ill. 44.
38. Berlioz used both the German (Es) and the French (Mi♭) indications to represent the English 'E♭'.
39. For more on the development of the Boehm flute see Powell 2002, pp. 164–85.
40. Howe 2003b, p. 104.
41. I'm grateful to Robert Howe for this observation.
42. *La France musicale*, 27 August, 1843, p. 278.
43. Robert Howe (personal communication) suggests that this may have been because Sax presumed this would more easily facilitate the reading of bassoon music, without the need to transpose.

44. See Howe 2003b, pp. 121–3, for further details. Howe observes that even this interpretation is problematic, since the shapes of the saxophones in the patent vary from the modern equivalents such pitch nomenclature implies.
45. McBride 1982, p. 114.
46. See Rice 2008 and Rice 2009b, p. 86.
47. For more on the demise of the ophicleide-shaped bass saxophone see Howe 2003b, pp. 131–2.
48. Kastner 1846, Cokken 1846, Hartmann 1846.
49. Kastner 1846, p. 26.
50. These key numbers are different from the 1846 printing because the two octave keys, previously identified as numbers 16 and 20, are described in the 1850 printing as keys A and B.
51. See for example Carse 1939, p. 176, or Marcuse 1975, p. 727.
52. Fewer than 5 per cent of surviving Adolphe Sax saxophones are in F or C, and these amount to: one C soprano, two F altos and four C tenors. Of these, all except the C tenors were made before 1855. See Howe 2003b, p. 162.
53. Although when Franz Rath, a saxophone player with the Fred Innes band in Denver Colorado wanted a C tenor sax in the mid 1890s, Buffet in France were apparently happy to make one specially for him. See 'The Saxophone in the Orchestra', *Metronome,* May 1916, p. 20.
54. Sax's original letter is reproduced in full in Haine 1980, p. 220.
55. For more extensive discussion of the arguments against the existence of a family of F/C saxophones, see Howe 2003b, pp. 162–7.
56. Cokken 1846, p. 1.
57. The ophicleide-shaped saxophone did not entirely disappear after 1850. One specimen, an E♭ baritone in high pitch, appears to have been made by Pélisson Frères around 1875. Al Rice (personal communication) suggests that the instrument may have been made as a corollary to a number of ophicleide-shaped bass clarinets in brass that could be found in France, Germany, Austria, and Italy in the mid/late nineteenth century. A picture of the instrument (mistakenly identified as being in F) is given in Dullat 1999, p. 34. An ophicleide-shaped saxophone was being offered by the Roth firm of Milan as late as 1895.
58. For a discussion on the use of the parabola by Boehm, Sax and Mahillon, see De Keyser 2003, pp. 240–5.
59. Some of this confusion is summarised in Hemke 1975, pp. 59–70.
60. Kool 1987, pp. 82–3.
61. Kool 1987, p. 84.
62. Hemke also undertook similar measurements in the 1970s and concurred with Kool's assertion. See Hemke 1975, pp. 57–70.
63. Howe 2003b, p. 149.
64. Kool 1987, pp. 84 and 87.
65. Scavone 1997, p. 73.
66. See Appendix.
67. See Berlioz: 'Instrumen[t]s de Musique: M. Ad. Sax', *Journal des débats,* 12 June 1842, p. 3, and Kastner 1844, p. 39.
68. Cokken 1846, p. 3.
69. French patent no. 139884, p. 3.
70. Belgian patent no. 5469, submitted 7 December 1850, granted 16 January 1851: 'Instrument de musique dit saxophone' (Brevet français no. 3226, granted 21.3.1846).
71. For a more detailed comparison between the 1846 and 1850 patents see McBride 1982.
72. See Howe 2003b, p. 136 and Haine 1980, p. 58.
73. See Howe 2003b, p. 149 for a comprehensive overview of bell diameters on extant Adolphe Sax saxophones.
74. Saxophone no. 6497, Musée de la musique, Paris.
75. These posters are reproduced in Haine 1980, pp. 110 and 66.
76. For further details see Howe 2003b, pp. 153–4.
77. Berlioz 1860, p. 284.
78. Patent no. 70894, 31 May 1866, 'Perfectionnements apportés aux instruments de musique, dits saxophones'.
79. Patent no. 139884, 16 January 1881, 'Perfectionnements au saxophone et autres instruments à vent, tels que le basson et la clarinette', p. 3.
80. For more on the relationship between saxophone and sarrusophone see Joppig 1986, pp. 77–88.

81. This was later marketed in Italy by the Orsi company as the 'saxorusophone', doubtless in part to exploit something of the saxophone's then popularity. See Joppig 1986, pp. 94–5.
82. Pontécoulant 1861, p. 513.
83. French Patent no. 72930, 7 August 1866, Fr. Millereau: 'Un système de musique à vent et en cuivre dit saxophone-Millereau'.
84. For more on the 'Système George' saxophone, see Kampmann 2006.
85. French patent no. 79612, 1 May 1868, 'Améliorations et changements apportés à diverses parties des saxophones'.
86. 'Le doigté du saxophone dans la main gauche a toujours été très difficile, et ce n'est qu'après des années d'étude que l'on finit par o'en tendre maître'. Patent no. 109817 (1), 1875, 'Système de saxophone dit: Système p. Goumas et Cie.', p. 1.
87. French patent no. 175287 (1), 1 September 1886: 'Perfectionnements aux saxophones'.
88. French patent no. 175287 (2), submitted 2 January 1887: 'Perfectionnements aux saxophones'.
89. French patent no. 186154, 5 January 1888: 'Un système de clef augmentant d'une note grave l'étendu du saxophone'.
90. Evette and Schaeffer's first patent, no. 184066, submitted 1887, was described as 'Un saxophone système Evette et Schaeffer'. Many of the subsequent patents are simply titled 'Perfectionnements aux saxophones'. French patent numbers and years are as follows: 246847 (1), 1895; 246847 (2), 1895; 260754 (1) 1896; 260754 (2) 1896; 310741, 1901; 372036, 1907; 378268 (1), 1907; 378268 (2) 1907; 439508, 1912.
91. See also 'The Apogée Key System of Evette Schaeffer', *Saxophone Journal*, 1993, vol. 17, pp. 6–8.
92. French patent no. 189198: 'Un système de saxophone'.
93. French patent no. 193722, 1888: 'L'application du système Boehm aux saxophones'.
94. Lecomte's innovation appears to have been prefigured by Jean Baptiste Soualle in the early 1860s on his turcophone. See p. 113.
95. Philip Bate and William Waterhouse: 'Heckel (i)', *Grove Music Online*, accessed 3 January, 2010.
96. Bro 1992, p. 25.
97. Bro 1992, p. 27.
98. American patent number 1,119,954, granted 8 December 1914: 'Musical Wind Instrument'. Haynes was an important flute manufacturer, and the process was originally intended to make better flutes. But Haynes could see that it might be more widely adopted, and the patent mentions saxophones also.
99. From the mid 1990s the Selmer company also offered a third octave key as an option on some of its models, marketed as 'Harmonic' versions of standard instruments.
100. Bro 1992, p. 72.
101. Bro 1992, p. 76.
102. US patent numbers 1401872 (granted 1921); 1611993 (1926); 1702962 (1929). All patents were titled 'Key-pad for wind musical instruments'.
103. Conn advertisement of 1928, reproduced in *Saxophone Journal*, vol. 14 (5), 1990, p. 11.
104. US Patent number 1166971, titled 'Reed Musical Instrument'. The patent was not granted until January 1916. Although the term Conn-O-Sax is not used there is an unmistakable morphological similarity between the two instruments, and the patent text itself notes that the instrument 'is somewhat analogous to the so-called English horn'. No keywork is shown in the patent, which instead suggests that either 'the Boehm key system, the ordinary Albert system, or a combination of these two systems, or any other system may be used' (p. 1).
105. Conn advertisement, *The Metronome*, May 1922, inside front cover, original emphasis.
106. US Patent number 1605101, p. 1.
107. Buescher advert from c. 1928 at http://www.drrick.com/straightalto/straightalto1.html, accessed 22 Feb 2009.
108. Davis 1932, p. 18.
109. US patent 1497939, 'Slide Saxophone', Waterhouse 1993, p. 322.
110. *The 'Swanee' Sax*, Lowe & Brydone Printers, London, c. 1930.
111. See Paul Cohen, 'The One-handed Saxophone', *Saxophone Journal*, vol. 12(3), 1987, pp. 4–8.
112. The patent application, US no. 2232151, granted in 1941, spells this surname 'Trew', but elsewhere it appears as 'True'.
113. For more on the oboe-sax see Howe 2003b, pp. 51–2.
114. King company catalogue, 1924, Quoted in Bro 1992, p. 148.

115. For more on Loomis's 'double resonance' saxophone, see Paul Cohen, 'Allen Loomis and the Incredible Double Resonance Alto Saxophone', part I, *Saxophone Journal*, vol. 15 (4), 1991, pp. 8–10, and part II, vol. 15 (5), 1991, pp. 8–11.
116. Although marketed by Selmer US these padless altos were in fact made as stencils by the Buescher company.
117. These were lodged at the Patent Office in London: Provisional Specifications Nos. 604,407 and 604,418 were applied for on 14 December 1945, with Complete Specifications for both patents being lodged on 13 December 1946 and 13 January 1947 respectively. These were finally granted on 2 July 1948.
118. Patent Number 604,407, 1945, p. 2.
119. The name 'Grafton' was taken from a street in north London where Sommaruga initially established his company.
120. Some of these details on the Grafton alto saxophone are taken from Wally Horwood's article 'The Grafton Story', published in the magazine of the Clarinet and Saxophone Society of Great Britain, December 1985.

Chapter 3   *The saxophone in the nineteenth century*

1. See Ehrlich 1990, pp. 92–8, for details of this trend in relation to Victorian England.
2. Weber 1975, p. 159.
3. Haine 1991, p. 103.
4. Haine 1980, pp. 195–205.
5. Haine 1991, p. 106.
6. Haine 1985, p. 175.
7. Waterhouse 2006, p. 122.
8. Haine 1991, p. 113.
9. Haine 1991, p. 118.
10. See Haine 1985, p. 84 and Weber 1975, p. 24.
11. Haine 1985, p. 85.
12. *RGMP*, 3 December 1848, p. 379.
13. Haine and de Keyser 1980, pp. 221–2.
14. Haine 1980, pp. 127–8. I have assumed in calculating this figure that the 19 *saxophones en la bémol* (A♭) listed were in fact saxophones, the key of which was wrongly recorded. If I am wrong then the percentage would be even lower.
15. For further information on the manufacturing licences issued by Sax at this time see Haine 1980–1.
16. See Haine 1980–1, p. 199.
17. Waterhouse 1993, p. 90.
18. *Musical Times*, 1 April 1854, p. 16.
19. Rice 2010, p. 94. Buffet Crampon was in fact owned by Goumas & Cie from 1865, but continued to use the Buffet Crampon marque for their saxophones.
20. For a more exhaustive list of saxophone manufacturers and dealers in the nineteenth century, see Rice 2010, p. 94.
21. A full list of the plates auctioned is given in Haine 1980, pp. 182–6.
22. Ronkin 1987, pp. 24–5.
23. *RGMP*, 22 August 1852, p. 278.
24. Dahlhaus 1989, p. 243.
25. Macdonald 2002, p. 3.
26. *RGMP*, 10 September 1843, p. 315.
27. Berlioz 1860, p. 284.
28. Comettant 1860, p. 47.
29. *L'Illustration*, 5 February 1848, p. 387.
30. *La France musicale*, 12 June 1842, p. 218.
31. Hanslick 1863, p. 441.
32. Saint–Saëns's *Les noces de Prométhée* op. 19, (1867), provides an exception to this general rule, since it includes parts for three E♭ saxophones (2A/B).
33. The second suite from this work, which also includes a saxophone, was put together by Ernest Guiraud after Bizet's death.

34. De Keyser 2006, pp. 165–6.
35. Berlioz 1843.
36. The *Chant sacré* was published as no. 6 of the song collection *Irlande* (1830). Its original incarnation was as a 'Prière' (prayer) in an unpublished cantata Berlioz composed in 1828. See Macdonald 1965–66, p. 34. The concert was warmly reviewed by the critic Maurice Bourges in *RGMP*, 4 February 1844, pp. 43–4.
37. Macdonald 2002, p. 301.
38. Berlioz 2002, p. 527. Berlioz did not, in fact, include saxophones in the completed work (which comprises the first two acts of the opera *Les Troyens*, written between 1856 and 1858).
39. There is a suggestion, however, that the part may have been played on a saxophone in B♭. See Howe 2003, p. 116, n. 50.
40. Jean–Marie Londeix (2004, p. 2) has suggested that François Bazin included a saxophone in the incidental music for his comic opera *Maître Pathelin*, first heard at Paris's Salle Favart on 12 December 1856. However there is no evidence of this in the score, nor any reference to the participation of a *banda* in which a saxophone might have been included.
41. In his memoirs Saint-Saëns's observes that 'as a compliment to Adolphe Sax [Fétis] substituted a saxophone for the bass clarinet the author indicated. This resulted in the suppression of that part of the aria *O Paradis sorti de l'onde* as the saxophone did not produce a good effect.' See Saint-Saëns 1921, pp. 248–9.
42. See De Keyser 2006, pp. 136–7.
43. De Keyser 2006, p. 152.
44. Terrier 2003, p. 147. For more on Mayeur's contribution to the saxophone in the nineteenth century, see Greenwood 2005.
45. Bickley 1914, p. 34.
46. Cairns 2000, p. 585.
47. Wagner's letter is reproduced in Terrier 2003, p. 178. He writes 'Comme il n'y aura pas assez des cors à Paris, M. Sax devrait être prié d'en faire remplacer une partie par des instruments du même timbre de son inventions, peut-être par des Saxaphones [*sic*].' De Keyser (2006, p. 147 n. 66) notes that he found only parts for horns in the *banda* material for this work at the Opéra. There is some circumstantial evidence that Wagner heard the saxophone at some point. An obituary for E. A. Lefebre notes that Lefebre was 'playing at the Schützen House, Leipzig, where the musical instructor of the Gewand House [*sic*] advised him to play for the great Richard Wagner, who was there striving hard to invent some brass instruments for special use in certain of his grand operas. The soft and sympathetic tone of the Saxophone, together with its almost unlimited power, proved to them to be the very instrument the great Wagner had been searching for so long.' No date is attributed to this event. See 'Death of E. A. Lefebre, The Famous Saxophone Soloist', *The Metronome*, 27 (April 1911), p. 16.
48. *La France musicale*, 3 August 1862, p. 244.
49. Sax's letter of 30 July 1883 is reproduced in full in Haine 1980, pp. 218–20.
50. See Rorive 2004, p. 255.
51. See Weber 1975, p. 109.
52. This was a pun on the word 'cornamusa' (cornemuse in English) which was applied to a type of bagpipe common in rural France at this time. Soualle's performance was widely advertised in the contemporary English press. See for example, *The Morning Chronicle*, 18 November 1850, p. 4.
53. See Rendall 1941–2, p. 79, and *New York Times*, 21 December 1853, p. 1.
54. *Musical World*, 13 October 1849, p. 656, and 3 November 1849, p. 704.
55. *Illustrated London News*, 7 July 1849, p. 5.
56. *Musical World*, 10 January 1852, p. 22.
57. *RGMP*, 23 February 1851, p. 67.
58. *Journal des débats*, 13 April 1851, p. 2.
59. Quoted in Harvey 1995, pp. 11–12.
60. There are many references to Soualle's performances in New Zealand during 1855. The Auckland *Daily Southern Cross* of 13 March 1855 (p. 2), for example, advertised that a grand concert would take place 'on FRIDAY next, when Ali-Ben-Sou-Alle will be assisted by Monsieur Valere and a full band.'
61. See also Rice 2010, pp. 92–3.
62. All quotes taken from Haan 1989, pp. 198–9.
63. *RGMP*, 21 June 1857, p. 204.

64. 18 August 1864. Concert programme in the McCann Collection, Royal Academy of Music, London, reproduced at http://www.yorkgate.ram.ac.uk/emuweb/pages/ram/Display. php?irn=4541 (accessed 20 March 2010).
65. *Musical Times*, 1 September 1864, p. 350.
66. This work appears to have been collated in Paris by L. Parent in 1865, under the title 'Royal Album for Saxophones'.
67. According to the Archives départmentales du Pas-de-Calais: http://www.archivespasdecalais. fr/ (accessed 20 December 2011).
68. *RGMP*, 30 November 1851, p. 387.
69. Carse 1951, p. 76.
70. *RGMP*, 11 July 1852, p. 230, and 22 August 1852, p. 278.
71. See Carse 1951, pp. 71–89.
72. *RGMP*, 11 July 1858, p. 232.
73. Rivière 1893, pp. 126–7.
74. Laurence 1981, p. 324.
75. Hemke 1975, pp. 383–4.
76. *New York Times*, 21 December 1853, p. 1.
77. *RGMP*, 22 January 1854, p. 32.
78. This phrase is taken from a note attached to the manuscript of the symphony; see Upton 1946, p. 26.
79. Hemke 1975, pp. 392–4.
80. 'University of Vermont', *New York Times*, 4 Aug 1866, p. 5. A selection from *Il Trovatore* was again among the repertoire performed.
81. Although born in Holland, much of Lefebre's life and work took place in America. Thus E. A. Lefèbre often Americanised the spelling of his surname to Lefebre, and I have retained this orthography.
82. Noyes 2000, p. 18.
83. 'Death of E. A. Lefebre' *The Metronome*, April 1911, p. 16.
84. *Benham's Musical Review*, vol. 10 (3), March 1875; quoted in Noyes 2000, p. 34, n. 26.
85. This enterprising group comprised Franz Walrabe (S), Edward A. Lefebre (A), Henry Steckelberg (T), and William F. Schultze (B). For further information see Noyes 2000, pp. 29–31 and two articles by Noyes on Lefebre in *Saxophone Journal*: vol. 23/5 (May/June 1999), pp. 6–10, and vol. 23/6 (July/August 1999), pp. 6–10. The seemingly idiosyncratic spelling of the word 'quartette' – presumably borrowed from the French – was conventional in much of the English-speaking world at the time,.
86. *Saxophone Journal*, vol. 23/5 (May/June 1999), p. 8.
87. Hindson 1992, p. 27.
88. *Musical Courier*, 13 August 1880, p. 406; quoted Noyes 2000, p. 32.
89. Noyes 2000, p. 41.
90. Caryl Florio was actually a pseudonym adopted by this English-born composer, whose real name was William James Robjohn.
91. The manuscript of the *Variation* is only 70 per cent complete and the work appears not to have been finished, although Paul Cohen notes that 'circumstantial evidence suggests that [Lefebre] possessed the completed copy of the score and parts and that performances took place'. See 'The New 19th Century Saxophone Part II', *Saxophone Journal*, vol. 16 (5), 1992, p. 11, and also Kelleher 1990.
92. 'Mr Florio's Concert', *New York Times*, 30 April 1880, p. 5.
93. Noyes 2000, p. 55.
94. 'Entertainment of the Arbeiter Union', *New York Times*, 28 March 1870, p. 8.
95. Noyes 2000, p. 60.
96. 'What is Going On?', *New York Times*, 4 May 1890, p. 8.
97. Noyes 2000, pp. 135–8.
98. Quoted in Noyes 2000, p. 149.
99. *RGMP*, 22 May 1853, p. 187.
100. See Davison 1912, pp. 214–16. The saxophones employed are somewhat confusingly described as: 2 saxophones in B flat, 2 saxophones in E flat, tenor, and 1 in B flat, bass.
101. *Musical Times*, 1 November 1858, p. 329.
102. See Haine 1985, p. 98.

103. Adolphe Sax, *De la nécessité des musiques militaires*, Paris, Librairie centrale, 1867.

104. Adapted from Neukomm 1889, pp. 165–8. In the Guides band Neukomm appears to list the soprano as 'un saxophone contralto', but two alto saxophones are listed separately.

105. Kappey 1894, pp. 91–2.

106. Murphy 1994, p. 5.

107. Hanslick 1863, pp. 442–3.

108. Ventzke, Raumberger, et al. 1987, p. 159.

109. *RGMP*, 22 August 1852, p. 278.

110. Rice 2010, p. 89.

111. Cited in Kappey 1894, pp. 91–2.

112. Tosoroni 1850, p. 25.

113. Pace 1943, p. 217. I am grateful to Albert Rice for bringing this reference to my attention.

114. In a letter to the King, Rossini writes of the 'new [instruments] we owe to Sax' as being the 'only advance of our days'. But it is not clear whether he is referring to Sax's innovations in general, or the saxophone in particular. See Weinstock 1968, p. 361.

115. Farmer 1960, p. 26.

116. Farmer 1950, p. 211.

117. Mandel was in fact appointed as Assistant Director in 1857, but acceded to the Directorship after the founding Director was dismissed in 1859. See Binns 1959, p. 58.

118. Mandel 1859, p. 19. By 'seraphim' Mandel was probably referring to a small reed organ, known as a 'seraphine' in the USA and England around this time. See Baines 1992, p. 300. I am grateful to Albert Rice for bringing this entry to my attention.

119. *Musical Times*, 1 December 1890, p. 722.

120. Zealley and Hume 1926, p. 13.

121. Kappey 1894, p. 43.

122. Miller 1912, p. 36.

123. 'Wind-Band', *Grove Dictionary of Music and Musicians* (fourth edition), 1948, vol. 5, p. 735.

124. *Musical Courier*, 22 July 1885, p. 36. Farmer, writing in 1912, notes that by then Mexico had a very fine Artillery band which was 'seventy-five strong, the instrumentation being on the French model, and embracing the entire family of saxophones'. Farmer 1912, p. viii.

125. 'Musical Filipinos', *The Lewiston Daily Sun*, 22 August 1898, p. 8.

126. http://www.policensw.com/info/band/policeband1.html (accessed 20 March 2010).

127. 'Books', *The Southern Cross*, 10 December 1873, p. 1.

128. 'Band Music Then and Now', *The New York Times*, 29 June 1879, p. 10. In the same interview Dodworth also claims that members of his family invented a valved brass instrument very similar to a saxhorn some time before Sax himself.

129. The musicians were listed by Oscar Comettant (1894, p. 92) as Cambray (soloist), Pégot, Canua, Bonner, Lebreton and Nivert, the latter – at least – having been a student of Sax at the Paris Conservatoire. However, Thomas Ryan (1885, p. 197) asserts that the Garde band comprised 'a double quartette of saxophones', leaving some ambiguity as to the actual disposition of saxophones employed.

130. *Boston Daily Evening Transcript*, 21 June 1872, p. 2. Quoted in Hemke 1975, pp. 397–8.

131. *Chicago Tribune*, 19 July 1872, p. 6. Quoted in Hemke 1975, p. 403.

132. See Hemke 1975, p. 409.

133. Hindson 1992, p. 6.

134. Mead 1889, p. 787. C. A. Cappa was director of the 7th Regiment Band of New York.

135. See also Hemke 1975, pp. 411–13, and Noyes 2000, p. 114.

136. Schwartz 1957, p. 169.

137. Schwartz 1957, p. 129.

138. http://hwww.ibew.org.uk/vbbp-uk.htm (accessed 20 March 2010).

139. See Bierley 2006, p. 148 and Mayer 1960, p. 54.

140. Mayer 1960, p. 56.

Chapter 4 Early twentieth-century light and popular music

1. Vermazen 2004, p. 8.

2. Quoted in Vermazen 2004, p. 9.

3. *Variety*, 3 February 1906, p. 16.
4. *Variety*, 13 April, 1907, p. 31.
5. *Variety*, 21 May 1910, p. 32
6. *New York Age*, 15 February 1912, p. 6.
7. See Kent 1983, pp. 42 and 45.
8. *New York Times*, 26 January 1896.
9. Quoted in Büchmann-Møller 1990, p. 8.
10. According to Whitney Balliott, quoted in Büchmann-Møller 1990, p. 8.
11. 'The Saxophone is Coming Fast', *The Dominant* 23 (July 1915), pp. 66–7.
12. Vermazen 2004, p. 41.
13. Vermazen 2004, p. 36.
14. Vermazen 2004, p. 238, n. 44.
15. Vermazen 2004, p. 9.
16. Büchmann-Møller 1990, p. 7. For more on Irma Young's saxophone skills see Placksin 1985, pp. 66–7.
17. Eileen Southern notes that the black W. A. Mahara Minstrels had a thirty-piece band for day parades and a forty-two piece band for night shows. See Southern 1997, p. 236.
18. Klitz 1989, p. 50.
19. Handy suggests that the saxophonists had left because of homesickness. Handy 1944, pp. 63–4.
20. See Southern 1997, p. 319.
21. *Metronome* 36 (11), November 1920, p. 75.
22. Perhaps there was a clearer understanding of the difference between 'ragtime' and 'jazz' in terms of performance, however. Ted Gioia writes of Jelly Roll Morton demonstrating for Alan Lomax two different ways of playing Joplin's 'Maple Leaf Rag', one a ragtime style, the second a more jazz-inflected approach. See Gioia 1997, p. 21.
23. Vermazen 2004, p. 9. The Majestic Musical Four toured widely on the vaudeville circuits. In 1905, for example, the group was advertised as comprising 'Collins, Terrill Brothers, and Simon' at the Star Theater in Brooklyn, New York. See Wertheim and Bair 2000, p. 199.
24. Wertheim and Bair 2000, p. 383.
25. American Saxophone Quartette promotional material, quoted in Plugge 2003, p. 155.
26. Noyes 2000, pp. 172–3.
27. *C. G. Conn's Truth* 6, no. 1 (July 1905) p. 3, quoted Noyes 2000, p. 173.
28. *C. G. Conn's Truth* 9, no. 10 (January 1912) unpaginated, quoted Noyes 2000, p. 173.
29. A picture of the Dorsey family quartet is given in Levinson 2005, facing p. 162.
30. Letter from Clay Smith to Harry P. Harrison, 7 November 1914, quoted in Smialek 1991, p. 38.
31. 'Saxophone Article', *The Dominant* 24 (January 1917), pp. 80–81, quoted in Smialek 1991, p. 68. From May 1924 *The Dominant* was absorbed by its competitor, *The Metronome*. The revamped *Metronome* featured saxophone articles by Ben Vereecken – who had contributed to the latter magazine prior to the merger – and Rudy Wiedoeft, in preference to those by Smith and Holmes.
32. Advertisement, *Variety*, 14 August 1909, p. 32.
33. Advertisement, *Variety*, 4 September 1909, p. 36, original emphasis.
34. Advertisement, *Variety*, 9 October 1909, p. 35.
35. Handy 1944, pp. 64–6.
36. Advertisement, *Variety*, 10 December 1920, p. 158. The repeated association of xylophone and saxophone in these groups may appear curious, but, notwithstanding its long history in different guises and cultures, the two-rack xylophone familiar today only evolved around the turn of the twentieth century. Like the saxophone, therefore, it may have appeared to audiences of the time as something of a novelty.
37. *Hamilton* [Canada] *Evening Times*, 7 January 1908, quoted in Lotz 1997, p. 131.
38. *Buffalo Enquirer*, 29 September 1911, quoted in Lotz 1997, p. 136.
39. Isabele Taliaferro was a significant figure in her own right. She was a tenor saxophone specialist who graduated from both the New England Conservatory of Music and the Juilliard School of Music, no mean feat for a black woman at this time. She went on to become an influential music educator in the New York area. See http://www.nypl.org/ead/3988 (accessed 31 December 2011).
40. Quoted in Lotz 1997, p.140. Joplin's opera, completed in 1910, remained unstaged at his death in 1917, although a concert performance had been given around 1911 with Joplin accompanying at the piano (see Berlin 1994, pp. 214–15). He gave a 200-page score of the entire work to William

Spiller, perhaps in the hope that Spiller could help arrange a production of it (see Lotz 1997, pp. 139–40). This clearly did not happen, since the work was not given its first full professional outing until 1972. Joplin's assistant in preparing this score was Sam Patterson, one of the Musical Spillers, providing yet more evidence for the strong link between the Spillers and the composer.

41. See Lotz 1997, pp. 132–5.
42. Lotz 1997, p. 143.
43. Vermazen 2004, pp. 43–4.
44. Vermazen 2004, p. 194.
45. 'The Five Brown Brothers', *Variety*, 11 December 1909, p. 50.
46. 'Alhambra', *Variety*, 18 February 1911, p. 18.
47. 'Brighton Theatre', *Variety*, 20 May 1911, p. 23.
48. Buescher company advertisement, *Metronome*, June 1921, p. 6.
49. *Variety* observed that 'The Browns have been a very valuable feature with "Chin Chin!" on the road because of the number of talking machine records of selections by them which have been sold.' 'Tom Brown's Saxophone Band', *Variety*, 30 March 1917, p. 20.
50. 'The Play', *New York Times*, 6 October 1920, p. 13.
51. For more details on the fractious relationship between Markwith and Tom Brown, see Vermazen 2004, pp. 152–3.
52. Vermazen 2004, pp. 152–3.
53. *New York Age*, 25 March 1915, p. 6.
54. Hindson 1992, p. 33.
55. http://sdrcdata.lib.uiowa.edu/libsdrc/details.jsp?id=/davidjb/1 (accessed 26 September 2010).
56. C. G. Conn's *Musical Truth*, vol. 5 no. 4, supplement, p. 3, quoted in Noyes 2000, pp. 174–5.
57. Vermazen 2004, p. 269, n. 98.
58. *Musical Truth*, April 1916, quoted in Hindson 1992, p. 32.
59. *Musical Truth*, November 1919, quoted in Hindson 1992, p. 33.
60. *Musical Truth*, October 1922, quoted in Hindson 1992, p. 34.
61. Hemke 1975, p. 450.
62. 'Tom Brown's Saxophone Band', *Variety*, 30 March 1917, p. 20.
63. Advertisement, *Variety*, 29 December 1922 p. 24K.
64. Charles D. Nicholls, *How to Conduct Saxophone Bands*. Libertyville, IL, Nicholls Band Circuit, 1921. Quoted in Levinsky 1997, pp. 268–9.
65. Another performer in this group was Georges Longy, who had previously directed the Boston Orchestral Club with which Miss Elise Hall performed.
66. The Boston Saxophone Orchestra Makes Its Appearance', *Metronome*, 1 January 1926, p. 14.
67. Vermazen 2004, p. 226 n. 6. lists several contemporaneous occurrences of this phrase.
68. See 'Vintage Saxophones Revisited', *Saxophone Journal*, 14(1), July/August 1989, p. 10.
69. During the First World War, for example, the army ordered more than 3,000 saxophones from American manufacturers (distributed as 89/959/1009/1093 S/A/T/B respectively), according to the Chief Inspector for Musical Instruments of the time. See 'Quicksteps and Army Jazz', *Metronome*, September 1922, pp. 63–4.
70. Bro 1992, p. 12.
71. Bro 1992, p. 16, Priestley, Gelly et al. 1998, p. 102.
72. Lindemeyer 1996, pp. 33 and 45.
73. *Music Trade News*, August 1924. Quoted in Koenig 2002, p. 345.
74. 'The F Alto Saxophone Part 2', *Saxophone Journal*, 14(5), March/April 1990, p. 11.
75. Hemke 1975, p. 452.
76. 'Vintage Saxophones Revisited', *Saxophone Journal*, 10(4), 1984, p. 7.
77. Powell 2002, p. 203.
78. Catalogue of Sears, Roebuck and Company, Spring 1908, p. 211.
79. Carl Fischer advertisement, *Metronome*, February 1918, p. 53. By 1921 these prices had risen by around 20–25 per cent.
80. King company advertisement, *Metronome*, July 1921, p. 22.
81. Vermazen 2004, p. 44.
82. Powell 2002, p. 230.
83. Catalogue of Sears, Roebuck and Company, Spring 1919, p. 745.
84. Ehrlich 1990, p. 141.
85. Selmer company advertisement, *Metronome*, 1 August 1925, pp. 10–11.

86. Selmer company advertisement, *Metronome*, 1 September 1925, pp. 12–13.

87. *Music Trade News*, August 1924, quoted in Koenig 2002, p. 344.

88. 'Vintage Saxophones Revisited', *Saxophone Journal*, 10(4), 1984, p. 7.

89. Quoted in Vermazen 2004, p. 11.

90. *The Story of the Saxophone*, Buescher Band Instrument Co., Elkhart, Indiana, p. 18.

91. Buescher advert, *The Metronome*, 15 January 1926, p. 49.

92. Noyes 2000, p. 119.

93. See Levinsky 1997, pp. 230–86.

94. *The Thompson Progressive Method for the Saxophone*, Kathryne E. Thompson. Los Angeles, CA, 1922, p. 2.

95. *Illustrated Five-Minute Course for Saxophone*, possibly written by M. M. Cole. The M. M. Cole Company, 1927; this was one of a series of 'five minute' courses on a variety of instruments. *Saxophone Made Easy: A New Method for Playing the Saxophone Without a Teacher*, Ben Bonnell. USA, Bonnell, 1923. *Eclipse Self-Instructor for Saxophone*, Paul DeVille. Boston, Carl Fischer, 1928.

96. Boyer 1996, pp. 191–2. On a more sombre note, Jones later writes that the company to which he had originally been assigned was all but wiped out in one particular offensive. In his particular case learning to play the saxophone – and thus being transferred to the infantry band rather than staying with the company – probably saved his life. See Boyer 1996, pp. 193 and 198.

97. Carter 1946, p. 356; Hyland 2003, p. 21.

98. *The Ernst Modern System of Improvising and Filling in for the Dance Saxophonist*, Ruby Ernst. New York, Irving Berlin Standard Music Corporation, 1928.

99. *Practical Studies in Bass Clef for Saxophone*, Kathryne E. Thompson. Los Angeles, F. J. Hart, 1922, p. 2.

100. Vereecken 1917, pp. 6–7.

101. Vereecken 1919, p. ii.

102. *Sax-Acrobatix* by Henri Weber, New York, Belwin Inc., 1926. Advertised in *Metronome*, 15 April 1926, p. 6.

103. Quoted in Hindson 1992, pp. 35–6.

104. Quoted in Vermazen 2004, p. 76, original source unknown.

105. Waller 1992, p. 12.

106. Vermazen 2004, p. 154 notes that the Brown Brothers fulfilled an eight-week engagement in Chicago movie palaces in 1922.

107. As heard, for example, on her recording of 'Irish Maggie' from 1913 (Jumbo 1045).

108. The Brown Brothers' technical execution, and the sophistication of the arrangements, progressed as their career unfolded. Nevertheless, by the time their popularity had waned in the mid 1920s, the technical ability of many other saxophonists had surpassed them.

109. 'Saxophone Celebrities', *Dominant*, May 1916, p. 74, quoted in Vermazen 2004, p. 243, n. 25.

110. A programme from 18 August 1894 suggests that in 1891 Moeremans was a 'Medallist at the Paris Conservatory', but this is unlikely, given the lack of a saxophone class there at that time (although he may also have been studying clarinet). A Conn advert from 1918 suggests that Moeremans 'entered the International Contest held in Paris where he obtained the Medal and Diploma, the highest honors extended'. See Hester 1995, p. 25, n. 9. Some kind of competition success, therefore, would appear closer to the truth, although this does not appear to have been recorded in the Parisian press at the time.

111. Bierley 2006, p. 69.

112. Bierley 2006, p. 27.

113. *London Daily News*, 13 April 1903 and *Daily Mail*, 13 April 1903, quoted in Hester 1995, pp. 33–4.

114. *Sheffield Independent*, 17 March 1903, quoted in Hester 1995, p. 33.

115. Bierley 2006, pp. 75–6.

116. Hindson 1992, p. 22.

117. *Kohler Wisconsin Sheboyhan Press*, 21 October 1919, quoted in Hester 1995, p. 55.

118. 'Jascha Gurewich', *Metronome*, 15 May 1927, pp. 14–15.

119. Wiedoeft 1927, p. 4.

120. *Down Beat*, 15 April 1940, quoted in Gushee 2005, p. 209.

121. Vallée 1962, p. 22.

122. Wiedoeft 1927, p. 45.

123. Wiedoeft 1927, p. 39.

124. Wiedoeft 1927, p. 57.

125. Priestley 2005, p. 12.
126. 'Rudy Wiedoeft Says', *Wireless Age*, June 1922, p. 33.
127. 'Rudy Wiedoeft Sets Precedent in Aeolian Hall Concert', *Metronome*, 1 May 1926, p. 24.
128. Prior to this technological innovation, recordings had been made acoustically, that is, without any electrical amplification of the sound entering the recording apparatus.
129. Gracyk 2000, p. 380.
130. Jim Walsh, 'The Wiedoefts: further glimpses into their musical lives', *The Saxophone Symposium*, 6(3), Summer 1981, p. 12.
131. *New York Age*, 27 Sept 1889, quoted in Badger 1995, p. 24.
132. Various minstrel groups in the late nineteenth and early twentieth centuries adopted the word 'Students' as part of their name, in an attempt to emulate the international success of the Fisk Jubilee Singers, who actually were students from Fisk University, Nashville. See Badger 1995, p. 29.
133. Quoted in Badger 1995, p. 30.
134. Quoted in Badger 1989, p. 50.
135. Badger 1995, p. 75.
136. Brooks 2004, p. 301.
137. Fletcher 1984, p. 261.
138. Tucker 1996, p. 145.
139. 'Editorial Notes', *Metronome*, vol. 32 no. 3, March 1916, p. 15.
140. Handy 1944, p. 95.
141. Badger 1995, p. 287, n. 20. One of Jim Reese Europe's collaborators, Noble Sissle, was working with this band at the time.
142. *Literary Digest*, 26 April 1919, quoted in Koenig 2002, p. 132.
143. Gracyk 2000, p. 306.
144. Gracyk 2000, p. 261.
145. Walker 1990, p. 15. However Vermazen (2004, p. 211) suggests this did not happen until as late as 1919.
146. The saxophone/clarinet players on Handy's seminal September 1917 recordings were Wilson Townes, Alex Poole, Charles Harris and Nelson Kincaid; see Brooks 2004, pp. 417 and 419, and Handy 1944, pp. 95 and 100.
147. Both the picture and this recording (Columbia A2419) can be found at http://www.redhotjazz.com/handy.html
148. Walker 1990, p. 10.
149. Like many saxophonists of the time, Doerr started as a violinist. He was a concert master and leader of a 32-piece orchestra in San Jose, California, before he joined Hickman's band. Doerr was interviewed by the American concert saxophonist Cecil Leeson in 1970, some three years before his death. Some of the results of that interview are available online at http://www.gracyk.com/clydedoerr.shtml (accessed 3 March 2010).
150. One can also often hear the slide whistle – a piston-operated instrument with a fipple, like a recorder – on these early Whiteman recordings. It too seems to have been identified as part of the reed section, either playing with the others saxes, or taking the melody line under which the other saxes provided harmonic support.
151. Victor 18803.
152. 'What is Jazz doing to American Music', *Etude*, vol. 42 no. 8, August 1924, p. 523.
153. These 1939 recordings were released on Decca 2467(A/B) and 2698 (A/B).
154. Whiteman and McBride 1974, p. 193.
155. Harry L. Alford, 'The Make-up of a Modern Orchestra', *Metronome*, July 1923, p. 56.
156. Frank J. Gibbons, 'Pre-Jazz, Post-Jazz', *Metronome*, September 1923, p. 155.
157. Vocalion B 14926.
158. Lange 1926, p. 40.
159. Weirick 1937, p. 1.
160. Lange 1926, p. 99.
161. Brunswick 7923 (*Sleepy Time Gal*) and 7915 (*Time on My Hands*).
162. See Schuller 1989, pp. 55–6.
163. See Peress 1993, p. 155.
164. 'The Saxophone Is Coming Fast', *Dominant*, July 1915 p. 66, quoted in Vermazen 2004, pp. 11–12.

165. Ernest Cutting, 'Instrumentation for the Theater Pit and Dance Orchestras', *Metronome*, December 1923, p. 80.
166. Harry L. Alford, 'The Make-up of a Modern Orchestra', *Metronome*, July 1923, p. 56.
167. Levinson 2005, p. 27.
168. For Gallodoro's own reflections on playing with Whiteman, see 'Alfred Gallodoro', *Saxophone Journal*, 14(2), 1989, pp. 12–20.
169. 'What is Jazz doing to American Music', *Étude*, vol. 42 no. 8, August 1924, p. 524.
170. Ed Chenette, 'Town Clef Topics', *Metronome*, March 1923, p. 35.
171. George T. Simon, 'Dance Band Reviews', *Metronome*, July 1936, p. 16.
172. All quotes taken from Davis 1932, pp. 164–6.
173. *Sax-Clarinet Doubling Studies* or *Sax Section Studies: For 2, 3, or 4 Sax Teams*. Both published by David Gornston, New York, 1937.
174. Advertisement, *Metronome*, April 1915, p. 41, and January 1916, p. 19.
175. Advertisement, *Metronome*, February 1918, p. 53.
176. Ed Chenette, 'Town Clef Topics', *Metronome*, March 1923, p. 35.
177. 'For Better or For Worse', *Musical Digest*, Feb 1924, quoted in Koenig 2002, p. 287.
178. Quoted in Vermazen 2004, p. 74.
179. Harrison 2006, p. 243.
180. Annand, H. H.: *Block Catalogue of the Cylinder Records Issued by the US Phonograph Company, 1890–6*, Hillingdon, 1970.
181. Koenigsberg 1969, p. 133.
182. Fagan 1983, p. 36.
183. Victor 16244 provides one version of Moeremans performing *Carnival of Venice*; Benne Henton's performance of *Scenes That Are Brightest* can be heard via the digitisation project of the University of California, Santa Barbara (http://cylinders.library.ucsb.edu/index.php).
184. Victor 18117-A.
185. Edison 5046-L (*Valse Erica*) and Columbia 4076 (*Souvenir*).
186. Büchmann-Møller 1990, p. 23.

Chapter 5 *The saxophone in jazz*

1. Sudhalter 1999, p. 9.
2. *The Etude*, September 1924, vol. 42 (9), p. 595. For an extensive overview of the etymology of the word 'jazz' see Gabbard 2002.
3. It has been suggested that neither Buddy Bolden nor musicians who played with him ever played in brothels; nor, with the exception of a few pianists, did they know anybody who had (see Marquis 1978, p. 58). Sidney Bechet, despite the unreliability of his colourful autobiography, also suggests that the frequently asserted connection between early jazz and prostitution is not entirely correct; see Bechet 1975, p. 53.
4. Hennessey 1994, p. 18.
5. Schafer (1977, p. 98) asserts that the Holmes Band contained saxophones, but a picture of the band from around this time shows no evidence of the instrument. See Rose and Souchon 1967, pp. 285–7.
6. Charters 1983, p. 29.
7. Pathé 20145 (A/B); 20147 (A/B); 20167 (A/B). The discs were released only two months after those made by the Original Dixieland Jass Band, often taken to be the first ever jazz recordings.
8. Quoted in Miller 1995, p. 159.
9. Jelly Roll Morton later observed that 'Buddy Bolden was the most powerful trumpet in history [. . .]. Any time it was a quiet night at Lincoln Park because maybe the affair hadn't been so well publicised, Buddy Bolden would publicise it! He'd turn his big trumpet around toward the city and blow his blues, calling his children home, as he used to say'. Lomax 1991, p. 60.
10. Sidney Bechet, for example, notes in his autobiography that 'the blues, they've got that sob inside, that awful lonesome feeling'. Bechet 1975, p. 213.
11. Gioia 1997, p. 50.
12. Quoted in Blesh 1946, p. 190.
13. Ernest Ansermet, 'Sur un orchestre nègre', *La Revue Romande*, 15 October 1919, p. 13.
14. Chilton 1987, p. 32.

15. Bechet 1975, p. 126.
16. Bechet 1975, p. 127.
17. Quoted in Gioia 1997, p. 50.
18. Victor 27485.
19. Parlophone R 3419.
20. Quoted in Porter 1991, p. 158.
21. The goofus was a small, saxophone-shaped instrument activated by blowing down a pipe. Internal metal reeds were controlled by sprung valves, operated by the fingers and laid out following a piano keyboard. The 1950s melodica worked on similar principles (albeit that the two instruments looked very different). The 'hot fountain pen' was a type of flageolet fitted with a clarinet-type single reed mouthpiece. Pitched in E♭, it had a thin but penetrating clarinet-type sound.
22. Chilton 1990, p. 5.
23. Gioia 1997, p. 110.
24. Schuller 1989, p. 426.
25. Quoted in Chilton 1990, p. 7.
26. Chilton 1990, p. 10.
27. Chilton 1990, p. 15.
28. Bluebird 10523A.
29. Quoted in Chilton 1990, p. 104.
30. Chilton 1990, p. 389.
31. Quoted in Sudhalter 1999, p. 172.
32. Quoted in Lawrence 2001, p. 400.
33. Gioia 1997, p. 114.
34. Porter 1985, p. 5.
35. Quoted in Porter 1985, p. 8.
36. Quoted in Büchmann-Møller 1990, p. 29.
37. Porter 1985, p. 34.
38. Quoted in Büchmann-Møller 1990, p. 25.
39. For more on Young's use of false fingerings as a representation of speech, see Daniels 1985, p. 317.
40. Quoted in Daniels 1985, p. 318.
41. Quoted in Porter 1985, p. 17.
42. For more on Young's idiosyncratic language and his various neologisms, see Daniels 1985.
43. Quoted in Porter 1985, p. 27.
44. The state line dividing Kansas and Missouri runs through the middle of Kansas City.
45. Gioia 1997, p. 206.
46. Gioia 1997, p. 206. One source suggests Parker started on the ubiquitous C-melody sax, but this is uncorroborated elsewhere. See Reisner 1975, p. 34.
47. Quoted in Reisner 1975, p. 139.
48. See Woideck 1996, pp. 11–12. These were likely to have been the 1936 Basie recordings described, for contractual reasons, as being played by 'Jones-Smith incorporated'.
49. Quoted in Reisner 1975, p. 137.
50. Parker's recording of *Lady Be Good* can be found on Stash STCD 542, Young's on many reissues, including Columbia CK 64966.
51. There are several stories advanced as the origin of this nickname. One relates to Parker's inclination to be 'as free as a bird'. A more plausible scenario is that when touring with Jay McShann in the late 1930s they accidentally hit a chicken (a yardbird) with their car and Parker made them stop to pick it up so he could have his landlady cook it for him. For further discussion see Woideck 1996, pp. 20–1.
52. Woideck 1996, p. 27.
53. Quoted in Porter 1991, p. 155.
54. Quoted in Peretti 1992, pp. 152–3.
55. For a more complete analysis of Parker's style, see Owens 1995, pp. 28–45.
56. Owens (1995, pp. 38–9) cites Shapiro and Hentoff (1966, p. 354) as an example. Further evidence in support of his assertion can be found in Russell 1996, p. 105, or Gioia 1997, p. 207.
57. This bright sound relates to Parker's work on alto. On the few recordings where he is heard on tenor his sound is more warm and full.

58. Quoted in Reisner 1975, p. 67.
59. For a detailed analysis of issues relating to pitch variation and vibrato in the 1948 recording of 'Parker's Mood', see Owens 1974.
60. Reisner 1975, p. 90.
61. Woideck 1996, p. 172.
62. Gioia 1997, p. 232.
63. Quoted in Porter 1998, p. 63.
64. For a more extensive appraisal of Adderley's style see Owens 1995, pp. 55–9.
65. Prestige PRLP 7079.
66. Capitol T792.
67. Quoted in Owens 1995, p. 69.
68. Quoted in Porter 1998, p. 30.
69. Porter 1998, p. 63.
70. Nash 1946, Rascher 1942.
71. Porter 1998, p. 79.
72. Quoted in Thomas 1975, p. 116.
73. Porter 1998, p. 126. It may be relevant that Coltrane had notoriously bad teeth, requiring extensive dental treatment.
74. Quoted in Porter 1998, p. 90.
75. Quoted in Thomas 1975, p. 58.
76. Quoted Porter 1998, p. 94.
77. Quoted in Porter 1998, p. 111.
78. Quoted in Porter 1998, p. 133.
79. Gioia 1997, p. 303.
80. Quoted in Porter 1998, p. 181.
81. Porter 1998, p. 232.
82. Quoted in Porter 1998, p. 275.
83. Porter 1998, pp. 202–4.
84. Miller (1995) provides an overview of saxophonists emanating from this Texas tradition. See especially p. 159.
85. Quoted in Litweiler 1992, p. 79.
86. Quoted in Litweiler 1992, p. 10.
87. Quoted in Litweiler 1992, p. 18, original emphasis.
88. For a sophisticated appraisal of Coleman's relationship with prevailing masculine paradigms of jazz music, see Ake 1998.
89. Quoted in Litweiler 1992, p. 31.
90. Litweiler 1992, p. 30.
91. Litweiler 1992, p. 67.
92. These various reactions to Coleman's playing – and others – are all listed in Litweiler 1992, pp. 62–7.
93. These words are from liner notes written for two of Coleman's Atlantic recordings. They are quoted in Porter 1998, p. 203.
94. Litweiler 1992, p. 54.
95. Whitney Balliett, 'Jazz Concerts: Historic', *New Yorker*, 5 December 1959, quoted in Litweiler 1992, p. 64.
96. Atlantic 1317.
97. Atlantic 1364.

Chapter 6 *The classical saxophone*

1. Peress 1993, p. 150.
2. Peress 1993, p. 153.
3. Grainger expanded on this theme in his 1929 preface to *Spoon River*, where, in a section titled 'Orchestral Use of Saxophones' he notes that 'If the saxophone [. . .] is not the loveliest of all wind instruments it certainly is *one* of the loveliest – human, voicelike, heart-revealing'. Reproduced as: Percy Grainger, 'The orchestral use of saxophones', Grainger Journal 7(20), 1985, p. 30.
4. Forsyth 1935, p. 491, original emphasis.

5. Piston 1955, p. 186.
6. Kennan 1953, p. 271.
7. Carse 1964, p. 291.
8. In a draft of the lecture on orchestration in which Elgar makes these observations, he originally described the saxophone as 'that beautiful sweet-toned instrument'. See Elgar 1968, pp. 242–3.
9. Trier 1998, p. 104.
10. Trier 1998, p. 103.
11. See Dean 1965, p. 203 n. 1.
12. The theme played by the saxophone in *L'Arlésienne* was in fact recycled from an unfinished *opéra-comique* titled *Grisélidis*, on which Bizet had been working in 1870–1. See Dean 1960, p. 243.
13. Dean 1965, p. 203.
14. Howes 1954, p. 310. For a more thorough appraisal of the relationship between Vaughan Williams's score and Blake's illustrations, see Weltzien 1992.
15. *The Times*, 30 April 1948, p. 7.
16. For more on the relationship between Mussorgsky's original suite and Hartmann's pictures, see Frankenstein 1939.
17. Britten used the saxophone extensively in other works, although not with these kinds of associations: in the opera, *Paul Bunyan*, the ballet *The Prince of the Pagodas*, the early song cycle *Our Hunting Fathers* and his orchestral piece *Sinfonia da Requiem*. He also employed it in several film scores, including *Love from a Stranger* and *The Way to the Sea* (both 1936), and in incidental music for a radio drama, *The Rescue* (1943), where it is associated with a lament by the Greek goddess Penelope.
18. For more on the oboe's role in musical orientalism see Burgess and Haynes 2004, pp. 236–40.
19. Larner 1996, p. 202.
20. Carner 1936, pp. 64–5.
21. Darius Milhaud, 'The Jazz Band and Negro Music', *Living Age*, 18 October 1924. Reproduced in Koenig 2002, p. 360.
22. Milhaud 1995, p. 98.
23. Hindemith clearly had strong convictions about the inclusion of the instrument, however, since a note in the score indicates that 'if a tenor saxophone is unavailable, this part can be taken by a heckelphone, although the effect intended by the composer will not be achieved.'
24. Danzi 1986, p. 58.
25. For more on Krenek, Schoenberg and *Zeitopern*, see Cook 1988, pp. 85 and 182.
26. Berg acknowledged in a letter to Schoenberg that for some time in 1932 he kept a copy of the score of *Von Heute auf Morgen* on his piano. See Brand, Hailey et al. 1987, p. 433.
27. Berg and Webern may well have been introduced to the saxophone and jazz via recordings played to them by the architect Adolf Loos, the dedicatee of Webern's Op. 22 'saxophone' quartet. Adorno also later recalled an evening in a Viennese bar when Berg first showed an interest in jazz. See Bell 2004, p. 90.
28. For a more extensive reading of *Lulu* as *Zeitoper*, see Jarman 1991, pp. 91–101.
29. The original incidental music for the play *Egyptian Nights* had two saxophones, but the subsequent rescored orchestral suite has only one tenor. As elsewhere, saxophones were reasonably common in Russian theatres of the 1930s.
30. 'Soviet Audiences and My Work' by Sergey Prokofiev. Originally in *Soviet Travel*, 1934, no. 3, quoted in Petchenina and Abensour 2004, pp. 17–18.
31. Bertensson and Leyda 2001, p. 361.
32. Engel 1925, p. 326.
33. Street 1983, p. 21.
34. Charles Martin Loeffler was German by birth, background and education, but aligned himself with France and took French nationality in protest at the Prussian treatment of his father. Ultimately he became based in Boston. He was part of Elise Hall's social circle, which explains this relatively large number of works for her.
35. Debussy 2005, p. 740.
36. Debussy 2005, p. 742.
37. Debussy 2005, p. 758.
38. For a thorough overview of the genesis of Debussy's *Rapsodie*, see Noyes 2007.
39. Rousseau 1982, p. 6.
40. Rousseau 1982, p. 83.

41. Rousseau 1982, p. 85.
42. The opening phrases of Mule's 1937 recording of the second movement of the Ibert *Concertino da camera*, for example, range between 200 and 240 undulations per minute.
43. Rousseau 1982, pp. 10, 40 and 84.
44. See Powell 2002, pp. 208–24.
45. A complete – and extensive – list of works dedicated to Mule is given in Gee 1986, pp. 223–5.
46. Rousseau 1982, p. 59.
47. 'Musical Notes from Abroad: Berlin', *Musical Times*, February 1933, p. 174.
48. See Robinson 1997, p. 339.
49. Sobchenko 1997, p. 68.
50. Quoted in Sobchenko 1997, pp. 68–9.
51. Rascher 1942.
52. *Hollywood News*, 12 June 1931, quoted in Hulsebos 1989, p. 70.
53. Quoted in Hulsebos 1989, p. 80; no date given.
54. Later in life Creston also composed other works involving the saxophone, including a *Rapsodie* (1976) for saxophone and piano or organ, and a saxophone quartet (1979).
55. 'Saxophone Soloist with Philharmonic', *Rochester Times Union*, 14 January 1938. Quoted in Hulsebos 1989, pp. 130–1.
56. In an unpublished memoir, Tuthill observes that he wrote the sonata for Leeson in 1939 without telling him he was doing so, and then sent it to him. Leeson appears to have forgotten the work, but rediscovered it some 25 years later on a shelf in his office. He then asked Tuthill's permission to publish it, and commissioned several further works at that point. See Burnet C. Tuthill, *Recollections of A Musical Life: 1888–1973*, unpaginated.
57. Hulsebos 1989, pp. 122 and 49–58.
58. *The Basis of Saxophone Tone Production: A Critical and Analytical Study*. Chicago Musical College, 1955.
59. 'In Defense of the Saxophone', *Musician*, November 1934, p. 466. Quoted in Hulsebos 1989, p. 87.
60. Of particular use for saxophonists are Londeix's extensive repertoire listings. See Londeix and Ronkin 2003.
61. Rorive 2004, p. 255.
62. *France Musicale*, 7 January 1844, p. 432.
63. 'Portrait of Debussy. 7: Koechlin and Debussy'. *Musical Times*, November 1967, p. 996.
64. Stravinsky and Craft 1962, p. 91. In fact Stravinsky did score for alto and baritone saxophones in the original version of Circus Polka completed in the spring of 1942. The saxophones were omitted in the orchestral version completed later the same year. See White 1969, p. 373.
65. Clarkson 1999, p. 385.
66. Moldenhauer and Moldenhauer 1979, p. 424.
67. Smalley 1975, pp. 29–30.
68. Rudolf played cello in the professional Amar Quartet with Paul Hindemith. The latter was dismayed when Rudolf decided to become a jazz musician in Frankfurt, leading to the break-up of the Quartet. See Hindemith 1995, p. 49.
69. 'Potter Hall, Longy Club', *Boston Daily Evening Transcript*, 20 January 1905, quoted in Street 1983, p. 75.

Chapter 7 Modernism and postmodernism

1. Capitol ST 2987.
2. Atlantic SD 1495.
3. Porter 1998.
4. The Lyricon was an analogue synthesiser (i.e. it used electro-mechanical components to generate sounds), while the Yamaha and Akai versions are MIDI (Musical Instrument Digital Interface) controllers. The latter rely entirely on digital technology, and can thus be allied to a wide range of computers and processing units.
5. Elektra 9 60441-2.
6. For more on the Synthophone see http://robosax.com/synthophone (accessed 21 August 2010).

7. Gilbert 2000, p. 159.
8. For more on the Metasaxophone see Burtner 2002.
9. *Institut de Recherche et Coordination Acoustique/Musique*, a research and performance centre established under the direction of Pierre Boulez in Paris in 1977.
10. Bumcke 1926.
11. Kientzy 1982.
12. The rapid alternation between a 'true' note and its 'false' alternative, a form of microtonal trill, is properly known as *bisbigliando*. The word is borrowed from harp terminology, where it refers to playing the same notes on different strings, producing a tremolo effect.
13. See Londeix and Ronkin 2003. This is an updated and considerably expanded version of Londeix 1971. That an update to the original was felt necessary after 30 years is testament to the significant amount of new material generated during this period.
14. A fuller list of names up to 1998 is given in Ingham 1998, pp. 45–50. Gee (1986) gives more detailed information on a range of soloists up to 1985.
15. See for example Kenneth Radnofsky's 'Worldwide Concurrent Premieres and Commissioning Fund' (http://www.kenradnofsky.com/wwcp/index.html) or Andy Scott's 'World Tenor Saxophone Consortium' (http://www.andyscott.org.uk/world-tenor-saxophone-consortium.htm). Accessed 21 August 2010.
16. For more on John Coltrane's influence on these composers, see various entries in Potter 1999.
17. This work has presently been withdrawn by the composer.
18. Potter 1999, p. 64. The Indian *shanai* or shawm is the smaller relative of the *nagaswaram*, both of which are double-reed 'oboe'-type instruments. Other saxophonists performing contemporary music in the 1970s and 80s also experimented with fixing a double reed to the instrument via a bespoke attachment, a practice that resonates with Gautrot's invention of the sarrusophone in the 1850s (see above, pp. 66–7).
19. The Aurelia Quartet, founded in 1982, has been particularly proactive in commissioning repertoire for the saxophone quartet genre.
20. Unfortunately Getz died in 1991, before he could perform this work.
21. A deeply unscientific but rapid way of arriving at this statement was to compare the number of methods available for various instruments from the specialist UK wind and brass literature supplier, June Emerson Wind Music. While the company's website registered 157 flute methods and 146 clarinet methods, there were 125 methods for saxophone. Similar proportions pertained to the overall amount of material available for each instrument. http://www.juneemerson.co.uk/index.aspx (accessed 17 August 2010).
22. For a list of saxophone quartets established since the 1970s (as of 1998), see 'The Saxophone Quartet' in Ingham 1998, pp. 65–74.
23. Ingham 1998, p. 200, n. 2 gives a brief list of some of these larger ensembles as of 1998.
24. Pressing 2002, p. 204.
25. Sony 89251.
26. Jazz rock is sometimes also known as fusion, although Nicholson (2002, pp. 231–3) argues that these terms describe two rather different approaches, with jazz rock seen as more innovative and experimental, and fusion as essentially a commercial spin-off.
27. Columbia GP 26.
28. Columbia KC 30661.
29. This part pedagogic, part autobiographical text was published in France by Outre Mesure in 1995; it was reprinted in 2006.
30. The straight Buescher E♭ alto is a rare instrument, having been manufactured for only a short time between about 1927 and 1929.
31. *Officium*'s combination of saxophone and early music vocal group was so successful that two follow-ups were released: *Mnemosyne* (1999) and *Officium Novum* (2010).
32. The individual members of The Hollywood Saxophone Quartet were Russ Cheever (soprano), Jack Dumont (alto), Morrie Crawford (tenor), and Bill Ulyate (baritone).
33. Niehaus is also a saxophonist who went on to become a well-known film score composer. He oversaw the innovative soundtrack for Clint Eastwood's biopic of Charlie Parker, *Bird* (1988), in which Parker's original recordings were remastered so that his performances were accompanied by modern players rather than the original sidemen.
34. The founder members of the New York Saxophone Quartet were Ray Beckenstein (soprano), Eddie Caine (alto), Al Epstein (tenor), and Danny Bank (baritone).

35. The correct spelling of this name is in fact Pompillii, but the final 'i' was dropped on publicity and record covers some time during the 1950s.
36. Sonet 696.
37. This title is likely to have been the inspiration for Boots Randolph's 1963 *Yakety Sax*, although the tunes are rather different.
38. Sonny Rollins's contribution to *Waiting on a Friend* (1981) by the Rolling Stones provides one exception to this general principle.
39. Dick Parry's solos on Pink Floyd's 1973 *Dark Side of the Moon* also provides an exception to this general rule.
40. *Your Latest Trick* was released as a single in 1986. The opening sax solo became so well known that entire audiences would sing along to it during live performances. Mark Knopfler (the band leader and songwriter) is reported later to have observed that the tune was often played by people trying out saxophones in music shops, in much the same way as guitarists would try out the opening of Led Zeppelin's *Stairway to Heaven* (1971). In addition to the now famous hook, the album version of *Your Latest Trick* does in fact fade out with a long solo from Brecker.
41. www.riaa.com, accessed 22 August 2010.
42. See for example Booth 1996–7, p. 63, and Booth 1990, p. 253.
43. See Booth 1996–7, pp. 68–9.
44. Gonsalves should not be confused with the saxophone player of the same name who later featured in Duke Ellington's band.
45. For more on the development of jazz in India see Pinckney 1989–90.
46. Kadri Gopalnath, 'Adapting the Saxophone to Carnatic Music'. Paper given at the Chembur Fine Arts Society, Mumbai, February, 2000.
47. Collins 1989, p. 222.
48. Collins 1986, p. 13.
49. Collins 1986, p. 11.
50. Collins 1989, pp. 225–6.
51. For fuller details on these bands and this particular form of highlife, see Collins 1989.
52. The word 'mabaqanga', roughly translating as 'homemade', is also used to describe this genre.
53. Dodson 1947, p. 259.
54. For a more extensive discussion of the role of saxophones in the orquesta típica of the Mantaro valley, see Romero 2001, especially pp. 67–90.
55. In his 2001 book (p. 71) Romero suggests that saxophones became common in the area from the 1940s, but in an earlier paper Romero (1990, p. 21) he suggests that the instruments were commonly added to these groups in the 1920s, a time-scale that would better explain the use of the C-melody model.
56. Romero 2001, p. 85.
57. Romero 2001, pp. 72–3.
58. Austerlitz 1998, p. 4.
59. Austerlitz 1998, p. 4.
60. Hernández 1991, p. 112.

Chapter 8   The saxophone as symbol and icon

1. *Musical World*, 10 January 1852, p. 22.
2. Hemke 1975, p. 357.
3. *RGMP*, 22 November 1868, p. 371.
4. Henry F. Gilbert, 'Concerning Jazz', *The New Music Review*, December 1922, quoted in Koenig 2002, p. 221.
5. Although McNair played it on board – NASA released a promotional photograph of him doing so – the performance was not heard on Earth. A space broadcast was apparently planned for a later trip, in January 1986. Unfortunately the shuttle exploded shortly after takeoff, and McNair and the rest of the crew lost their lives.
6. Clay Smith and G. E. Holmes, 'Saxophone Article', *Dominant* 26 (September 1918), p. 63. Quoted in Smialek 1991, p. 103.
7. *Metronome*, June 1924, p. 64.
8. Smialek 1991, p. 120.

9. This observation was reprinted in *Musical Times*, February 1925, p. 160.

10. For an examination of similar advertising trends in relation to Germany and Austria, see Eggert and Vockeroth 2003, pp. 93–168.

11. 'Is Jazz the Pilot of Disaster?', *Étude* 43(1), January 1925, pp. 5–6.

12. Quoted in Segell 2005, p. 89.

13. Isador Berger, 'The Saxophone: Siren of Satan', *San Francisco Chronicle*, 14 January 1917, magazine section, p.1, quoted in Vermazen 2004, pp. 12–13.

14. 'Our Jazz Symposium', *Music News*, 12 December 1924, quoted in Koenig 2002, p. 368.

15. 'Religio Musici', *Music and Letters*, 10 (1), January 1929, p. 71.

16. See Horwood 1980, p. 161.

17. Nuzum 2001, p. 5.

18. 'Women Judge Saxophone; One Calls It Immoral, Another Respectable If Treated Right', *New York Times*, 2 August 1925.

19. 'Messrs. Wiener and Doucet', *Musical Times*, 1 June 1928, p. 549.

20. 'Ad Libitum', *Musical Times*, 1 May 1932, p. 410.

21. 'Gramophone Notes', *Musical Times*, 1 July 1928, pp. 614–6.

22. 'The Promenade Concerts', *Musical Times*, October 1936, p. 937.

23. 'Sax and the Saxophone', *The Times*, 1 May 1933, p. 15. The reference to 'Alice' here is of course to Lewis Carroll's *Alice in Wonderland*.

24. Southern 1997, p. 255.

25. These acts were not confined only to white entertainers: African Americans themselves also performed as blackface minstrels, similarly using burnt cork to indicate their adoption of caricatured minstrel personas, and creating material that would today be described as racist. While this may seem paradoxical, for African Americans in what was an increasingly segregated society, opportunities for both work and individual advancement were few; minstrelsy, which in any case went beyond simple comedy routines to include individual and ensemble singing as well as a range of speciality acts, provided one route by which they might generate a livelihood. See Vermazen 2004, pp. 128–9.

26. Said 1995, p. 72.

27. Quoted in Vermazen 2004, p. 21.

28. Peretti 1992, p. 73.

29. Peretti 1992, p. 76.

30. Fitzgerald 1922, p. 338.

31. Quoted in Litweiler 1992, p. 83.

32. For a fuller reading of Douglas's picture, see Cassidy 1997, pp. 115–46.

33. Quoted in Cassidy 1997, p. 140.

34. Du Bois 1953, p. 17.

35. See Porter 1999.

36. See Gebhardt 2001, pp. 80–1.

37. Quoted in Gebhardt 2001, p. 83.

38. Quoted in Laubenstein 1929, p. 622.

39. *The Times,* 1 May 1926, p. 15

40. *Monthly Musical Record*, 'Jazz and the Modern Serpent', November 1926, reproduced in Koenig 2002, p. 490.

41. Kater 1992, p. 16.

42. Kater 1992, p. 67.

43. Robinson 1994, p. 115.

44. Weiner 1991, pp. 475–6.

45. Weiner 1991, p. 478.

46. Hesse 1965, pp. 146 and 56.

47. Lareau 2002, p. 29.

48. Cook 1989, p. 41.

49. Quoted with translation in Bell 2004, p. 51.

50. Kater 1992, p. 46.

51. Bell 2004, p. 69.

52. Quoted with translation in Bell 2004, p. 72.

53. The exhibition then toured widely around Europe and the USA.

54. Quoted with translation in Bell 2004, pp. 74–5.

55. Starr 1983, p. 42.
56. Starr 1983, p. 42.
57. Starr 1983, p. 85.
58. Starr 1983, p. 216.
59. See Ellis 1999, pp. 235–6.
60. Ellis 1999, p. 225.
61. See Rousseau 1982, pp. 121–43.
62. See Street 1983, p. 53.
63. Charles 1995, p. 184.
64. Quoted in Charles 1995, p. 184.
65. Tucker 1999, p. 96.
66. For more on the marginalisation of all-women bands at this time see Tucker 1998, especially p. 286, n. 28.
67. Dahl 1984, p. 47.
68. Abeles and Porter 1978, p. 68.
69. Hallam, Rogers et al. 2005, p. 99.
70. Adorno uses the word 'zwischengeschlechtlicher', literally 'between genders', to describe the saxophone's sexual ambiguity. For more on Adorno and the saxophone see Jay 1973, pp. 187–8, and Bell 2004, pp. 77–84.
71. Shepherd 1991, pp. 167–8.
72. Shepherd 1991, p. 164.
73. Wiedoeft 1927, p. 39.
74. Miller 1995, p. 170.
75. Miller 1995, p. 161.
76. Taylor 1982, p. 6.
77. Gates 1988, p. 64.
78. Quoted in Horn 2002, p. 31.
79. Fitzgerald 1925, p. 218.
80. Quoted in Segell 2005, p. 229.
81. See Segell 2005, pp. 227–8.
82. See Morcom 2001, pp. 68–70.
83. Quoted with translation in Philippot and Messinger 1964, p. 136. Ansermet's book title may be translated as 'The Foundations of Music in Human Consciousness'.
84. See, for example, Shepherd 1991, pp. 96–127.

Bibliography

Abeles, H. F. and S. Y. Porter (1978). 'The Sex-Stereotyping of Musical Instruments'. *Journal of Research in Music Education* 26: 65–75.

Ake, D. (1998). 'Re-Masculating Jazz: Ornette Coleman, "Lonely Woman", and the New York Jazz Scene in the Late 1950s'. *American Music* 16 (1): 25–44.

Austerlitz, P. (1998). 'The Jazz Tinge in Dominican Music: A Black Atlantic Perspective'. *Black Music Research Journal* 18 (1/2): 1–19.

Badger, R. R. (1989). 'James Reese Europe and the Prehistory of Jazz'. *American Music* 7 (1): 48–67.

Badger, R. R. (1995). *A Life in Ragtime: A Biography of James Reese Europe.* New York, Oxford University Press.

Baines, A. (1967). *Woodwind Instruments and Their History.* London, Faber.

Baines, A. (1992). *The Oxford Companion to Musical Instruments.* Oxford, Oxford University Press.

Bechet, S. (1975). *Treat It Gentle.* New York, Da Capo Press.

Bell, D. M. (2004). 'The Saxophone in Germany, 1924–1935'. Diss., University of Arizona.

Berlioz, H. (1843). *Die Kunst Der Instrumentierung. Aus dem Französischen übersetzt von J. A. Leibrock.* Leipzig.

Berlioz, H. (1860). *Traité d'instrumentation et d'orchestration.* Paris, Lemoine.

Berlioz, H. (2002). *The Memoirs of Hector Berlioz,* trans. and ed. D. Cairns. London, Everyman.

Berlin E.A. (1994). *King of Ragtime: Scott Joplin and His Era.* New York. Oxford University Press.

Bertensson, S. and J. Leyda (2001). *Sergei Rachmaninov: A Lifetime in Music.* Bloomington, Indiana University Press.

Bickley, N. (1914). *Letters from and to Joseph Joachim.* London, Macmillan.

Bierley, P. E. (2006). *The Incredible Band of John Philip Sousa.* Urbana and Chicago, University of Illinois Press.

Binns, P. L. (1959). *A Hundred Years of Military Music: Being the Story of the Royal Military School of Music, Kneller Hall.* Gillingham, Dorset, Blackmore.

Blesh, R. (1946). *Shining Trumpets: A History of Jazz.* New York, Knopf.

Booth, G. D. (1990). 'Brass Bands: Tradition, Change, and the Mass Media in Indian Wedding Music'. *Ethnomusicology* 34 (2): 245–62.

Booth, G. D. (1996–7). 'The Madras Corporation Band: A Story of Social Change and Indigenization'. *Asian Music* 28 (1): 61–86.

Boyer, D. R. (1996). 'The World War 1 Army Bandsman: A Diary Account by Philip James'. *American Music* 14 (2): 185–204.

Brand, J., C. Hailey, et al., eds. (1987). *The Berg–Schoenberg Correspondence: Selected Letters.* New York, Norton.

Bro, P. A. (1992). 'The Development of the American-made Saxophone: A Study of Saxophones Made by Buescher, Conn, Holton, Martin, and H. N. White'. Diss., Northwestern University.

Brooks, T. (2004). *Lost Sounds: Blacks and the Birth of the Recording Industry, 1890–1919.* Urbana, University of Illinois Press.

Büchmann-Møller, F. (1990). *You Just Fight for Your Life: The Story of Lester Young.* New York, Praeger.

Bumcke, G. (1926). *Saxophon Schule,* Hamburg, A. J. Benjamin.

Burgess, G. and B. Haynes (2004). *The Oboe.* New Haven and London, Yale University Press.

Burtner, M. (2002). 'The Metasaxophone: Concept, Implementation and Mapping Strategies for a New Computer Music Instrument'. *Organised Sound* 7 (2): 201–13.

Cairns, D. (2000). *Berlioz: Servitude and Greatness, 1832–1869.* London, Penguin.

Carner, M. (1936). 'The Exotic Element in Puccini'. *Musical Quarterly* 22 (1): 45–67.

Carse, A. (1939). *Musical Wind Instruments*. London, Macmillan.

Carse, A. (1951). *The Life of Jullien*. Cambridge, Heffer

Carse, A. (1964). *The History of Orchestration*. New York, Dover.

Carter, E. (1946). 'Walter Piston'. *Musical Quarterly* 32 (3): 354–75.

Cassidy, D. M. (1997). *Painting the Musical City: Jazz and Cultural Identity in American Art, 1910–1940*. Washington, Smithsonian Institution Press.

Charles, M. A. (1995). 'The Age of a Jazzwoman: Valaida Snow, 1900–1956'. *Journal of Negro History* 80 (4): 183–91.

Charters, S. B. (1983). *Jazz – New Orleans, 1885–1963: An Index to the Negro Musicians of New Orleans*. New York, Da Capo Press.

Chilton, J. (1987). *Sidney Bechet: The Wizard of Jazz*. Basingstoke, Macmillan.

Chilton, J. (1990). *The Song of the Hawk: The Life and Recordings of Coleman Hawkins*. London, Quartet Books.

Clarkson, A. E. (1999). 'Stefan Wolpe in Conversation with Eric Salzman'. *Musical Quarterly* 83 (3): 378–412.

Cokken, J. F. B. (1846). *Méthode complète de saxophone, applicable à tous les saxophones des différents tons*. Paris, E. Gérard.

Collins, J. (1986). *E. T. Mensah: The King of Highlife*. London, Geoffrey Shrubsall.

Collins, J. (1989). 'The Early History of West African Highlife'. *Popular Music* 8 (3): 221–30.

Comettant, O. (1860). *Histoire d'un inventeur au dix-neuvième siècle: Adolphe Sax, ses ouvrages et ses luttes*. Paris, Pagnerre.

Comettant, O. (1867). *La Musique, les musiciens et les instruments de musique*. Paris, Michel Lévy.

Comettant, O. (1894). *La Musique de la garde républicaine en Amérique*. Paris, La nouvelle France chorale

Cook, S. C. (1988). *Opera for a New Republic: The Zeitopern of Krenek, Weill and Hindemith*. Ann Arbor, MI; London, UMI Research Press.

Cook, S. C. (1989). 'Jazz as Deliverance: The Reception and Institution of American Jazz during the Weimar Republic'. *American Music* 7 (1): 30–47.

Dahl, L. (1984). *Stormy Weather: The Music and Lives of a Century of Jazzwomen*. London, Quartet Books.

Dahlhaus, C. (1989). *Nineteenth-Century Music*. Berkeley and Los Angeles, University of California Press.

Daniels, D. H. (1985). 'Lester Young: Master of Jive'. *American Music* 3 (3): 313–28.

Danzi, M. (1986). *American Musician in Germany, 1924–1939: Memoirs of the Jazz, Entertainment, and Movie World of Berlin during the Weimar Republic and the Nazi Era, and in the United States*. Schmitten, Ruecker.

Davis, B. (1932). *The Saxophone: A Comprehensive Course*. London, Henri Selmer.

Davison, H. (1912). *From Mendelssohn to Wagner; Being the Memoirs of J.W. Davison*. London, William Reeves.

Dean, W. (1960). 'Bizet's Self-Borrowings'. *Music and Letters* 41 (3): 238–44.

Dean, W. (1965). *Georges Bizet: His Life and Work*. London, Dent.

Deans, K. N. (1980). 'A Comprehensive Performance Project in Saxophone Literature with an Essay Consisting of Translated Source Readings in the Life and Work of Adolphe Sax'. Diss., University of Iowa.

Debussy, C. (2005). *Correspondance: 1872–1918*, ed. F. Lesure and D. Herlin. Paris, Gallimard.

De Keyser, I. (2003). 'The Paradigm of Industrial Thinking in Brass Instrument Making during the Nineteenth Century'. *Historic Brass Society Journal* 15: 233–58.

De Keyser, I. (2006). 'Adolphe Sax and the Paris Opéra'. *Brass Scholarship in Review: Proceedings of the Historic Brass Society Conference, Cité de la Musique, Paris 1999*, ed. S. Carter. Hillsdale, NY, Pendragon Press: 133–70.

Dodson, L. (1947). 'Hill Country Tunes: Instrumental Folk Music of Southwestern Pennsylvania (Reviewed)'. *William and Mary Quarterly* 4 (2): 258–9.

Du Bois, W. E. B. (1953). *The Souls of Black Folk*. New York, Fawcett.

Dullat, G. (1999). *Saxophone: Erfindung und Entwicklung einer Musikinstrumenten-Familie und ihre bedeutenden Hersteller*. Nauheim, G. Dullat.

Eby, W. M. (1925). *Eby's Scientific Method for Saxophone*. 4 vols, Hollywood, CA, Walter Jacobs.

Eggert, A. and M. Vockeroth (2003). *The Saxophone in Advertising*. Frankfurt am Main, Peter Lang.

Ehrlich, C. (1990). *The Piano: A History*. Oxford, Oxford University Press.

Elgar, E. (1968). *A Future for English Music and Other Lectures*. London, Dobson.

Ellis, K. (1999). 'The Fair Sax: Women, Brass-Playing and the Instrument Trade in 1860s Paris'. *Journal of the Royal Musical Association* 124 (2): 221–54.

Engel, C. (1925). 'Charles Martin Loeffler'. *Musical Quarterly* 11 (3): 311–30.

Fagan, T. (1983). *Encyclopedic Discography of Victor Recordings*. Westport, CT, Greenwood.

Falvy, Z. (1997). 'Tárogató as a Regional Instrument'. *Studia Musicologica Academiae Scientiarum Hungaricae* 38: 361–70.

Farmer, H. G. (1912). *The Rise and Development of Military Music*. London, William Reeves.

Farmer, H. G. (1950). *History of the Royal Artillery Band, 1762–1953*. London, Royal Artillery Institution.

Farmer, H. G. (1960). *Handel's Kettledrums, and Other Papers on Military Music*. Second edition. London, Hinrichsen.

Fétis, F. J. (1866–8). *Biographie universelle des musiciens et bibliographie générale de la musique. Deuxième édition*. Paris, Firmin-Didot.

Fitzgerald, F. S. (1922). *The Beautiful and the Damned*. New York, Charles Scribner's Sons.

Fitzgerald, F. S. (1925). *The Great Gatsby*. New York, Charles Scribner's Sons.

Fletcher, T. (1984). *100 Years of the Negro in Show Business*. New York, Da Capo Press.

Forsyth, C. (1935). *Orchestration*. London, Macmillan.

Frankenstein, A. (1939). 'Victor Hartmann and Modeste Musorgsky'. *Musical Quarterly* 25 (3): 268–91.

Gabbard, K. (2002). 'The Word Jazz'. *The Cambridge Companion to Jazz*, ed. M. Cooke and D. Horn. Cambridge, Cambridge University Press: 1–6.

Gates, H. L. (1988). *The Signifying Monkey: A Theory of Afro-American Literary Criticism*. New York, Oxford University Press.

Gebhardt, N. (2001). *Going for Jazz: Musical Practices and American Ideology*. Chicago, University of Chicago Press.

Gee, H. R. (1986). *Saxophone Soloists and Their Music, 1844–1985, an Annotated Bibliography*. Bloomington, IN, Indiana University Press.

Gilbert, M. (2000). 'Michael Brecker'. *Masters of Jazz Saxophone*, ed. D. Gelly. London, Balafon: 154–61.

Gioia, T. (1997). *The History of Jazz*. Oxford, Oxford University Press.

Gracyk, T. (2000). *Popular American Recording Pioneers, 1895–1925*. New York, Haworth Press.

Greenwood, N. L. (2005). 'Louis Mayeur, His Life and Works for Saxophone Based on Opera Themes'. Diss., University of British Columbia.

Gushee, L. (2005). *Pioneers of Jazz*. Oxford, Oxford University Press.

Haan, J. H. (1989). 'Thalia and Terpsichore on the Yangtze: A Survey of Foreign Theatre and Drama in Shanghai, 1850–1865'. *Journal of the Hong Kong Branch of the Royal Asiatic Society* 29: 158–251.

Haine, M. (1980). *Adolphe Sax (1814–1894): sa vie, son œuvre et ses instruments de musique*. Brussels, Editions de l'Université de Bruxelles.

Haine, M. (1980–81). 'Les Licences de fabrication accordées par Adolphe Sax à ses concurrents – 26 juin 1854–13 octobre 1865. [Manufacturing Licenses Awarded by Adolphe Sax to His Competitors, 26 June 1854–13 October 1865.]'. *Belgisch tijdschrift voor muziekwetenschap/Revue belge de musicologie* 34–5: 198–203.

Haine, M. (1985). *Les Facteurs d'instruments de musique à Paris au XIXᵉ siècle*. Brussels, Editions de l'université de Bruxelles.

Haine, M. (1991). 'Les Facteurs d'instruments de musique à l'époque romantique'. *La Musique en France à L'époque Romantique*. Paris, Flammarion: 101–24.

Haine, M. and I. de Keyser (1980). *Catalogue of Sax Instruments in the Musée Instrumental de Bruxelles; suivi de la liste de 400 instruments Sax conservés dans les collections publiques et privées*. Brussels, Musée Instrumental de Bruxelles.

Hallam, S., L. Rogers, et al. (2005). *Survey of Local Authority Music Services 2005*. London, Institute of Education.

Handy, W. C. (1944). *Father of the Blues: An Autobiography*. New York, Macmillan.

Hanslick, E. (1863). 'Classe Xvi, Musikalische Instrumente'. *Österreichischer Bericht über die Internationale Ausstellung in London 1862*. Vienna, J. Arenstein.

Harrison, M. (2006). *Rachmaninoff: Life, Works, Recordings*. London, Continuum International Publishing Group.

Hartmann (1846). *Méthode élémentaire de saxophone*. Paris, Schoenberger.

Harvey, P. (1995). *Saxophone*. London, Kahn and Averill.

Hemke, F. L. (1975). 'The Early History of the Saxophone'. Diss., University of Wisconsin.

Hennessey, T. J. (1994). *From Jazz to Swing: African-American Jazz Musicians and Their Music, 1890–1935.* Detroit, Wayne State University Press.

Herbert, T. (2006). *The Trombone.* New Haven and London, Yale University Press.

Hernández, D. P. (1991). "'La Lucha sonora": Dominican Popular Music in the Post-Trujillo Era'. *Latin American Music Review* 12 (2): 105–23.

Hesse, H. (1965). *Steppenwolf.* London, Penguin.

Hester, M. E. (1995). 'A Study of the Saxophone Soloists Performing with the John Philip Sousa Band: 1893–1930'. Diss., University of Arizona.

Hindemith, P. (1995). *Selected Letters of Paul Hindemith.* New Haven and London, Yale University Press.

Hindson, H. B. (1992). 'Aspects of the Saxophone in American Musical Culture, 1850–1980'. Diss., University of Wisconsin, Madison.

Hoeprich, E. (2008). *The Clarinet.* New Haven and London, Yale University Press.

Horn, D. (2002). 'The Identity of Jazz'. *The Cambridge Companion to Jazz*, ed. M. Cooke and D. Horn. Cambridge, Cambridge University Press: 9–32.

Horwood, W. (1980). *Adolphe Sax 1814–1894: His Life and Legacy*, Bramley Books.

Howe, R. S. (2003a). 'The Boehm System Oboe and Its Role in the Development of the Modern Oboe'. *Galpin Society Journal* 56: 27–60.

Howe, R. S. (2003b). 'The Invention and Early Development of the Saxophone, 1840–55'. *Journal of the American Musical Instrument Society* 29: 97–180.

Howes, F. (1954). *The Music of Ralph Vaughan Williams.* London, Oxford University Press.

Hulsebos, M. (1989). 'Cecil Leeson: The Pioneering of the Concert Saxophone in America from 1921–1941'. Diss., Ball State University.

Hyland, W. (2003). *George Gershwin: A New Biography.* Westport, CT, Praeger.

Ingham, R., ed. (1998). *The Cambridge Companion to the Saxophone.* Cambridge, Cambridge University Press.

Jardin, A. and A.-J. Tudesq (1983). *Restoration and Reaction, 1815–1848.* Cambridge, Cambridge University Press.

Jarman, D. (1991). *Alban Berg: Lulu.* Cambridge, Cambridge University Press.

Jay, M. (1973). *The Dialectical Imagination: A History of the Frankfurt School and the Institute of Social Research 1923–1950.* London, Heinemann.

Jobard, J. B. (1841). *Industrie française: Rapport sur l'exposition de 1839.* Brussels, the author; Paris, Mathis.

Joppig, G. (1986). 'Sarrusophone, Rothphone (Saxorusophone) and Reed Contrabass'. *Journal of the American Musical Instrument Society* 12: 68–106.

Kampmann, B. (2006). 'Le Saxophone "Système George"'. *Le Larigot* 37: 20–26.

Kappey, J. A. (1894). *Military Music. A History of Wind-Instrumental Bands.* London, Boosey.

Kastner, G. (1844). *Supplément au Traité général d'instrumentation.* Paris, Prilipp.

Kastner, G. (1846). *Méthode complète et raisonnée de saxophone. Dédiée à Monsieur Ad. Sax.* Paris, Troupenas. Rev. edn: Paris, Brandus, 1850.

Kastner, G. (1848). *Manuel général de musique militaire.* Paris, F. Didot.

Kater, M. H. (1992). *Different Drummers: Jazz in the Culture of Nazi Germany.* Oxford, Oxford University Press.

Kelleher, D. (1990). '"Quartette (Allegro De Concert), Soprano, Alto, Tenor and Baritone Saxophones, Caryl Florio; Richard Jackson". *Notes* 47 (2): 561–3.

Kennan, K. W. (1953). *The Technique of Orchestration.* New York, Prentice-Hall.

Kent, G. (1983). *A View from the Bandstand.* London, Sheba Feminist Publishers.

Kientzy, D. (1982). *Les Sons multiples aux saxophones.* Paris, Salabert.

Klitz, B. (1989). 'Blacks and Pre-Jazz Instrumental Music in America'. *International Review of the Aesthetics and Sociology of Music* 20 (1): 43–60.

Koenig, K. (2002). *Jazz in Print (1856–1929): An Anthology of Selected Early Readings in Jazz History*, Hillsdale, NY, Pendragon Press.

Koenigsberg, A. (1969). *Edison Cylinder Records, 1889–1912.* New York, Stellar Productions.

Kool, J. (1987). *Das Saxophon (The Saxophone): An English Translation of Jaap Kool's Work.* Baldock, England, Egon Publishers (Eng. trans. of *Das Saxophon,* Leipzig, Weber, 1931).

Lange, A. (1926). *Arranging for the Modern Dance Orchestra.* New York, A. Lange.

Lareau, A. (2002). 'Jonny's Jazz: From *Kabarett* to Krenek'. *Jazz & the Germans: Essays on the Influence of "Hot" American Idioms on 20th-Century German Music.* M. J. Budds. Hillsdale, NY, Pendragon Press. 17: 19–60.

Larner, G. (1996). *Maurice Ravel*. London, Phaidon.

Laubenstein, P. F. (1929). 'Jazz – Debit and Credit'. *Musical Quarterly* 15 (4): 606–24.

Lawrence, A. H. (2001). *Duke Ellington and His World*. New York, Routledge.

Levinsky, G. B. (1997). 'An Analysis and Comparison of Early Saxophone Methods Published between 1846–1946'. Diss., Northwestern University.

Levinson, P. J. (2005). *Tommy Dorsey: Livin' in a Great Big Way*. Cambridge, MA, Da Capo Press.

Liebman, D. (2004). *Developing a Personal Saxophone Sound*. Medfield, MA, Dorn Publications.

Lindemeyer, P. (1996). *Celebrating the Saxophone*. New York, William Morrow.

Litweiler, J. (1992). *Ornette Coleman: The Harmolodic Life*. London, Quartet Books.

Lomax, A. (1991). *Mister Jelly Roll*. London, Virgin Books.

Londeix, J.-M. (1971). *125 Ans De Musique Pour Saxophone*. Paris, Leduc.

Londeix, J.-M. and B. Ronkin (2003). *Comprehensive Guide to the Saxophone Repertoire 1844–2003*. Glenmoore, PA, Northeastern Music.

Londeix, J. M. (2004). *Pour une véritable histoire du saxophone*. Conference paper given at Saint-Maur des Fossés, November, 2004.

Lotz, R. E. (1997). *Black People: Entertainers of African Descent in Europe and Germany*. Bonn, Birgit Lotz Verlag.

McBride, W. (1982). 'The Early Saxophone in Patents 1838–1850 Compared'. *Galpin Society Journal* 35: 112–21.

Macdonald, H. (1965–66). 'Berlioz's Self-Borrowings'. *Proceedings of the Royal Musical Association* 92: 27–44.

Macdonald, H. (2002). *Berlioz's Orchestration Treatise: A Translation and Commentary*. Cambridge, Cambridge University Press.

Mandel, C. (1859). *A Treatise on the Instrumentation of Military Bands*. London, Boosey.

Marcuse, S. (1975). *A Survey of Musical Instruments*. Newton Abbot, David and Charles.

Marquis, D. M. (1978). *In Search of Buddy Bolden, First Man of Jazz*. Baton Rouge, Louisiana State University Press.

Mayer, F. N. (1960). 'John Philip Sousa: His Instrumentation and Scoring'. *Music Educators Journal* 46 (3): 51–9.

Mayeur, L. (1867). *Grande Méthode complète de saxophones*. Paris, Leon Escudier.

Mead, L. (1889). 'The Military Bands of the United States'. *Supplement to Harper's Weekly*: 787–8.

Milhaud, D. (1995). *My Happy Life*. London, Marion Boyars.

Miller, D. (1995). 'The Moan within the Tone: African Retentions in Rhythm and Blues Saxophone Style in Afro–American Popular Music'. *Popular Music* 14 (2): 155–74.

Miller, G. (1912). *The Military Band*. London, Novello.

Moldenhauer, H. and R. Moldenhauer (1979). *Anton von Webern: A Chronicle of His Life and Work*. London, Gollancz.

Morcom, A. (2001). 'An Understanding between Bollywood and Hollywood? The Meaning of Hollywood-Style Music in Hindi Films'. *British Journal of Ethnomusicology* 10 (1): 63–84.

Murphy, J. (1994). 'Early Saxophone Instruction in American Educational Institutions'. Diss., Northwestern University.

Nash, T. (1946). *Studies in High Harmonics, for Tenor and Alto Saxophone*. New York, MCA Music.

Neukomm, E. (1889). *Histoire de la musique militaire*. Paris, Baudoin.

Nicholson, S. (2002). 'Fusions and Crossovers'. *The Cambridge Companion to Jazz*, ed. M. Cooke and D. Horn. Cambridge, Cambridge University Press: 217–52.

Noyes, J. (2000). 'Edward A. Lefebre (1834–1911): Pre-Eminent Saxophonist of the Nineteenth Century'. Diss., Manhattan School of Music.

Noyes, J. (2007). 'Debussy's *Rapsodie pour orchestre et saxophone* Revisited'. *Musical Quarterly* 90 (3/4): 416–45.

Nuzum, E. (2001). *Parental Advisory: Music Censorship in America*. New York, HarperCollins.

Owens, T. (1974). 'Applying the Melograph to 'Parker's Mood''. *Selected Reports in Ethnomusicology* 2 (1): 167–75.

Owens, T. (1995). *Bebop: The Music and Its Players*. Oxford, Oxford University Press.

Pace, T. (1943). *Ancie battenti: Storia-fisica-letteratura*. Florence, Cya.

Peress, M. (1993). 'My Life with "Black, Brown and Beige"'. *Black Music Research Journal* 13 (2): 147–60.

Peretti, B. W. (1992). *The Creation of Jazz: Music, Race, and Culture in Urban America*. Urbana and Chicago, University of Illinois Press.

Petchenina, L. and G. Abensour (2004). 'Egyptian Nights – in Search of the 'New Simplicity". *Three Oranges: The Journal of the Serge Prokofiev Foundation* 7: 10–15.

Philippot, M. and E. Messinger (1964). 'Ansermet's Phenomenological Metamorphoses'. *Perspectives of New Music* 2 (2): 129–40.

Pinckney, J. W. R. (1989–90). 'Jazz in India: Perspectives on Historical Development and Musical Acculturation'. *Asian Music* 21 (1): 35–77.

Piston, W. (1955). *Orchestration*. New York, Norton.

Placksin, S. (1985). *Jazzwomen: 1900 to the Present: Their Words, Lives, and Music*. London, Pluto.

Plugge, S. D. (2003). 'The History of the Saxophone Ensemble: A Study of the Development of the Saxophone Quartet into a Concert Genre'. Diss., Northwestern University.

Pontécoulant, A. Le Doucet, Comte de (1861). *Organographie. Essai sur la facture instrumentale*. Paris, Castel.

Porter, E. (1999). '"Dizzy Atmosphere": The Challenge of Bebop'. *American Music* 17 (4): 422–46.

Porter, L. (1985). *Lester Young*. Boston, Mass, Twayne Publishers.

Porter, L. (1991). *A Lester Young Reader*. Washington, Smithsonian Institution Press.

Porter, L. (1998). *John Coltrane: His Life and Music*. Ann Arbor, MI, University of Michigan Press.

Potter, K. (1999). *Four Musical Minimalists: La Monte Young, Terry Riley, Steve Reich, Philip Glass*. Cambridge, Cambridge University Press.

Powell, A. (2002). *The Flute*. New Haven, Yale University Press.

Pressing, J. (2002). 'Free Jazz and the Avant-Garde'. *The Cambridge Companion to Jazz*, ed. M. Cooke and D. Horn. Cambridge, Cambridge University Press.

Price, R. (1987). *A Social History of Nineteenth-Century France*. London, Hutchinson.

Priestley, B. (2005). *Chasin' the Bird: The Life and Legacy of Charlie Parker*. New York, Oxford University Press.

Priestley, B., D. Gelly, et al. (1998). *The Sax & Brass Book*. London, Balafon Books.

Prod'homme, J.-G. (1935). 'Chabrier in His Letters'. *Musical Quarterly* 21 (4): 451–65.

Rascher, S. M. (1942). *Top Tones for the Saxophone*. New York, Carl Fischer.

Raumberger, C. and K. Ventzke. 'Saxophone.' *Grove Music Online*. Retrieved 3 August, 2008.

Reisner, R. G. (1975). *Bird: The Legend of Charlie Parker*. New York, Da Capo Press.

Rendall, F. G. (1932). 'The Saxophone before Sax'. *Musical Times* 73 1077–9 (1078).

Rendall, F. G. (1941–42). 'A Short Account of the Clarinet in England During the Eighteenth and Nineteenth Centuries'. *Proceedings of the Musical Association* 68: 55–86.

Rice, A. R. (2003). *The Clarinet in the Classical Period*. New York, Oxford University Press.

Rice, A. R. (2008). 'The Earliest Known Saxophone'. *Newsletter of the American Musical Instrument Society* 31 (1): 11–12.

Rice, A. R. (2009a). *From the Clarinet d'amour to the Contra Bass: A History of Large Size Clarinets, 1740–1860*. New York, Oxford University Press.

Rice, A. R. (2009b). 'Making and Improving the Nineteenth-Century Saxophone'. *Journal of the American Instrument Society* 35: 81–122.

Rivière, J. (1893). *My Musical Life and Recollections*. London, Sampson Low, Martons.

Robinson, J. B. (1994). 'Jazz Reception in Weimar Germany: In Search of a Shimmy Figure'. *Music and Performance During the Weimar Republic*, ed. B. Gilliam. Cambridge, Cambridge University Press: 107–34.

Robinson, S. (1997). '"An English Composer Sees America': Benjamin Britten and the North American Press, 1939–42'. *American Music* 15 (3): 321–51.

Romero, R. R. (1990). 'Musical Change and Cultural Resistance in the Central Andes of Peru'. *Latin American Music Review* 11 (1): 1–35.

Romero, R. R. (2001). *Debating the Past: Music, Memory, and Identity in the Andes*. Oxford, Oxford University Press.

Ronkin, B. E. (1987). 'The Music for Saxophone and Piano Published by Adolphe Sax'. Diss., University of Maryland, College Park.

Rorive, J.-P. (2004). *Adolphe Sax 1814–1894: Inventeur de génie*. Brussels, Éditions Racine.

Rose, A. and E. Souchon (1967). *New Orleans Jazz: A Family Album*. Baton Rouge, Louisiana State University Press.

Rousseau, E. (1982). *Marcel Mule: His Life and the Saxophone*. Shell Lake, WI, Etoile Music.

Russell, R. (1996). *Bird Lives: The High Life and Hard Times of Charlie (Yardbird) Parker*. New York, Da Capo Press.

Ryan, T. (1885). *Recollections of an Old Musician*. New York, E. P. Dutton.

Said, E. W. (1995). *Orientalism*. Harmondsworth, Penguin.

Saint-Saëns, C. (1921). *Musical Memories*. London, Murray.

Sax, A (1867). *De la nécessité des musiques militaires*. Paris, Librairie centrale.

Scavone, G. P. (1997). 'An Acoustic Analysis of Single-Reed Woodwind Instruments with an Emphasis on Design and Performance Issues and Digital Waveguide Modeling Techniques'. Diss., Stanford University.

Schafer, W. J. (1977). *Brass Bands and New Orleans Jazz*. Baton Rouge, Louisiana State University Press.

Schuller, G. (1989). *The Swing Era: The Development of Jazz 1930–1945*. New York, Oxford University Press.

Schwartz, H. W. (1957). *Bands of America*. New York, Doubleday.

Segell, M. (2005). *The Devil's Horn: The Story of the Saxophone, from Noisy Novelty to King of Cool*. New York, Farrar, Straus and Giroux.

Shafer, B. (1950). *Through History with J. Wesley Smith*. New York, Vanguard Press.

Shapiro, N. and N. Hentoff (1966). *Hear Me Talkin' to Ya: The Story of Jazz by the Men Who Made It*. New York, Dover.

Shaw, G. B. (1981). *Shaw's Music: The Complete Musical Criticism*, ed. D. H. Laurence. 3 vols, London, Bodley Head.

Shepherd, J. (1991). *Music as Social Text*. Cambridge, Polity.

Smalley, R. (1975). 'Webern's Sketches (Ii)'. *Tempo* 113: 29–40.

Smialek, J. T. W. (1991). 'Clay Smith and G. E. Holmes: Their Role in the Development of Saxophone Performance and Pedagogy in the United States'. Diss., University of Georgia.

Sobchenko, A. (1997). 'Letters for Glazunov: The Saxophone Concerto Years'. *Saxophone Journal* 22 (2): 66–70.

Southern, E. (1997). *The Music of Black Americans*. New York, Norton.

Starr, S. F. (1983). *Red and Hot: The Fate of Jazz in the Soviet Union 1917–1980*. New York, Oxford University Press.

Stravinsky, I. and R. Craft (1962). *Expositions and Developments*. London, Faber.

Street, W. H. (1983). 'Elise Boyer Hall, America's First Female Concert Saxophonist: Her Life as Performing Artist, Pioneer of Concert Repertory for Saxophone and Patroness of the Arts'. Diss., Northwestern University.

Sudhalter, R. M. (1999). *Lost Chords: White Musicians and Their Contribution to Jazz, 1915–1945*. New York, Oxford University Press.

Taylor, C. (1982). "Salt Peanuts': Sound and Sense in African/American Oral/Musical Creativity'. *Callaloo* 16: 1–11.

Terrier, A. (2003). *L'orchestre de l'opéra de Paris de 1669 à nos jours*. Paris, Éditions de La Martinière.

Thomas, J. C. (1975). *Coltrane: Chasin' the Trane*. New York, Doubleday.

Tosoroni, A. (1850). *Trattato pratico di strumentazione*. Florence, Guidi.

Trier, S. (1998). 'The Saxophone in the Orchestra'. *The Cambridge Companion to the Saxophone*, ed. R. Ingham. Cambridge, Cambridge University Press: 101–8.

Tucker, M. (1996). 'In Search of Will Vodery'. *Black Music Research Journal* 16 (1): 123–82.

Tucker, S. (1998). 'Nobody's Sweethearts: Gender, Race, Jazz, and the Darlings of Rhythm'. *American Music* 16 (3): 255–88.

Tucker, S. (1999). 'The Prairie View Co-Eds: Black Women Musicians in Class and on the Road during World War II'. *Black Music Research Journal* 19 (1): 93–126.

Upton, W. T. (1946). *The Musical Works of William Henry Fry in the Collections of the Library Company of Philadelphia*. Philadelphia, PA, Free Library of Philadelphia.

Vallée, R. (1962). *My Time Is Your Time: The Story of Rudy Vallée*. New York, Ivan Obolensky.

Ventzke, K., C. Raumberger, et al. (1987). *Die Saxophone: Beiträge zu Ihrer Bau-Charakteristik, Funktion und Geschichte*. Frankfurt am Main, Erwin Bochinsky.

Vereecken, B. (1917). *Foundation to Saxophone Playing: An Elementary Method*. New York, Carl Fisher.

Vereecken, B. (1919). *The Saxophone Virtuoso: An Advanced Method*. New York, Carl Fischer.

Vermazen, B. (2004). *That Moaning Saxophone: The Six Brown Brothers and the Dawning of a Musical Craze*. New York, Oxford University Press.

Wagner, R. (2007). *My Life (Complete)*. Teddington, Middlesex, Echo Library.

Walker, L. (1990). *The Wonderful Era of the Great Dance Bands*. New York, Da Capo Press.

Waller, G. A. (1992). 'Another Audience: Black Moviegoing 1907–16'. *Cinema Journal* 31 (2): 3–25.

Waterhouse, W. (1993). *The New Langwill Index: A Dictionary of Musical Wind-Instrument Makers and Inventors*. London, Tony Bingham.

Waterhouse, W. (2006). 'Gautrot-Aîné, First of the Moderns'. *Brass Scholarship in Review: Proceedings of the Historic Brass Society Conference, Cité de la Musique, Paris 1999*, ed. S. Carter. Hillsdale, NY, Pendragon Press: 121–32.

Weber, W. (1975). *Music and the Middle Class: The Social Structure of Concert Life in London, Paris and Vienna between 1830 and 1848*. London, Croom Helm.

Weiner, M. A. (1991). 'Urwaldmusik and the Borders of German Identity: Jazz in Literature of the Weimar Republic'. *German Quarterly* 64 (4): 475–87.

Weinstock, H. (1968). *Rossini: A Biography*. Oxford, Oxford University Press.

Weirick, P. (1937). *Dance Arranging. A Guide to Scoring Music for the American Dance Orchestra*. New York, Witmark Educational Publications.

Weltzien, O. A. (1992). 'Notes and Lineaments: Vaughan Williams's "Job: A Masque for Dancing" and Blake's "Illustrations"'. *Musical Quarterly* 76 (3): 301–36.

Wertheim, A. F. and B. Bair, eds (2000). *The Papers of Will Rogers: Wild West and Vaudeville: April 1904–September 1908*. Norman, OK, University of Oklahoma Press.

Whiteman, P. and M. M. McBride (1974). *Jazz*. New York, Arno Press.

Wiedoeft, R. (1927). *Complete Modern Method for Saxophone*. 2 vols, New York, Robbins.

Woideck, C. (1996). *Charlie Parker: His Music and Life*. Ann Arbor, MI, University of Michigan Press.

Wood, G. (c. 1833). *Complete Instructions for the Alto Fagotto, an Instrument Which Embraces the Sweetest & Most Admired Notes of the Clarinet & Bassoon, & Eminently Calculated to Accompany the Human Voice, or to Perform Solos & Concertos in Orchestras or Military Bands*. London, the author.

Zealley, A. E. and J. O. Hume (1926). *Famous Bands of the British Empire*. London, J. P. Hull.

Index